Analytical Methods for Lawyers

Howell E. Jackson
James S. Reid, Jr., Professor of Law
Harvard Law School

Louis Kaplow
Finn M. W. Caspersen and
Household International Professor of Law and Economics
Harvard Law School

Steven M. Shavell
Samuel R. Rosenthal Professor of Law and Economics
Harvard Law School

W. Kip Viscusi
University Distinguished Professor of
Law, Economics, and Management
Vanderbilt University Law School

David Cope
Lecturer on Law
Harvard Law School

© 2003 FOUNDATION PRESS
© 2011 By THOMSON REUTERS/FOUNDATION PRESS
     1 New York Plaza, 34th Floor
     New York, NY 10004
     Phone Toll Free 1–877–888–1330
     Fax 646–424–5201
     foundation–press.com
Printed in the United States of America

ISBN 978–1–59941–921–3

Mat #41090617

To Robert C. Clark

Preface

This text was created to accompany a course we have taught for the past four years at Harvard Law School. The course and the text grew out of our joint realization that the traditional law school curriculum, with its focus on the development of analogical reasoning skills and legal writing and research, left many law students inadequately prepared for upper-level law courses and, more importantly, for legal practice in the modern world. Lawyers, whether corporate counsel or public interest advocates, must work in settings where effective argumentation and the giving of sound legal advice often depend on mastery of language and techniques derived from disciplines such as economics, accounting, finance, and statistics, staples of the modern business school curriculum, but notably absent, in introductory form, from law school classrooms.

True, a number of students arrive at law school well equipped with knowledge of these areas from undergraduate experience as economics, finance, or business majors. Equally true, however, is that many, perhaps the majority, of law students are woefully under-prepared in these areas. Furthermore, many self-select away from those upper-level courses in which their inadequate preparation would severely disadvantage them. These students will graduate from law school without a set of basic skills, the absence of which will hamper their development in almost any of the careers that law graduates now pursue. It has been our experience that the students who lack background in these critical areas are themselves acutely aware of their deficiency (or are made aware of it when they encounter their first law and economics discussion in torts or contracts). Such students are eager to enroll in a course such as ours that promises to demystify analytical concepts and quantitative techniques that they see as clearly relevant to success in their other law school classes and, ultimately, to success in their chosen careers. It is primarily for these students that this text has been written.

I

Unlike traditional introductory treatments, this book is not a dry or technical text, far removed from the world of law. Quite the opposite. Virtually every concept is introduced, explained, and applied in legal contexts. The translation from theory to practice is not left for students to develop after graduation; instead, it is at the very heart of the text.

Chapter One introduces students to decision analysis, a set of techniques traditionally taught to first-year MBA students. Increasingly, practicing lawyers make use of decision trees to review litigation strategies and settlement offers. With a few relatively simple tools, decision trees help lawyers unpack complex decisions and advise clients choosing among various possible courses of action. The chapter introduces concepts such as probability, expected value, sensitivity analysis, risk aversion, and the value of obtaining additional information. It's hard to imagine a lawyer giving effective advice without a familiarity with these basic analytical tools, yet the explicit study of decision analysis is totally absent from the traditional law school curriculum.

Chapter Two expands on decision analysis to introduce basic game theory, with an emphasis on strategic challenges raised by incomplete information. In many contexts where lawyers offer advice, the decisions of their clients will depend in part on what they expect to be the actions and reactions of others. Game theory offers an analytical structure to help students recognize and evaluate problems of this sort. In a similar spirit, the chapter introduces students to the basics of information theory, including the concepts of moral hazard and adverse selection. While students will have heard these terms mentioned in other law school classes, many don't have a clear understanding of their meaning or how they can complicate negotiations and contracts. Nor have students been exposed to standard solutions to the prisoner's dilemma or other similarly recurring problems.

Chapter Three presents an overview of the function of contracts and a tool box for designing effective agreements — contracts that will accomplish clients' objectives and avoid common pitfalls. In contrast to most first-year contract courses, which emphasize legal doctrines governing contract formation and damage awards, this chapter offers students a practical framework for determining what kinds of provisions contracts should include, for instance, when to use a cost-plus as opposed to a fixed payment fee structure or how to formulate a contract to ensure that work is completed on time. In addition to reviewing actual terms from real contracts, the chapter considers the avoidance and resolution of contract disputes, topics also typically absent from first-year contracts courses.

In Chapter Four, we turn to analytical skills often associated with business practice: accounting and the interpretation of financial statements. All lawyers — not just corporate counsel — should have a basic understanding of these topics. Accounting is pervasive in modern legal practice. Family lawyers negotiating divorce agreements or child custody arrangements must be able to interpret and critique financial statements. Employment agreements often include compensation provisions that are expressed in terms of accounting standards. Non-profits and government agencies all measure their performance in accordance with financial accounting standards. Much information obtained in discovery is of a financial nature. Without a passing acquaintance with balance sheets and income statements, law school graduates face a serious handicap when they enter the world of practice, whatever their area of specialization.

Chapter Five offers an introduction to the field of finance. Our task here is threefold. In terms of basic skills development, the core of the chapter is an introduction to the time value of money: the most basic concept in finance and the one that new lawyers must fully internalize in order to be able to represent their clients sensibly in a variety of legal contexts, from contract negotiations to litigation settlements. We then introduce a series of more advanced concepts in finance theory such as diversification, the relationship between risk and return, and rudimentary coverage of asset pricing models and valuation techniques. The chapter also provides a selection of excerpts from classic writings in the field of finance. We include these excerpts to expose students to an intellectual tradition that will be familiar to their classmates who have studied economics and finance as undergraduates and that is often taken for granted in upper level courses on corporations and advanced commercial topics. These readings also offer an important alternative perspective on the goals of financial analysis.

Chapter Six presents a primer in microeconomics. While many students have been exposed to economics, some have not and a large number will have taken introductory courses at the undergraduate level that make no effort to relate the basic concepts of microeconomic analysis to problems that lawyers are likely to encounter in practice. Accordingly, in this chapter, we review the basic tools of microeconomics — including supply and demand, public goods, externalities, and marginal analysis — and then relate these concepts to common legal problems.

Chapter Seven is an introduction to the field that has become known as law and economics, the hallmark of which is attention to the effect of law on the behavior of individuals and firms. Here the basic ideas of law and economics are discussed for the core areas of law — property, tort, contract, and crime — as well as for litigation. For example, in torts, we discuss how rules of negligence and strict liability influence incentives to reduce risk and we also examine the relationship between tort liability and insurance. Students will sometimes have encountered law and economics thinking in small doses in other courses, but a systematic treatment is a different and highly valuable enhancement to their usual exposure.

Finally, in Chapters Eight and Nine, we turn to empirical techniques. In Chapter Eight, Fundamentals of Statistical Analysis, we begin by introducing the basic elements of descriptive statistics, including various measures of central tendency and variability, with a particular emphasis on the value of visual presentations of data in histograms and other graphic formats. We then turn to the basic elements of sampling and survey design, concepts that many treatments of empirical method often overlook. Finally, the chapter offers an informal presentation of the two most important tools of inferential statistics: hypothesis testing and estimation.

Chapter Nine concludes our treatment of empirical methods with an introduction to multivariate analysis. We start off with simple linear relationships between two variables and the techniques of correlational analysis and simple linear regressions. We then extend the discussion with a presentation of multiple regression in the context of discrimination litigation. The chapter ends with brief treatment of some of the most common difficulties in making inferences using multiple regression analysis: the omission of important explanatory variables, the inclusion of irrelevant variables, the effect of multicollinearity, and the problem of two-way causation.

II

At most law schools, Analytical Methods for Lawyers will be a new offering and, as a result, a number of questions are likely to arise as to how the course would best fit into the curriculum. While many approaches are possible — and we welcome input from those who adopt the course — here are our preliminary thoughts on some key issues.

First, which law students should take courses in analytical methods? At one extreme, one could imagine making the course a requirement for all students, perhaps as part of the first-year curriculum. For some law schools, a mandatory course might make sense, but there are also certain pitfalls with this approach. Many schools will no doubt prefer — at least initially — to make the class optional, as we have at Harvard Law School.

A further practical question is when such a course should be offered to students. At Harvard, our choice originally was to schedule the course in the Spring Term so that students can take it during the second half of their first year. At that point, the students know something about legal doctrine and civil procedure, and are beginning to understand the various roles that lawyers are called upon to play in both litigation and transactional settings. As a result, it is possible to use problems that draw upon their legal training: for example, considering how to decide whether to hire an expert witness for a civil trial or what kind of compensation provision to put into a personal service contract. While students would have even greater knowledge of legal problems by the second or third year, there are important offsetting costs of delaying the timing of the course. Many of the skills that we teach in Analytical Methods are essential building blocks for upper level courses. Accounting and finance provide important background for corporations classes and other commercial courses. Knowledge of statistical methods is useful in upper level courses on employment discrimination and many other areas of public policy analysis. Particularly for students most in need of quantitative skills training — the French literature major who dropped math after eleventh grade — we strongly recommend that the course not be postponed till late in the second or third year of law school lest these students be needlessly disadvantaged in other upper-level courses.

Next, there is the issue of feedback and examinations. In other areas of the university where analytical skills are taught, a critical component of instruction is the weekly problem set or laboratory exercise, and that is the model we have adopted in our teaching of the course. In our experience, the best way for students to internalize new analytical skills is through regular written exercises and prompt feedback. Over the course of the semester, students are expected to complete approximately ten such exercises, which together account for about a quarter of their course grade. While there is a cost associated with these weekly exercises — preparing and grading weekly exercises is time consuming — the offsetting benefit is considerable. Students feel empowered when they have actually used — successfully — their newly acquired skill. Moreover, students generally seem to enjoy the opportunity to complete much of their work in one course before the end of the semester. For the balance of the grade we use two "mid-term" examinations, each approximately an hour and a half in length and each covering roughly one half of the course. (A teachers' manual, which is available to instructors upon request, includes a large number of sample exercises and written assignments.)

A separate practical concern relates to the issue of what kind of faculty member should teach a course on Analytical Methods. In our view, the concepts covered in this book are either already known, or easily enough understood, so that most instructors who teach commercial, corporate, or economic courses would find themselves entirely comfortable presenting most of the topics covered in the text. Formal training in the subject matter is not necessary. (And our teachers' manual offers substantial assistance for the uninitiated.) The course lends itself to team teaching, with each faculty member responsible for covering different chapters of material. We also typically employ a teaching assistant to help grade the weekly written exercises. Many schools, whether due to instructor preferences, limited class hours, or overlaps with other offerings, may well choose to offer only a selection of modules. Our text is designed so that this is readily accomplished, for each chapter (or group of two) is entirely self-contained.

Finally, there is a question of how a course in analytical methods relates to other semester-long law school courses, such as corporate finance, analysis of financial statements, economic analysis of the law, or empirical methods in the law. At least at Harvard, we have tended to view Analytical Methods as an optional gateway to these upper level offerings. Students with no prior training in quantitative methods will take our Analytical Methods course and then choose to go on to advanced upper level courses on related subjects. This strikes us as entirely appropriate. (We do, however, impose some limits on students who have taken two or more upper level courses in related fields from enrolling in the overlapping modules in our Analytical Methods class.)

* * * *

Chapters One, Two and Three of this book were written primarily by Louis Kaplow and Steven Shavell; Chapters Four and Five by Howell Jackson; Chapters Six and Seven by Steven Shavell; and Chapters Eight and Nine by David Cope and Kip Viscusi. Many others have also contributed to the development of the book. To begin with, the John M. Olin Foundation, through its grants to the John M. Olin Center for Law, Economics, and Business at Harvard Law School, provided generous and sustained support for the development of this book and associated research efforts at the Law School. We benefited from a different, but equally important, kind of support from our students at Harvard who suffered through early versions of the manuscript, endured with good humor not-always-successful experiments in pedagogical innovation, and offered invariably helpful and creative suggestions for improvements in the manuscript. We are also extremely grateful for the excellent and extraordinarily patient editorial assistance that we received from Peggy Burlet and Diane Long, as well as help from Matt Seccombe in preparing the index and providing a final proofing of the manuscript. Finally, we want to express our appreciation and gratitude to Robert C. Clark, to whom this book is dedicated, for his unwavering support for our efforts in developing this book and the Analytical Methods for Lawyers course upon which it is based.

Cambridge, Massachusetts
September, 2003

Preface to the Second Edition

The first edition of this text has been used now for seven years in our Analytical Methods for Lawyers course at Harvard Law School, which, as an elective, has attracted between 100 and 200 students each year. The popularity of the course can, we believe, be attributed to the continuing presence at the law school of large numbers of students who arrive without background in many or all of the subjects covered in the text and who recognize that success at the law school and in law practice will require that they achieve a degree of familiarity with the concepts and techniques presented in it. We are acutely aware of the fact that our core constituency is a group of students who can be expected to be not only beginners in the various areas we cover, but also, though intelligent and highly motivated, not fully comfortable with quantitative methods. Making subjects like economics, statistics, accounting, and finance accessible to this group is a difficult pedagogical task, and we have greatly benefitted in it from our interactions over the years with the many students who have taken the course. A good deal of our effort and concern in preparing this second edition has been devoted to improving the presentation of key ideas, primarily in the accounting and statistics chapters, based on their detailed feedback, and on many helpful suggestions from faculty using the text at other law schools. In addition, where needed, we have updated the text, including new references at the end of each chapter. Those faculty already using the text will be pleased that we have retained the coverage of the first edition and that much, if not all, of the material in the teacher's manual will remain viable.

We are grateful for support provided for the development of this new edition by the John M. Olin Center for Law, Economics and Business at

Harvard Law School. We would also like to acknowledge the first-rate work of Sandra J. Badin in editing the manuscript, and of Sharon D. Ray in preparing it for publication.

Cambridge, Massachusetts
November, 2010

Contents

Analytical Methods
for Lawyers

1
Decision Analysis

1. Introduction

Lawyers have to make all kinds of decisions — some of them quite complex — when conducting litigation or counseling clients. Obviously, lawyers and clients would like all their decisions to be the best ones possible. The surest way to reach this goal is by proceeding through the decision-making process in an organized and methodical way. Decision analysis provides a tool for doing just this. It's an organized method of making decisions — indeed, an enthusiast might even say that it is *the* rational way to go about making decisions — that is especially valuable when decisions have to be made in the face of uncertainty and when one decision must be followed by subsequent decisions.

Here are several typical decision-making problems of the types that you might encounter in your practice of law:

- *Automobile accident settlement negotiation.* You're the lawyer for a plaintiff who was in an automobile accident, and you're involved in settlement negotiation with the defendant's lawyer. If you go to trial, there will be three possible outcomes. First, you might win and prevail on the major issue of damages: lost wages. In this event, your client will receive a total award of $100,000. The likelihood of this outcome, in your opinion, is 50%. Second, your client may win at trial but not obtain lost wages. In this case, she'll receive only $20,000 for the damage to her car. You think that the chances of this outcome are 30%. Third, your client might lose at trial and thus win nothing. In your estimation, the probability that this will be the outcome is 20%. Going to trial would cost $10,000. The defendant has offered $40,000 to settle the case. Should you advise your client to accept this offer?

- _Land purchase decision._ Your client, who wishes to build a restaurant, is trying to decide which of two parcels of land to buy. Parcel A has been offered at $300,000 and Parcel B at only $250,000. They seem equally attractive, so your client initially thinks that purchasing the cheaper one, Parcel B, is the way to go. However, in questioning the sellers about the parcels, you learn that Parcel B may have an environmental problem because wastes have been dumped on it, whereas no problems are associated with Parcel A. You find that if the wastes on Parcel B are hazardous, the law would require your client to clean up the site and that the cost of cleanup would be $200,000. You figure that the odds of Parcel B having this problem are 50%. But before your client decides which parcel to buy, you can hire an environmental testing firm to determine definitively whether your client would have to clean up Parcel B. Having the environmental firm do the testing would cost your client $20,000. Should you advise your client to have the testing done? Or should he just buy Parcel A? Or Parcel B?

- _Tax deduction advice._ You're a tax lawyer advising a client about a tax matter and don't know whether a particular tax deduction — one that would save her $80,000 — is allowable (it's a judgment call that involves no ethical issue). If she takes the deduction, she'll be audited with probability 75% (she's in a group that's often audited for such deductions). If she's audited, the odds that the deduction will be found to be allowable are 50%. If she's audited and the deduction is disallowed, she won't obtain the $80,000 benefit, and she'll have to pay a penalty of $20,000. Should you advise her to claim the deduction?

- *Medical decision and negligence issue.* You are a lawyer helping a health maintenance organization formulate a medical treatment policy that will prevent it from being sued for negligence. For patients with a certain kind of heart ailment that will lead to immediate death if untreated, there are two options, both involving substantial risk. The first is a course of drug treatment, which will be successful 50% of the time but will also fail to prevent death 50% of the time. The second option is corrective surgery. The operation will be successful 33a% of the time. It won't go well and will result in patient death 10% of the time. The rest of the time it won't solve the problem and will leave the patient in a weakened condition. In this case, the patient's only option will be treatment with the drug, but now the drug has only a 25% chance of working. Neither the drug treatment nor the corrective surgery is very expensive in relation to any reasonable valuation of life, so it would be negligent not to choose some method of treatment. The question is, to avoid a finding of negligence, which method should be chosen (assuming that cost is not taken into consideration in the negligence determination)? What do you advise the health maintenance organization to adopt as its treatment policy?

We'll use decision analysis to work through some of these problems, as well as some others, a little later in this chapter. But, as an experiment, you might try to solve them right now on your own, if only to see how difficult the process sometimes can be.

Decision analysis is useful for a number of reasons. Some decisions are quite complicated to make — because of the number of choices, the number of possible consequences and their likelihoods, and the significance of decisions at each stage for later decisions. Therefore, more than intuition is often needed to see through to an answer, and decision analysis can fill this void.

Decision analysis is also useful because it forces us to be explicit about the considerations relevant to making a decision. It requires that we write down all the factors that might influence us. This process itself frequently yields significant dividends. In addition, listing all the potential consequences of a decision, assessing the likelihood of each, and noting all subsequent decisions that might have to be made down the road commonly reveals relevant issues and possibilities that would otherwise have been overlooked. In this regard, the sketches above may be a bit misleading, because the relevant events, their likelihoods, and future actions were laid out. In real life, we have to figure out for ourselves what they are.

As is obvious from the sketches, decision analysis can be relevant and helpful both to lawyers who are involved in active litigation and to lawyers who are advising clients before disputes arise. Much of the work that's necessary in making decisions to help clients is work that has to be done by lawyers: it is the lawyers who are often in the best position to identify many relevant contingencies, their likelihoods, and their significance. For instance, in the settlement negotiation sketch, the lawyer will have the best knowledge of the odds of winning this or that amount in the judgment. In the land purchase example, the lawyer might be the person who will be on the lookout for possible environmental problems (the environmental issue might not be on the radar screen of someone who doesn't purchase land very often), who will know what types of wastes have to be removed and precisely what the cleanup obligation entails, who will be familiar with waste-testing firms, and so forth. For such reasons, many lawyers themselves explicitly use decision analysis. Some hire consultants to teach them how to work through the decision analysis process. Others hire consultants to do the decision analyses. (If you go to the website of the decision analysis software company men-

---

Box 1-1
Is Decision Analysis Ethical?

Is using decision analysis always ethical when doing so would be helpful to your client? For example, is employing decision analysis always ethical when giving tax advice? The answer, of course, is that your general ethical and legal obligations as a lawyer should guide you in providing advice to your client. There's nothing special per se about legal advice that makes use of decision analysis. Thus, if your client is seeking tax advice in the face of uncertainty about the interpretation of tax laws (as in our tax deduction example), decision analysis is good to employ. But if your client is trying to evade taxes clearly owed, it's wrong to knowingly aid your client, be it with decision analysis or in any other way.

---

tioned at the end of this chapter, you'll see that it has many top-flight law firms as customers.)

Moreover, decision analysis is a mainstay of business and government decision making and is increasingly used in the medical world and in other arenas. A knowledge of decision analysis will prove useful to you in your practice not only because it will be of direct value to when you're making decisions but also because it will allow you to better understand the situation at hand and to communicate more effectively with your clients.

2. Decision Trees

The first step in decision analysis is to convert a problem into a standard format: a *decision tree.* This format, which is quite intuitive, has proven to be very helpful. It displays all the decisions that are possible and all the consequences that are possible, along with their probabilities and their importance, the latter often being expressed in monetary terms. (How this information is obtained is another matter, which we'll explore a little later. For now, we'll assume that the decision maker has it.) Once a decision tree is displayed, it has to be solved. The process of solving a decision tree, like the format itself, is intuitive.

A. A Simple Problem

Let's begin by focusing on an extremely simple settlement decision. Suppose that your client is the plaintiff in a contract case. If he proceeds to trial, he will surely win, because the case is a slam-dunk: there was a clear breach of contract. The amount your client will receive if he goes to trial is $100,000, and legal costs will be $20,000, so your client will net $80,000. The defendant has offered your client $70,000.

The tree diagram for this scenario is shown in Figure 1-1. As we can see, it begins on the left with a box, a *decision node.* Two lines, referred to as *decision branches,* emanate from the box. They represent each of the two possible decisions that you can make: Settle (i.e., accept the settlement offer) and Trial (i.e., reject the offer and go to trial).[1] The $70,000 written along the Settle branch is the amount your client will receive if he settles. This is the *payoff,* or *consequence,* corresponding to the decision branch Settle. A negative amount, –$20,000, is noted along the Trial decision branch. This is the cost of going to trial. The payoff notation is followed by $100,000, the amount won at trial. Determining which branch to choose, Settle or Trial, is readily apparent in this tree: if you settle, you get $70,000, and if you go to trial, you net $80,000. You would, obviously, choose Trial.

To indicate that a decision branch has been eliminated, we strike two lines through that line branch (see Figure 1-2). Similarly, the payoff when the best decision is made at a decision node is written underneath the decision node (e.g., the $80,000 in Figure 1-2).

Striking off eliminated decision branches and recording under the decision node the best possible payoff is conventional practice in decision analysis. This practice may seem unnecessary to you at this point, but it proves to be very helpful when dealing with more complicated decision problems, as will soon become clear.

---

1. In a decision tree, the number of lines extending from a decision node always equals the number of decisions that are possible.

Figure 1-1
Settlement versus Trial

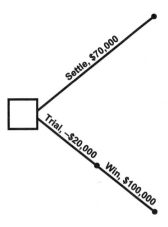

Figure 1-2
Settlement versus Trial: The Best Decision

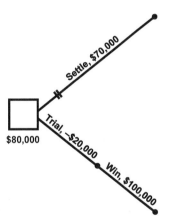

B. Uncertainty

Now let's introduce the element of uncertainty into our story. Suppose that your case for breach of contract is not a sure thing, because the other side has a possible counterargument. You think that the odds of prevailing at trial are only about 60%. If the decision doesn't come down on your side, your client will lose and collect nothing. This scenario is illustrated in Figure 1-3.

Notice that a circle is drawn at the end of the decision branch Trial. This circle, a *chance node,* signifies that chance will play a role in what

Figure 1-3
Settlement versus Trial: Uncertainty

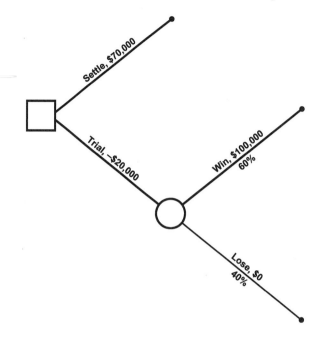

next happens. In our example, your client either will Win and gain $100,000 or will Lose and receive $0. Each outcome is indicated along a *chance branch,* and its likelihood is written under the branch. Thus, the tree diagram in Figure 1-3 contains all the relevant information provided by the verbal description of the problem.

Now that we have a visual representation of the problem, how do we evaluate the uncertain payoffs from trial? Let's focus on just a part of the decision tree, the uncertain chance branches for Trial (see Figure 1-4). How does it make sense to evaluate this situation, where there's a 60% chance of gaining $100,000 and a 40% chance of obtaining nothing? Plainly, if the chances of winning $100,000 were 100%, the evaluation of the situation would be $100,000. Just as clear is that, if the chances of winning anything were 0%, the evaluation of the situation would be $0. What we're confronted with, however, is a situation where you will Win with a probability of 60% and Lose with a probability of 40%. Intuition suggests that the evaluation of the situation should be somewhere between $100,000 and $0.

Figure 1-4
Chance Branches

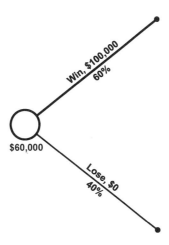

How do we decide what amount between $100,000 and $0 to use? The natural choice would seem to be the *expected value,* which is the probability of the payoff multiplied by the amount of the payoff. In this case, the expected value is $60,000 (i.e., 60% × $100,000 = $60,000). The expected value is the obvious, natural number to use as an evaluation because it is the average payoff a person would obtain if repeatedly faced with a risky situation similar to the type in question. Suppose that you find yourself repeatedly in trial situations in which you feel the odds of winning $100,000 are 60% (and the odds of winning $0 are 40%). You don't know what will happen in any one trial, of course, but you would know what your average winnings would be over the course of many of these trials: about $60,000. In other words, if you were to repeat the situation under discussion 100 times and anticipated obtaining $100,000 in 60 trials and gaining nothing in the other 40 trials,[2] your total gain would be $6,000,000 (i.e., 60 × $100,000 = $6,000,000), and thus your average gain would be $60,000 (i.e., $6,000,000/100 = $60,000).

For the time being, let's accept expected value as an appropriate measure or value of chance events and return to the decision tree in

_____

2. This distribution of trial outcomes, 60 and 40, is suggested by the probabilities 60% and 40%. The actual number of outcomes of each type might well be different, but usually the number of wins in 100 trials would be close to 60 if the likelihood of winning each is 60%.

Figure 1-4. In this example, $60,000 is the expected value of the chance events following from the decision to go to trial, so we write $60,000 under the chance node. This notation indicates that we evaluate the chancy situation as if it were worth $60,000.

If we look again at the full decision tree, in Figure 1-5, we can see that we're now in a position to compare the two decision branches, Trial and Settle. It's apparent that Trial is worse than Settle. Trial requires an expenditure of $20,000 and leads to the chance node worth $60,000, yielding a net of $40,000, whereas Settle is worth $70,000. Hence, Settle is the better decision. We therefore strike off the decision branch Trial, leaving Settle as the better of the two possible decisions that you can make with your client. We also note the payoff — $70,000 — under the first decision box to indicate that this is the amount that will be obtained if you make the best decision, Settle.

C. Risk Aversion

You might be thinking that your client wouldn't necessarily have assigned a $60,000 value to the chancy situation in which $100,000 is won with a 60% probability and $0 gained with a 40% probability. Perhaps your client is scared of the possibility of ending with nothing (in addition to having to spend $20,000 on litigation) and really needs to wind up with some positive amount of money. In such a case, your client would evaluate the chancy situation as worth less than $60,000, maybe only $50,000. A client who treats a risky situation as worth less than its expected value is called *risk averse*, and the lower the client's evaluation of the situation, the more risk averse the client is said to be.

Risk aversion is often relevant where the amounts in question are large in relation to a party's wealth and where the party might be left with low assets. It helps to explain why people like to purchase insurance. It also suggests why people ordinarily are reluctant to commit too much of their assets to one investment and, instead, tend to diversify. However, risk aversion would not necessarily be relevant where the amounts at stake don't constitute a significant proportion of a party's assets. For instance, risk aversion might not be relevant to a wealthy person or to a large corporation in a litigation involving a sum like $100,000.

Figure 1-5
Settlement versus Trial: Uncertainty and the Best Decision

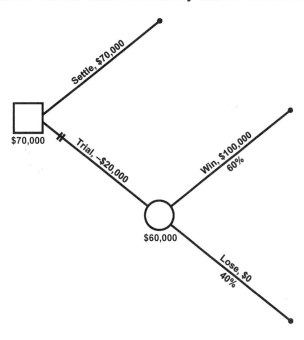

If risk aversion is relevant when you're using a decision tree, your evaluation of a chancy payoff should be a number lower than the expected value — for example, a number like $50,000 or $40,000, rather than $60,000 in our hypothetical case. You can use your intuition or judgment to arrive at an appropriate lower number.[3] Better yet, discuss it with your client.

Mainly for convenience, expected value will be used as the evaluation of risky situations in the material that follows.

D. Application: Settlement Negotiation

Let's go back to the first example described at the beginning of the chapter: settlement negotiation following an automobile accident. The decision tree, in Figure 1-6, is similar to the one for the contract case with an uncertain outcome that we just discussed (see Figure 1-6).

---

3. Alternatively, you could use a more systematic approach to find the right lower number, which is often called the *certainty equivalent*. If you'd like to learn about this, be sure to check the sources mentioned at the end of the chapter.

Figure 1-6
Automobile Accident Litigation

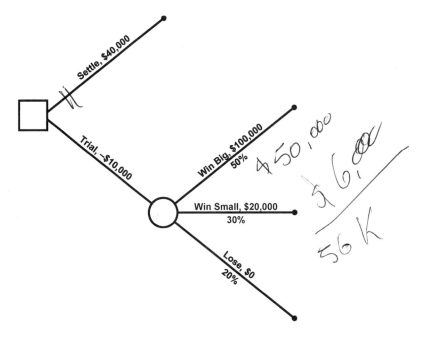

The initial decision is whether to accept the settlement offer or to go to trial, so we begin with a decision node that has two decision branches extending from it, Settle and Trial. Along the Settle decision branch, we write $40,000 as the payoff, which was stated to be the settlement offer. Along the Trial branch, we now write –$10,000, the stated legal expense of trial for this case. At the end of the Trial branch, we draw a chance node, because the outcome of trial is uncertain. There are three possible outcomes of going to trial in this example, so we must have three chance branches coming off the chance node. First, as indicated on the uppermost chance branch, the client can Win Big and obtain $100,000 in damages. The probability of this outcome is 50%. Second, as noted on the middle chance branch, the client can Win Small, receiving only $20,000. The likelihood that this would be the outcome is 30%. Third, as represented by the lowermost chance branch, the person may Lose and emerge from trial with nothing. The odds of this outcome are 20%. (It's worth noting again that the decision tree contains all the information that's in the verbal description and displays it in a fashion that shows the sequence in which decisions are made and events unfold.)

Figure 1-7
Trial: Chance Branches

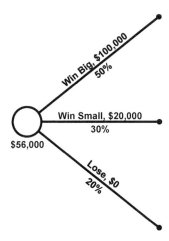

We solve this decision tree in much the same way that we solved the one in the contract case. Let's start by paying particular attention to the chance node and the chance branches corresponding to going to trial (see Figure 1-7). We have to figure out what the expected value is, taking into account the three possible outcomes: gaining $100,000 with a probability of 50%, gaining $20,000 with a probability of 30%, and losing with a probability of 20% (in other words, gaining $0 with a probability of 20%). As we can see from Table 1-1, the expected value is (50% × $100,000) + (30% × $20,000) + (20% × $0), or $56,000.[4] We can interpret this figure — $56,000 — as being the amount that your client would obtain, on average, after repeated litigation if your assessment of the odds of the three outcomes were those we used here. We record the expected value, $56,000, under the chance node.

The decision tree can be solved now, so let's return to the full tree as it appears in Figure 1-8, which includes all the information from Figure 1-7. Because $56,000 is the evaluation of the chance node following Trial, the evaluation of the branch Trial is $46,000 (i.e., $56,000 – $10,000 = $46,000). When we compare this amount ($46,000) with the value of

---

4. In general, the expected value of a risky situation with many possible payoffs is found as follows: multiply each payoff amount by its probability, and then add these figures.

Table 1-1
Computing the Expected Value

Chance Branch	Amount	×	Probability	=	Product
Win Big	$100,000	×	50%	=	$50,000
Win Small	$ 20,000	×	30%	=	$ 6,000
Lose	$ 0	×	20%	=	$ 0
				Expected value:	$56,000

Figure 1-8
Automobile Accident Litigation: The Best Decision

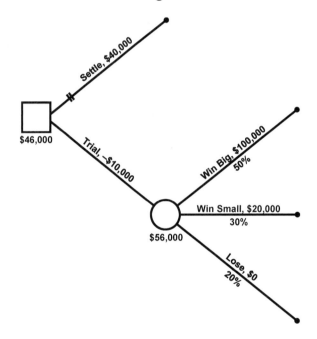

Settle, $40,000, it's apparent that Trial is superior. So we strike off Settle and write $46,000 under the beginning decision node. We've solved this decision problem: Trial, with an evaluation of $46,000, is the better of the two possible decisions.[5]

E. Application: Land Purchase

We're now ready to tackle the land purchase decision outlined at the beginning of the chapter. Even though this problem is more complex

---

5. Consider how a highly risk-averse client might assess this situation.

than the ones we've already worked through, no new conceptual apparatus is required to solve it.

The first thing that we have to do is to translate the problem into decision-tree format. A good way to do this is to think about the problem in chronological order. Let's begin by determining what is the first decision that has to be made. Recall that your client has to decide whether to purchase Parcel A or Parcel B and whether to test Parcel B for hazardous wastes. In other words, your client must, in fact, initially decide among three options. Hence, the decision tree begins with a decision box from which three decision branches emanate: Buy A, Buy B, and Test B. The additional labels in Figure 1-9 — $300,000, $250,000, and $20,000 — reflect, respectively, the purchase prices of Parcel A and B and the cost of testing Parcel B for hazardous wastes. (Minus signs aren't used here because all the outcomes are expenses and all the payoffs are written with this understanding in mind.)

Figure 1-9
The Initial Land Purchase Problem

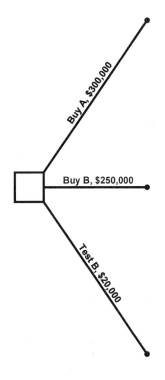

Figure 1-10
The Complete Land Purchase Problem

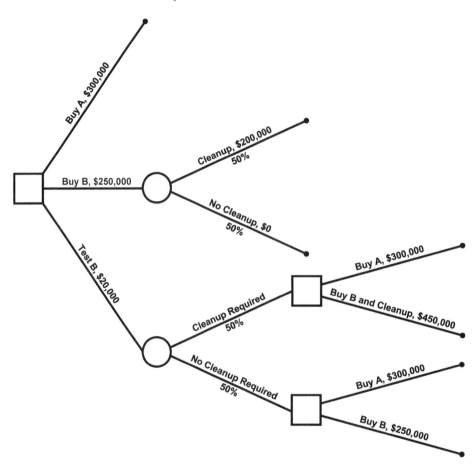

Now we have to extend the tree to take into account what, if anything, happens after the initial decision is made. As we can see from Figure 1-10, a chance node follows decision branch Buy B, because one of two events will occur if your client decides to buy Parcel B: your client will discover that hazardous wastes have to be cleaned up or that hazardous wastes don't have to be cleaned up. So one possibility is Cleanup, which was said to involve an expense of $200,000, as indicated along with its probability of 50% on the upper chance branch. The other possibility, represented on the lower chance branch, is No Cleanup, which involves no additional expense and which also has a probability of 50%.

A chance node also follows decision branch Test B because testing for hazardous waste can result in either of two outcomes — Cleanup

Required and No Cleanup Required — each of which, as noted in Figure 1-10, has a probability of 50%.

If testing results in Cleanup Required, your client then decides which parcel to buy, so another decision node is added to the tree. If your client chooses Buy A, the cost will, of course, be $300,000. If your client instead elects Buy B, the total cost will be $450,000: $250,000 (the price of Parcel B) plus $200,000 (the cost of cleaning up Parcel B) because cleanup is required.

If testing for hazardous wastes results in No Cleanup Required, your client again decides which parcel to buy, and a decision node with two branches is added: Buy A and Buy B. If your client opts for Buy A, the cost will be $300,000. If your client chooses Buy B, the cost will be the Parcel B purchase price — $250,000 — and no more, because the parcel doesn't have to be cleaned up.

Now that the decision tree reflects all the possible decisions that can be made and all the possible events that can occur, it can be solved.[6] Let's

---

Box 1-2
The Value of Information

When we figure out whether testing for hazardous wastes is worthwhile, we'll be solving a problem of a pretty general type: is a particular amount worth paying for information? Decision theory allows us to answer this question, because it enables us to take into proper account how much better off we will be in light of how we would use the information we get.

---

work through the solution, which appears in Figure 1-11. We begin with the topmost decision branch, Buy A. Evaluating this branch is straightforward: the cost is $300,000. In evaluating decision branch Buy B, we have to consider the chance node following it. That is, we have to calculate

---

6. The tree could be drawn in a different way: it could begin with a choice between Test and Don't Test. Can you see how it would then continue? And can you verify that its solution is equivalent to what we find here?

Figure 1-11
The Land Purchase Problem: The Best Decisions

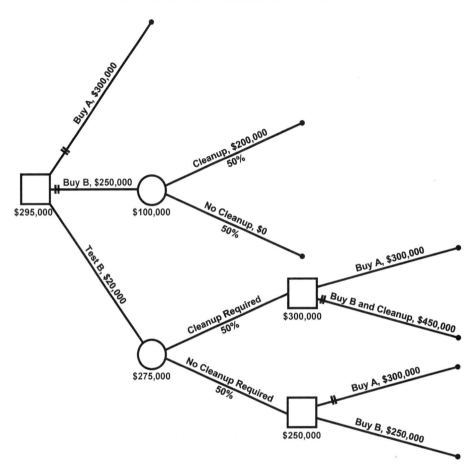

the expected cleanup cost: 50% × $200,000 = $100,000. In other words, if Parcel B is purchased, the expected cleanup cost will be $100,000. So $100,000 is noted below the chance node. Consequently, if the client buys Parcel B, the evaluation is $350,000 (i.e., the $250,000 purchase price plus the $100,000 expected cleanup cost). The $350,000 evaluation exceeds the $300,000 cost of Buy A, so Buy B can be struck off because it's a worse decision than Buy A is. (As you can see, Buy A is also struck off in Figure 1-11. We'll get to the reason for this in a moment.)

Let's consider the remaining decision branch, Test B. Two possible chance outcomes follow this branch — Cleanup Required and No Cleanup Required — but we can't evaluate this chance node yet, because we haven't determined what decisions would be made later or their value. What we do in this situation is work backward. Starting with Cleanup Required, we see from the tree that Buy A is better than Buy B in this situation, because $300,000 is less than $450,000. This, of course, accords with the intuition that paying $300,000 for Parcel A is better than paying $250,000 for Parcel B and then having to spend an additional $200,000 to clean it up, bringing the total cost of Parcel B up to $450,000. Given that Buy A is the optimal decision in this case, Buy B is struck off and $300,000 is noted under the decision node.

Now for the other possibility, a test result of No Cleanup Required: Buy B is better than Buy A, because $250,000 is less than $300,000. In other words, paying $250,000 for Parcel B (which we know in this situation doesn't require cleaning up) is better than paying $300,000 for Parcel A. Because Buy B is the optimal decision, Buy A is struck off, and $250,000 is written under the decision node.

We're now in a position to evaluate the chance node that follows Test B. The evaluation is $300,000 for a test outcome of Cleanup Required and $250,000 for a test outcome of No Cleanup Required. So the expected value of the decision node following Test B is $275,000 — i.e., (50% × $300,000) + (50% × $250,000) = $275,000 — and this figure is written under the chance node.

Finally, we have the information we need to evaluate decision branch Test B. The evaluation is $295,000 (i.e., $20,000 to perform the test and an expected payout of $275,000 once the test is completed). This figure is lower than the $300,000 evaluation of Buy A, so the Buy A decision is inferior and thus can be struck off. Hence, Test B emerges as the optimal decision, and $295,000 — the expected value of the Test B decision — is noted under the first decision node.

At this point, it's worth stepping back for a moment to look at what we've just done in solving this problem and to put some kind of perspective on it.

First, not only have we found the best initial decision for you and your client to make — Test B — but we've also formulated a complete set of instructions for what you're supposed to do throughout the process. We

---

Box 1-3
Government Policy Design and Decision Analysis

Suppose that the EPA often wants people (and corporations) to test land for hazardous wastes so that they'll undertake cleanup right away if hazardous wastes are found. Does the government have to subsidize testing or give tax credits for such testing in order to motivate people to do the testing? The EPA can find out whether people will want to test for hazardous wastes, given the current cost of testing, by using decision analysis. More generally, decision analysis can help government to predict people's behavior and thus enable government to design its policies intelligently.

---

can see this by examining the tree and going down the decision branches that aren't struck off. Specifically, you begin by choosing Test B, because the other two decision branches are struck off. Then you find out whether or not cleanup is needed. You're now at one or the other of the two decision nodes at the bottom right of the tree. For each of these, only one buy decision is available, the other having been struck off, so you can tell from the tree what your client should do: buy Parcel A or buy Parcel B, depending on whether or not toxic wastes have to be cleaned up from Parcel B.

Second, if you reflect on what we did to evaluate the Test B decision branch, you'll realize that we started at the right-most aspect of the tree and worked leftward. And we did this naturally, intuitively. Indeed, we had to work this way. For example, we couldn't know how to evaluate Cleanup Required without knowing whether your client would ultimately purchase Parcel A or Parcel B after the testing results were known for Cleanup Required. And we couldn't evaluate the Test B branch without knowing what decision you and your client would later make about purchasing for each of the possible test results. We had to do this because, in effect, we have to *look before we leap* in order to know what to do.

F. Generalizations

Some generalizations that are applicable in solving any decision tree can be derived from what we've done in the preceding examples:

- Start at the right side of the tree — that is, with the last group of chance events or last group of decisions. (It doesn't matter where on the right side you begin.) Where there are chance events at the right end of the tree — that is, branches stemming from a chance node — compute the expected value, and write it under the chance node. Where a decision has to be made at the right end of the tree, figure out what decision is the best one, and strike off the other possibilities to indicate that you've ruled them out. Be sure to write the value of the best decision under the decision node.
- Repeat this process for all of the right-most decision and chance nodes.
- Move one level to the left, repeat the preceding steps, and keep working leftward until you've finished with the tree.

One point that merits emphasis is truly good news: you really can't do the wrong thing in solving a decision tree, because it's impossible to evaluate any node without having already evaluated everything to the right of it. So, in a sense, you don't have to remember the specific technique described here. By simply attacking the tree, you will automatically be led to proceed from right to left, thereby reaching the correct solution.

G. Test Your Skill

Let's consider one more example of a decision-making problem, one more complicated than those we've already solved. If you can follow how this one is translated into a decision tree — and most likely you can — then you'll know that you have a good grasp of how to construct trees.

Suppose that you're advising a plaintiff and you're unsure about the magnitude of her losses (say, losses due to lost business resulting from a breach of contract). You can hire an expert to obtain a preliminary estimate of losses, and you figure that the preliminary estimate has an equal probability of being low ($200,000) or high ($400,000). The cost of hiring the expert is $20,000.

You'll have time before trial to develop support for the expert's estimates, but doing so will be costly. Specifically, if you spend $10,000 on supporting the low estimate, you'll receive $200,000 at trial for sure, whereas if you don't spend the $10,000, you'll have only a 50% chance of receiving $200,000 and a 50% chance of receiving $150,000. Similarly, if you spend $10,000 on supporting the high estimate, the probability is 80% that you'll receive $400,000 and 20% that you'll receive $350,000, whereas if you don't spend the $10,000, the odds are 70% that you'll receive $400,000 and 30% that you'll receive $350,000.

If you don't hire an expert, you won't have time before trial to support the estimate because you'll have no real idea of what the losses are and no guidance from an expert as to what facts you should try to demonstrate. You figure that, in this situation, trial has a 50% chance of resulting in a $150,000 judgment and a 50% chance of resulting in a $350,000 judgment, depending on the information revealed at the time of trial.

What should you do? The answer can be derived from the decision tree in Figure 1-12. This tree has two initial decisions branches: Hire Expert and No Expert.

Let's begin with the upper branch: Hire Expert. A cost of $20,000 is incurred, so this figure is noted on the branch. A chance node follows the branch, and it indicates the two possible estimates that the expert can discover: Low Estimate, which is $200,000, and High Estimate, which is $400,000. Their probabilities, 50% each, are noted on the chance branches. The decision node at the end of each chance branch indicates that a decision is to be made. The possibilities are Spend, $10,000 (i.e., spend $10,000 on trial preparation) and Don't Spend (i.e., spend nothing on trial preparation). If the expert reports the low estimate and you then opt to spend $10,000 on trial preparation, you're certain to win $200,000. If, on the other hand, you get the low estimate from the expert but don't spend on trial preparation, you might receive $200,000, but you're equally likely to get only $150,000, as indicated at the chance node that follows the Don't Spend decision branch.

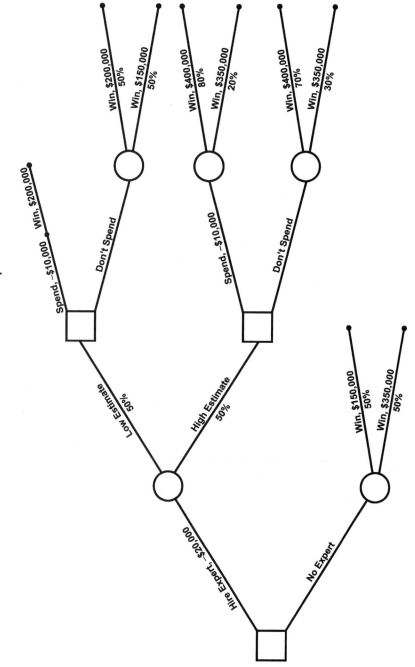

Figure 1-12
Should You Hire an Expert?

We've just worked through the Hire Expert, Low Estimate part of the tree. The part just below — the Hire Expert, High Estimate section — is very similar. We're left with the No Expert decision branch. This branch is followed by a chance node from which two possibilities emanate: receiving $150,000 and receiving $350,000, each of which has a probability of 50%.

At this point, solving the tree should be straightforward. You might want to give it a try, either now or at a later time, as a review exercise. As you do so, see whether you can explain to yourself the intuition behind the best decisions to make.

3. Acquiring the Necessary Information

In the foregoing examples, the information needed to construct the decision trees was provided to us. We didn't have to gather it or develop it. But, in real life, being presented with such neat thumbnail sketches isn't at all typical. In fact, much of the information pertinent to making a decision often isn't readily available. And not all of the possible decisions may be obvious, because no one has methodically worked them out. So how can you, in your practice of law, get your hands on the information you need?

If we analyze the decision analysis process, we find that the information you'll require is of three basic types: (1) descriptions of the possible decisions and possible outcomes — in other words, information relevant to the structure of the decision tree; (2) the probabilities of the various chance events that are part of the tree; and (3) the numerical (or other) payoffs or costs associated with all the options.

A. Structure

Before you can do anything else, you'll have to ascertain the structure of the problem facing you. You'll have to identify the initial decision, determine what can happen as a result of each possibility, and so on. You may do this yourself. More often, though, the information will emerge from discussions with others, notably, with your client and sometimes with your lawyer colleagues, experts, and others. The process of describing the problem will frequently proceed chronologically, from the left of the decision tree to the right. This exercise will often provide a great deal of clarity, because it will force you — indeed, impose an inescapable discipline on you — to be precise and reasonably complete.

As pointed out earlier, your legal knowledge and your practical experience as a lawyer will play an important role in the structuring of the decision tree. If, for example, the problem at hand involves regulatory rules, you'll know them or learn them. If it involves potential liability for negligence, you'll know how the standard of care is determined. If it involves the conduct of litigation, you'll know about the pertinent legal procedure (e.g., the motions that might be filed, the discovery process, and trial itself). Frequently, you'll have, in addition, experience that your client doesn't have but that is relevant even though, strictly speaking, it isn't legal experience. For instance, you'll be aware that there are firms that test for hazardous wastes on land if you've already done many land transactions (and you'll know of specific firms that do such testing), whereas your client, having been involved in few, if any, transactions of this kind, may well be unaware that testing firms even exist (or even that testing for hazardous wastes may be necessary or desirable).

Another common benefit of formally constructing a decision tree is also worth noting: it may reveal that the number of possible decisions and the number of possible outcomes is greater than was originally thought. (However, you'll sometimes want to do a bit of simplifying and consolidating, especially of outcomes, to prevent the tree from becoming unwieldy.)

B. Probabilities

Once you've worked out the structure of the decision tree, you'll need to plug in the probabilities of events. But how will you figure out what the probabilities are? In some cases, you'll have access to hard data that are helpful. For instance, for the probability that you'll win a particular case, you might use the percentage of similar cases in which your side has prevailed. Similarly, in giving tax advice, you might use the audit rate. In other cases, relevant data won't be immediately available, but you'll have an opportunity to obtain it at some cost. For example, you might conduct mock trials to help predict the odds of winning at trial, or you might hire an expert to ascertain the likelihood that your client's conduct constituted negligence.

Box 1-4
How Are Probabilities Determined in Practice?

Probabilities are often found by asking people to compare bets, just as described in the text. In fact, one very successful consultant uses a "betting wheel" that has an adjustable red wedge, which represents the "winning" area, and a black background, which represents the "losing" area. He starts with just a thin sliver of red and asks his client if she thinks the outcome in question is more likely to occur than the thin sliver of red would be to come up on a spin of the betting wheel. If she says no, he makes the red wedge progressively larger until she says, "Gee, I guess my outcome is about as likely to occur as the red wedge now is to come up on a spin of the betting wheel."

Often, however, you'll have to rely on subjective judgments in formulating probabilities. When trying to determine the likelihood of winning a case, you might find that data on very similar cases are insufficient or lacking altogether. You might not be able to locate information that would enable you to estimate the likelihood that the other party to a contract will breach it. In situations like these, probability estimates are unavoidably subjective. But, you might be asking, how can a specific probability be derived for use in such cases?

This question is most easily answered by example. Let's say that you're trying to ascertain the probability that you'll win a particular case. You can start by asking yourself, Would I prefer to place a bet in which I collect if I win my case or to place a bet in which I collect if any number between 1 and 30 turns up when a fair roulette wheel with 100 numbers on it is spun? If your answer is that you prefer the bet on your case, your subjective probability of winning is greater than 30%. If so, compare the bet on your case to a bet on the roulette wheel in which you win if any number between 1 and 40 comes up. If you still prefer the bet on your case, this means that you feel the odds of winning exceed 40%. Continue

Box 1-5
Time, Hassle, and Other Nonmonetary Payoffs

Don't forget to include in your assessment of payoffs factors that aren't purely financial. Various decisions and outcomes will involve the expenditure of time, which you'll definitely want to take into account and probably convert to some monetary equivalent. Another example: a client might want to avoid the emotional cost of trial or embarrassment of some type. You'll want to take a stab, with the help of your client, at incorporating such non-monetary elements into your figures: a guesstimate is a lot better than ignoring these often important factors.

doing this type of comparison, adjusting the range of winning numbers on the roulette wheel up or down, until you reach a resting point — the point where you're indifferent between the bet on your case and the bet on the roulette wheel. This will tell you what your subjective probability is. For example, if you're indifferent between a bet on your case and a bet on the roulette wheel when any number between 1 and 60 turns up, your subjective probability of winning the case is 60%. Two points are worth noting about this method. First, even though it's subjective — a matter of your opinion — the result is influenced by the information you have. Second, you and others who use it might arrive at similar subjective probability estimates. And, when you don't, the discussion produced by your disagreement will often be illuminating and should provide a basis for formulating your best estimate.

You should keep in mind that many probabilities are ones that you, as the lawyer, will have to supply or have your client produce. Probabilities pertaining to legal outcomes are ones that you'll have to provide (or, at the least, play an important role in furnishing). It will be your responsibility to determine the odds of prevailing in a case or on an element of a case. Your client will be able to bring certain types of facts to the table that, in combination with your knowledge, will make it possible to arrive at probabilistic judgments about what will happen.

C. Payoffs

Payoffs (and costs) can be estimated by methods similar to those used in determining probabilities. You'll often find yourself obtaining information from clients to estimate payoffs and hiring experts to refine your estimates. Again, as a lawyer, you will have unique information to contribute. For instance, in determining payoffs in the form of possible damage awards, your knowledge of which elements of losses are included as damages will be relevant. You will also, in contrast to most of your clients, know such things as the costs of legal services and of various types of experts.

4. Sensitivity Analysis

As is probably evident by now, a recurring problem in constructing and solving decision trees is the problem of finding estimates for probabilities and final outcomes that are sufficiently reliable to make us feel reasonably confident in the outcomes of our analyses. Sometimes even our best efforts fail to yield a numerical estimate that we feel comfortable about. In such cases, it's natural to ask whether our decisions would be affected if the data on which they're based changed. Would we make a different decision if our probability assessments were different by some amount or if the profits we wrote down were altered by some amount? In considering this type of question, we're engaging in *sensitivity analysis*. This analysis process is so named because its object is to find out whether the best decision is sensitive to particular changes in the data.

One way of ascertaining how sensitive our answer is to the data is by asking how much our estimate of the probability or a payoff amount can vary without changing what we've found to be the best set of decisions. Sometimes we'll find that the optimal decision remains the same over a wide range of plausible estimates for the value under consideration. In other words, the decision is robust with respect to that value. In other cases, however, we'll find that even a small change in an estimated value leads to a different preferred decision. In cases of this type, we have good reason to seek further information in an attempt to improve our estimates.

Let's return to the problem represented in the first decision tree we looked at to see how sensitivity analysis works (see Figure 1-13). As

Figure 1-13
Settlement versus Trial: The Best Decision

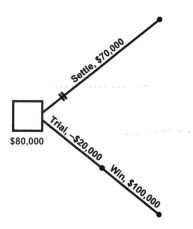

pointed out earlier, the correct solution is trivial as long as you accept these estimates as accurate. Suppose, however, that you have reason to doubt the accuracy of the estimate of net recovery if you go to trial. Perhaps the expense of going to trial depends in part on how vigorously the defendant opposes you. Perhaps a jury wouldn't award the predicted amount. You'd want to know how far off your estimate of net recovery would have to be for you to change your decision from Trial to Settle. The answer is obvious. Only if you reduced your estimate of the trial outcome from $100,000 to less than $90,000, which reduces the net recovery from $80,000 to less than $70,000 (i.e., the settlement offer), would you change your decision. Thus, an estimate of a trial outcome of $90,000, for a net recovery of $70,000, is a *crossover point* for the sensitivity analysis. In other words, if you cross over this point, you're going to change your decision. Crossover points often become focal points for reflection on the reliability of decision analyses.

Suppose that you can spend money to refine your information and that, in doing so, you might end up with information that would cause you to change one or more of your decisions. You can determine whether you should obtain the additional information (which itself is a decision problem, similar to the land purchase problem) in the following way: First, ascertain what your expected payoff is without having more information. Second, calculate what your expected payoff would be if you had the additional information (realizing that your best decision will generally depend on the type of information that you obtain). Finally, if this second value (the expected payoff with information) exceeds the first value (the expected payoff without information) by more than the cost of the information, you should obtain the information.

To illustrate, consider again the decision tree in Figure 1-13 and suppose that, right now, you're uncertain about the amount you would recover at trial. You think that you have a 50% probability of winning $150,000 and a 50% probability of winning only $50,000. You can, however, at a cost of $10,000 hire an expert on damages in advance to determine for sure whether you'd collect $50,000 or $150,000 at trial. See if you can construct a decision tree reflecting this situation and can use it to verify the following: If you don't hire the expert, your expected payoff is $80,000. If you hire the expert and he tells you that you would win $50,000 at trial, you would net $30,000 from trial, so you would decide to take the settlement of $70,000. If the expert tells you that you would win $150,000 at trial, you would net $130,000 from trial, so you would choose to go to trial. The expert's advice therefore increases your expected payoff from $80,000 to $100,000. Hiring the expert costs only $10,000, so it's desirable for you to do so.

5. Suggestions for Further Reading

If you're interested in delving further into decision analysis, there are a number of good treatments to which you may turn. An excellent practical presentation, at a slightly more advanced level than our chapter, may be found in S. Christian Albright, Wayne L. Winston and Christopher J. Zappe, *Data Analysis and Decision Making*, 3rd ed. (Mason, OH: South-Western, 2009), chapter 7. This chapter is intended as an introduction to decision analysis for graduate students in business. Readers with more mathematical sophistication may prefer chapter 13 of Wayne L. Winston, *Operations Research*, 4th ed. (Belmont, CA: Brooks/Cole, 2009).

Another recommendation is TreeAge Software's website, www. TreeAge.com, where you can find software that facilitates drawing and solving complex decision trees. Be sure to check out their client list: it includes many of America's premier law firms.

Much recent research in decision analysis has been conducted by psychologists who are interested in understanding the errors that are common in actual human decision-making. Reid Hastie and Robyn M. Dawes' *Rational Choice in an Uncertain World*, 2nd ed. (Thousand Oaks, CA: Sage Publications, 2010) is an excellent non-technical introduction to this work that should be of value to anyone who wishes to improve their decision making skills.

Some students may be interested in a classic by Howard Raiffa, one of the founders of decision analysis, *Decision Analysis* (Reading, MA: Addison-Wesley, 1968), or in his more recent advanced-level text, Howard Raiffa, John Richardson, and David Metcalfe, *Negotiation Analysis: The Science and Art of Collaborative Decision Making* (Cambridge, MA: Harvard University Press, 2002). Current work in decision analysis can be found in *Theory and Decision*, a multidisciplinary journal that's accessible to a general scholarly audience, and *Decision Analysis* — the official journal of the Decision Analysis Society (the professional organization of decision analysts, http://www.informs.org/Community/DAS).

2
Games and Information

1. Introduction to Game Theory

In many situations, people decide on an action based in part on how others are likely to act, on how they themselves are likely to react to the actions of others, or both. This is often true of actions chosen by players in many games. A chess player decides which piece to move and where to move it on the basis of what he anticipates his opponent's response will be. Similarly, in business, legal, and social interactions, parties frequently take into account the anticipated behavior of others when making their decisions. The price that an airline chooses to set on a particular route depends on whether it expects competitors to match or undercut its price. Whether a lawyer files a motion will depend on what she thinks the opposing side will do as a consequence of the motion. In deciding whether to extend a dinner invitation to someone, the host will take into account how he expects the person to behave at the party and whether the invitee is likely to reciprocate.

Game theory deals with such situations. The foundations of this discipline were laid in the 1920s and 1930s, and the study of military tactics during World War II stimulated its development. Game theory, now highly developed, provides a useful, flexible way to organize thinking about strategic decision making. For lawyers, it's valuable for these general reasons and for the aid it furnishes in designing contracts, formulating litigation strategy, and conducting all sorts of negotiation. In addition, a knowledge of game theory is a prerequisite to understanding much writing in law as well as areas of business of interest to lawyers, such as corporate takeovers and anticompetitive behavior.

2. Description of Games

A game involves *players*. In many cases, there are two players, as in a chess game or a legal case involving a plaintiff and a defendant. But sometimes there are more than two, as in some poker games, a legal case involving a plaintiff and two defendants, or three airlines competing on a route.

Each player chooses one or more *actions*, which can be anything from moving a chess piece to filing a legal motion to setting the price to charge for an item. The actions available to a player may vary over time. For instance, a chess player is able to move only pawns and knights at the beginning of a game but can move other pieces as well several moves later.[1]

Each player also has certain *information.* This, too, may change during the course of a game. For instance, the defendant might have little knowledge about the plaintiff's losses at the outset, whereas after discovery he might have substantial information about the plaintiff's losses.

The *timing* and *order of moves* are important aspects of games. The players often move after one another. For instance, chess players alternate moves. In litigation, if the plaintiff decides to file suit (the first move), the defendant then either files an opposing motion or offers to settle for some amount, and so forth. Sometimes, however, the parties act simultaneously or choose acts without knowing what acts the others are selecting. Consider, for instance, sealed bids submitted at auction or pleadings that opposing litigants are required to furnish to the court at the same time.

---

1. In game theory, a *strategy* is a plan that specifies the action to be chosen at every possible juncture. In chess, for instance, a strategy would tell you what move to make as a function of where all the pieces are on the chessboard.

The objective of each player is to end up with the maximum possible *payoff*. Payoffs encompass all things that matter to a player, positively or negatively, at any time during the game. For instance, in litigation, payoffs include not only any payment that the litigant ultimately makes or receives through settlement or trial judgment but also the time and money that she expends as well as any pleasure or displeasure that she experiences from the negotiation or trial process.

One device that's sometimes useful when working with games, especially when two players are involved, is the *game table*. The easiest way to explain a game table is by example. Let's suppose the following: (1) Amy and Bill are two opposing litigants, each of whom claims ownership of some asset, say, from an inheritance. (2) Amy can choose one of two actions: Discovery or No Discovery. (3) Bill can select one of three actions: Expert Witness (hire an expert witness), Consultant (hire just a consultant), or Do Nothing. A game table representing this situation can be created, as in Table 2-1, by assigning each of Amy's possible actions (Discovery and No Discovery) to a row and each of Bill's possible actions (Expert Witness, Consultant, and Do Nothing) to a column. Then, a particular cell in the game table corresponds to one of Amy's possible actions and one of Bill's possible actions. For instance, the cell in the first row and the first column corresponds to Amy's choosing Discovery and Bill's choosing Expert Witness. In general, the payoff to each player will depend on the action that each takes. The players in a game are presumed to know (or to estimate) the payoffs they would get as a result of their actions.

How are the payoffs written in the game table? In each cell, the payoffs for the players are written for the actions of that cell. By convention, the

Table 2-1
Game Table: Bill and Amy

		Bill's Action		
		Expert Witness	**Consultant**	**Do Nothing**
Amy's Action	**Discovery**	3, 4	5, 7	9, 2
	No Discovery	2, 10	8, 8	12, 4

Table 2-2
Game Table: The Prisoners' Dilemma

		Baxter's Action	
		Confess	**Deny**
Chester's	**Confess**	10, 10	0, 15
Action	**Deny**	15, 0	1, 1

payoff of the player whose actions are listed to the left (in Table 2-1, this would be Amy's payoff) is the first number in the cell, and the payoff of the player whose actions are listed at the top (in Table 2-1, Bill's payoff) is the second number. So, if Amy chooses No Discovery and Bill chooses Expert Witness, the bottom left cell tells us that they get 2 and 10, respectively. Similarly, if Amy chooses Discovery and Bill chooses Consultant, Amy gets 5 and Bill gets 7, according to the entry in the top center cell.

A famous example of a game that can be represented by a table is the *prisoners' dilemma*. In this game, there are two prisoners, Baxter and Chester, who in fact are guilty of a theft. They are questioned separately. If both confess, each will be sentenced to 10 years in prison. If both deny their guilt, each will be sentenced to 1 year in prison, because the prosecution will be able to prove only a lesser offense. If one confesses and the other denies guilt, the deal with the prosecutor will be that the one who confesses will go free, and the other will receive a 15-year sentence. In this game, both players have the same two options — Confess to the theft or Deny guilt — and payoffs are measured in number of years in prison (see Table 2-2).[2] Note that, in each cell, the first payoff is Chester's (because it's his possible actions that are listed on the left), and Baxter's payoff is written second. Thus, if Chester chooses Confess and Baxter opts for Deny, Chester gets off scot-free and Baxter goes to jail for 15 years, so the payoffs are entered as 0, 15. (We'll return to Chester and Baxter a little later to figure out what they might be expected to do.)

---

2. The payoffs could have been written as negative numbers rather than as positive numbers.

Figure 2-1
A Simple Litigation Game Tree

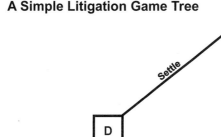

Game trees, which are similar to decision trees, provide an alternative way of representing games. They're especially helpful when players' actions are sequential. Again, let's consider a simple example. Suppose that a victim suffers a loss and can choose either of two actions: Sue or Lump It (do nothing and just accept the loss). If the victim sues, suppose that the defendant, in turn, can choose either of two actions: Settle (settle the suit for what the plaintiff asks — we're simplifying here) or Go to Trial. The tree representing the game tree to this point appears in Figure 2-1. Note that the initial box — a *decision node* — is labeled P (short for *plaintiff*), because it's the plaintiff who first chooses an action (in this case, either Sue or Lump It).[3] Each possible decision is indicated by a *decision branch.* At the end of the Sue branch, there's another decision node. This one is marked D (for *defendant*), because the defendant has a decision to make at this point if the plaintiff has filed suit. The two possible actions are Settle and Go to Trial, each with its own decision

3. As you'll recall from the Decision Analysis chapter, we don't label decision nodes when we construct decision trees. Doing so is unnecessary because the assumption in decision analysis is that just one person makes decisions.

branch. After the defendant makes this choice, whichever action it is, the game ends.

It's worth noting that this game, as simple as it is, can't be represented by a game table. The reason is that, in a table, each possible action of one player appears in combination with *each* possible action of the other player. But this isn't the case here. Lump It can't, for example, be paired with Go to Trial; the combination makes no sense. The defendant's possible actions — Settle and Go to Trial — are available for consideration *only* if the plaintiff has chosen Sue. A table in which possible actions are arranged in rows and columns doesn't allow for the representation of situations where players move in sequence and the action of one player subsequently affects the set of actions available to the other player.

Continuing with our example, let's say that it was the plaintiff's loss of $10,000 in an accident that gave rise to the game, and let's assume that filing suit would cost the plaintiff $3,000, that the defendant would pay $8,000 if the case were settled, and that each side would bear $2,000 in expenses and the judgment would be for $9,000 if the case went to trial.[4]

Payoffs can be incorporated into a game tree as shown in Figure 2-2. Any payoff associated with a possible action is noted along the corresponding decision branch, and the accumulated, final payoffs (i.e., the net payoffs) for each possible pathway are written next to the decision node representing the end of the game for that pathway. By convention, the plaintiff's payoff is entered first, because he moves first, and the defendant's payoff is entered second, because he moves second.

For example, in Figure 2-2, the first amount at the uppermost end node of the tree (the one following Settle) is $5,000. This would be the plaintiff's payoff — the amount that she would end with (i.e., if she spent $3,000 to file suit and received $8,000 in a settlement, her net return would be $5,000).[5] The second amount written after the same end node is –$8,000, which would be the defendant's payoff. It's written as a negative number

---

4. The plaintiff might, for example, not be able to establish $1,000 of his loss. Hence, the judgment would be for only $9,000 rather than the full $10,000 loss. These amounts are the payoffs for this game.

5. For convenience, we've disregarded the $10,000 loss that the plaintiff sustained before the game began. We took into account only amounts spent or received during

Figure 2-2
A Simple Litigation Game Tree with Payoffs

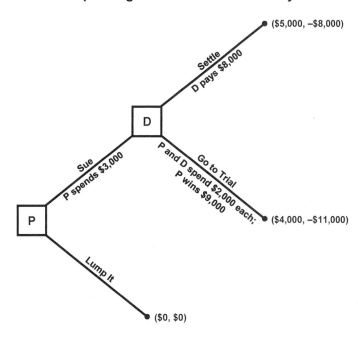

because he spends $8,000 on the settlement. Similarly, at the next end node (the one after Go to Trial), the plaintiff's payoff is $4,000 (i.e., she would spend $3,000 to file suit and $2,000 to go to trial and would obtain a judgment of $9,000), and the defendant's payoff is –$11,000 (i.e., he would spend $2,000 on trial and $9,000 on the judgment). At the bottom end node (after Lump It), because neither the plaintiff nor the defendant would pay or receive anything, the payoff for each is $0.[6]

Chance plays a role in many games, and it, too, can be reflected in game trees, in much the same way that it is in the decision trees of the Decision Analysis chapter. For example, perhaps a $9,000 outcome isn't a certainty for the plaintiff in our example if she goes to trial. Perhaps,

---

the game. However, it would be all right to add in to each of the plaintiff's final payoffs the amount the plaintiff had when the game began.

6. A point about game trees that's worth keeping in mind is that the payoffs are not always indicated along the way but including them at the end nodes is conventional. Another point to note is that, in the decision trees that we considered in the Decision Analysis chapter, we didn't write down accumulated payoffs at the end nodes, although some analysts do so.

Figure 2-3
A Litigation Game Tree

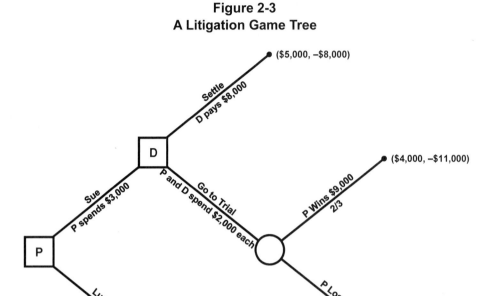

instead, she has a two-thirds probability of winning and receiving the $9,000 and a one-third probability of losing and receiving nothing.

The tree in Figure 2-3 (a modified version of the one in Figure 2-2) shows how such a situation can be represented. A *chance node* follows the Go to Trial branch, and two *chance branches* extend from this node. The probability of each outcome is written under the corresponding branch: 2/3 for P Wins $9,000 and 1/3 for P Loses. And, as before, the final payoffs for the plaintiff and the defendant are noted at the end nodes following the branches: $4,000 for the plaintiff and –$11,000 for the defendant after P Wins $9,000, and –$5,000 for the plaintiff (i.e., the net after spending $3,000 to file suit and $2,000 to go to trial) and –$2,000 for the defendant (i.e., all he spends is $2,000 in trial) after P Loses.

It should be apparent from the foregoing discussion that trees provide a great deal of flexibility for the representation of games.

3. Solving Games

Solving a game means figuring out what each player will do if he's rational. In effect, then, solving a game is making a prediction about what

Table 2-2
Game Table: The Prisoners' Dilemma

		Baxter's Action	
		Confess	Deny
Chester's Action	Confess	10, 10	0, 15
	Deny	15, 0	1, 1

will happen when each player tries to achieve the outcome that's the best one for himself. Let's begin by working through the prisoners' dilemma. To see how this is done, let's start by looking again at Table 2-2.

For Chester, Confess is better than Deny, no matter what action Baxter selects: *if Baxter confesses,* Chester is better off confessing than denying because his sentence will be 10 years rather than 15 years; *if Baxter denies guilt,* Chester is better off confessing because he'll end up with no sentence rather than with a 1-year sentence. Likewise for Baxter, Confess is better than Deny, regardless of Chester's action: *if Chester confesses,* Baxter is better off confessing than denying because he'll be sentenced to 10 years rather than 15 years; *if Chester denies,* Baxter is better off confessing because he'll get no sentence rather than a 1-year sentence. Hence, both Chester and Baxter will choose Confess. Now that we've figured

---

Box 2-1
Why Is the Prisoners' Dilemma So Important?

The prisoners' dilemma represents a very typical problem: one in which people wind up in a bad situation relative to where they could be had they *coordinated* their actions. Do you understand why the following might — or might not — be considered (by some) to be the undesirable outcomes of prisoners' dilemmas?

- Athletes take harmful drugs, such as steroids, to boost their performance.
- Countries engage in an arms race.
- Students study hard for exams.

out what Chester's and Baxter's decisions will be, we can determine the outcome of the game: each will receive a 10-year sentence.

You may have noticed that the outcome could have been better for both Chester and Baxter. If both had chosen Deny, the sentence for each would have been 1 year rather than 10 years, which we arrived at in solving the game. The game is said to be a dilemma for the prisoners because they jointly make themselves worse off when each attempts to pursue his interest.

Of the two possible actions open to each player in the prisoners' dilemma game, one is the best for the player to choose regardless of the action selected by the other player. In other words, a *dominant strategy* is available to each player, and this is the one — Confess — that the player selects. In such situations, where each player has a dominant strategy, games are easy to solve. In many games, however, there are no dominant strategies. What is best for a given player to do depends on what the other player does.

Box 2-2
How Can the Prisoners Get Out of Their Dilemma?

If the prisoners could communicate with each other to coordinate their strategy and somehow commit themselves to deny their guilt, they'd get the outcome they want. Another possibility is that both have developed in past encounters a reputation for denying guilt, so each would expect the other to continue to do so. A great deal of discussion in game theory literature revolves around these two avenues of escaping the bad outcome of the prisoners' dilemma.

Let's reconsider the game in which Amy and Bill are the players (see Table 2-1). Amy has no dominant strategy: for example, she's better off choosing Discovery if Bill chooses Expert Witness but No Discovery if Bill chooses Consultant. (Can you explain why?) Nor does Bill have a dominant strategy: his best option is Consultant if Amy selects Discov-

Table 2-1
Game Table: Bill and Amy

		Bill's Action		
		Expert Witness	**Consultant**	**Do Nothing**
Amy's Action	**Discovery**	3, 4	5, 7	9, 2
	No Discovery	2, 10	8, 8	12, 4

ery but Expert Witness if she selects No Discovery. (Can you explain why?[7]) Thus, for Amy and for Bill, the best action depends on what the other one does.

Another simple example of a game in which players don't have dominant strategies concerns which side of the road a driver would choose to drive on (were there no traffic laws). Clearly, if everyone else drives on the right, the best action for the driver in question is to drive on the right, in order to avoid accidents. On the other hand, if everyone else drives on the left, the best action for this driver is to drive on the left. Hence, an individual driver doesn't have a dominant strategy: the side of the road that's best for this person to drive on depends on which side other drivers choose to drive on.

Even when dominant strategies aren't available and players determine what their best actions are on the basis of what they believe others will choose to do, we can often say something about what might happen. For example, let's assume that all drivers believe that all other drivers will drive on the right. It's rational, then, for Jill to drive on the right. Driving on the right is a rational choice for Jack as well, as it is for every other driver. Hence, we can predict that a status quo in which drivers drive on the right and believe that others will drive on the right will persist: all drivers will continue to believe that all other drivers will drive on the right, and, because of this belief, all drivers will continue to behave exactly as they have been behaving — that is, all will continue to drive on the right.

Such a situation — one in which beliefs and choice of actions reinforce one another and persist — is an *equilibrium*, or a *Nash equilibrium*. That

---

7. You should also explain why Bill will rule out Do Nothing.

is, a list of named actions (e.g. in the preceding example, each drives on the right), one for each player, is a Nash equilibrium, if each player's action is the best one for him, given what the other players are doing. It is a no regret situation, in that none of the players feels he could have done better by making a different choice. To test whether a given set of choices constitutes a Nash equilibrium, check to see if each player's choice is the best possible choice for him in response to the other player's choices. In the driving example, everyone driving on the right is a Nash equilibrium, because no individual would do better to drive on the left. Equally, everyone driving on the left is also a Nash equilibrium. (Are there one or more Nash equilibria in the Prisoner's Dilemma game?)

The concept of a Nash equilibrium is a very important one. The main reason is that a Nash equilibrium is a situation that we would naturally say would exist and persist if parties were rational and somehow came to believe that the other parties would choose their Nash equilibrium actions.

Why or exactly how a particular Nash equilibrium arises isn't always immediately obvious, even though such an equilibrium would tend to persist *were* it to arise. If there's more than a single Nash equilibrium, why does one rather than another occur? For instance, why would an equilibrium in which all drivers drive on the right emerge rather than one in which all drivers drive on the left? Why would any equilibrium at all emerge? If some people drive on the left and others drive on the right, why would we expect all people to gravitate to a uniform belief about which side of the road everyone will drive on?

Focal points — beliefs about behaviors that have some kind of psychological salience — provide one possible answer to such questions. For

---

Box 2-3
John Nash

The idea of Nash equilibrium was pioneered in the 1950s by John Nash, a mathematician at Princeton. Nash won a Nobel Prize in economics largely for his development of this equilibrium concept. He is the subject of a book and hit movie, *A Beautiful Mind*.

Figure 2-4
Litigation Game Tree and the Nash Equilibrium

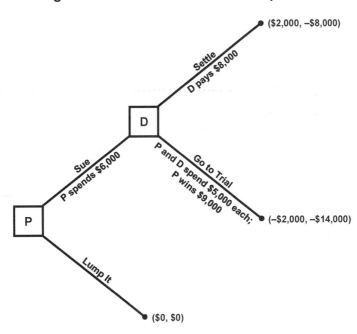

instance, given that people tend to walk on the right, people might think that they would drive on the right as well. In other words, driving on the right might be a focal-point behavior. Another example is this: Two friends are supposed to meet at noon in Paris, but they forgot to decide on a specific meeting place. Both might well go to the Eiffel Tower at noon, expecting the other to do the same, given that it's one of the most famous landmarks in the city. In this case, meeting at the Eiffel Tower might be a focal point.

Notions other than focal points sometimes allow players in games to figure out which of several possible Nash equilibrium outcomes is likely to occur. To illustrate, let's consider a variation of the game concerning suit and possible trial that we discussed before. This game is described in Figure 2-4 (which is the same as Figure 2-2 except for some of the payoffs).

One Nash equilibrium in this game is for the plaintiff to Lump It and for the defendant to Go to Trial. To see why this is so, suppose that the plaintiff believes that the defendant will Go to Trial. If the plaintiff were to select Sue, she would wind up losing $2,000: she would spend $6,000 on suit and $5,000 more on trial but win only $9,000. (This is the reason for writing –$2,000 at the end of the Go to Trial node.) On the other hand, if the plaintiff chose Lump It, she would end up with nothing, which is better. So the plaintiff will choose Lump It, given her belief that the defendant will choose Go to Trial. Conversely, suppose that the defendant believes that the plaintiff will choose Lump It. The defendant's choice between Settle and Go to Trial doesn't matter — it's irrelevant to him. Thus, for him to choose Go to Trial is a rational option. Hence, we've confirmed that the defendant's choosing Go to Trial and the plaintiff's choosing Lump It constitute a Nash equilibrium.

But there's also a second Nash equilibrium in this example: the plaintiff chooses Sue, and the defendant chooses Settle. To see why, suppose that the plaintiff believes that the defendant will Settle. If the plaintiff chooses Sue, she'll net $2,000: she'll spend $6,000 on suit and receive $8,000 in settlement. If the plaintiff Lumps It, she'll get nothing. So the plaintiff will clearly choose Sue. What about the defendant? If he thinks that the plaintiff will Sue, he's better off choosing Settle and paying $8,000 than he is choosing Go to Trial and winding up losing $14,000. Consequently, it's a Nash equilibrium for the plaintiff to Sue and the defendant to Settle.

Which Nash equilibrium is more plausible? Most of us would say that the second one is. The first equilibrium is unlikely because it's implausible that the defendant would choose Go to Trial. In particular, it would be irrational for the defendant to choose Go to Trial *were* the plaintiff to Sue: if the plaintiff were to Sue, the defendant would then be better off settling for $8,000 than losing $14,000 in trial. This point — that the defendant would not choose Go to Trial — can be expressed in various ways. One way is to say that Go to Trial isn't a credible action, isn't a credible threat to the plaintiff, because it wouldn't be carried out if the plaintiff decided to Sue. Another way of putting the point is to say that the only actions that a player ought to believe another player will choose are ones that are rational to choose if and when the choice about the actions actually arises. In the jargon of game theory, such actions are called *subgame rational* or *subgame perfect,* because they are rational to make in the part of the game that remains when a choice actually comes up (like

---

Box 2-4
Can Empty Threats Be Made Credible?

As we discussed, the plaintiff in the litigation game will think that the defendant won't go to trial and thus will settle if sued. But the defendant would like to make the plaintiff believe that he would go to trial. He could do this by having developed a reputation of going to trial. Another possibility would be for the defendant to make some kind of commitment to go to trial (e.g., by having a lawyer on retainer or a staff of salaried lawyers in-house).

---

the choice between Settle and Go to Trial for the defendant, once the plaintiff chooses Sue).

You've now been introduced to some of the important concepts that will enable you to solve games: Sometimes players will have dominant actions, so they'll choose these actions (as in the prisoners' dilemma game). Sometimes they won't, but there will be a Nash equilibrium. If there's more than one Nash equilibrium, the one that will occur will often involve a focal point (e.g., meeting at the Eiffel Tower) or will involve only actions that are subgame perfect (e.g., ruling out empty threats). These concepts should help you in thinking about how individuals and firms are likely to behave in real life. And, as noted earlier, they should also help you to understand writing that refers to game theory and uses its vocabulary. We have, of course, merely scratched the surface of a very large subject. And you might be interested in looking over the books mentioned at the end of this chapter and select one to use to pursue game theory further.

4. Moral Hazard and Incentives

We're going to switch from game theory to some important topics involving situations in which a party lacks information possessed by another. This subject is relevant to many legal problems; we consider it here because of its particular significance for game theory, though we will note a range of applications. Afterwards, we will turn to a specific game theoretic context in which incomplete information is important, namely, bargaining.

Our first topic on information concerns a phenomenon that got its name from the insurance industry. This industry became aware quite some time ago that ownership of insurance increases the risk that insured parties will incur losses: owning insurance tends to dull the incentive for insured parties to take actions to help prevent losses. For instance, people are naturally less concerned about property losses and thus less careful in preventing fires if they own fire insurance policies than if they don't. The insurance industry dubbed this phenomenon *moral hazard*.

The insurance example of moral hazard typifies an overarching phenomenon: after a contract is made, a party to it may have incentives to act in a way that's detrimental to the other party to the contract. For instance, an employee who's been hired may work less hard than her employer would want. Or a CEO of a corporation may make poorer decisions than its shareholders would like. Or a lawyer who has a contract to be paid by the hour may work more hours than his client would wish. Or a recipient of government welfare benefits may not try hard to find a job or to obtain good job training even though the government would want her to.

The moral hazard problem isn't just that having a contract may change the incentives of one party to the disadvantage of the other party. It's

---

Box 2-5
Moral Hazard and Information

The moral hazard problem is often considered a part of the economics of information. The reason is that the moral hazard problem of undesirable incentives in a contractual relationship is rooted in one party's lack of information about the other party's behavior – such as an insured's fire precautions or an employee's work effort. If the information can be obtained, the problem can be avoided by writing the terms of the contract accordingly.

that incentives tend to be altered in a way that hurts *both* parties to the contract. To illustrate, let's consider a fire insurance example. Suppose that an insured person can very easily take a precaution — such as closing the fireplace doors when a fire is burning in the fireplace and he's leaving home (closing the doors will prevent embers from escaping into the house and setting it on fire) — and that the cost of the precautionary effort is $10 a year. Suppose, too, that if an insured person takes this precaution, the insurance company would save, on average, $100 a year (according to its actuarial tables). Taking the precaution would be in the mutual interests of the insured individual and the insurer: if the insured would bear the $10 precaution cost, the insurer could afford to reduce the insured's annual insurance premium by more than $10 — say, by $50 — given that the insurer would save $100, so both the insured and the insurer could wind up better off. But, unfortunately, the very fact that the individual is protected by insurance against fire-related losses may lead him not to take the precaution of closing the fireplace doors when he leaves home. Thus, both the insured and the insurer are worse off than they might be.

How can the moral hazard problem be solved? One possibility is for the insurer to *obtain information* about the insured's precautionary behavior. If the insurer can somehow tell whether the insured takes the precaution of closing the fireplace doors, the insurer can induce the insured to do so. For instance, the insurer could lower the annual premium only if the insured closes the fireplace doors, or the insurer could deny coverage for losses if they were caused by failure to close the fireplace doors. More generally, moral hazard problems can be cured if one party to the contract can get information about the possibly problematic behavior or situation of the other party. If an employer can tell how hard an employee is working, the employer can prevent the problem of laxity of effort by rewarding the employee for proper effort or by penalizing the employee for improper effort. If the client who has hired a lawyer on an hourly basis can figure out how many hours the legal task really requires, the client can limit in the contract the number of hours to that number. If the government can find out how hard a welfare recipient searches for a job, it can condition the continuation of benefits on the recipient's exercising proper search effort.

Box 2-6
Insurance Policy Terms and Moral Hazard

Can you explain the following features of insurance policies in view of the moral hazard problem? How do they avoid moral hazard?

- If a worker is disabled, the disability insurance policy will usually limit coverage to, say, 60% of the worker's wage.   *incentive*
- If death is due to suicide, a life insurance policy won't pay benefits.   *Sanction*
- If belongings stored in a basement sustain water damage because the basement floods, a homeowner's flood insurance policy won't pay.

Solving the moral hazard problem with information is one thing. Obtaining the information is another matter. How does an insurer get information about what measures an insured takes to prevent fires? How does an employer obtain information about how hard the employee is working? How do shareholders apprise themselves of the information about business opportunities open to the CEO? How does a client determine how many hours a case ought to take the lawyer?

It depends. Sometimes obtaining information is easy. For instance, it's probably fairly easy for a fire insurer to inspect a person's home to see where smoke detectors are installed. And it's probably not too hard for an employer to find out whether an employee shows up for work and puts in a full day. On the other hand, for an insurance company to determine whether an insured person really closes the fireplace doors when doing so would be appropriate or for an employer to find out whether an employee is taking too many breaks might not be easy. Likewise, ascertaining what business opportunities are available to a CEO or what number of hours is proper for a lawyer to work on a case could be a daunting task.

Difficulty in solving the moral hazard problem through acquisition of information leads to problems for the contracting parties. One problem is that, although they may solve their problem, they will have to spend money to obtain the information to do so. The insurer may be able to find out whether an insured has installed smoke detectors, but the process of finding out will require paying someone to visit the insured's premises. Another problem is that the acquired information may be fuzzy and imperfect — for example, an employer's information about how hard an employee works or a client's assessment of how many hours a case ought to take may not be very reliable. Therefore, the ability of the employer to motivate the worker properly or the client to set the appropriate number of hours for the lawyer to spend on the case might be poor.

There's a second major way in which moral hazard can be combated: through the use of an *output-based incentive* of some type, such as basing an employee's pay on the employee's contribution to profits. For instance, *e.g. commission* if the wage of a salesperson in a department store depends on his volume of sales, he'll have a natural incentive to work harder than he would if he were paid only by the hour. If the compensation of a CEO depends significantly on corporate profits, perhaps through stock options, she'll have a motive to choose business opportunities that will increase corporate profits. If an insurance policy doesn't cover losses fully — for example, because it includes a deductible feature or a ceiling on coverage — the insured party will bear part of the loss and will therefore have a reason to reduce the risk of fire. (This is an output-based incentive of a sort, in that the occurrence or nonoccurrence of a fire is an output of whether or not the insured party takes precautionary efforts.)

However, output-based incentives have a big drawback: they impose risk on people. If a CEO's pay is based in substantial part on stock options, her pay will be risky, because the amount will depend on chance elements. If an insured individual is only partially covered against loss, he will, by definition, bear some risk, but risk is exactly what he wants to avoid by purchasing insurance. As a consequence, although output-based incentives can reduce the moral hazard problem, they're often disliked because of risk imposition and are thus of limited utility. More specifically, if too much risk is imposed on a risk-averse contracting party, this party will demand higher compensation (as in the case of a CEO or an employee) or a lower price (as in the case of an insured person), and the cost to the other contracting party may be too high to be worthwhile.

Another difficulty with output-based incentives is that output may be hard to measure. For instance, determining just how much a salesperson contributes to sales may be quite difficult (perhaps one salesperson helps a customer but a different salesperson rings up the sale). Output-based incentives may be hard to fashion in such cases.

In the end, therefore, although moral hazard can be alleviated by two general methods, it typically can't be eliminated. Hence, moral hazard often remains.

A final point is that the existence of moral hazard isn't an argument for government intervention, as is sometimes mistakenly thought to be the case. If workers don't work as hard as would be best or if insured people aren't as careful to prevent loss as would be ideal, this is because the employer or the insurance company is unable to find a worthwhile way to overcome the moral hazard problem by obtaining information or using output-based incentives. Because the government doesn't typically have a superior ability to obtain information or design output-based incentives, there is no call for the government to do anything when moral hazard arises in the private sector.

5. Adverse Selection

Now we're going to turn our sights to another important phenomenon that, like the moral hazard problem, involves asymmetry of information and contracts. It's called *adverse selection*, and it arises in situations in which individuals who differ from each other in important ways selectively choose to enter into contracts.

A famous instance of adverse selection is that of used-car sales and is known as the *lemons problem*. We'd expect to find a larger proportion of cars with problems — so-called lemons — in the used-car market than in the general population of cars. The reason is that people who own lemons would be more likely to try to sell their cars than people whose cars are running well would be. Of course, we wouldn't expect all cars on the used-car market to be lemons. There are, after all, a variety of reasons for wanting to sell perfectly good cars (e.g., the owner might want to buy a new car or might decide to move to a distant city and not drive the car there).

In any case, most prospective used-car buyers will know that used cars carry a relatively high risk of being lemons. Because of this risk, the price that they'll be willing to pay for used cars will tend to be low — that is, lower than it would be if the used-car market included few, if any, lemons. The low price will often be unacceptable to potential sellers of reasonably good used cars, however, and will discourage them from putting their cars up for sale. With fewer cars in decent shape entering the used-car market than would otherwise be the case, the percentage of lemons in the market increases. Hence, the quality problem associated with used cars is exacerbated.

Ultimately, many potential mutually beneficial transactions — between sellers of good used cars and buyers willing to pay an acceptable price for them — will never occur, because the disproportion of lemons lowers the price of used cars. In other words, the tendency for lemons to be selected for sale in the used-car market adversely affects the market in that it prevents the market from functioning in a desirable way.

Adverse selection can be involved in the insurance context as well. Let's consider fire insurance again. We might expect people whose fire risks are relatively high because of the character of their property (e.g., people whose homes don't have good wiring) to be more likely than property owners in general to buy fire insurance. As a consequence, a fire insurer will receive more claims and have to charge higher premiums than it otherwise would. The higher premiums, in turn, will deter some property owners at low risk for fire from buying insurance (or lead them to buy less coverage), even though they'd be willing to pay lower premiums that the insurer would be willing to accept to cover them if it could identify them as the low-risk prospects that they are. In the end, people at high risk for fire tend to buy more insurance coverage. And this adversely affects the functioning of the insurance market by causing premiums to rise and thus leads some people at low risk to buy less coverage than otherwise.

Let's consider one more example: loans, such as bank loans to owners of new restaurants to help them get their restaurants established. We might expect bank loans to be more attractive to owners of restaurants with a lower chance of success than to owners of restaurants with a

---

Box 2-7
Can Warranties Cure Adverse Selection?

In some cases, warranties can be used to avoid the adverse selection problem. For example, a used-car dealer who knows that his cars aren't lemons could guarantee buyers that they aren't — perhaps by agreeing to pay maintenance costs for a year or to take back a car that's frequently in need of repairs. How would this sidestep the adverse selection problem?

---

higher chance of success. The owner of a restaurant that isn't likely to be successful may view a loan as relatively cheap: if the restaurant fails and goes bankrupt, the loan won't have to be repaid. Also, if it's not particularly likely to succeed, its owners (and their friends) might be somewhat reluctant to invest a lot of their own money in the venture. What's the implication of the tendency for the owners wanting to take out loans to be those whose restaurants are more likely to go bankrupt? It means that the banks will have to charge higher interest rates so as to cover their losses when borrowers go bankrupt. But the higher interest rates discourage borrowing. This also means that owners of some promising new restaurants won't take out loans, even though banks would be willing to lend them money at lower, affordable interest rates if the banks knew these restaurant owners to be unlikely to go bankrupt and thus to be good bets. The problem in the loan market is adverse selection, in which the restaurant owners who take out loans tend to be those who are relatively less likely to repay the loans.

What can be done about adverse selection? One basic response of contracting parties who lack information is to obtain the information they need about their contracting partners. If a prospective buyer of a used car can determine its quality — for instance, by taking it to a service station for inspection — the adverse selection problem will be eliminated: lemons will be recognized as such and sell for low prices, and good used cars will be recognized as well and will sell for appropriately high prices. Therefore, someone contemplating selling a good used car will put the car on the market because he knows that he'll be able to get a fitting price for it, and a buyer who wants such a car, knowing that it isn't a lemon, will willingly pay the fitting price for it. Likewise, in the insurance example, we can imagine that the insurance company will obtain information about the fire risk of prospective policy buyers (e.g., by inspecting their houses to determine the condition of the wiring) and charge those at higher risk more for coverage. Hence, a low-risk buyer wouldn't have to pay a high premium, and the problem of adverse selection would be averted. Note that the adverse selection problem is analogous to the moral hazard problem in that both are due to an asymmetry of information and can be ameliorated in similar ways: by obtaining the appropriate necessary information.

Of course, acquiring information to prevent adverse selection is costly. Some effort is required to have a car inspected to determine whether it's a lemon, and money must be spent to ascertain which risk category a fire insurance purchaser falls into. Hence, information acquisition is, in general, an imperfect remedy for the adverse selection problem. Though it will at times substantially alleviate the problem, often it will not.

One more aspect of the adverse selection problem is that sometimes government action can help to ameliorate it. For example, consider the context of insurance where high-risk individuals cause premiums to go up and the high premiums discourage low-risk individuals from purchasing coverage. In this situation, a rule requiring all individuals to purchase coverage and to pay premiums equal to the average risk might be beneficial, but the details of why are beyond our scope.

6. Bargaining

In ending this chapter, we're going to take a look at bargaining — something that lawyers do all the time, of course, in making contracts, reaching settlements in litigation, and so forth. For the sake of simplicity, we'll assume that the only issue of concern in bargaining is price. The goal of a party in bargaining is to obtain as large a slice of the available "pie" as possible, but without being so aggressive in making demands that an agreement isn't reached. If either side is too greedy, the deal might fall through, and then no one will be able to enjoy any of the pie. As will become apparent in a moment, this is yet another setting in which asymmetry of information is a crucial issue.

How does a party go about bargaining so as to achieve the goal of obtaining a large slice of the pie without preventing a mutually beneficial deal from being made? One very important factor is a party's *reservation price* — the most that a buyer will pay or the least that a seller will accept. Let's use an example to illustrate the concept of reservation price and why having information about it is valuable.

Suppose that you're selling a piece of land that the prospective buyer would like to build a restaurant on. The buyer's reservation price is the maximum amount that the she'd be willing to pay for the land. This price would be determined by what the restaurant's profits are likely to be, given the location, by how much alternative sites would cost, and so forth. Suppose also that you know the buyer's exact reservation price, that it's $1,000,000. For simplicity, suppose, too, that you can credibly make a single best-and-final demand — a demand that's your only and final one. If you insist on a price that's virtually $1,000,000 — say, $999,000 — you have reason to expect that you'll get this amount.[8] The prospective buyer, truly believing that you'll walk away if she refuses your demand, will rationally accept any price you demand as long as it's less than $1,000,000. You'd thus get the largest possible slice of the contractual pie, and, because your demand wouldn't exceed the buyer's reservation price, you wouldn't prevent the contract for the sale of land from being made.

In practice, of course, you won't know the other side's reservation price. And in trying to get as much as possible, you might end up asking for too much — for an amount that turns out to exceed the buyer's reservation price, which you don't know at the outset — in which case your demand will be rejected. In other words, the more you demand, the better off you'll be *if* a contract is made but the less likely a contract is to be made. As a result, you'll end up having to make a tradeoff: a higher price will result in a lower likelihood of making the contract. So your best bargaining strategy will usually be one that's less aggressive than it otherwise would be.

---

8. Can you think of reasons that you might not?

This issue is worth considering in greater detail, and we can do this by elaborating on the land-sale example. Suppose again, for simplicity, that you'll make one demand, a take-it-or-leave-it demand that the buyer must either accept or reject. Suppose also that, if you don't sell the land to this buyer, your next-best alternative is to sell to another buyer, one whom you know to be willing to pay $400,000. (That is, your own reservation price is $400,000.)

You must consider what the first potential buyer's reservation price might be. In contrast to the situation we looked at earlier, however, in this case you aren't certain what it is, but suppose that you do know that it is either $700,000 or $1,000,000 (the assumption that it has only two possible values is for convenience only). Suppose, too, that you know that its odds of being $700,000 are 75% and its odds of being $1,000,000 are 25%. If you demand $700,000 (or, rather, slightly below), the buyer will accept regardless of whether her valuation is $700,000 or $1,000,000, and you'll receive $700,000, $300,000 more than the $400,000 from the alternative buyer.

If you demand $1,000,000 (or, rather, slightly below) and the buyer accepts, you'll receive $1,000,000, $600,000 more than from the $400,000 alternative. But the likelihood that this will happen is only 25%. And there's a 75% probability that the buyer's valuation is $700,000, in which case she'll walk away, leaving you with no profit. So, if you ask for $1,000,000, the expected gain over the $400,000 alternative is 25% × $600,000, or $150,000. And this is less than $300,000, the amount you're certain to gain if you ask for $700,000. Hence, you should choose to demand $700,000: demanding $1,000,000 is too aggressive to be in your interest.

Sometimes, however, being tough may make sense for you. In the scenario that we just considered, for example, suppose that there's a 75% chance that the buyer's valuation is the higher amount, $1,000,000. Then insisting on $1,000,000 nets you $600,000 more than the $400,000 alternative 75% of the time. So your expected gain is 75% × $600,000, or $450,000, which is more attractive than the $300,000 gain from the $700,000 demand (unless you're very risk averse).

Having worked through a couple of versions of the land-sale scenario, what generalizations can we make about bargaining strategy?

First, when your bargaining strategy is rational, a mutually beneficial agreement won't necessarily be consummated. The reason is that it may be rational, given your knowledge, to adopt a bargaining stance that's sufficiently tough that, sometimes, the other side will reject it. This was the case in the second version of the land-sale example, the one in which the rational demand was $1,000,000. Demanding this higher amount was rational because the odds were pretty good — 75% — that the buyer placed a high valuation on the land and thus would accept the high demand. But if this turned out to be incorrect and the buyer placed a low valuation on the land, she would reject the demand.

Second, the main lessons that the land-sale scenario drives home are robust: they carry over to more complicated and realistic descriptions of the bargaining process involving, for example, multiple rounds of bargaining. Most bargaining, needless to say, consists of a series of offers and counteroffers. In such settings, as in our land-sale scenario, parties can rationally formulate the demands that they ought to make, given their uncertain knowledge of each other's situation. Sometimes deals will fall through because a party attempted to grab too large a piece of the pie and misgauged the other side's reservation price.

Third, when you're considering how to go about bargaining, you'll most likely find that the kinds of calculations we used in the example will serve you well as a benchmark. This is not to deny that bargaining is, in many respects, an art. Admittedly, there are elements of the other side's psychology that aren't easily assessed or summarized but are important in determining the result that you'll achieve. Nevertheless, you'll find that using calculations of the type illustrated in the example will help you to systematically compare different types of bargaining stances against one another.

7. Suggestions for Further Reading

Many books on game theory have been published. Here are a few recommendations for you to examine if you're interested in exploring the subject further. Thomas Schelling, *The Strategy of Conflict* (Cambridge, Mass.: Harvard University Press, 1960), is a famous early study of game theoretic issues and is written in an informal accessible style. Avinash Dixit and Barry Nalebuff, *The Art of Strategy: A Game Theorist's Guide to*

Success in Business and Life (New York: Norton, 2010), is a modern wide-ranging nontechnical book on game theory and is highly readable. A work of special interest for lawyers is Douglas Baird, Robert Gertner, and Randall Picker, *Game Theory and the Law* (Cambridge, Mass.: Harvard University Press, 1994). An easy-to-digest chapter on game theory in a microeconomics textbook is chapter 13 of Robert S. Pindyck and Daniel L. Rubinfeld, *Microeconomics*, 7th ed. (Englewood Cliffs, N.J.: Prentice-Hall, 2008). A more technical but well-exposited book on game theory is Eric Rasmusen, *Games and Information*, 4th ed. (Malden, Mass.: Wiley-Blackwell, 2006). An advanced, comprehensive treatment of the subject of game theory is contained in the modern classic, Drew Fudenberg and Jean Tirole, *Game Theory* (Cambridge, Mass.: MIT Press, 1991).

For references on moral hazard, adverse selection, and bargaining, you'll find Baird et al., Rasmusen, as well as chapter 17 of Pindyck and Rubinfeld to be useful.

3
Contracting

1. Introduction

Writing contracts is an important part of a lawyer's job. The bread-and-butter work of many lawyers is transactional. Notably, they make agreements for the production of goods and the provision of services, for the sale and development of real estate, for the licensing of intellectual property, for corporate deals, or for financial arrangements — all of which are quintessentially contractual. Such transactional work is common in the public sector as well as in the private sector. After all, government and nonprofit entities spend more than one-third of this country's GNP, much of it to purchase goods and services, and they also manage massive transfer and grant programs. These expenditures are usually mediated by contracts. Additionally, lawyers involved in litigation of all types settle the vast majority of their cases. Settlement agreements are contracts in their own right, and they can be quite involved, whether in a business context or in a personal context (just think of divorce and custody agreements). Obviously, then, designing contracts is a major aspect of legal practice for most lawyers. Additionally, understanding

61

contract design is valuable for lawyers engaged in litigation involving contractual disputes. So it's important for you to learn how to design the best contracts possible and how to analyze contract design.

① purpose
② problems
③ avoid

Having an organized idea of the purposes that contracts serve, the problems that can arise after they're written, and the ways that these problems can be avoided is a good starting point for drafting effective contracts. For instance, a client who wants to have a building constructed might ask you whether to use a flat-fee or a cost-plus payment arrangement. Regardless of which is chosen, your client will want to anticipate the problems that could arise (e.g., under a flat-fee contract, the contractor might buy low-quality materials) so that you can incorporate into the contract provisions that will safeguard against these problems (e.g., specify in the contract what quality of materials are to be used in order to avoid the possibility that a flat-fee contractor will use inferior materials). In addition, your client will want to know what the legal consequences will be if the contract is breached (e.g., how damages will be calculated if the building isn't completed on time). Your client will also want to know whether including an arbitration clause would be wise. Thus, you'll also be putting to use your knowledge of contract law.

2. Why Contracts Are Made

At the most general level, there is only one reason why a person would want to make a contract: to obtain an advantage of some kind. Ordinarily, however, the other party would also want to make a contract in order to secure an advantage. Contracts, it would seem then, are typically made only because they are *mutually* advantageous.

Let's take a look at a few of the factors that make them so. The examples that we'll cover should help to illuminate the sources of the benefits that parties secure when they make contracts.

A. Differences in Valuation

In many contexts, the owner of something will place a lower value on it than another party will. For example, a homeowner who has to move to another city will place a lower value on his home than will many people seeking a residence in the area where he currently lives, and a business that installs new office furniture will no longer need its old furniture and will place a lower value on it than will another business that can use it. Obviously, when the owner of something places a lower value on it than another party does, it's possible for the two parties to enter a mutually beneficial contract for the transfer of ownership (or for lease). If the owner values the property she owns at $1,000 and someone else values it at $2,000, any contract under which the owner sells the property to the other person at a price between the two figures — say, $1,500 — will benefit both parties.

B. Advantages in Production

Often, one party wants an item produced or a service performed and finds that another party can do it more cheaply or more ably than he himself can. For example, a person may want his home renovated, and doing the work himself may be expensive in time and effort, whereas someone who makes his living from renovating homes can perform the work that the owner wants done at a much lower cost. Moreover, a specialist in renovation probably can do much higher quality work. Similarly, a restaurant owner may want a sign made, and a sign-making firm can do the job more cheaply and more elegantly than the restaurant owner herself can. In other cases, a party simply can't do what he wants done or can't do it very well. I may want my watch repaired but don't even know how to open it up. I may want my hair cut, but cutting it myself will be a disaster; my skill level just isn't anywhere near a professional's.

Why might a party have a cost or quality advantage that allows him to produce more cheaply or effectively than another? There are a number of general reasons: economies of scale in manufacturing an item, specialization in performing a task, having a particular ability or characteristic, to mention three of importance.

Clearly, when a task that one party wants done can be done more cheaply or better by a second party, entering into a contract for the task may well be mutually beneficial. For example, let's assume that I value a project that I can't do myself at $200 and that someone could do it for me for $100. Then I might pay this person $150 to do the job, and he'd be willing to do it for me for this amount. In such a case, all the elements for a mutually beneficial agreement are present, so it would serve both of us well to enter into a contract.

C. Complementarities

It frequently happens that two parties' capabilities mesh well in producing goods or performing services. For example, a computer software engineer who has developed a new product and a person skilled in marketing may, by joining forces, be able to offer the product, whereas neither alone could do so or do as well. Or a firm that specializes in drilling for oil and another that builds pipelines may combine their efforts and thus be able to bring oil to market more inexpensively and more profitably than could otherwise be done. When parties can increase joint profits by combining their complementary skills and capabilities, they're in a position to make a mutually beneficial contract.

D. Borrowing and Lending

An extremely common situation is for parties to need funds. A firm may want to initiate a new venture; an individual may want to purchase a home, send a child to college, or pay off a debt for medical care. At the same time, other individuals or financial institutions may be interested in lending or investing funds. In such settings, mutually beneficial contracts are possible. If one party obtains funds from another party on the condition that the first party repays the second party the amount borrowed plus interest or gives a share of the profits to the second party, both parties stand to benefit.

E. Allocation of Risk

Contracts may also be mutually beneficial when they allocate risk between parties, especially when the parties differ in their ability or willingness to bear risk. A classic case is an insurance policy, a contract between an insurance company and an individual or other entity. The insurance company is willing to insure the policyholder, who, in turn, is happy (or at least willing) to pay the premium in exchange for being covered against the risk. Investment partnership agreements are examples of another kind: the partners, as a group, are willing and able to take on the risk because it's distributed among them, whereas, as is often the case, no single partner is willing or able to absorb the entire investment risk.

F. Different Expectations

Predictions about the price of real estate, currencies, securities, and the like nearly always vary, at least to some degree, among parties. In such cases, parties may find it mutually beneficial to contract. For example, one party, expecting prices of real estate to drop, might sell to another party, one who believes that prices will rise. Or one party might buy futures in yen with the expectation that it will rise against the dollar, while another party sells these futures, thinking that the exchange rate will change in the oppose direction.

A point worth noting before we move ahead is that most contracts are not made for a single reason but for a combination of reasons. For instance, an agreement to produce may also involve elements of borrowing and lending, as is the case when the buyer advances money to the seller, implicitly giving the seller a loan, and in exchange obtains a lower price than if payment had not been made until the seller delivered on his end of the deal.

3. Principles and Checkpoints for Contracting

A number of fairly general principles and checkpoints are worth bearing in mind when you're making contracts for your client. The focus here will be on a few of the more important ones. They'll make many reappearances in the remainder of the chapter, as we put them to work in the context of specific types of contracts.

A. Enlarging the Contractual Pie

One of the most general principles of contract design is that the "contractual pie" should be as large as possible. The reason is obvious: the larger the pie, the larger the slice that can be given to each party to the contract and thus the better off each party will be. In other words, maximizing the size of the contractual pie is in the *mutual* interests of the parties; they both want it. This principle is important even when the other party isn't well represented: your client will usually be able to benefit from any increase in the size of the pie that you can figure out how to bring about because you generally can come up with a way for your client to receive some of the gain.

In practice, the contractual pie is enlarged by including terms that increase the net value of the contract to the parties. Suppose, for example, that your client, the buyer of goods, has to have the goods earlier than the supplier would typically deliver them — say, December 1 as opposed to December 15. And suppose that the early delivery is worth an additional $3,000 to your client and would cost the seller $1,000 more. Early delivery thus creates an additional net value of $2,000 (i.e., $3,000 – $1,000 = $2,000) for the two parties and, according to the pie metaphor, should be mutually valuable to them.

But why, exactly, is it in the seller's interest to agree to delivery by December 1 if doing so will cost her $1,000 more? The answer is that your client, the buyer, should be willing to raise the price by enough to make delivery by December 1 worth the seller's while, because your client values early delivery more than it costs the seller. If your client offers to increase the contract price by, say, $2,000 for moving the delivery date up to December 1, the seller can be expected to agree to it. She makes an extra $1,000 in profit (the $2,000 increase in the price minus the $1,000 increase in cost), and your client is better off by $1,000 too (paying $2,000 for something worth $3,000).

The important lesson to draw from this example is that, whenever a term adds net value to a contract — when it adds more value for one party than it costs the other party — there will exist a way to include the term so that *both* parties end up better off. This is so because, as long as the additional value garnered by the party who benefits from inclusion of the term (e.g., the buyer in the example we just looked at) is more than the cost to the party hurt by its inclusion (the seller), it's possible for the first party to compensate the second party for more than the cost incurred and still come out ahead.

A kind of converse of this principle also holds: if a contractual term *reduces* the net value of a contract, it is possible to remove the term in a way that helps both parties. For instance, suppose that a delivery contract calls for special packing of the goods and that this method of packing costs the seller $5,000 but is worth only $1,000 to the buyer, who is your client. If your client offers to exclude the special-packing term in exchange for a price reduction of at least $1,000 — let's say $2,000 — and the seller agrees (which he would certainly be glad to do), both your client and the seller are better off than they would be otherwise: your client by $1,000 (price falls by $2,000 but value falls by only $1,000) and the seller by $3,000 (costs fall by $5,000 but price falls by only $2,000).

The take-home message is a very important one to bear in mind: a contractual term is in the mutual interests of the parties when and only when it adds more to the value of the contract than it costs. Indeed, most terms in contracts are included precisely because including them is in the combined interests of the parties: they add more to combined value than they cost.

The lesson here is that, when you're making a contract, if it lacks a term that you want or includes a term that you don't want, you may well be able to have the term included or excluded, respectively, by paying for it. By exploring the value of the term to your client and the cost of it to the other side, you can figure out whether your client will gain by paying the price it would take to induce the other side to acquiesce. Likewise, when the other party wants to include or exclude, you can determine whether the other party is offering enough to make it worthwhile for your client to agree. This principle is so central to contract design that overemphasizing it is virtually impossible. Indeed, much of what we'll be covering in the remainder of this chapter can be viewed and understood as aspects of this principle: addressing contractual issues in a way that increases the total value of a contractual arrangement tends to be mutually advantageous to the parties involved.

B. Incentive Issues

When guiding your client through making a contract, you must be aware of the incentives that it creates. You have to ask yourself, Given the terms of the contract, what will the other side do if certain events take place? For instance, if you make a construction contract that calls for a fixed price, will the builder have an incentive to buy low-quality materials? If he's likely to, should you try to avoid that problem by specifying in the contract the quality of materials to be used? Or what if the contract contains a liquidated damage clause stating that $2,000 will be paid for a breach? Isn't it possible that this clause, intended to protect your client, could actually provide an incentive to the other side, the builder, to breach? For example, if completing the project would leave

the builder with a loss of more than $2,000, wouldn't it be to his advan-
tage to breach? If so, should you try to increase the amount of damages
even though your client would then have to pay a higher price for the
contract? Careful evaluation of the incentives — unintended as well as
intended — established by the contract terms is vitally important when
fashioning a contract. Doing so influences the value of the contract to
your client as well as to the other party and may make other contractual
provisions appropriate to include.

As important as it is to think about and evaluate the incentives in a
contractual relationship, it would be an oversimplification to suppose
that parties to contracts are driven solely by the desire for immediate
personal gain. In fact, many contracting parties will want to behave in
ways that are generally viewed as desirable, regardless of contractual
incentives. They are prompted to behave correctly in a contractual context — that is, to adhere to contractual terms and otherwise act with
good faith — by a belief that they have an ethical duty to do so or by a
desire to protect their reputations (both in general and with regard to
future dealings with current contracting partners). Nevertheless, most
contracting parties are not saints. In many settings, assuming that narrow
self-interest will significantly influence behavior is eminently reasonable.
In such circumstances, it's generally better — often much better — for
contractual terms to provide financial incentives that encourage productive rather than exploitative behavior. Even though we'll focus on
immediate financial rewards when we address incentives a little later
in the chapter, you should keep in mind that a sense of ethical duty or
a concern for reputation often helps to ensure good results.

C. Uncertainty and Risk Bearing

Dealing effectively with uncertainty is another aspect of designing a
good contract. In most contractual situations, there are numerous contingencies, and many will be problematic for one party or the other. So
it's helpful to enumerate them and plan for them. For example, what if
the contractor erecting the building for your client runs into unexpected
costly problems? What if your client, because of a financial reversal of his
company, wants to back out of the deal after the contract has been signed
and the contractor has begun the work? You might want to include a

provision that specifies how the building plans will be altered or, if the project is terminated prematurely, how much will be paid to whom. In other words, you have to think about how, in light of troublesome contingencies, to substantively alter the contract and allocate the risks.

D. Practical Enforceability of Contractual Conditions

For a contractual term to be workable — that is, for it to succeed in inducing the desired outcome — any condition on which it depends must be readily understood and its occurrence (or nonoccurrence) must be verifiable at reasonable cost. Let's suppose that a construction contract contains a term that excuses the builder from performance if the prices of material inputs exceed a specified amount. An adjudicator can readily verify whether these prices have indeed surpassed the threshold for nonperformance. Hence, the term is workable: if prices of inputs rise above the threshold level, the builder can abstain from performance and be confident that he would prevail in adjudication if the promisee sued for breach. Likewise, if costs haven't risen above the threshold, the other party knows that the builder can't use an alleged price increase to wriggle out of the contract.

But what if difficulty in digging the foundation is included in the contract as grounds for nonperformance? Such a term may be unworkable or impractical for the parties. On one hand, the foundation may, in fact, be hard to dig, but the builder may have a hard time establishing that it is, so the clause doesn't necessarily protect him. Demonstrating to an adjudicator that a foundation is hard to dig — perhaps because the builder encounters numerous stones that are difficult to remove or perhaps because water keeps leaking into the excavated area — may not be so straightforward or may even be impossible. On the other hand, if the foundation is, in fact, not hard to dig and the builder decides, for some reason, to claim that it is, the other party may be vulnerable because he may not be able to disprove the builder's claim. In either case, the parties may well face high litigation expenses in attempting to prove whether the requirements of the term have been satisfied.

Obviously, then, when you want to include a term in a contract that you're writing for a client, you must think about whether the conditions on which the term depends are readily interpretable and verifiable by courts or arbitrators. If they aren't, you may at least be able to figure out a way to make the conditions less difficult to apply — perhaps through an expenditure or an effort of some kind, for example, by specifying that an outside expert in construction be brought in to inspect the site and determine whether the foundation is hard to dig. This issue — of the kinds of conditions that can be interpreted and verified by adjudicators — is a very important one. Another point worth keeping in mind is that it is lawyers, not clients, who are likely to be knowledgeable about the feasibility and cost of determining the applicability of contractual provisions when disputes arise.

E. Disputes and Their Resolution

No matter how careful you are in crafting a contract, there's always a possibility that a dispute will arise. This is yet another consideration that you have to take into account when writing a contract.

One basic question for you to decide is whether to specify liquidated damage for breach of contract (i.e., to spell out what is to be paid to whom in the event of various types of breach) and, if you decide to do so, in what amount. As long as such terms are clearly delineated, they can provide definite incentives to avoid breach, and they can also minimize the costs of dispute resolution if a breach does occur.

Another basic question is whether to stipulate in the contract that disputes, should any arise, will be settled by arbitration rather than by the courts. Arbitration holds certain advantages for parties to a contract. It allows them to bypass the often expensive and time-consuming legal process of the courts, because the parties can determine the arbitrator and agree to the procedure (which often turns out to be a simplified one) in advance. It also allows the parties to have their disputes adjudicated by someone experienced in their field rather than by a judge or jury, who may know little about the subject of their contract. Because of these benefits, many contracts specify that disputes will be subject to arbitration. And the holdings of arbitrators are generally enforced by courts. Indeed, entire industries rely primarily on arbitration, and the practice is also widespread in international agreements.

Finally, you have to determine whether to include a choice-of-law provision — that is, a specification of which jurisdiction's law shall govern — in the contract. Many parties find it useful to do so, whether the agreement is to be enforced through arbitration or through the courts. Provisions of this kind may reduce uncertainty or enable the parties to avoid litigation over the issue in question. In addition, they may benefit a party involved in large numbers of contracts by providing economies of scale.

A later section in this chapter focuses specifically on these and other issues concerning disputes and their resolution, so we'll be coming back to the topic in a little while.

4. Production Contracts

Contracts for the production or construction of things are very common. They come in two classic types: *cost-plus* and *flat-fee*. Under a cost-plus contract, the party requesting the work pays the party doing the work whatever the costs turn out to be plus something extra. The "something extra" may be either a fixed amount or an amount based on costs (e.g., a percentage of costs). Under a flat-fee contract, the amount paid is fixed and is specified in the contract. Suppose, for example, that your client signs a contract to have an apartment building that she owns renovated. If it is a cost-plus contract and specifies that the something extra is, let's say, 20% of the costs and if the contractor's costs total $150,000, your client ends up paying $180,000 (i.e., $150,000 + 20% × $150,000 = $180,000). On the other hand, if it's a flat-fee contract and it calls for your client to pay $175,000, this is the amount she pays, regardless of the contractor's costs or any other consideration.

Which kind of production contract would work better for your client? The answer is, It depends. Various features of the two types come into play, and you have to evaluate these features against the backdrop of your client's circumstances — to figure out not only which one is preferable but also whether certain kinds of provisions would be desirable additions. Several specific incentive issues as well as some of the other checkpoints that we covered also enter into the equation.

A. Incentives and Component Prices

A cost-plus contract contains no incentive for the contractor to find low prices for components. Let's assume, for instance, that renovation of your client's apartment building includes the purchase and installation of new windows. To find the best deal on windows, the contractor has the burden of searching for the best price, which may involve spending time on the phone or the Internet, driving to a distant supplier, and the like. So, if he's to be paid an extra 20%, let's say, on top of his total costs, what financial incentive is there under a cost-plus arrangement for him to go to all the trouble of finding windows at the lowest price? The answer is, None. Indeed, he may even have a perverse incentive to find high-priced windows: under this type of cost-plus contract, the higher the window price, the greater the contractor's profit. Suppose that the windows are available for $400 from a discounter but $500 elsewhere and the contractor decides to buy them at full price (i.e., $500). Your client winds up paying $600 for each window (i.e., $500 + 20% × $500 = $600) when she could have paid $480 (i.e., $400 + 20% × $400 = $480) apiece.

By contrast, under a flat-fee contract, the contractor has an incentive to search for low prices: because he receives a fixed amount regardless of the prices he pays for components, the lower his costs are, the greater his profit is. Let's say that the contract for renovation of your client's apartment building is a flat-fee contract specifying that the contractor is to be paid $200,000. He receives this amount — $200,000 — whether he pays $400 or $500 for the windows. It's to his advantage to get the windows for $400. Buying the more expensive ones would mean wasting his own money — in effect, paying $100 out of his own pocket for each one. So, without a doubt, he will install the $400 windows instead of the $500 ones.

As we can see, then, all other things being equal, your client may well be better off with a flat-fee contract. Under this kind of contract, which induces the contractor to search for the best prices, your client pays less to have her apartment building renovated than she would under a cost-plus contract, which rewards the contractor for paying unnecessarily high prices that ultimately inflate the cost of the project to your client.

Alternatively, you might attempt to circumvent the incentive problem caused by the cost-plus contract. One possibility is to include language in the contract that places a cap on how much the contractor can charge your client for various components of the project. For example, you might set a ceiling of $400 for windows in the apartment-building renovation.

To do this intelligently, however, you have to know what is a good price for the component. For example, the price of windows is not likely to be something that you or your client knows with any kind of precision off the top of your heads, so you'd have to do some homework before specifying a $400 cap. Another possibility is to insist that the contractor get your client's okay on a price before he buys the component or that your client, rather than the contractor, be permitted to purchase it. But this approach requires your client to know about current prices for the component and is often inconvenient. Hence, even though additions to a cost-plus contract may enable your client to lessen the problem — the lack of incentive for the contractor to search for low prices — they aren't likely to be sufficient to eliminate the problem or, even if they are, they may not be feasible to implement.

Up to this point, we've looked at things as if you're representing the person doing the hiring, and we found that a flat-fee contract tends to be better than a cost-plus contract for your client. But what does the situation look like from the other perspective? What if your client is the person being hired? Is a flat-fee contract likely to be better for this party as well? The answer is yes, and the reason is that the flat-fee contract lowers the total cost of the renovation project and, as we've already seen, enlarging the contractual pie ordinarily is *mutually* advantageous.

To see how a flat-fee contract can enlarge the contractual pie, let's focus again on a single aspect of the renovation project — the installation of new windows. The windows can be purchased for either $400 or $500. Suppose that both parties start out by considering two contracts for the project, one cost-plus and one flat-fee. According to the cost-plus contract, the contractor would pass on to the building owner the cost of the windows and would, in addition, charge a 20% fee. The flat-fee contract, on the other hand, might call for the owner to pay the contractor $550 per window.

Under the cost-plus contract, the contractor would, of course, buy the $500 windows in order to maximize his profit. Hence, the building owner would end up paying the contractor $600 for each window (i.e., $500 + 20% × $500 = $600), and the contractor would realize a profit of $100 on each (i.e., $600 − $500 = $100).

Now let's see what would happen under the flat-fee contract. The contractor would, in this situation, buy the $400 windows. He would make a profit of $150 (i.e., $550 – $400 = $150) on each one — $50 more than it would be under the cost-plus contract.[1] The building owner would come out better too, spending $550 per window (as specified in the contract) rather than $600. Given that both parties would do better under the flat-fee contract, they shouldn't have any trouble agreeing on which contract they should sign.

The take-home message, which we've encountered before, is this: if you can identify a contractual provision that is in the interest of the buyer and that increases the size of the contractual pie, this provision really will be in the mutual interest of the parties because it enables both parties to have a larger slice. This point is relevant to the rest of the material in this chapter, but in the interest of expositional ease, we will not continue to repeat it. It is important, nevertheless, that you keep it in mind.

B. Incentives and Component Quality

As we just saw, under a flat-fee contract, the contractor has a financial incentive to find the best price for components of the job he's hired to do: doing so lowers his costs, thereby saving him money and maximizing his profit. For the same reason, this type of contract also provides a financial incentive for him to find the lowest-quality components (assuming that quality and price go hand in hand).

A cost-plus contract, on the other hand, contains no such incentive. The contractor passes the cost of components, whatever they are, on to the person who hires him, so he has nothing to gain by searching for low-quality components in order to keep his costs down. In fact, locating and purchasing low-quality products is to his disadvantage if the "plus" part of the contract is a percentage of costs. The incentive is, then, for him not to use components of low quality — or, in other words, for him to use high-quality and high-priced components. From the perspective of the hiring party, it's obviously undesirable for the contractor to have a motive to buy low-quality components, as is the case under a flat-fee

---

1. The cost of the contractor's effort in obtaining the windows at the lower price under the flat-fee contract has to be offset against the $50 gain per window. Let's suppose that this added cost is less than $50 per window.

contract. So a cost-plus contract seems preferable for the hiring party in this respect.

How can your client enter into a flat-fee contract and yet be protected against the problem of low-quality components? One approach is to insert a clause requiring the contractor to obtain your client's approval before purchasing components, such as the windows, for the apartments. This is a cumbersome process, however, adding time and trouble to the project. For instance, it takes time for the contractor to track your client down to get her okay. Or if the contractor happens upon a great bargain, he isn't able to make the purchase on the spot, and the opportunity may be lost because of the delay. In addition, the contractor — whose fee, as you recall, is fixed — may be concerned that your client will withhold approval unreasonably (e.g., by insisting on materials of extremely high quality) or try to extract some unrelated concession in exchange for approving a purchase.

Another approach is to specify in the flat-fee contract the quality of components to be used — for example, the brand and model of the windows. But to do this means that your client has to know, at the time you write the contract, what kind of windows she wants, which ones are of high quality and which ones aren't, and so forth. Gathering the information necessary to make such determinations in advance isn't always easy or practical. The investigation may well be time consuming and expensive.[2]

Despite these limitations, a contract term requiring advance approval of purchases or one specifying the quality of components can be helpful in many settings.

Even under cost-plus contracts, however, there is the potential for quality-related problems: quality may be *too* high. For instance, the contractor your client hires to renovate her apartment building may buy windows that are fancier and thus more expensive than need be. If he is to be reimbursed for his costs and paid an additional percentage, anything he does to increase his costs is to his advantage: increased cost translates into increased profit. Hence, he has an incentive to spend as

---

2. Note that, even though your client has to determine the appropriate quality of windows under an approval arrangement as well, the difference is that she doesn't have to do so in advance in this situation.

much as possible on windows, even if their quality and price aren't justifiable from your client's perspective.[3] You can protect your client in the cost-plus contract just as you did in the flat-fee contract: by writing it in a way that requires the contractor to obtain your client's approval before buying the windows or that specifies the quality of windows he is to buy.

In summary, unacceptably poor quality is a risk under flat-fee contracts but not under cost-plus contracts, whereas unnecessarily high quality is a risk under cost-plus contracts but not under flat-fee contracts. Problems relating to quality of components that the hired person buys can be avoided in either type of contract by including language that requires purchases to be approved in advance or specifies the quality. Neither approach, however, is without its difficulties.

C. Uncertainty and Renegotiation

Uncertainty is a fact of life, and it gives rise to several important issues that you have to consider when deciding which type of contract to go with, cost-plus or flat-fee. Contract renegotiation is one of them.

Suppose that your client's plans and desires change midway through the renovation project. She decides that a different kitchen configuration makes the apartments significantly more attractive to potential tenants or that recessed lighting is better than the standard kind. Under a cost-plus contract, your client's change of plans necessitates no (or very little) renegotiation, assuming that the contract permits your client to insist on some modifications. The contractor usually is willing to accept such a contract provision under a cost-plus contract. After all, he won't bear any of the extra costs himself. He would simply charge them to your client.[4] By contrast, under a flat-fee contract, you would have to renego-

---

3. Another possible reason for the contractor to want to buy high-priced windows is to build up implicit credit with the appliance dealer — or to get a kickback.

4. There's one qualification here: If the changes end up significantly expanding the renovation job and if the contractor's profit is a fixed amount (as opposed to a percentage, as in our example), the contractor, in addition to passing on the extra costs to your client, will want his own payment (his profit) to rise, so some renegotiation will be necessary.

tiate your client's contract, because you're asking the contractor to bear more costs than originally agreed on.

From the perspective of your client, the hiring party, renegotiation has two drawbacks. First, it's costly in time and effort. Second, the contractor most likely has an advantage over your client. By the time renegotiation becomes an issue, it's typically too late for your client to turn to someone else to complete the project (and the contract may well not allow this). Hence, the contractor already on the job is in a position to take your client for a ride in the renegotiation by charging her an unreasonably large amount. This is an example of what is often called a *holdup problem*. The need for renegotiation and the associated twin problems of costliness and holdup can be minimized by making sure at the outset that your client has thoroughly thought everything through and knows — and accurately communicates to you — what it is that she wants. But this process itself is costly. Furthermore, it's unlikely that your client (or you) can anticipate every change that she could possibly want to make down the road. All in all, then, in the face of uncertainty, the potential need to renegotiate argues in favor of a cost-plus contract over a flat-fee contract.

D. Uncertainty and Risk Bearing

Another issue associated with uncertainty that has to be taken into consideration is risk bearing. By definition, financial risk is borne by the buyer under a cost-plus contract. Whatever the costs turn out to be, low or high or anywhere in between, the buyer pays them. The greater the uncertainty, the greater the cost is for a risk-averse buyer. On the other hand, a cost-plus contract insulates the contractor from risk.

Under a flat-fee contract, the situation is reversed: the contractor bears the entire risk, absorbing the total costs, whether they turn out to be low or high, because his fee is fixed in advance. And if the contractor is risk averse and the costs turn out to be high, bearing them is a major disadvantage to him. But now the buyer is protected against risk.

Which type of contract is a better arrangement from the perspective of risk allocation (i.e., putting aside all the other issues that enter the equation)? The answer clearly depends on who is better able to absorb the risk. Suppose, for instance, that the risk is no big deal for the contractor — perhaps it's a large company that's involved in many unrelated

Box 3-1
Flat-Fee versus Cost-Plus Contracts in a Nutshell

- *Flat-fee* contracts are often cheaper than cost-plus contracts because they induce contractors to search for the lowest prices (and their charges tend to reflect only these prices). The problem that prices will be too high under *cost-plus* contracts can be avoided by using price caps or requiring advance approval of purchases.

- *Cost-plus* contracts are often better than flat-fee contracts because they don't induce contractors to buy low-quality components to save money (though they may lead contractors to buy components that are too high in quality). The problem that quality will be inappropriate under *flat-fee* contracts can be avoided by specifying quality or requiring advance approval of purchases.

- *Cost-plus* contracts have the advantage of usually not having to be renegotiated when changes are made, whereas *flat-fee* contracts often do. Renegotiation is costly, and it subjects parties to holdup.

- *Flat-fee* contracts tend to be good on risk-sharing grounds when buyers are relatively risk averse. *Cost-plus* contracts tend to be good when contractors are relatively risk averse.

This list of comparisons of flat-fee and cost-plus contracts isn't exhaustive, but it does cover the most important points that you should take into consideration.

projects, or perhaps it's part of a conglomerate enterprise. And suppose that the buyer is unable to bear much risk — maybe it's a fledgling business with meager assets. In this setting, it makes sense from the perspectives of both sides to use a flat-fee contract.

Conversely, suppose that the buyer is a large corporation and that the seller is a small construction company with limited assets and can't afford to take significant risks. Here, in terms of risk allocation, a cost-plus contract is desirable. The small construction company bears no risk and thus is more likely to agree to a cost-plus than to a flat-fee arrangement with the buyer. And the buyer willingly makes a cost-plus contract because it can tolerate the risk. (The buyer doesn't favor a flat-fee contract, on the other hand, because the construction company charges a lot to compensate for the risk it bears.)

E. Application: School Gymnasium

Suppose that you're the lawyer for a small private school that wants to build a new gym. The school is negotiating with a large construction company. What should the basic structure of the contract look like?

Before we get down to the specifics of figuring this out, two aspects of the general approach to drafting any production contract are worth emphasizing: (1) when you're deciding between a cost-plus contract and a fixed-fee contract, it's always important to think about the principles we've discussed, carefully considering them in light of your client's situation; and (2) whichever route you go, you should do everything possible to protect your client from the predictable kinds of pitfalls that we've discussed. Now let's work through the example methodically, taking into account our discussion points that seem most relevant.

A flat-fee contract seems good for the usual reason — it would motivate the contractor to search for low prices. Under a cost-plus contract, on the other hand, the contractor would lack an incentive to find low prices. This disadvantage presupposes that your client and its architect don't know enough about prices of the relevant components to be able to impose fitting price caps or require advance approval of purchases in order to ensure that the contractor secures good prices. In other words, the presumption is that your client doesn't know much about construction costs, the costs of materials, the best suppliers, and so forth. Thus,

Box 3-2
Common Contractual Provisions

Can you relate the contractual terms in the excerpts below to points we've covered?

Flat-fee contract. The following terms are from a flat-fee contract between a city and a contractor:

> *Article 3.01. Contractor's Responsibility.* The Contractor shall do all the work . . . at his own cost. . . . [T]he work must be performed in accordance with the best modern practice, with materials as specified and workmanship of the highest quality, all as determined by and entirely to the satisfaction of the [City] Engineer. . . .The means and methods of production shall be . . . subject . . . to the approval of the Engineer. . . .
>
> *Article 3.03 Inspection.* The City shall have the right to reject materials and workmanship which are defective.*

Cost-plus contract. The following terms are from a cost-plus contract between a company and a contractor that calls for a fixed additional fee to be paid to the contractor:

> *Article 6. Authority of Company Engineer.* Company shall provide a competent Company Engineer, who shall have authority to direct all phases of work and to approve all authorized costs. . . . The Company Engineer shall have authority to reject work and material which [do] not conform to the contract. . . .
>
> *Article 8. Procurement of Materials.* . . . Contractor shall submit all purchase orders to Company for its prior approval. Company reserves the right to purchase any items directly on its own account. . . . Company also reserves the right to furnish materials and equipment from its own surplus.†

---

* Dib, 1994, chapter 3E-93.
† Dib, 1994, chapter 3E-71.

under a cost-plus contract, your fear would be that your client, the school, will be taken to the cleaners. Your choice, then, would probably be to go with a flat-fee agreement.

If you do opt for a flat-fee contract, you'll have to protect your client against the possibility that the construction company will chisel your client on the quality of the gym it builds. For you to be able to ensure that the quality of the gym meets your client's expectations, your client would have to spend time investigating the ins and outs of gyms so that it can identify precisely what it wants and you can pin down the specifics in the contract. In other words, your client would have to spell out the details for the whole spectrum of components — type of gym floor, brand of fold-down bleacher seats, and type of shower facilities and heating plant, to name just a few. But because your client probably doesn't know very much about such things and their costs, the investigative task would be time consuming and difficult. On the other hand, it might be possible for the architect to provide plans that are sufficiently detailed to circumvent the quality problem. Under a flat-fee contract, you'd want to be as specific as possible so that the contractor wouldn't have an opportunity to shortchange your client on quality.

You'll want your client to think very carefully about its plans. Are they an accurate reflection of what your client wants? Can your client anticipate any changes that it might want to make down the line? Decisions are best made up front, because modifications made after work begins on the project would be add-ons to the contract that would require separate negotiation. So thinking ahead would really pay off in terms of saving time and trouble and expense later. Remember the holdup problem: if your client decides halfway through the job that it wants the gym to have a balcony with additional bleachers, the contractor, having your client over a barrel, might well attempt to charge excessively for the addition.

A flat-fee contact would mean that your client won't be bearing any risk. This may be a big advantage: your client can't really afford to absorb the risk because it might have difficulty raising additional money on short notice. Moreover, the construction company, being large and easily able to absorb any risk inherent in a project like gym construction,

---

> **Box 3-3**
> **What If Your Client Does Change Its Plans?**
>
> We've explained why a flat-fee contract is probably best for the school and why, given this kind of contract, it would be bad for the school to change its plans during construction. Ideally, the school will think about everything in advance. Realistically, though, it probably won't. Maybe a new regulation will require a design change, for instance. Think about this as a remedy: any change in the plans will be paid for on a cost-plus basis. What are the pros and cons of this supplement to your flat-fee contract?

probably wouldn't charge a lot more under a flat-fee contract to bear the risk of fluctuating construction costs.

In summary, it appears that your choice would be to go for a flat-fee contract, but you'd make very sure that you specify in the contract the quality standards to be met and, to prevent the need to renegotiate the contract, that your client tries to anticipate everything that it's going to want.

By the way, how many of all these pros and cons do you think the school will have considered? If you present your analysis and recommendations laying out the kinds of issues just discussed, it's quite likely that you'll contribute substantially to the making of the right kind of contract, that you and your client can together fashion a much better contract than otherwise.

F. Developing Arguments in Contract Litigation

What we've learned in this section is useful not only in drafting production contracts but also in coming up with points to use in litigation involving contract disputes. Suppose, for instance, that you specified in the contract for the school gym that a certain type of roofing material be used, a material recommended by the architect because of its durability. And let's say that the contractor chose an unusual, low-quality brand of roofing material that isn't particularly durable but which he claims is essentially equivalent to that specified in the contract.

A general term in the contract calls for "good faith" on the part of the contractor. You're thinking that this term might be interpreted in your favor to require the contractor to replace the low-quality material. At the same time, you're worried because the contractor might assert that your client made the flat-fee contract (rather than a cost-plus contract) so that costs (and the contract price) would be held down and thus so that he (the contractor) had a reason to economize — which he claims is just what he did. Given this possible counter to you, wouldn't it be better to make a more pointed argument than merely to invoke the duty of good faith and then throw yourself at the mercy of the court?

Armed with the principles we've covered, you could do so. You could answer the contractor with this argument: contractors have an excessive incentive under flat-fee contracts to choose cheap, low-quality components. Accordingly, your client attempted to avoid this problem by incorporating into the contract specific provisions to protect against being shortchanged on quality. This is, in fact, exactly why you specified the type of roofing material to be used. You can — and will — demonstrate that the particular brand of roofing material the contractor used is of very poor quality for your client's purposes.

More specifically, you might prove that the material could easily lead to a leaky roof in just a few years and that the necessary repairs would cost $30,000. You might also prove that the contractor saved only $5,000 by purchasing the low-quality material. Therefore, this unusual brand of roofing material isn't one that you would have agreed to had you discussed it, and the contractor, given his experience, presumably knew this. If the court rejects your argument, you can go on to say, then flat-fee contracts in the future will have a negative effect on quality that reduces the size of the contractual pie. Hence, a ruling against your client would cause contracting parties in the future to suffer: it will lower quality and reduce the willingness of buyers to pay for contracts, or it will require parties to spend excessive amounts of time and money drafting contracts that are incredibly detailed (e.g., by listing every brand that may not be used) in order to prevent behavior that isn't in their mutual interests.

This constitutes a more specific and more powerful line of argument to make to a court or arbitrator than does a general plea that your client was hurt by the use of low-quality roofing material and that it was simply bad faith for the contractor to have chosen the brand that he did. And it demonstrates how an understanding of the purposes of contracts and particular provisions within them can help you develop useful arguments and types of proof in litigation that might not otherwise have occurred to you.

5. Principal and Agent Contracts

A common situation is for one party, a *principal,* to contract with another, an *agent,* to do something: a person hires a lawyer to undertake a legal task; an individual hires a real estate agent to look for property; a store owner hires someone to manage the store; a taxpayer hires an accountant to handle tax matters; a landowner hires a farmer to grow crops; and so forth. A principal need not, however, be an individual. Indeed, when a company hires an employee, the company can be considered the principal and the employee an agent. Obviously, then, the principal-agent relationship covers a lot of territory.[5]

There are three major types of principal-agent contracts: *performance-based* (also referred to as *output-based*), *input-based,* and *fixed-fee.* Under a performance-based contract, payment depends on productivity as measured by some specified criterion. A real estate agent might be paid for making a deal, with the amount of the payment based on the sale price of the property. A store manager might be rewarded if the store makes a profit or if a survey shows an increase in customer satisfaction. A salesperson might be paid on commission, perhaps a percentage of the revenues on goods sold. A lawyer might be paid a contingent fee, a percentage of the recovery or settlement obtained, if any. These are just a few examples.

---

5. The production contract that we just considered can be regarded as a type of principal-agent contract, one in which the contractor is the agent. In our discussion, we addressed issues specific to the production context and focused on two particular types of contract, flat-fee and cost-plus. Here, we'll consider a broader range of issues, settings, and contract types.

Under an input-based contract, on the other hand, payment is tied to input, such as time spent. For instance, a store employee or a lawyer might be paid on the basis of number of hours worked. Or a builder might be paid on the basis of his costs, as in the cost-plus construction contract that we considered earlier.

Under a fixed-fee contract, the agent is simply paid a stipulated amount for performing a service. Thus, an accountant might be paid a given sum for doing taxes, a lawyer for writing a will, a guide for providing a tour, or a builder for a construction project as in the flat-fee contract discussed earlier.

Many contracts are mixtures of these types, as in the case of a store manager who is paid a salary on the basis of the number of hours worked (an input) and also a bonus consisting of a percentage of profits (a measure of performance). For each general type of principal-agent contract, many decisions — such as what percentage of profits the store manager is to receive — have to be made to fully delineate the contract.

Performance-based, input-based, and fixed-fee contracts differ along a number of dimensions. In the examples that we discuss, we'll often assume that your client is the principal and decide from this perspective what kind of contract you should write.[6]

A. Incentives

Principals generally want incentives to be created that will enable them to achieve their goals. The store owner or land owner will want to end up with a profit, the client will want her lawyer to win a large judgment, and so forth. It can't, however, be taken for granted that agents will do their best to advance the principals' goals. Doing so requires effort, which agents may not be inclined to exert unless they have an incentive to do so. Moreover, it's often insufficient for a contract merely to specify "best efforts," because such a term is hard to interpret and an agent's efforts may be difficult for a principal to observe and to demonstrate

---

6. It's just for the sake of simplicity that we'll assume that your client is the principal. If your client were the agent, you'd end up going with the same kind of contract. The reason is one that should be quite familiar to you by now: the type of contract that's better for one party is also better for the other party — it's mutually beneficial — because it increases the size of the contractual pie.

to a tribunal. Hence, understanding the incentives created by different types of contracts is important.

Incentives under a performance-based contract are, obviously, directed toward performance. Basing a store manager's salary on profits serves as an incentive for him to try to maximize the store's profits. Tying a lawyer's compensation to a judgment or settlement is an incentive for her to obtain as much as possible for her client.

The strength of incentives under performance-based contracts depends on the specific nature of the contract. Consider the store manager. If his compensation is but a small percentage of profits — say, 5% — he has little incentive to increase profits. In contemplating whether to work over the weekend on a new advertising plan that would bring in an extra $2,000 in profits, for example, he may well decide not to because he realizes that he'd end up with only an extra $100 (5% of the $2,000), too little to justify the additional work.

For the manager's incentive to be better aligned with what the store owner wants, he would have to receive a higher percentage of the profits. A 25% share — which would translate into an additional $500 in this instance — might be enough to induce him to work over the weekend. But even this fraction of profits isn't necessarily high enough: if he values an alternative for the weekend at $700 (e.g., he's already made plans for a vacation, and his airline tickets aren't refundable), he'd choose not to work for the store, because he'd end up losing more than he'd gain from the additional $2,000 in store profits. For the manager to have a sufficient incentive to maximize total value, he must be induced to spend the weekend working whenever his personal valuation of the weekend is less than $2,000. But this means that he'd have to obtain for himself 100% — the full $2,000 — of additional profits the store would bring in as a result of his weekend's work. Likewise, for him to have the proper incentive to prevent losses, he'd also have to suffer 100% of any losses the store experienced.

However, a contract in which the manager both earns any extra profits the store makes and suffers any losses it experiences might not be desirable for the principal and would often be unworkable. If the manager were to receive all the profits relative to some benchmark level, his earnings might exceed what the principal is willing to pay.[7] In addition, because the manager's assets might not be sufficient to cover the losses, it's possible that he couldn't bear them. Both of these problems might be unavoidable even if the manager's share of the profits or losses were less than — perhaps much less than — 100%. For example, if a manager of a large corporation were to receive 5% of profits, his salary could be hundreds of millions of dollars — an amount greatly exceeding what shareholders are willing to pay.

The upshot is that the strength of the incentive to perform under an output-based contract depends on, among other things, the percentage of profits or losses that the agent will receive or bear. Yet contracts under which agents receive high percentages of profits and suffer high percentages of losses may be undesirable for principals or unworkable.

An alternative way to create an incentive for the agent is to opt for an input-based contract rather than a performance-based one. A store owner might want the manager to work more hours than is customary because more hours means larger profits for the owner, so he would specify in the contract that the manager is to be paid by the hour. If the manager is specifically paid extra for working over the weekend, he'll be more willing to do so.

Typically, however, the number of hours that a manager works isn't the only determinant of store profits. How the manager oversees the workers, treats customers, and behaves in many other dimensions also enters into the picture. Indeed, envisioning a manager who spends much of his time gossiping with other employees, even though he does work long hours, isn't at all difficult. More broadly, a store manager rewarded only on the basis of time put in won't have an incentive to oversee employees effectively, provide good customer service, or attend to business rather than to personal matters. This exemplifies a general difficulty with input-based contracts: they tend to base payment on only some of

---

7. To take this one step further, let's consider not just the manager, but all employees of the store. For each of them to have perfect incentives, each would have to be entitled to 100% of the additional profits — and the difficulty that this poses is impossible to miss.

the determinants of profits; hence, agents may not have much, or any, incentive to increase profits along other dimensions.

How can a principal attempt to ensure that the agent will perform as desired? The most direct solution is for the principal to pay to observe or otherwise assess the agent's performance. For instance, the owner of the store could hire a marketing firm to survey customers about their satisfaction. The information from the survey could be used to determine whether to pay a bonus or to decide whether to fire the manager. (Note that these uses of information introduce a performance-based element into the contract.) Such approaches to the problem of monitoring inputs that affect profits, however, are not only costly but also often provide only imperfect information about the inputs.

Finally, under a fixed-fee contract, there is no direct incentive for the agent to perform well. The principal may be relying entirely on the agent's good character, reputation, or desire for subsequent business from the principal. Or, as with the input-based contract, the principal could pay to monitor performance, perhaps making payment of the fee contingent on satisfactory effort or quality of the final product.

B. Risk Bearing

Another very important consideration in the choice of contract type is risk bearing — how great the risk is, who will bear it, and who is in the best position to bear it. Under a performance-based contract, the agent is the risk bearer (to the extent of the profit or other share), because random, unpredictable factors typically make it impossible for him to predict performance. For any of a number of reasons, the store manager can't be sure what sales will be: consumers' tastes might change, competing stores might open, the weather might affect demand, general economic conditions might change, and so on. If he's paid solely a percentage of profits, his income could be very risky, fluctuating widely from month to month. Similarly, if a lawyer is paid solely a percentage of awards or settlements gained, her income might be very risky, because of the vagaries of settlement negotiations and judicial decision making. Hence, from the perspective of agents, performance-based contracts that create good incentives by tying compensation substantially to profit or output have a major drawback: they impose significant risks.

By contrast, input-based contracts tend not to impose risk on agents. A store manager paid by the hour knows, given the number of hours he works, what his salary will be. By definition, whether profits turn out to be high or low is irrelevant. A lawyer paid on the basis of the amount of time she spends on a case often knows reasonably well (though not perfectly, because some uncertainties are inherent in time spent) what she'll make. The size of the recovery the case produces for the client doesn't matter.

Fixed-fee contracts also may impose little or no risk on agents. However, when the required amount of effort is highly uncertain up front,

---

Box 3-4
Performance-Based, Input-Based,
and Fixed-Fee Contracts in a Nutshell

- *Performance-based* contracts create incentives for performance. But the creation of strong incentives requires that the agent receive a high percentage of profits and bear a high percentage of losses, which may be undesirable for the principal and unworkable.

- *Input-based* contracts also create incentives for performance. But to the extent that contracts of this type leave out hard-to-observe or hard-to-measure dimensions of input that affect performance, incentives for performance are incomplete. Such dimensions of input can sometimes be monitored, but monitoring is costly and often imperfect.

- *Fixed-fee* contracts don't create incentives for performance. Here, too, monitoring can sometimes be a solution.

- *Performance-based* contracts impose risk on agents, which is a drawback if agents are more risk averse than principals.

- *Input-based* and *fixed-fee* contracts tend to protect agents against risk, which is an advantage if agents are more risk averse than principals.

the agent may bear substantial risk. Consider, for example, a lawyer who agrees to litigate a case for a fixed fee not knowing if or when it will settle.

Hence, agents who are risk averse tend to favor input-based or fixed-fee contracts, depending on the circumstances. Principals, though, bear risk under these kinds of contracts. The store owner bears uncertainty in profits if the manager is paid on the basis of time worked or a fixed salary. The client bears all of the risk in terms of the outcome of the case if the lawyer is paid on the basis of time worked or a flat fee. When principals aren't very risk averse relative to agents, on the other hand, both sides tend to prefer input-based or fixed-fee contracts.

Although agents might generally be thought to be more risk averse than principals are, often the opposite is true. Suppose, for instance, that the principal is a plaintiff in a lawsuit who has little in assets and the agent is a successful lawyer or law firm with a large portfolio of cases. That an input-based contract protects the lawyer from risk and imposes it entirely on the client instead is a disadvantage rather than an advantage for the lawyer. A performance-based contract — for example, one under which the lawyer receives a fraction of the settlement or judgment — would be superior in terms of risk allocation. The client still bears considerable risk under a contingent-fee contract under which the lawyer receives, say, 33% of any recovery, but in the event of a loss, the client doesn't have to pay legal fees, which otherwise may have been large.

C. Application: Coffee Shop Manager

Suppose that you're the general counsel for a new coffeehouse company that aspires to be another Starbucks. You're working on a contract that will govern the managers of all the company's cafes. The following points are made during in-house discussions.

- The kind of person the company is looking for to fill these positions usually makes in the neighborhood of $50,000 a year in a salaried position.
- The job of manager entails hiring and firing, overseeing employees (e.g., monitoring their diligence and their behavior with customers), ordering supplies from the

---

Box 3-5
Screenwriter's Contract

The following excerpts are from a principal and agent contract — specifically, a standard employment contract for a screenwriter on a British feature film. Can you relate the contractual terms to points we've covered? Try to identify why the various terms are in the mutual interests of the parties.

[The] writer undertakes under the Agreement to:

1. attend story conferences with the producer
2. carry out research and preparation for the script
3. write and deliver the treatment, first draft, second draft and principal photography script in accordance with the contract with the producer. Each manuscript should be clearly typed, and time is stipulated to be of the essence of the agreement
4. collaborate with others as necessary and render all reasonable services to the best of his ability . . .

The producer will not be obliged to accept or pay for any work which is more than fourteen days in arrears of any delivery dates set out in the agreement with the producer [unless] it is by illness or incapacity of the writer.

Payment for the above is 23,200 pounds. In addition, the screenwriter will be paid [per use on] US network prime time TV, 13,000 pounds[;] ROW free TV, 6,000 pounds[;] UK TV, 2,000 pounds[;] . . . PBS, 1,500 pounds.*

---

* Mosawi, 1997, at 83–90.

central warehouse and distribution system, among a host of other responsibilities (e.g., ensuring that the establishment is clean and opens on time).

• The company's computer system can track on a daily basis the receipts of each cafe and the costs of coffee and other supplies. In addition, you'll know how many employees work at each location and what their hourly wages are, and you'll be able to track the number of hours they work each day. The company expects to sell shares of stock to the public in the near future.

What kind of contract should you write for coffeehouse managers?

1. Performance-based contract. The company's computer system, by tracking and calculating revenues and costs for the individual coffeehouses, makes it possible to determine profits fairly readily. So a performance-based contract that ties the managers' salaries to the profits of their respective cafes seems workable.

In considering profit-based compensation, however, you know that you have to be mindful of the risk that each manager will bear. True, someone who seeks a management position at a retail establishment is someone who's more than likely to take the initiative and whose risk tolerance is probably greater than the average person's. Nevertheless, a person like this may well not be interested in a position where salary is overly dependent on random elements that could affect profits. Applicants that your company really wants to hire might consider an entirely profit-dependent salary that yields $70,000 on average less desirable than the alternative of a flat $50,000 salary (which, as you remember, is the typical alternative for the kind of employee your company wants to hire). Even though the profit-based salary would be higher on average, the risk that income will at times be very low might be quite unattractive to these candidates. For example, the company's coffeehouses might really catch on, resulting in a salary of $120,000, or they might be a flop, yielding a salary of $20,000 (or even nothing).

In order to entice the applicants to serve as managers, you might need to guarantee a base salary — say, $40,000 — and augment it with a profit-based component, perhaps a modest percentage of cafe profits.

(Observe that this approach combines fixed-fee and performance-based elements.)

If you decide on a profit-based component that you can reasonably expect to average $20,000, for example, a manager's salary would, in turn, average $60,000. Note that such an arrangement might be more attractive to applicants for the positions, because much less risk is associated with the salary, and that, at the same time, it would cost your company less on average: $60,000 instead of $70,000. The incentive for managers to maximize profits would, however, be weaker under this salary scheme, where the profit-based component is rather modest, than under the one where salary is entirely profit dependent.

Because your company is likely to go public, you also contemplate giving the coffeehouse managers stock options, which, it is commonly said, motivate managers. Perhaps each manager would receive options in 0.1% of the company's stock. But you wonder, given that you've been thinking about using profits as a performance-enhancing incentive, what additional motivation stock options would provide. You realize that stock options add essentially nothing to this incentive. The reason is that, because the company will be opening many coffee shops, the value of the stock of the whole company won't be affected in any significant way by the actions of a single store manager. Moreover, each manager would be given options to but a trivial percentage of the company's stock. Nevertheless, the stock options are a very risky form of compensation. Hence, on reflection, the case for including stock options in the managers' compensation packages seems weak.

2. Input-based contract. You're well aware that managers can affect profits of their cafes in many ways through their actions, behavior, and work style — that is, their input. The number of hours that managers work, for example, definitely bears on profits, so the contract should address this issue. It should probably include as well terms dealing with things that you want the managers to have an incentive to do. Unfortunately, a lot of this won't be observable or verifiable to a tribunal. For instance, profits will be affected by how well the staffs serve customers — how professionally, efficiently, and courteously they do their jobs. And it will be the managers' duty to ensure that their staffs perform appropriately — by making sure not only that their staffs understand what's

---

Box 3-6
Coffeehouse Manager's Contract

Managers of coffee shops of a well-known chain receive a base salary and are eligible for two types of bonus. A profit bonus is paid if the profits of a shop exceed a target figure, which is set on the basis of the shop's past performance. This kind of bonus is paid quarterly and is capped at 20% of the manager's base salary. A "snapshot" bonus is based on an evaluation, as reflected in the report of a secret shopper, of the store's adherence to the company's official policies. It can potentially be almost as large as the maximum profit bonus. All bonuses are split — 70% and 30% — between the manager and the assistant manager, both of whom also receive sizable discounts on merchandise, including coffee.*

---

* David Cope, interview with a manager, January 2000.

---

expected of them but also, through direct supervision, that they are in fact doing their jobs at the level expected. In other words, the managers will have to be skilled at handling and motivating employees. Obviously, it isn't easy to monitor and evaluate such aspects of managerial effort. One way to evaluate managerial behavior — a costly one — would be through unannounced spot checks by company representatives posing as customers. But then you'd have to take this cost into account.

3. Fixed-fee contract. You could, of course, just offer managers a fixed salary of $50,000. They would bear no risk, but neither would they have an incentive to exert effort. The company could employ monitoring of inputs and performance to improve manager behavior under this kind of contract.

4. Your decision. After considering all of these points, you'll probably want to write a contract that has some performance-based component, probably in the form of percentage of coffee-shop profits. And you may also want to build into the contract one or more input-based components — at the least, one tied to amount of time spent working at the cafe.

Note that under this contract managers must be compensated for the risk that they would bear owing to the performance-based component. Yet the higher cost would be worthwhile for the fledgling company if, as seems likely, the quality of managers' efforts will be important to the success of the coffeehouses.

6. Other Types of Contracts

There are, of course, many important types of contracts in addition to the two we've discussed, and we'll take a brief look at several of them. The goal isn't to be comprehensive. Rather, it's to illustrate that, for each type of contract, you have to think about the general factors in the checklist set out earlier in the chapter and how to apply them. (Recalling the reasons we discussed earlier about why contracts are made, try to explain why those we are about to discuss were agreed to.)

A. Joint Undertakings

A partnership agreement among a group of lawyers or physicians; an agreement between two drug companies under which one is to develop a new drug and the other is to market it; a contract among a group of investors to start a company, where one takes on a primary managerial role; an agreement between a venture capitalist with many connections and with know-how in the business world and an inventor with relatively little business experience — these are just a few examples of contracts made by parties that want to engage in *joint undertakings* — in which possibly many parties do different things. Such agreements are as common as they are varied. And they are much more general than either production or principal-agent contracts, both of which involve "joint" undertakings in which only one party is doing something.

Incentives are important in contracts that govern joint undertakings. What you must think about in particular is what each party has to be motivated to do. For a partnership among lawyers where all the partners are in roughly the same situation, for example, you'd have to build into the agreement incentives for each to bring in new clients and to work hard and succeed. One way to do this would be by linking compensation to the generation of new business and to the number of hours worked. In the agreement between the two drug companies, on the other hand, you'd want the incentives you fashion to be very different for the two companies, because they have distinct roles (one is to develop the drug, and the other is to market it). Hence, you must think about what specific provisions you can include in the contract that will furnish effective incentives for each company. Perhaps the company that is to develop the drug should receive a payment based on whether and when the drug is approved by the FDA, and perhaps the payment to the marketing company should be based on drug sales revenue net of advertising costs.

Other considerations when you're drafting joint-venture contracts are uncertainty and risk sharing, which vary widely from context to context. For instance, in a partnership agreement among lawyers, the risk of a low salary may be a concern. To get around this problem, you might be tempted to draw up a contract in which the partners share profits more evenly than they would if rewards went to those who brought in business or worked long hours during the year. This approach would shield individual partners from excessive risk, but it would also compromise incentives. So including some input-based or performance-based features in the contract would be necessary.

Risk may have to be allocated in the drug companies' joint venture as well. If the drug-developing company is a relatively small firm with low assets, it wouldn't be well suited to absorb the substantial risks attending the development, testing, and approval processes. The contract you design would have to call for the large marketing company to bear a substantial fraction of these risks. Because this approach would dilute the incentives of the small company, you might have to set up contractual mechanisms that would allow the large company to monitor the small company's effort level.

These examples also serve to illustrate another point that we've covered: whether or not a behavior is observable and can be verified to a tribunal is important. Can the small company's efforts to develop a drug of high quality, to develop it quickly, and so forth really be determined by outsiders? If experts in drug development were hired to monitor the small company's progress, would this monitoring be sufficient? And how much would it cost? Can the expenses incurred by the small company in developing the drug be ascertained with any degree of accuracy? (If it buys a centrifuge and claims that it's for use in the development of

---

Box 3-7
Law Firm Partnership Agreements

The following excerpts are from samples of two types of law firm partnership arrangements. Think about them and, in particular, compare them in terms of incentives and risk allocation.

Formula schedule for distribution of earnings. One arrangement begins by defining a number of terms, including the following:

> *"Work credit"* shall mean . . . eighty-five per cent (85%) of the gross fees allocated to a . . . Partner or associate for legal services. . . . *"Associate profit"* shall mean the excess of associates' work credit over all associates' direct expenses. . . . *"Client credit"* shall mean the amount added to the participation of a . . . Partner . . . based on clients attributable to such Partner. . . . *"Participation"* shall mean the total share of each Partner in the profits of the Firm.

The contract then goes on to specify what the partners will earn:

> Each Partner is guaranteed a minimum participation . . . of $___ in each fiscal year. . . . The normal participation of each Partner shall be the sum of the following: . . . work credit; . . . client credit . . . ; per capita share of other firm profits; per capita share of associate profit.*

Equal partners system. Under an equal partners arrangement, the partners, it stated in the sample contract, "shall have equal allocations of firm profits . . . during each year." According to the commentary that accompanies the sample,

> [T]he equal partners system is probably used most often by newer or smaller law firms. It implies that the participants are in practice for better or worse with the intention to share the burdens and the rewards equally. The goal of such a system . . . is to make the partner with higher objective statistics aware of the importance the law firm places on the different set of contributions of a partner with lower statistics. Conversely, such a compensation system encourages the partner with lower statistics to close the gap . . . [with] the partner who has contributed more statistically.†

What do you think of this reasoning?

---

* Corwin and Ciampi, 1998, Section 5.04[2].
† Corwin and Ciampi, 1998, Section 5.04[3].

the drug in question, how can the large firm know whether this is true?) Issues concerning the ability to observe or measure variables that you'd like to include in a contract are important, and you have to think about them in detail in advance in order to figure out whether they are, in fact, workable and appropriate to incorporate as terms in the contract you're preparing.

B. Sale or Lease of Property

Another prevalent kind of contract is one in which property is conveyed, either in a sales transaction or in a lease. For these contracts, too, incentives of various sorts enter into the equation.

Parties that are planning to buy or lease property are often concerned about its condition. This is an issue that you can address directly by contractual terms. For example, if your client wants an apartment to be clean, the hot water to be hot, and so forth, you can specify as conditions in the contract that these criteria are to be met. If your client is purchasing a home, you might condition the deal on an inspection of the property as of a particular date. Including a term like this gives the other side a clear incentive to make sure that the home remains in good condition for your client.

On the other side of the coin, a lessor might like to have some assurance that the lessee will maintain the property in good condition during the period of a lease. If you represent the lessor, you can include contractual terms that deal directly with this matter and supplement them with provisions that, for example, give your client the right to inspect the property while the lease is in effect, require the lessee to put down a security deposit to cover the cost of repairs should they be necessary, and impose a penalty on the tenant (such as termination of the lease) for failure to maintain the property. Should your client (the owner) not want to allow the property to be sublet (e.g., because of the possibility that the sublessor would be less careful than the lessor), you can specify this in the contract too.[8]

---

8. In practice, when determining whether to grant a lease, property owners typically assess prospective lessees on a number of dimensions to judge how likely they are to maintain the property or to disturb other tenants.

For contracts covering the delivery of goods, you might want to think about incentives aimed at reducing the chance that the property will be damaged during transport. All other things being equal, it would be appropriate for the risk of harm or loss to be borne by the selling party, as that party packs the goods and arranges for them to be transported. A contract term specifying this would motivate the seller to take proper precautions.

The incentive issue is very different when it comes to the matter of disclosure. Often, one side — usually the seller but sometimes the buyer — has information that the other side doesn't have about the condition of the property. For example, the seller but not the buyer might know that toxic wastes have been dumped onto a parcel of land or that the basement of a house leaks. In such a case, the knowledgeable party would have an incentive to withhold unfavorable information — and might not be required by law to disclose it. It's always important to keep

---

Box 3-8
Apartment Rental Agreement

Why would the following terms be in a rental agreement for an apartment?

The Lessee shall not paint, decorate or otherwise embellish and/or change . . . the leased premises . . . No washing machine, air-conditioning unit, space heater, television aerials . . . shall be installed without the prior written consent of the Lessor . . .

The Lessee shall maintain the leased premises in a clean condition . . .

The Lessor may enter upon the leased premises to make repairs thereto, to inspect the premises, or to show the premises to prospective tenants . . .

The Lessee shall not assign nor underlet . . . the leased premises . . . without first obtaining the assent in writing of the Lessor.

this possibility in mind. You could protect your client (the buyer) with contracting options that provide for disclosure, require inspection, spell out guarantees that allow your client to seek redress if particular adverse circumstances arise, and so forth. For example, you might include a term specifying that the seller of land will indemnify the buyer for any environmental cleanup costs that turn out to be necessary.

Many kinds of risk are associated with the transfer of property. Being thorough in identifying and assessing them will help you figure out how they would best be allocated. If you're the buyer's lawyer, risks related to titles, liabilities (e.g., for environmental harms), and loss or theft of property prior to delivery are particularly relevant. Another risk is that the seller will turn around and sell to someone else, breaching the contract. If you represent the seller, on the other hand, you'd want to anticipate that the buyer might try to back out of the deal — because of a simple change of mind, a financial reversal, or a chance to take advantage of a better opportunity. In addition to specifying in the contract who is to bear what risks, you might also want to suggest that your client insure against some of them — say, by arranging for title insurance or liability coverage. Assigning risk will, of course, also affect incentives. (As we saw just a minute ago, for example, the selling party that packs the goods can be expected to do a better job if it bears the risk of harm during transport than if it doesn't.) The parties may, however, have different capacities to bear risk or abilities to insure against it.

C. Loan Contracts

Loans, which constitute yet another category of contract, are an omnipresent feature of economic activity: individuals borrow and lend and so do businesses, nonprofit institutions (e.g., museums, schools), and governments. The kinds of incentive issues that borrowers and lenders face are numerous, and we'll look at just a few, first from the perspective that your client is the lender and then from the perspective that your client is the borrower.[9]

---

9. Other financial arrangements, such as taking an equity stake in a firm, raise similar concerns, but in the interest of brevity, we'll restrict our focus to loans.

One thing you'd want to take into account in looking out for a lender's best interests is that the borrower might sell his assets and end up being unable to pay off the loan. To guard against this possibility, you could take out security interests (such as a mortgage) or employ covenants (i.e., clauses that would, for example, prohibit the sale of assets without your client's permission). Another approach would be to put controls on the borrower's expenditures (e.g., by including in the contract a covenant requiring the borrower to obtain your client's permission before making significant outlays).

You'd also want to anticipate the possibility that the borrower will seek out particularly risky opportunities, thinking that everything will be rosy if he succeeds but knowing that bankruptcy is a fallback if he fails. Should the deal not pan out for the borrower, however, your client will be left without repayment. You could address this problem of excessive risk taking through contractual terms that allow your client to control the borrower's investment decisions.

However, the degree to which the borrower's activities can be controlled by your client is limited. Moreover, your client wouldn't want to impose such constraints that the borrower would be prevented from conducting business reasonably well (thereby jeopardizing repayment of the loan) — or, indeed, be dissuaded from taking out the loan in the first place.

No matter how many precautions you take to ensure that the borrower will be able to repay your client, bankruptcy remains as a possibility, and you might want to provide for this eventuality in the contract. To the extent that commercial and bankruptcy law doesn't already adequately protect your client and allows you to contract for additional protection, you could incorporate terms that prevent other creditors from seeking and receiving priority over your client for repayment.

If you were representing the borrower, on the other hand, many of your concerns would mirror those of the lender's lawyer (e.g., ones having to do with controls over the borrower's monetary outlays and business decisions). You should keep in mind that restrictions on your client are not an unmitigated evil, however. In fact, without them, your client might not be able to borrow at all, or the lender might insist on a higher interest rate to compensate for the greater risk of default. If this

---

Box 3-9
Loan Contract Secured by a Home

Why would the following provisions appear in a standard loan contract secured by a home?

> Borrower shall keep . . . the Property insured against loss by fire . . . and any other hazards, including floods, . . . for which the Lender requires insurance. . . . The insurance carrier shall be chosen by the Borrower subject to the Lender's approval. . . .
>
> Borrower shall occupy . . . and use the Property as Borrower's principal residence within sixty days . . . and shall continue to occupy the Property . . . for at least one year. . . . Borrower shall not destroy, damage or impair the Property. . . .
>
> If Borrower fails to perform covenants . . . then Lender may do . . . whatever is necessary to protect the value of the Property and Lender's rights. . . .
>
> Lender . . . may make reasonable entries upon and inspections of the Property. . . .
>
> . . . Any forbearance by Lender in exercising any right or remedy shall not be a waiver or preclude the exercise of any right or remedy.*

---

* Lefcoe, 1997, at 1407–1420.

---

strikes you as being another illustration of our recurring theme — that enlarging the contractual pie is mutually beneficial to the parties, even if the term that enlarges it (viewed in isolation) is disadvantageous for one party — you're right on the mark. The party for whom the term is unfavorable can be compensated by the other party in exchange for agreeing to include the term in the contract. In the case at hand, in exchange for yielding some control over its own operations, the borrower (your client) is compensated by the lender with a lower interest rate than would otherwise be prudent. In this context, the interest rate functions as the price.

From your perspective as the borrower's lawyer, other issues might warrant consideration as well — for example, early repayment of the loan. Having the option to repay without penalty might be worthwhile in some circumstances: perhaps your client will have the opportunity to refinance through a cheaper source or will earn a great deal more than anticipated. Early repayment can be undesirable for the lender, however, so including such a term would make sense only if the advantage to the borrower outweighs the disadvantage to the lender.

7. Resolving Contractual Disputes

As a lawyer drafting a contract, you naturally have to anticipate problematic outcomes and legal trouble down the road and figure out how to avoid such pitfalls or, should they arise, how to handle them. Contingent provisions, damages for breach, and arbitration are three tools that you have at your disposal to help you do just this.

A. Contingent Provisions

Some potential problems that might lead to disputes can be avoided through the use of contingent contractual provisions. If you carefully think about a problem that could arise, you'll often find that you can write a contingent provision that addresses the issue and thereby heads off a dispute. Suppose that your client is a small firm that makes components for a GM plant and that GM is entering into a contract with your client for a steady supply of electronic parts. If workers at your client's factory go on strike, however, your client may need its obligation to supply these parts to be suspended because having to raise the cash to pay damages would disrupt its business. By thinking ahead, you can include in the contract a clause that excuses your client in the event of a strike. The cost to your client shouldn't be very high if a strike is unlikely, yet the clause may be a very important protection for your client if a strike does take place.

The more contingencies you plan for in advance, the better off your client will be. Contingent provisions are not without costs, however. So you'll want to be somewhat selective and address a contingency only if

---

Box 3-10
Apartment Rental Agreement
and Construction Contract: Contingent Terms

Why is the following term from an apartment lease in the mutual interests of the parties?

> *Fire, Other Casualty.* If the leased premises . . . shall be destroyed or damaged by fire . . . then this lease . . . shall terminate at the option of the Lessor. . . . If this lease . . . is not so terminated . . . then in case of any such destruction . . . rendering [the apartment] . . . unfit for occupation, a just proportion of the rent . . . shall be suspended or abated. . . . If the leased premises have not been restored by the Lessor . . . within thirty days . . . the Lessee may terminate this lease.*

How well do you think the following two contingent terms from a standard cost-plus construction contract would function?

> *29. Delay.* Contractor will be excused for delay caused by inclement weather, labor disputes, acts of public agencies . . . or other events beyond the reasonable expectation and control of Contractor. . . .
>
> *30. Unanticipated Concealed Conditions.* In the event that Contractor encounters adverse concealed conditions that could not reasonably have been anticipated, the Guaranteed Maximum Cost will be equitably adjusted, and the cost of dealing with such unanticipated conditions will become a Cost of the Work.†

---
* Lefcoe, 1997, at 1407–1420.
† Acret, 1990, at 47.

---

its likelihood and its importance are sufficient to justify the additional effort in negotiation and drafting. In addition, for each contingency you're concerned about, you'll want to use your general knowledge of contract law to estimate how likely a tribunal would be to interpret a simpler contract (one without the contingency provision) in a way that would suit your client's needs just as well (e.g., maybe a tribunal would excuse your client should a strike occur even if the contract didn't mention this contingency). Of course, relying on a tribunal's fixing your contract can be risky and result in greater litigation costs.

B. Damages for Breach

The issue of damages for breach of contract becomes important when certain types of contingencies arise. If breach occurs and you haven't specified in the contract that damages are to be paid and how much they'll be if breach should occur, the tribunal will decide the amount. In such cases, damages are usually expectation damages as calculated by the court (typically by a jury) or by an arbitrator. But, as we've already briefly discussed, it's often in your client's interest to specify the level of damages — that is, to name liquidated damages — in the contract rather than to risk having others determine the amount of damages in the event of breach. (Keep in mind, however, that if liquidated damages are set too high in relation to what expectation damages would likely be, they might not be enforceable, because the court will regard them as penalties. So you are, in practice, constrained in the level of liquidated damages that you can set.)

An important advantage of specifying liquidated damages for breach is that doing so can result in savings for the parties at the time of a breach. When the parties name the level of damages in advance, the amount to be paid in the event of breach is clear. When they don't, the level of damages is often contested, and more resources than necessary end up being consumed to resolve the disagreement, and more uncertainty is introduced into contractual disputes.

In setting the level of liquidated damages, you have to think about several factors. One is the effect that the level you decide on will have on performance. The prospect of having to pay damages spurs performance. So breach is less likely if damages have to be paid than if they don't. Having to pay damages when delivery is late, for instance, serves as an incentive for the supplier not to miss the delivery date and thereby lessens the odds that delivery will be late. More specifically, the effectiveness of damages in preventing breach goes hand in hand with the level at which they're set: at a low level, damages aren't very effective and not very likely to prevent breach; at a moderate level, they're somewhat more effective and somewhat more likely to prevent breach; and at a high level, they're very effective and very likely to prevent breach, often even when performance would be very expensive or disadvantageous to the promisor. Hence, the goal is to set damages at a level that's mutually advantageous: high enough to ensure performance as long as performance makes sense but not so high as to elicit performance once performance no longer makes sense. The challenge is for you to figure out what this level is.

Thus, incorporating liquidated damages into the contract allows you to fine-tune the incentives for performance so that they match your client's needs. If late delivery would be very costly to your client, setting damages high for breach might be desirable in order to maximize the likelihood of timely delivery.

Another function of damages, including liquidated damages, is to protect the party that is the potential victim of breach from risk. Whether such protection is mutually desirable depends on whether and the extent to which the potential victim is risk averse. For instance, a large firm might not be in obvious need of this kind of protection, whereas the insurance aspect of damages might be very valuable to a small, risk-averse firm that's really counting on performance (perhaps because it's barely eking by and faces ruin if the other party commits breach). For a very risk-averse party that might have to commit breach, on the other hand, the very possibility of having to pay damages constitutes a risk. Hence, not having to pay any damages when performance would be onerous — that is, being excused from having to meet contractual obligations under certain circumstances — might be desirable on grounds of risk bearing. In any event, we can see that naming liquidated damages in a contract allows you to select the degree of protection against risk that meets your client's needs.

The level at which damages are set also affects the contract price. The greater the damages that a promisor would have to pay for committing breach, the higher the price that the promisor will insist on at the outset. The higher price is, in effect, compensation for the higher risk that the higher level of damages reflects. If your client wants the contractor to pay very high damages for committing breach, the contractor may well want your client to pay a much higher price. As discussed previously, you should be setting liquidated damages at a level that's mutually advantageous; if you do, then there should be a contract price adjustment that leaves both you and the other party better off.

When you're drafting contracts for your clients, it's important that you think about all of these aspects of damages in general and liquidated damages in particular.

C. Arbitration

Another significant issue when a legal dispute arises is whether it will be resolved through arbitration or by the courts. It should be noted at the outset that when a dispute is resolved through arbitration, the decision will generally be *enforced* by the courts. Otherwise, arbitration would be robbed of its advantages. And, as we've already seen, it does have advantages.

Dispute resolution is typically cheaper and faster by going through arbitration than by going through the courts. It lacks the cumbersome procedures — such as extensive discovery and time-consuming, expensive motions, countermotions, and appeals — that so often bog down the judicial process.

When parties turn to arbitration, they themselves get to decide who the adjudicator will be. If they would like the dispute to be settled by someone knowledgeable about their business, they can make a point of selecting an arbitrator with the pertinent expertise. Construction disputes, for example, are commonly arbitrated by people who have experience in the construction industry. The alternative is to go before a court-assigned judge who tries all manner of cases or a jury drawn from the general population, neither of which is likely to have any kind of expertise in the relevant field. Although going before an arbitrator is usually preferable to going before a judge, it isn't always: a judge is generally preferable to an arbitrator with limited experience in dispute resolution. This is a caveat you'll want to be sure to take into account when you're deciding whether to opt for arbitration and, if you do go the arbitration route, who to select as the arbitrator.

Parties that go to arbitration are in an important sense choosing for themselves what rules will govern the resolution of their disputes. In contrast, parties that turn to the judicial system have little or no say in the matter and are bound by whatever rules the courts employ. Sometimes the parties may find that using rules of their own design is best, and arbitration arrangements make it possible for them to do so. They don't usually start from scratch, however. Instead, they typically adopt rules that an arbitration association has on hand or invoke the rules of a trade association. The wide latitude that parties have in specifying rules usually works to their advantage.

Arbitration affords privacy to the parties involved in a dispute. Because the proceedings aren't a matter of public record, there's no obligation to reveal the details of the dispute and its resolution.

Because of its advantages, arbitration is assuming an increasingly important role with regard to contracts. A significant percentage of contracts are now governed by arbitration clauses. Indeed, as noted earlier, some industries rely almost entirely on arbitration, and many agreements involving international transactions make use of arbitration. So it's vitally important for you, as a lawyer, to keep its advantages clearly in mind.

8. Negotiating the Contract

We've discussed the kind of contract that you want to write for your client, but what's the best way to go about negotiating it? As you know, negotiation is a highly developed subject area, and a thorough discussion is beyond our scope. The points that we will cover here might seem obvious or intuitive. Nevertheless, they merit explicit articulation: in addition to being innately important, these principles provide a framework for approaching a negotiation methodically. And being methodical and following these principles is often very helpful.

A. Both Sides Should Understand How to Enlarge the Pie

Very often, as you know by now, a contractual term is advantageous to both parties. Sometimes, however, a term is mutually advantageous, but only one party recognizes that it would benefit both sides. Unless the second party can be convinced that the term (perhaps combined with other adjustments) works to its advantage as well as to the advantage of the first party, the two sides are likely to hit an impasse, and the term will be omitted from the contract.

Consider, for example, the term stipulating on-time performance that we looked at earlier in the chapter. Let's assume that you're negotiating this term for your client. It's obvious to you that it — along with the price adjustment — is advantageous for the promisor as well as for your client. The promisor, on the other hand, doesn't see what its own benefit could possibly be. So you have to explain. Guaranteeing on-time performance will, you admit, cause the promisor's costs to increase by $1,000. But on-time performance is so important that your client is willing to pay, in exchange for the guarantee, an additional $2,000 to offset the promisor's additional costs. Hence, including the term along with the price adjustment in the contract benefits not only your client but the promisor as well. If you're unsuccessful in getting the promisor to understand this reasoning, the on-time performance term most likely won't appear in the contract, even though it is, in fact, mutually advantageous.

A point to keep in mind is that your client's payment to the other party for agreeing to include a term doesn't necessarily have to be monetary. Your client could, instead, pay the other party by agreeing to include terms that help the other party. Sometimes this alternative will be at least as good for your client as paying a higher price would be.

B. Be Greedy but Not Too Greedy

In addition to you and the lawyer for the other party having settled on the kind of contract to draw up — ideally, one in which all the contractual terms are mutually advantageous — the two sides need to agree on an overall price. Overall price is a crucial issue, because it determines how the contractual pie will be split up. Your goal, of course, is to obtain for your client as large a slice as possible. But you don't want to go after so large a slice — you don't want to be so greedy — as to prevent a contract from being made. In fact, if either side is too greedy, the deal will fall through, in which case there will be no contractual pie for either side to enjoy. How to go about bargaining so as to achieve your goal — obtaining a large slice of the pie for your client — and not prevent consummation of a mutually beneficial contract was discussed in the Games and Information chapter.

9. Suggestions for Further Reading

An excellent theoretically-informed but practical book on employee and managerial contracts is Edward P. Lazear and Michael Gibbs, *Personnel Economics in Practice* 2nd ed. (Hoboken, NJ: John Wiley, 2009). For a more formal treatment of the incentive problem, see chapter 15 of *Managerial Economics and Organizational Architecture* 5th ed. (Boston: McGraw-Hill, 2008) by James Brickley, Clifford W. Smith and Jerold Zimmerman. We also recommend a number of books on contracting practice that, among other things, contain sample contracts:

James Acret, *Construction Industry Formbook,* 2nd ed. (Colorado Springs: Shepard's/McGraw-Hill, 1990).

Leslie D. Corwin and Arthur J. Ciampi, *Law Firm Partnership Agreements* (New York: Law Journal Seminars-Press, 1998).

Albert Dib, *Forms and Agreements for Architects, Engineers, and Contractors,* vol. 1, release 36 3/94. (Deerfield, Ill.: Clark Boardman Callaghan, 1994).

John F. Dolan, *Fundamentals of Commercial Activity* (Boston: Little, Brown, 1991).

George Lefcoe, *Real Estate Transactions, Finance and Development* 6th ed. (New York: LexisNexis, 2009).

Mark Litwak, *Dealmaking in the Film and Television Industry: From Negotiations to Final Contracts* 3rd ed. (Los Angeles: Silman-James Press, 2009).

Anthony Mosawi, *Entertainment Law: A Guide to Contract in the Film Industry* (London: Butterworths, 1997).

Kit Merremeyer, *Understanding and Negotiating Construction Contracts* (Kingston, MA: R. S. Means, 2006).

Aaron Wise and Bruce Meyer, *International Sports Law and Business,* vol. 1 (The Hague: Kluwer, 1997).

4
Accounting

1. Introduction

Contrary to what you may believe, there is nothing mysterious about accounting. It is simply a way of organizing financial information. Accounting offers a common language that can be used to communicate anything from a simple business plan of an entrepreneur seeking her first bank loan to the annual performance of an amateur theater company to a comprehensive rendering of the financial position of a multinational conglomerate. Lawyers of many sorts routinely deal with accounting statements. Family lawyers, litigators, government regulators, counsel to nonprofit organizations, labor lawyers, and even public-interest lawyers must work with financial statements as part of their day-to-day practices. Having a basic understanding of the language of financial accounting is thus a prerequisite to providing effective representation in all sorts of legal contexts.

Neither is there anything new about accounting. When Christopher Columbus first set sail across the Atlantic, one of his crew was a royal controller of accounts, assigned to the voyage to keep track of whatever gold and spice might be uncovered. Our modern system of accounting can be traced back to the merchants of Florence and Venice in the four-teenth and fifteenth centuries. Prior methods of record keeping based on textual entries and Roman numerals were simply inadequate to deal with the explosion of trade and commercial activity that accompanied the European Renaissance. Modern accounting developed to fill this void.

Nor is accounting a monolithic discipline. Although many people associate accounting with the highly stylized (and often voluminous) financial statements that public corporations must distribute periodically to their shareholders, there are many other applications of accounting in our economy and legal system. Governmental entities have their own systems of financial statements, which are related to but distinct from the accounting conventions applied to entities in the private sector. Cost accounting is a subset of accounting rules designed to illuminate the costs of undertaking particular activities, whether developing a new form of medicine or mounting a fundraising effort for a local charity. A range of accounting conventions are routinely written into legal contracts, loan applications, applications for licenses and other government benefits, tax returns, and a host of other documents that lawyers are often called on to prepare. Although the specific accounting rules used vary from context to context, all are variants of a common language.

The first half of this chapter introduces the fundamentals of financial accounting. It begins with an overview of the three basic components of financial statements: the balance sheet, the income statement, and the cash flow statement. It then explores the double-entry bookkeeping system, upon which accounting statements are traditionally built, before turning to some of the conceptual foundations underlying modern accounting conventions. If you understand these basic principles, you will have a clear sense of both the strengths and the weaknesses of financial state-ments and an appreciation of the problems that recur in their creation and interpretation.

The second half of the chapter introduces more practical and institu-tional aspects of accounting. It discusses the legal and professional rules governing the creation of financial statements and the role of auditors. The chapter concludes by briefly introducing financial ratio analysis, a technique that lawyers and financial analysts use to investigate and compare financial statements of different entities at different times.

2. Three Basic Accounting Formats

A typical financial statement has three basic components: a balance sheet, an income statement, and a cash flow statement. Each provides a particular kind of information. To get a complete picture of an entity's overall financial status, lawyers routinely consult all three (as well as any related footnotes and textual descriptions accompanying financial statements).

A. Balance Sheets

In many respects, the most intuitive form of financial statement is the balance sheet. We can think of a balance sheet as a series of snapshots of an entity's financial position at specific times. A typical one includes two snapshots: one at the beginning of the period being reviewed (say, January 1) and one at the end of the period (say, December 31). By convention, information ordinarily is reported under three headings: assets, liabilities, and owners' equity. The asset side of the balance sheet of an internet start-up firm is presented in Figure 4-1 and the other side of the balance sheet — liabilities and owners' equity — in Figure 4-2.

1. Assets. The asset side of a firm's balance sheet is a listing of a firm's economic resources at a particular time. Under established accounting principles, assets are resources with "probable future economic benefits obtained or controlled by an entity resulting from past transactions or events." Although this definition may generally comport with the common understanding of the term *asset,* the accountant's definition has important peculiarities. To begin with, it has both retrospective and prospective elements. For an accountant to consider a resource an asset, (1) it must arise out of "past transactions or events," *and* (2) it must have "probable future economic benefits." In addition, it must be "owned or controlled" by the entity.

The accountant's definition of assets implicitly excludes a variety of resources that may be quite important to a firm's prospects. For example, resources with only a possibility — as opposed to probability — of yielding future benefits are not assets under the accountant's definition. In addition, resources must arise out of specific "past transactions or events" if they are to be considered assets. Thus, many important resources — e.g., inventions and other forms of intellectual property, reputation for

Figure 4-1
Balance Sheet: Assets
(in thousands)

	DECEMBER 31,	
	1997	1996
ASSETS		
Current Assets		
Cash and cash equivalents	$109,810	$6,248
Short-term investments	15,256	—
Inventories	8,971	571
Prepaid expenses and other	3,298	321
Total current assets	137,335	7,140
Property Plant and Equipment	12,899	1,295
Less accumulated depreciation	3,634	310
Deposits	166	146
Deferred charges	2,240	—
Total assets	$149,006	$8,271

providing good service, the CEO's sister-in-law being vice president of an important customer — do not meet the criteria for assets and typically would not be included on a firm's balance sheet.

By convention, assets are listed in a particular order on balance sheets. Cash and things that are equivalent to cash (e.g., bank accounts) are listed first, and they are followed by other *current assets*. This category includes assets that are likely to be exchanged for cash in the relatively near future, typically within a year. For example, inventory available for sale is typically listed as a current asset, whereas an investment in real estate is usually not. More permanent assets (including plant, equipment, and other properties not likely to be sold soon) appear at the bottom of the asset side of the balance sheet.

Much can be learned from the asset side of a balance sheet, such as the one for an internet start-up company in Figure 4-1. For example, we can see that the firm's reported assets have increased from about $8.3 million at the beginning of the year to $149 million at the end. Its cash and

Figure 4-2
Balance Sheet: Liabilities and Owners' Equity
(in thousands, except share and per share data)

	DECEMBER 31,	
	1997	1996
Current Liabilities		
Accounts payable	$32,697	$2,852
Accrued advertising	3,454	598
Accrued product development	—	500
Other liabilities and accrued expenses	6,167	920
Current portion of long-term debt	1,500	—
Total current liabilities	43,818	4,870
Long-term portion of debt	76,521	—
Long-term portion of capital lease obligations	181	—
Stockholders' Equity		
Preferred stock, $0.01 par value:		
Authorized shares — 10,000,000		
Issued and outstanding shares — none and		
569,396 shares in 1997 and 1996, respectively	—	6
Common stock, $0.01 par value:		
Authorized shares — 100,000,000		
Issued and outstanding shares — 23,937,169 and		
15,900,229 shares in 1997 and 1996 respectively	239	159
Additional paid-in capital	63,792	9,873
Deferred compensation	(1,930)	(612)
Accumulated deficit	(33,615)	(6,025)
Total stockholders' equity	28,486	3,401
Total liabilities and stockholders' equity	$149,006	$8,271

investments have increased by about $119 million. In fact, every category of assets is way up. The firm is expanding at a very rapid pace. Where are all these new assets coming from? There are three basic possibilities: (1) the firm made a lot of money last year; (2) the firm borrowed money; and (3) investors contributed money in return for shares of the firm's stock (capital contributions). These are not mutually exclusive. In fact, start-ups will often grow based on all three sources of assets.

The lawyer's perspective

Suppose your client were the proprietor of a retail store having a substantial resource that was not represented on its balance sheets — for example, being located at the site where a new subway station was about to open. (Construction of a subway is not the sort of transaction or event that accountants would typically factor into financial statements.) In negotiating on your client's behalf for a bank loan, how could you persuade the bank that this resource was substantial? How could you assure the bank that it would not be dissipated before the loan was repaid? These questions have various possible answers. For example, you might present evidence about the market price of the property, or you might offer the store's commitment not to dispose of the property without the bank's permission. In neither case, however, would your client's balance sheet be particularly useful.

2. Liabilities and owners' equity. The other side of the firm's balance sheet — liabilities and owners' equity — is presented in Figure 4-2, again for both the beginning and the end of the period. This side of the balance sheet itemizes certain claims on the firm's resources, usually divided into claims of creditors (liabilities) and claims of the owners (owners' equity). Liabilities tend to be further divided into current liabilities (those likely to be reduced to cash payments within a year) and other liabilities (longer-term ones). For the typical U.S. corporation, where the owners are its shareholders, owners' equity consists of funds originally contributed by shareholders (capital stock in Figure 4-2) plus accumulated profits (retained earnings).

The terms *liabilities* and *owners' equity* have special meanings for accountants. Liabilities are defined as "probable future sacrifices of economic benefits arising from present obligations to transfer assets or render services in the future as a result of past transactions or events." A liability is thus the inverse of an asset. It arises out of an *obligation* incurred in the past, and it represents a *probable sacrifice* in the future. Accountants recognize many forms of liability, but not all future "sacrifices" of an entity will be encompassed by this definition. For example, a policy of retaining workers during recessions may result in a future sacrifice, yet the sacrifice may not arise out of a present obligation (e.g., if the employment relationship is an at-will one). Similarly, there may be a chance that a firm will be forced to pay a million dollar punitive damage award in a pending law suit; however, despite the substantial sacrifice that such a payment would represent, it would not be included as a liability on the balance sheet if the accountants conclude (in consultation with lawyers) that the award is not sufficiently likely to be made.

The accountant's definition of owners' equity relies on the definitions of assets and liabilities presented above: it is the "residual interest in assets of an entity after subtracting its liabilities." For this reason, the sum of total liabilities and owners' equity is always exactly equal to total assets.

While the asset side of the balance sheet has revealed that our example firm has greatly expanded, it has not revealed the sources of the funds fueling the expansion. The liabilities and owners' equity side of the balance sheet, however, will tell us the sources of funding for the new assets. Looking at Figure 4.2 we see that liabilities have increased enormously during the year. Accounts payable, representing the firm's obligations to pay for goods and services it has received, has grown by almost $30 million (a 10-fold increase) from the beginning to the end of the year. In addition, the firm has taken on a new liability in the form of a large long-term loan. These two liabilities between them account for over $100 million of the new assets that have appeared during the year, but they are not the whole story. Additional paid-in capital has grown by almost $54 million. This represents money paid to the firm in exchange for part ownership interest. So, the firm's enormous growth was primarily funded by a large long-term loan, contributions by investors, and a short-term loan from its suppliers. What, then, can we say about our firm's prospects based upon our reading of its balance sheet? Well, one further important fact needs to be taken account of: the balance sheet reveals that despite the generally upbeat picture painted by the firm's enormous growth and the apparent confidence of lenders, suppliers, and investors in the future prospects of the firm, the firm has lost over $33 million (Accumulated deficit) since its inception — $27 million of which was lost in the last

Figure 4-3
Income Statement
(in thousands)

	YEARS ENDED DECEMBER 31,	
	1997	1996
Net sales...	$147,758	$15,746
Cost of sales...	118,945	12,287
Gross profit...	28,813	3,459
Operating expenses		
Marketing and sales...	38,964	6,090
Product development...	12,485	2,313
General and administrative......................................	1,831	749
Depreciation and amortization	4,742	286
Total operating expenses...................................	58,022	9,438
Loss from operations.......................................	(29,209)	(5,979)
Interest income..	1,898	202
Interest expense...	(279)	—
Net loss..	$(27,590)	$(5,777)

year. Why is the company losing money? Is it likely to produce a profit in the future? Why are investors pouring more money into a company that so far has a track record of accelerating losses? Additional information about the company's financial situation and future prospects, which may help answer these and other questions, is available from the company's income statement, which appears in Figure 4-3.

B. Income Statements

The second basic component of a financial statement is the income statement. Unlike balance sheets (which present snapshots of a firm's condition at particular times), the income statement provides a summary of financial activity over time, again typically a year (see Box 4-1). More specifically, it summarizes revenues and expenses during an accounting period. When revenues exceed expenses, the entity is said to

---

Box 4-1
The Income Statement

The income statement is designed to reflect an entity's financial performance during some period of time. Its central feature is the comparison of the entity's revenues and expenses during the relevant period. Revenues and expenses are critical terms for accountants.

Revenues are defined as "increases in equity resulting from asset increases and/or liability decreases from delivering goods or services or other activities that constitute the entity's ongoing major or central operations."

Expenses are defined as "decreases in equity from asset decreases or liability increases from delivery of goods or services, or carrying out any activities which constitute the entity's ongoing major or central operations."

---

have earned a profit. When expenses exceed revenues, as in the income statement in Figure 4-3, the entity has suffered a loss (e.g. $27.6 million for our start-up firm in its most recent year.) Hence, income statements are sometimes called *profit and loss statements*. In other contexts, they are referred to as *results of operations*.

The foregoing description of income statements is deceptively simple because, in reality, these documents harbor much of the complexity of financial accounting. What are revenues and expenses? How are they allocated to particular periods? What is the relationship between a balance sheet and the corresponding income statement? Which is more important for assessing the financial health of an entity? Exactly which lines in the income statement should analysts focus on in assessing the health or potential of companies? Before we address these questions, let's focus on a few fairly straightforward features of income statements.

First, income statements typically begin with a measure of total revenue (e.g., "Net sales" in Figure 4-3), from which is deducted a figure roughly equal to the direct cost of producing this revenue. The direct cost is often denominated *cost of goods sold* (in Figure 4-3, "Cost of sales"). Subtracting the direct cost from sales revenue yields the *gross margin* (in Figure 4-3, "Gross profit"), a measure of profitability. A firm, however, incurs a number of additional expenses in the course of doing business, and to determine the net income for the period, all of these must be deducted from the gross margin. By convention, accountants usually first subtract operating expenses (e.g., salary and administrative expenses), to arrive at operating earnings and then deduct financial expenses (most importantly, interest charges on loans or other forms of borrowing) and income tax. After all these calculations are performed, the final remainder is the net income (or profit). If expenses exceed revenues during the period, net income will be negative and the entity will have suffered a loss. Depending on the nature of the entity and the preferences of the accountant preparing the statement, the designations of line items of an income statement can vary considerably. However, the basic structure of all income statements is the same: total revenues reduced by a cascade of expenses.

A second fundamental point about income statements has to do with their relationship to balance sheets. When a balance sheet is constructed, net income for the period is, in essence added to retained (or accumulated) earnings. As a result, for a typical corporation net income ends up being included in owners' equity, which conforms with our intuition that a corporation's profits belong to its shareholders. Retained earnings can either be left in the corporation for future use or distributed to shareholders (as a dividend or in some other form). Where, as in our example firm, a corporation suffers a net loss, that loss is subtracted from owners' equity (accumulated deficit).

So, will our example firm continue to lose money at an ever-increasing rate? Will it turn profitable? Are there any hints in the income statement that might suggest one direction or the other? The income statement reveals that the company's gross profit is not adequate to cover its operating expenses at its current level of sales. One possibility is that there are economies of scale in the operation of the business. If so, then, as sales and gross margin grow at a rapid pace, operating expenses will grow more slowly, and eventually the firm will turn profitable. But there are many other possible futures for this corporation! At the end of the chapter we shall look at one powerful technique — ratio analysis — for using financial statement information to make educated guesses about a corporation's future prospects.

The lawyer's perspective

Frequently, attorneys have to incorporate the concept of profit or loss into legal documents. If a client were the author of a best-selling novel and wanted to sell the movie rights for a percentage of the film's profits, the lawyer would have to translate this concept into a contractual term. Similarly, a plaintiff seeking to recover damages for a fire that prevented a factory from operating for a year would have to prove how much had been lost in profits as a result. Concepts of these sorts are also employed outside the commercial context. For example, if you represented a charitable institution that was thinking of hiring a new fundraising director, you might have to advise it about how to determine whether this person would make a net contribution (akin to profit) for the organization.

C. Cash Flow Statements

The third basic form of accounting format is the cash flow statement. Like an income statement, the cash flow statement reports financial performance during some period. Whereas an income statement summarizes a firm's profitability, a cash flow statement highlights the manner in which the entity obtains and uses cash. Our example firm's cash flow statement appears in Figure 4-4.

The purpose of the cash flow statement is to illuminate the changes in an entity's cash position during an accounting period. When we were looking at balance sheets, we noted that the cash balance of our example firm had increased by $103,562,000 during the year in question. The cash flow statement in Figure 4-4, which in its final line reports a $103,562,000 increase in cash during the period, confirms this fact. Although this information can be gleaned from both documents, the cash flow statement provides much more detail about the factors that contributed to the increase. The statement begins with the firm's reported net loss for the period, $27,590,000 (see Figure 4-3). This net loss is adjusted to account

Figure 4-4
Cash Flow Statement
(in thousands)

	YEAR ENDED DECEMBER 31,
	1997

OPERATING ACTIVITIES

Net Loss	($27,590)
Adjustments to reconcile net loss to net cash provided by (used in) operating activities:	
Depreciation and amortization	4,742
Changes in operating assets and liabilities:	
Inventories	(8,400)
Prepaid expenses and other	(2,997)
Accounts payable	29,845
Other liabilities and accrued expenses	7,922
Net cash provided by (used in) operating activities	3,522

INVESTING ACTIVITIES

Maturities of short-term investments	5,198
Purchases of short-term investments	(20,454)
Purchases of fixed assets	(7,221)
Net cash used in investing activities	(22,477)

FINANCING ACTIVITIES

Proceeds from initial public offering	49,103
Proceeds from exercise of stock options and sale of common stock	518
Proceeds from sale of preferred stock	200
Proceeds from (repayment of) notes payable and long-term debt	75,000
Financing costs	(2,304)
Net cash provided by financing activities	122,517
Net increase in cash	103,562
Cash and cash equivalents at beginning of period	6,248
Cash and cash equivalents at end of period	$109,810

for changes during the reporting period in balance sheet entries related to operations. Such adjustments are in reality a bit complex. In general, however, increases in assets (and decreases in liabilities) use up cash and therefore are entered as negative numbers (i.e., they are cash outflows). For example, when a company buys additional inventory or pays off a loan, it uses up cash reserves. On the other hand, decreases in assets (and increases in liabilities) are positive numbers, because they add to the entity's cash. For example, when a firm sells inventory or takes out a loan, it increases its cash reserves. On balance, these adjustments in our example firm's operating accounts produced an additional $31,112,000 in cash and thereby increased its cash flow from operations to $3,522,000 (–$27,590,000 + $31,112,000 = $3,522,000).

By convention, cash flow statements also include information on cash used for longer-term investments (as opposed to operating activities) as well as information on cash flows associated with financial activities, such as borrowing money or paying dividends. The statement in Figure 4-4 indicates that during the year our example firm used $7,221,000 to purchase fixed assets, that is, had a cash outflow of $7,221,000 for this purpose. The statement also shows a net inflow of $122,517,000 from financial activities — primarily, the proceeds of a $75 million long-term loan, and almost $50 million from its initial public offering. As an exercise, you might check to see whether starting with the cash total at the beginning of 1997 — $6,248,000 — and adding in net cash provided or used by operating, investing, and financing activities, you end up with the cash total at the end of 1997 — $109,810,000.

As might be obvious from the foregoing, a cash flow statement is largely derived from information in an entity's balance sheets and income statement, and for now we will focus on these two other accounting formats. Cash flow statements are, nevertheless, extremely useful tools when an entity's liquidity (its ability to make payments on time) is the topic of interest. In many legal contexts, such as when an entity is financially strapped, its liquidity is paramount. And, as will become obvious in the Finance chapter, financial analysts are particularly interested in firms' cash flows.

3. Double-Entry Bookkeeping and the Accountant's Frame of Reference

The three basic categories of financial statement — balance sheets, income statements, and cash flow statements — are the ones with which lawyers typically deal. Although lawyers are not usually responsible for creating these statements — doing so is the province of accountants — they should have a basic understanding of how accountants go about doing the job so that they can appreciate the nature of financial statements and have some insight into what information can and cannot be found in them.

A. The Transactional Nature of Financial Statements

As you may remember, the accountant's definitions of assets and liabilities spoke in terms of resources and obligations arising out of past transactions or events. The attention to specific transactions and events stems from an important aspect of the logic that underlies accounting. Financial statements reflect an accumulation of transactions and events, which accountants record in accordance with certain conventions that have evolved over time. Typically, the transactions and events are initially recorded as temporary entries in *journals* or *T accounts*. Then, at the end of the accounting period, these accounts are *closed*, and the balances are transferred to the appropriate places on the entity's financial statements.

We will consider in a moment the manner in which these accounting entries are made. But as a preliminary matter, a bias inherent in the transactional foundation of accounting bears noting. It is best explained by example: When a company buys a piece of equipment or sells a widget, a transaction has occurred, and it will be recorded in T accounts and eventually reflected in the firm's financial statements. On the other hand, when consumer tastes change or the price of raw materials rises, such an event, even if of critical importance to the entity's financial health, typically does not constitute a transaction or event that is registered as an entry in the T accounts and therefore is not likely to be reflected in the firm's financial statements. This is one reason why financial statements may not present a complete picture of a firm's economic condition. (Although the reference here is to T accounts, other discussions of bookkeeping procedures may speak in terms of journal entries, which perform essentially the same function as T accounts.)

B. The Fundamentals of Double-Entry Bookkeeping

Double-entry bookkeeping is the system that accountants use to record transactions and events affecting the financial position of an entity. The transactions and events may be recorded using the graphic device of the T account.

Here is a frequently employed asset T account:

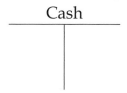

Cash

Here is a frequently employed liability T account:

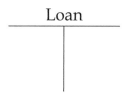

Loan

Each type of asset or liability has its own T account which is used to record increases or decreases in the monetary value of the asset or liability it is being used to track. To use a T account properly, you must know which asset or liability it is being used to track (the name on the top of the T account), when to make an entry in the T account (when a transaction or event affects the monetary value of the asset or liability), and which side of the T account is used to indicate an increase, and which side a decrease in the asset or liability being tracked. This last concern requires knowledge of a seemingly arbitrary convention. Asset T accounts are increased by left-hand entries and decreased by right-hand entries, while liability accounts are increased by right-hand entries and decreased by left-hand entries.

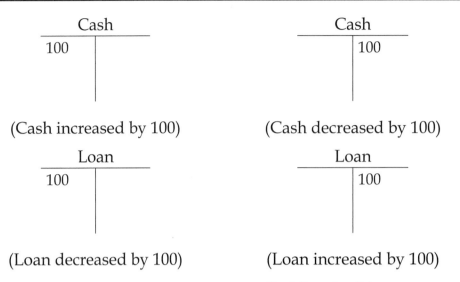

(Cash increased by 100)   (Cash decreased by 100)

(Loan decreased by 100)   (Loan increased by 100)

Right-hand entries in T accounts are called "credits" by accountants, and left-hand entries are called "debits." So another way of indicating an increase in cash of $100, without actually using a T account, would be to write "debit cash $100," and another way of indicating a decrease in cash of $100, would be to write "credit cash $100."

> **NOTE**: the words "debit" and "credit" as used in accounting are not consistent with the way they have come to be used in ordinary English, so do not be concerned if the accounting use of these terms surprises you.

Double-entry bookkeeping is so-called because each transaction or event is recorded in the account book by paired entries of equal amounts, one a debit entry and one a credit entry — i.e. an entry on the left-hand side of a T account is always paired with an equal entry on the right-hand side of a T account, and vice-versa.

Let's see how some simple transactions would be recorded in double-entry bookkeeping using T accounts.

Example 1:

> Suppose that a company used $500 of cash to purchase a computer. The changes that result are a $500 reduction in cash, an asset, and a $500 increase in computers, also an asset. Using the rules above, our T accounts should look like this after the transaction is recorded:

There are a couple of things to notice about this simple example. First, the bookkeeping consists of two paired entries — one on the left side of an account, and one on the right side of an account (a debit and a credit), in accord with the rule given above. And second, when recording the acquisition of an asset, the bookkeeping convention is to record its value as its cost to the entity acquiring it.

Example 2:

Suppose that the firm borrowed $50k from a bank to acquire a piece of land that cost $50k. Once again, the result will be a pair of left and right entries, but here, instead of changes to two asset T accounts, there is a change to one asset T account and one liability T account. The result looks like this:

Land		Loan	
50k			50k

The accounts show the acquisition of a piece of land (an asset) that cost $50k, and the undertaking of an obligation to pay $50k (a liability).

There is one additional account that is neither an asset account, nor a liability account, which, as we shall see, plays a central role in bookkeeping. It is called "owners' equity." It keeps track of *the difference* between the sum of all of the asset accounts, and the sum of all of the liability accounts, so that:

Total Assets minus Total Liabilities = Owners' Equity.

As with the liability T accounts, an increase in owners' equity is indicated by a right-hand entry in the owners' equity T account, and a decrease is indicated by a left-hand entry

Example 3 (a more complex example):

Suppose the firm sells the land acquired in Example 2 for $100k in cash. What changes have occurred in the firm's financial picture? Well, for one, it has acquired $100k cash. For another, it no longer has the land it sold. So, two T account entries are clear:

Cash		Land		(Total of land asset en-
100k			50k	tries is now zero, which reflects the fact that the company no longer owns the land.)

Cash is increased by $100k, and land is decreased by $50k.

However, if this were the entire bookkeeping treatment, it would violate the rule requiring pairs of equal left and right entries. The solution requires use of the newly introduced "owners' equity" T account which, as you may recall, is used to record changes in the difference between total assets and total liabilities.

How has this transaction affected owners' equity? Well, total assets — the total of all the asset accounts — has increased by $50k (increase of $100k in cash, decrease of $50k in land), and total liabilities has not changed. So total assets minus total liabilities has increased by $50k. Since owners' equity just is total assets minus total liabilities, owners' equity has increased by $50k as a result of the land sale.

Now, how should this be indicated in the owners' equity T account? The convention is that the bookkeeper records both the loss of the land asset and the gain of the cash as two simultaneous changes in owners' equity — a $50k reduction, reflecting the decrease in the value of the land asset account, and a $100k increase, reflecting the increase in the cash asset. (Remember, the owners' equity account is reduced by left entries and increased by right entries).

So, the bookkeeping treatment of the land sale looks like this:

Cash		Land		Owners' Equity	
100k			50k	50k	100k

The result is 4 entries, two pairs of equal left and right entries. Note that the value of the owners' equity account has changed by a net of 50k — an increase of 100k and a decrease of 50k, which does, indeed, reflect the change in total assets minus total liabilities (total assets increased by 100k in cash, but decreased by 50k reduction of the land asset, for a net increase of 50k in total assets and no change in total liabilities).

Two questions for you:

1. The Fundamental Equation of Accounting is: Total Assets = Total Liabilities + Owners' Equity.

   Why is this true, given the rules of double-entry bookkeeping?

2. Why should the Owners' Equity account be of particular interest to users of financial statements?

At the end of an accounting period, the bookkeeper uses the T accounts to prepare the end-of-period balance sheet in the form illustrated in figs. 4.1 and 4.2. Each T account is netted out — *i.e.* the positive entries are added up and the sum of the negative entries is subtracted to yield a single number which is entered on the balance sheet as the end-of-period value for each particular asset, liability or owners' equity account. So, for example, for the hypothetical firm whose accounts we have been following, the cash T account would have accumulated over the course of the accounting period, a negative (left-side) entry of $500 (purchase of computer), a negative (left-side) entry of $50k (purchase of land), and a positive (right-side) entry of $100k (sale of land). Netting out the cash T account (–$500 – $50k + $100k) yields an end of period net figure of $49.5k. This is the figure for Cash that would be entered on the end of period balance sheet. (In a more realistic example, there would be one additional entry in each T account representing the value of that account at the beginning of the accounting period, so that the $49.5k cash figure would have added to it the amount of cash that the firm possessed at the beginning of the period.)

The system of T accounts so far presented allows for the construction of balance sheets, but not for the construction of income statements. In order to construct income statements of the form presented in Figure 4.3, additional accounts are used which are called income statement accounts. Income statement accounts are used to collect additional information about changes in total assets minus total liabilities — *i.e.* about changes in owners' equity. The most important types of income statement accounts are called "expense accounts" and "revenue accounts". To understand their use it is necessary to master the accounting definitions of revenues and expenses (see Box 4-1). Revenues are "increases in equity" which arise in a particular way — *i.e.* "from delivering goods or services, or other activities that constitute the entity's ongoing major or central operations." An increase in equity just means an increase in total assets minus total liabilities, which, before we added income statement accounts, would have been recorded as a right hand entry in the owners' equity account. Now, when the increase results from "delivering goods and services . . ." we make a right hand entry in the revenue account. Similarly, expenses are "decreases in equity" which arise in a certain way, *i.e.* from "delivery of goods and services . . ." A decrease in equity just means a decrease in total assets minus total liabilities, which, before the addition of income statement accounts, would have been recorded as a left hand entry in the owners' equity account.

Let's revisit the land sale example we dealt with above to see how it would be handled using revenue and expense accounts. As you may recall, the land sale resulted in an increase in equity from the receipt of $100k cash coupled with a $50k decrease in equity resulting from the loss of the land asset, for a net increase in equity of $50k. Here is how that was recorded:

Cash		Land		Owners' Equity	
100k			50k	50k	100k

Now, how does the introduction of revenue and expense accounts affect the bookkeeping treatment of this transaction? Well, certain increases and decreases of owners' equity are no longer to be recorded in the owners' equity account, but instead, in the revenue and expense accounts. To decide whether to record an increase or decrease in equity in the revenue or expense accounts, the bookkeeper must judge whether the increase or decrease resulted from "activities that constitute the entity's ongoing major or central operations." Because we don't know the nature of the business our hypothetical company is engaged in, we cannot make this judgment, but let's suppose that the company is a land speculation company. In that case, increases and decreases in equity resulting from the land sale fit squarely into the revenue and expense categories. (Do you see why?) The appropriate T account treatment would look like this:

Cash		Land		Expense		Revenue	
100k			50k	50k			100k

A comparison of the two treatments yields three observations: first, the revenue T account increases on the right and the expense account increases on the left; second, the revenue entry in the 2nd version is the same as the right side entry in owners' equity in the 1st version and the expense entry in the 2nd version is the same as the left side entry in owners' equity in the 1st version, and third, more information is conveyed in the 2nd version than in the 1st version. (Why? What is the additional information?) To convey even more information about the source of changes in equity, most companies use many expense and revenue accounts, all of which meet the definition of revenue and expense, but which sort out different types of revenue and expense, as e.g., salary expense, interest expense, rent expense, etc.

At the end of the accounting period, to prepare the income statement, each income statement T account is netted out and the resulting number is entered into the end-of-period income statement. In our continuing example we have only 2 income statement accounts to consider — the cost of land sold account (an expense) and the sales revenue account (revenue).

The simple income statement prepared from these accounts would look like this:

Income Statement

Revenue from Sales	100k
Cost of Sales	(50k)
Net Income	50k

Real life income statements appear much more complicated than this, but they share the basic format of stating revenues from which are subtracted a list of expenses to reach a bottom line representing net income.

What sorts of increases and decreases in equity would not properly be recorded in an expense or revenue account? Suppose an investor contributes 100k cash to the company in exchange for a 10% ownership interest. Does the resulting increase in equity fit the definition of revenue? Suppose the company distributes a cash dividend to its investors resulting in a total payout of 100k. Does the resulting decrease in equity fit the definition of expense? (The answer to both of these questions is no.) There are many other changes in equity that do not fit into the revenue and expense categories. These changes must still be recorded on the balance sheet, so, in the absence of specific additional T accounts, they would be recorded directly in the owners' equity account. All the changes in owners' equity over the course of the accounting period will end up being recorded either in the owners' equity account itself, or in a revenue or expense account. How does the accountant determine what the value of owners' equity is at the end of the accounting period, if some or all of the changes to it are not actually recorded in the owners' equity T account, but in revenue and expense T accounts? It turns out to be surprisingly simple. The accountant computes revenue minus expenses and adds the result to the net value of the owners' equity T account. Revenue minus expenses will appear as "retained earnings" (or "accumulated deficit" in the case of a loss) in the owners' equity section of the balance sheet. The effect of adding retained earnings is just to include all the transactions affecting owners' equity (including those which were originally entered in revenue or expense accounts) in the computation of "total owners' equity."

The lawyer's perspective

Although lawyers are seldom responsible for maintaining double-entry bookkeeping accounts, they often play a role in ensuring that a client's internal accounting procedures are adequate to detect and prevent fraudulent activity. An unscrupulous sales manager could easily disguise poor performance by classifying too many transactions as entries for revenue accounts or too few as entries for expense accounts. Accordingly, a fundamental principle of internal control is to keep operational responsibilities separate from accounting responsibilities. To protect a client's interests, lawyers often are responsible for ensuring that such separation is maintained.

4. Some Fundamental Concepts

Now let's pull back a bit from the details we've been looking at and focus instead on the major principles and assumptions that underlie financial accounting — the critical lessons of this chapter. This information can be organized into four categories: the big picture, the conservative bias of financial statements, the matching principle and its implications, and boundary problems.

A. The Big Picture

Let's begin with a few points that may strike you as obvious but that are sufficiently important to warrant explicit notation.

1. The entity concept. An initial point to be made about financial statements is that they concern a particular entity — a corporation and not its shareholders, a partnership and not its suppliers or customers, and so on. Although this may seem intuitive when the entity is a large public corporation such as IBM, which has tens of thousands of shareholders, the division between owners and corporations can be less well defined for smaller entities or start-up ventures. For example, when a couple of young entrepreneurs establish a firm and operate the business in their garage, is the garage an asset of the firm or of its shareholders? What if the garage is leased by the firm for a dollar a year? For a million dollars a year?

The accounting profession has a number of conventions for reporting transactions between firms and related parties (such as owners and principal employees). This is also an area of particular scrutiny in federal securities regulation, corporate law, and the income taxation system, as the transactions between related parties present fertile ground for manipulation and abuse. Beyond these applications, however, the entity concept is an important building block for lawyers because it reveals a basic truth about legal obligations and the likelihood that they will be honored. In interactions with a legal entity, the resources of only that entity are presumptively available to stand behind its obligations. For example, a contract with a subsidiary of a large multinational corporation does not necessarily — or even ordinarily — represent a legal commitment on the part of the parent corporation or any other affiliate. For this reason, it is important for attorneys to focus on the financial wherewithal of the specific legal entity that enters into a contract. Financial statements are well suited to help them do so.

The lawyer's perspective

Suppose that your client were about to enter into a food-service contract with the subsidiary of a large firm and was concerned about the subsidiary's relatively modest balance sheet. How could you improve the likelihood that your client would be paid for the services it was about to provide?

2. The fundamental accounting equation. Although the basic accounting equation has already been stated (and subsequently referred to more than once), it is important enough to warrant repetition: *owners' equity is the amount by which a firm's total assets exceeds its total liabilities*. Or, with modest algebraic reformulation, *total assets are, by definition, equal to the sum of a firm's total liabilities and owners' equity*. These equations are true not just of corporations but also of nonprofit organizations, such as schools and religious organizations. The only difference is that outside the corporate realm owners' equity is associated, not usually with shareholders, but with other groups of claimants or residual owners. For this reason, in the context of nonprofits, the analogous accounting entry

Figure 4-5
The Fundamental Accounting Equation

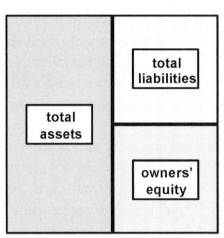

owners' equity = total assets – total liabilities
total assets = total liabilities + owners' equity

may be labeled *accumulated surplus* or *net assets.* Whatever label is used, the entry constitutes the difference between the entity's total assets and its total liabilities.

Figure 4-5 is a common graphical presentation of the fundamental accounting equation. For a variety of reasons, lawyers find it useful to keep this image in mind. For example, if a client is about to enter into a business contract with a firm, it is important for the attorney to know how many other obligations the firm has already undertaken — that is, what other liabilities are outstanding. In addition, it is wise for the attorney to have a sense of the comparative magnitudes of those liabilities and the firm's assets. For a firm with $10 million of assets, liabilities of $1 million would not be troubling, whereas for a firm whose balance sheet shows $500,000 in assets, $10 million in liabilities should raise some eyebrows. (What would the owners' equity be? Hint: Owners' equity can be negative.)

Occasionally, lawyers speak in terms of trying to move a client's interests up the right-hand side of a firm's balance sheet. They simply mean that they are attempting to improve the status of the client's claim relative to that of other claims against the firm. (On a balance sheet, more senior liabilities are typically listed above junior claims, and short-term debts —

liabilities to be repaid within a year — are at the top.) The seniority (i.e., priority) of a creditor can be altered by contract unless other creditors or someone else has imposed legal restrictions on the company's capacity to make such changes. Similarly, a corporation or individual borrower can pledge specific assets as collateral for certain claims. Under such an arrangement, the "secured" creditor has a special claim on those assets, which can be used to ensure that its obligation is repaid. Our bankruptcy system offers a statutory mechanism for sorting out the relative order of claims of creditors when an entity can neither honor all of its obligations as they become due nor work out an alternative mechanism for repayment to which all creditors are willing to agree. (Upper-level law school courses on commercial law and bankruptcy dedicate considerable time to these topics.)

B. The Conservative Bias of Accountants

During their training, accountants are encouraged to take a conservative, even skeptical posture with respect to the creation of financial statements. In part, this perspective reflects the profession's role as a counterweight to the tendency of individuals and firms to gravitate toward presenting their financial condition in the best possible light. But the conservative bias of accountants does affect the kinds of information they include in financial statements, and it is a factor that lawyers must appreciate and keep in mind when using financial statements. We have already seen one illustration of this phenomenon — the accountant's definitions of assets and liabilities, which restrict financial statements to resources and obligations arising out of past transactions or events. Here are two others:

1. The monetary unit concept. You may have noticed that all of the accounting entries we have discussed so far have been denominated in dollars. This is no coincidence. Under a convention known as the monetary unit concept, accountants are required to express all figures in a common monetary unit. So you will never see balance sheet entries expressed in terms of nonmonetary units (e.g., 10 bales of hay or 5 acres of land). Because of this accounting convention, accountants are reluctant to record occurrences that are not easily convertible to monetary units, such as changes in consumer taste.

2. Preference for historical costs over market values. Another traditional feature of financial accounting is a preference for relying on historical (i.e., original) cost rather than market value. For example, if a company purchased a piece of land in 1950 for $100,000, that land could still be recorded on the firm's financial statements half a century later as having the same value, even if its current market value exceeded $1 million or even $10 million.

The preference for using historic cost rather than market value may strike you as odd, but it provides some insight into the logic that underlies accounting. In an environment of gradually (or even rapidly) rising prices, historical cost tends to be more conservative, at least in assigning value to assets such as land. Moreover, historic costs tend to be based on actual transactions (e.g., in the preceding example, the $100,000 paid for the land in 1950). In many contexts, reliance on market value is more subjective and susceptible to manipulation. For example, the valuation of works of fine art is highly subjective; claiming that an art collection has great value doesn't make it so.

The divergence between historical cost and market value introduces another disconnect between financial statements and economic reality. When the historical cost significantly deviates from the current market value of an asset, the balance sheet does not offer an accurate reflection of the firm's financial health, and even the income statement can become misleading in certain respects. The norm in most areas of accounting, however, remains historical cost (but see Box 4-2).

C. The Matching Principle and Its (Profound) Implications

Another important tenet of accounting is the matching principle, according to which

- revenue should be allocated to the period during which effort is expended in generating it, and
- an expense should be allocated to the period in which the benefit from it will contribute to income generation

This principle and related concepts determine when transactions should be recorded as entries in revenue or expense accounts. (You might want to look back at the earlier discussion of double-entry bookkeeping). The

Box 4-2
Historic Cost vs. Fair Value

As we have seen, historic cost — the amount paid for an asset at its acquisition — is generally the value given to an asset when it first appears on an entity's balance sheet. At that time, it is reasonable to suppose that it fairly approximates the current or market value of the asset. Over time, however, historic cost loses its close connection to current value. Consider, e.g., real estate acquired in Manhattan 30 years ago. Its purchase price is very different from its current value. Consider also recent mortgage loan packages that were purchased at a price reflecting likelihood of loan repayment, which changed dramatically with the collapse of the housing market. While the historic cost balance sheet entries are reliable, in the sense that they are accurate records of what they purport to be — the price the entity paid for the assets — the entries are not very relevant for assessing the current financial position of the entity. In the one case, the real estate asset is likely to be vastly undervalued on the balance sheet (appreciation of real estate in Manhattan over 30 years). In the other case, in the changed mortgage market, the current value of the mortgage loan package is likely to be quite a bit less than its acquisition price. In response to the relevance concerns, fair value accounting has emerged as an alternative valuation method that has become more common over the last few decades. Under fair value accounting, an asset is valued at the price that would be received for the sale of the asset in an orderly transaction between market participants at the measurement date (FAS No.157). Using fair value accounting, asset values must be updated periodically to reflect existing market conditions. When done well, the use of fair values produces a balance sheet that is more relevant for investor and creditor decision making, though at the cost of continued revaluation of assets. Fair values turn out to be pretty easy to ascertain and relatively uncontroversial when the assets in question are traded daily in national markets, as e.g., shares in NYSE-listed companies. So, indeed, "mark-to-market" is the standard for publicly traded shares owned by an entity. But problems arise with application of the fair value standard where no such markets are available as ready sources of current valuations. Each piece of real estate has unique properties, so the best one can do is to find transactions in comparable real estate. For mortgage loan packages — e.g., 1,000 mortgages in South Florida — there are no markets where directly comparable assets are sold, so determining a current value requires a lot more than looking up today's stock price in the Wall Street Journal. In extreme cases, where no obviously relevant markets exist, a company's accountants are forced to do the best they can, producing complicated valuation formulas that have little direct connection to actual markets or transactions. The practice of producing value estimates via internally generated complex formulas and entering the results on the company's balance sheet — "marking-to-model" — is often criticized as allowing too much discretion and resulting in biased, self-serving balance sheet valuations.

matching principle accords with the intuition that an income statement is intended to summarize economic activity within a particular period. To do so, it must reflect all revenues and associated expenses from that period but no others.

If all transactions were completed within a single time period and if all items of input were consumed within a single period, the matching principle would be fairly easy to implement. Reality, however, is more complex. Customers buy products in one period and pay for them in the next. Companies purchase equipment that lasts for many years and contributes to revenue generation in multiple accounting periods. To deal with this messiness, accountants rely on yet additional conventions: *accrual* and *deferral*. These conventions allow accountants to allocate revenues and expenses to the appropriate time period even though cash payments for the associated transactions may not be received until a subsequent period and even though cash expenditures for some relevant inputs may have been made in earlier periods.

We will explore a few important examples of these concepts shortly. For the moment, what you should appreciate as a future lawyer who will have to make use of financial statements is that inherently discretionary judgment calls are an unavoidable outgrowth of the matching principle. Although accountants have many detailed rules governing accrual and deferral — and much professional effort has gone into making these rules as formally realizable as possible — the ultimate decision as to when revenues should be recognized or expenses allocated remains a matter of judgment. If a client's interests depend on a calculation of profit or loss, the attorney has to consider who is allocating the revenues and expenses from the underlying transactions and how that person's decisions will be monitored.

1. Recognition of income. By now, it is probably clear that income can be recognized (i.e., recorded in revenue accounts of an income statement) in various ways. Let's look at some examples by way of illustration.

Example 4-1

Assume that we are dealing with a law firm that has three clients: A, B, and C. The firm does work for Client A in Year 1, who stops by the firm before the year is over to settle the account by paying $100 in cash. The firm also does work for Client B in

Year 1, but sends Client B a bill for $200, which Client B has not paid by the end of the year. The firm does no work for Client C in Year 1 but does receive a retainer of $300 from this client, with the understanding that Client C will use the firm's services in Year 2. Under the matching principle, how should the firm account for each of these transactions?

Client A. This example is fairly straightforward, as all relevant transactions occur in Year 1. Accordingly, the appropriate treatment is to recognize revenue of $100 in that period. Under double-entry bookkeeping, the cash account would be increased by (debited) $100 and the revenue account also increased by (credited for) the same amount.

Example 4-1a: T Account Entries for Client A

Cash			Revenue	
(payment for services)	$100		$100	(payment for services)

Client B. In terms of the firm's effort, the work for Client B occurred during the same period as the work for Client A; as of year end, however, Client B's payment had not been made. In order to honor the matching principle, the firm's accountant has to have some way to recognize the revenue in Year 1, even though the bill remains outstanding. The standard way of handling this problem is by using an asset account known as accounts receivable (bills outstanding on which payment is expected shortly). So, to record the transactions with Client B, the law firm's revenue account would be increased by (credited for) $200, and the offsetting entry would be a $200 increase in (debit to) accounts receivable. Then, when the bill is paid, presumably in Year 2, cash will be increased (debited) and accounts receivable decreased (credited), with no effect on the firm's income statement for Year 2.

Example 4-1b: T Account Entries for Client B

Accounts Receivable		Revenue	
(billing of services) $200			$200 (billing of services)

Client C. This situation is the obverse of the preceding example. The firm receives cash but renders no services in Year 1. To adhere to the matching principle in this case, the accountant has to be able to note the receipt of cash in Year 1 but postpone the recognition of income to Year 2. A technique known as deferral is available for doing just this. The accountant would turn to a liability account known as deferred income. (It is a liability because it represents an obligation to be met in the future.) The bookkeeping entries would be as follows: the receipt of the money in Year 1 would constitute an increase in (debit to) cash of $300 and an increase in (credit for) the same amount to deferred income. In Year 2, when the firm provides the promised services, deferred income will be reduced by (debited) $300 and the revenue account increased by (credited for) $300. Hence, the transaction would be factored into the firm's income statement for Year 2.

Example 4-1c: T Account Entries for Client C

Cash		Deferred Income	
(retainer) $300			$300 (retainer)

2. Allocation of expenditures under accrual accounting. Similar complexities arise in the allocation of expenditures to expense accounts. As with the income recognition problems outlined above, the root of these difficulties is that cash payments for inputs necessary to generate income are not always made in the period during which the associated revenue is generated. The rules of accounting in this area are extraordinarily complex, and we will limit our discussion to two prominent illustrations.

a. Cost of goods sold. Our first example concerns the rules that govern the valuation of inventory purchased over time at various prices. Suppose that a firm enters into the business of supplying home heating oil and builds a new storage tank capable of holding 1,000 gallons. In January, it fills the tank with oil purchased at $1.00 a gallon and sells half of its inventory in March for $3.00 a gallon. In September, the firm replenishes its inventory by purchasing 500 gallons at $2.00 a gallon and in November sells 500 gallons for $3.00 a gallon.

The accounting treatments for the January purchase and March sale are straightforward (see Figure 4-6). The company's initial purchase of 1,000 gallons of oil constitutes a $1,000 decrease (credit) of cash offset by a $1,000 increase (debit) in inventory. Then the sale of 500 gallons reduces (credits) inventory by $500, with an offsetting increase (debit) to cost of goods sold, which is an expense account. Cash is increased by $1500 with a matching increase in revenue.

The purchase in September of 500 gallons of heating oil at $2 a gallon is also uncomplicated. Cash is reduced by (credited) $1,000 and inventory is increased by (debited) the same amount. But how should the accountant deal with the sale of 500 gallons in November? Once again, cash and revenue are up $1500, but what figure should be used for the changes in cost of goods sold and inventory? The accountant could use the earlier price of oil first — the so-called FIFO (first-in, first-out) approach — that is, value the oil sold in November at $1.00 a gallon. Alternatively, the accountant could use the most recent price of inventory — known as LIFO (last-in, first out) — and assign a value of $2.00 a gallon. FIFO would result in a gross profit from the transaction of $1000, while LIFO would result in a gross profit of half that much, $500. Is either a more accurate portrayal of the gross profit resulting from the sale? What are the advantages and disadvantages of each of these methods? Can you think of other ways to approach this problem? Which would be most consistent with the underlying logic of financial accounting?

Figure 4-6
Inventory with Two Alternatives: T accounts

Cash		
(March sale) $1500	$1000	(Jan. purchase)
(Nov. sale) $1500	$1000	(Sept. purchase)

Revenue	
	$1500 (March sale)
	$1500 (Nov. sale)

Inventory		
(Jan. purchase) $1000	$500	(March sale)
(Sept. purchase) $1000	???	(Nov. sale)

Cost of Goods Sold	
(March sale)	$500
(Nov. sale)	???

b. Capitalization and depreciation of expenditures. A related issue arises when inputs have readily determined costs (say, a computer purchased for $2,000) that contributes to income over several accounting periods. The problem here is figuring out, not what the appropriate cost of the input is, but when it should be reflected as an expense on the firm's income statement. Accountants solve this problem by allowing the capitalization of certain expenditures — that is, making them into assets — and then requiring them to be depreciated — reflected as expenses — over some fixed period that is supposed to correspond to the period during which the asset contributes to income generation.

In terms of bookkeeping, accountants do this by reducing (crediting) cash and increasing (debiting) equipment when the computer is purchased — neither of which transactions affects the firm's income statement. Then, over some predetermined period — say, five years — they make annual deductions (credits) to the equipment account and offsetting increases (debits) in an expense account for depreciation. So, for the preceding example, the computer would, as indicated in Figure 4-7, initially be capitalized as a $2,000 asset (1) and then be depreciated over five years, thereby generating an annual expense of $400 (one-fifth of

Figure 4-7
Capitalization and Depreciation: T accounts

Cash

	$2000 (purchase of) equipment) (1)

Property, plant, and equipment

(purchase of) equipment) (1)	$2000	$400	(depreciation of equipment in Year One) (2)

Depreciation expense

(depreciation of equipment in Year One (2)	$400	

$2,000) for each year (2). This combination of capitalization and depreciation allows accountants to match (more or less) the cost of purchased equipment to the periods during which the investment (i.e., the equipment) contributed to income.

The lawyer's perspective

Lawyers do, in fact, spend a good deal of time advising clients on capitalization and depreciation. In certain contexts (such as when financial statements are prepared for the investment community), clients have a strong desire to capitalize expenditures in order to reduce or postpone expenses and thereby increase reported earnings. In other settings (e.g., when income is calculated for tax purposes) they are likely to be less inclined to capitalize expenditures or at least to be interested in the quickest possible system of depreciation. Why? Because they want to lower their reported income and thereby their income taxes. Lawyers often play a role in helping clients make these accounting decisions and may even be called on to structure contracts so that subsequent accounting treatments will be more advantageous to the clients' interests. How might this be done?

D. Boundary Problems

So far, we have focused on fairly concrete examples of assets and liabilities, such as computer equipment and bank loans. The classification of economic activity is not always so straightforward, and many cases fall within the gray area between items that are supposed to be included within financial statements and those that are not. Intangible assets, contingent liabilities, and "extraordinary and unusual items" are three such categories that lawyers have to be aware of.

1. Intangible assets. Early on, we noted that not all economic resources are treated as assets when it comes to balance sheets. Various sorts of intangible assets (i.e., ones that lack any physical substance) fall into this category. They include intellectual property (e.g., trademarks and patents), favorable reputations, a well-trained workforce, and other factors that contribute to a successful enterprise. Given the accountant's convention of using historical cost (as opposed to market valuation) and a preference for conservatism in the face of uncertainty, intangible assets typically appear on the balance sheet only to the extent that they are the products of identifiable costs. Thus, many intangible assets have no impact on a firm's financial statements, their considerable economic importance notwithstanding.

Intangible assets are treated differently, however, if they have been purchased by an entity in an arm's-length transaction. For example, the Coca-Cola trademark — an extremely valuable brand name — may not be recorded as a material asset on the firm's balance sheet. If, however, General Mills were to purchase the trademark from Coca-Cola for $10 billion in cash, it would be recorded on the General Mills balance sheet as having a value of $10 billion (and then might be slowly amortized as an expense on the firm's income statement the number of years deemed to reflect its useful life). Thus, the same piece of intellectual property would have no impact on one balance sheet and a $10 billion impact on another.

The lawyer's perspective

Suppose that you were general counsel for a firm that was interested in obtaining the services of Joey Winkle, a 13-year-old computer genius who had a reputation for designing web pages that attract millions of viewers. A year ago, Joey set up his own company, in which he was the only employee. To date, he has paid himself an annual salary of $10,000 and has used the rest of his company's revenues to purchase fast food and the latest computer games, most of which are already obsolete. You are considering two ways of structuring the deal: (1) entering into a five-year exclusive service contract with Joey's company for $100,000 a year or (2) purchasing the company outright for $450,000, with the understanding that Joey would continue working for the company until he begins college in five years. What are the accounting implications of each of these two choices?

2. Contingent liabilities. An analogous, but more profound problem confronts accountants when they face obligations that a firm might, but will not necessarily, incur — liabilities that are contingent on future events. As it turns out, a great deal of economic (and legal) activity falls into this category. Common examples include the financial guarantee (i.e., a promise to repay another person's debts), which comes due only if the other party defaults; the warranty, which requires performance only if a product malfunctions; or liability in a lawsuit, which arises only if the plaintiff prevails. In none of these examples is future payment a sure thing, but it is a possibility in all of them. The accountant must resolve the issue of how to reflect such situations on financial statements.

The solution that the accounting profession has developed to deal with contingent liabilities is multifaceted. When it is probable that the liability will be incurred and the cost can be reasonably estimated — that is, for the least contingent of contingent liabilities — firms are supposed to accrue the loss for financial reporting purposes. (Bookkeeping entries: increase [credit] a liability account on the balance sheet, and increase [debit] an expense item to be reflected in the firm's income statement for the reporting period.) When the contingency is reasonably possible (i.e., more than remote but less than probable) or when the loss is probable but no reasonable cost estimate can be made, the normal practice is to disclose information about the contingency (frequently also providing an estimated cost or range of costs) in a footnote on the financial statements and often elsewhere as well, such as in SEC disclosure documents.

The lawyer's perspective

One of the most frequent points of interaction between attorneys and accountants is the discussion of contingent liabilities and how they should be reported on financial statements. To help accountants classify pending legal claims, attorneys are often asked to assess the likely outcome of pending litigation as well as to estimate possible damage awards. In addition, accountants routinely send law firms letters listing all pending or threatened litigation that the accountants are aware of and requesting the firms to confirm that they are not aware of any other pending or threatened actions. Suppose that you received such a letter and it did not mention an environmental problem that you are currently working on, a problem for which the company has potentially substantial, but not yet fully ascertained, legal exposure. How should you respond to the accountant's letter?

3. Extraordinary and unusual items. Another interesting boundary problem concerns the treatment of costs associated with events that are highly unusual, such as natural disasters, exceptional legal awards, unexpected deterioration of business assets, and corporate transactions such as mergers and acquisitions. These costs are similar to expenses that would ordinarily be charged to an entity's income statement, but because they are unusual, they are not tied to firms' ordinary operations and are therefore not likely to recur. Accounting conventions call for such unusual and nonrecurrent items to be distinguished from other expenses on income statements. Typically, these items appear on a separate line, beneath a line denominated "net income before extraordinary and unusual items" or words to that effect.

In recent years, several prominent officials (including former SEC Chair Arthur Levitt) have criticized firms for treating too many costs as extraordinary and unusual items. Inasmuch as these charges reduce net income (and therefore owners' equity) for the period in which they are taken, why do you think firms might have an incentive to be overly aggressive in this area?

5. The Institutional and Legal Structure of Accounting

An important part of a lawyer's education about financial accounting is learning about the institutional and legal context in which accounting standards are developed and applied. So far in this chapter, we have discussed various principles underlying financial statements and the conventions for implementing them. But how are they agreed on, and to what extent are they legally binding on private parties? Lawyers have to understand these institutional arrangements as well as the accounting conventions they support.

A. Institutions and the Creation of Accounting Standards

In the United States, the government's role in the development of accounting standards is relatively limited. The SEC, a federal entity, does play a role in defining a wide range of information that public companies must supply to their shareholders (e.g., annual reports and on certain occasions other disclosure documents, such as those required when securities are sold to the general public). However, these rules apply to only a very small fraction of U.S. firms (only some 15,000 to 20,000 companies — less than 1% of all U.S. businesses) at any given time. For these firms, the SEC has an elaborate system of disclosure requirements and accounting standards (known respectively as Regulation S-K and Regulation S-X). In addition, the SEC requires that the financial statements of public companies be maintained in accordance with a body of authority known as generally accepted accounting principles (GAAP, pronounced like the name of the store) and that these statements be reviewed (or audited) periodically by independent accounting firms.

In part because of the SEC's influence, GAAP has become the dominant accounting norm in this country. It either controls or heavily influences the accounting practices of nearly all firms that maintain financial statements in the U.S. — whether or not publicly owned — as well as an increasing number of entities in other jurisdictions. The conventions introduced during our discussion of accounting standards are, in fact, the basic elements of GAAP.

The institution primarily responsible for articulating GAAP is the Financial Accounting Standard Board (FASB, rhymes with frisbee). Founded in 1973 and located in Connecticut, FASB is an independent organization with five full-time board members. It articulates GAAP principally by issuing statements and interpretations. (For example, FASB Statement No. 5 deals with accounting for contingencies, whereas Interpretation No. 14 addresses reasonable estimation of losses.) Before FASB issues a new statement on a subject, the board typically appoints a task force to investigate the matter and engages in a prolonged period of notice-and-comment, during which interested parties (often including the SEC) provide input and reaction. FASB's statements and interpretative releases are the highest form of authority in the accounting profession, but they are supplemented by a host of lesser forms of guidance, including other sorts of FASB pronouncements as well as standards articulated by FASB's predecessor organization, the Accounting Principles Board (APB). (If you are interested in getting a sense of FASB's current reform agenda, you should view its website, http://www.fasb.org.)

Another important organization in the field is the American Institute of Certified Public Accountants (AICPA). The AICPA's Auditing Standards Board has traditionally performed a rule-making function in the development of generally accepted auditing standards (GAAS, pronounced like gas). These constitute a separate set of rules that prescribe procedures that outside accountants (also known as independent auditors) are supposed to follow prior to certifying that financial statements comply with GAAP. Mirroring FASB's role in the preparation of statements of accounting standards, the AICPA Audit Board promulgated rules governing audit practices. For example, the AICPA's Statement on Auditing Standard No. 12 explains how auditors should make inquiries of a client's lawyer concerning litigation, claims, and assessments. (This standard was promulgated in 1975, at the same time that the American Bar Association issued a companion statement of policy for lawyers.) In 2002, in the wake of the widespread scandals in corporate accounting for firms such as Enron and Worldcom, Congress mandated the creation of a new Public Company Accounting Oversight Board (PCAOB), a private sector, nonprofit corporation whose five members are appointed by the SEC, to oversee the auditors of public companies. PCAOB has now taken over the role of AICPA in developing and promulgating auditing standards for public companies and overseeing their auditors.

The most broadly based institution involved in the creation of financial statements is the accounting profession itself. At the core of this group are certified public accountants, who are licensed by state accounting boards (analogous to state bar associations for lawyers). To obtain certification as an accountant, a person must pass a test developed under the auspices of the AICPA and satisfy training and apprenticeship requirements, which vary from jurisdiction to jurisdiction. Certified public accountants work in numerous capacities — as corporate employees, most commonly in internal accounting or control departments, as government employees with auditing responsibilities, and as partners or other members of independent accounting firms. The most prominent of the independent accounting firms are the Big Four: Deloitte Touche Tohmatsu, Ernst & Young, KPMG, and PricewaterhouseCoopers.

Under SEC regulations, the financial statements of a public company must be audited periodically (usually annually) by an accounting firm that is independent of the company. Typically, the Big Four perform the audits of larger companies. Even firms that are not subject to SEC regulations often choose to subject themselves to independent audits, sometimes to supplement internal controls and other times to establish for third parties, such as creditors, customers, or contributors, the credibility of their financial statements. In many cases, firms are bound by contractual provisions to submit to independent audits annually. In gross numbers, substantially more financial statements are produced each year in response to contractual obligations — that is, private law drafted by attorneys — than as a result of SEC regulations governing public companies. Thus, a final institution responsible for the creation of financial statements in the United States is the legal profession — in other words, you.

The lawyer's perspective

A question that lawyers routinely have to decide is whether, in a given case, to require that financial statements delivered to them be audited by independent auditors. Sometimes they even have to decide whether to specify the kind of accounting firm (i.e., a Big Four firm or some less well known — and presumably less expensive — alternative) that should perform the audit. In reaching their decisions, they must balance the value of obtaining better financial information against the cost of imposing such requirements.

B. Finding Financial Statements and Related Information

The institutional structure outlined above is the engine that generates the financial statements of business organizations and other entities in the United States. And it is this structure that you have to understand in order to locate and use these financial statements and information associated with them. Imagine for a moment that you are a new associate in a law firm and your supervising partner, knowing that you are trained in analytical methods, sticks her head through your office door and says, "I'd like you to check out the financials on Company XYZ." What would you do?

A reasonable first step would be to ask the partner whether the firm is a public company and thus subject to the SEC disclosure and accounting requirements. If she doesn't know, there are a number of ways for you to find out for yourself. One of the simplest is to access the SEC's home page (http://www.sec.gov) and then click on EDGAR Database. (EDGAR, pronounced like the name of the author of *The Telltale Heart*, is an acronym for Electronic Data Gathering, Analysis, and Retrieval; the database contains the filings [i.e., disclosure and accounting documents] of nearly all public companies.) Once there, you can use various search engines and indices to determine whether the firm in question is a public company. If it is, you will have a large amount of financial information about the firm right at your fingertips, usually including its most recent financial statements.

Before we discuss the content of SEC disclosure documents, let's suppose that the partner had told you that the firm was privately owned and thus not subject to SEC regulation. What would you do in this case? A reasonable next question would be: Does Company XYZ have audited financial statements for the preceding year? Because many companies not subject to SEC requirements undergo annual independent audits (either voluntarily or by contractual commitment), independently audited financial statements may indeed be available for Company XYZ, and they may even have been audited by one of the Big Four and therefore be of the same quality as those included in the SEC filings (though not likely to be supplemented with other disclosures that the SEC requires of public companies). If available, these statements would offer valuable insight into the financial posture of Company XYZ.

What if audited financial statements are not available for the company (e.g., if it is family owned and the family has never felt the need to subject the company to an independent audit)? Is there anything else you might ask? One possibility would be to inquire whether the company has any financial statements that were prepared internally. The company would almost certainly generate financial information for its own purposes even if it didn't go to the trouble of having independent audits performed. Though less reliable on numerous dimensions than audited financials, internal statements offer at least some information on the financial status of a company and at times can even be extremely informative.

Let's briefly consider the kind of financial information likely to be found in the various categories of financial statements, starting with the least complete and moving up to SEC disclosure documents.

1. Internal financial statements. The content and quality of internal financial statements are highly variable. In general, we might expect at least the three basic formats (i.e., the balance sheets reporting the firm's year-end financial position for the two most recent years, an income statement for the preceding year or two, and a cash flow statement for the most recent year), although with smaller firms, all three formats may not be available. We would have no idea about the quality of the statements that are available. The firm may or may not have a CPA on staff; typically, it would not be obligated to. Some other person, who may be marginally trained or even untrained, may be responsible for preparing the documents. Moreover, without investigating further, we could not be certain that the statements fully satisfy GAAP standards, even though they most likely look as if they do. Financial statements do not necessarily conform to even the basic foundational principles that we have addressed, much less the detailed requirements articulated in FASB statements and related lines of authority. There are many reasons why these statements may deviate from GAAP and FASB standards. Perhaps no one on the company's payroll was qualified to prepare them in accordance with GAAP. Or they may have been prepared for a specific purpose where full GAAP compliance may not have seemed necessary — such as calculating bonuses for the sales staff. Another possibility is that they had been put together to show low income for tax purposes. What's more, internal financial statements do not necessarily fully reflect all

In Compl

or even most of the firm's economic activities. For example, we cannot possibly know, simply by looking at an internal balance sheet, if all of the company's liabilities appear on it.

2. Audited financial statements. Considering the limitations of and uncertainties about internally generated financial statements, the advantages of ones audited by independent accounting firms are obvious. Hiring an independent auditor is supposed to ensure quality, and this assurance is expressed formally in the auditor's report that accompanies audited financials.

A typical auditor's report appears in Box 4-3. This report is from audited financial statements included in the 2009 Annual Report of Amazon.com, Inc. If you look at it carefully, you will note that a number of statements speak to the quality of the financials and explain how they were prepared.

① First, notice to whom the report is addressed: the Board of Directors and Stockholders of Amazon.com, Inc. What's going on in the report is that the independent accountant — Ernst & Young, one of the Big Four — is reporting to these parties about Amazon.com, Inc.'s financial statements for the period 2008-2009.

② Second, the bottom line of the opinion (in the third paragraph of text) is that the financial statements attached to the auditor's report "present fairly, in all material respects" the company's financial position "in conformity with *generally accepted accounting principles.*" With this sentence, the independent auditor assures the members of the Board and anyone else who reads the report not just that the structure of the statements complies with the FASB rules but also that the statements are supplemented with appropriate footnotes and additional information that GAAP requires. (If you look at the excerpt from the Amazon. Com Annual Report appended to this chapter, you'll see that the three basic formats take up only a few pages starting on page 171, whereas the footnotes and supplemental statements run for a few dozen pages. Note 7 on pages 191-96, for example, discusses litigation and was almost certainly drafted with the assistance of attorneys.)

③ Third, the report speaks to the auditor's confidence that the financial statements do, in fact, reflect all of the firm's economic activity during the relevant periods. Importantly, the auditor does not claim to have

---

Box 4-3
Report of Ernst & Young LLP, Independent Registered
Public Accounting Firm

The Board of Directors and Stockholders
Amazon.com, Inc.

We have audited the accompanying consolidated balance sheets of Amazon.com, Inc. as of December 31, 2009 and 2008, and the related consolidated statements of operations, stockholders' equity, and cash flows for each of the three years in the period ended December 31, 2009. These financial statements are the responsibility of the Company's management. Our responsibility is to express an opinion on these financial statements based on our audits.

We conducted our audits in accordance with the standards of the Public Company Accounting Oversight Board (United States). Those standards require that we plan and perform the audit to obtain reasonable assurance about whether the financial statements are free of material misstatement. An audit includes examining, on a test basis, evidence supporting the amounts and disclosures in the financial statements. An audit also includes assessing the accounting principles used and significant estimates made by management, as well as evaluating the overall financial statement presentation. We believe that our audits provide a reasonable basis for our opinion.

In our opinion, the financial statements referred to above present fairly, in all material respects, the consolidated financial position of Amazon.com, Inc. at December 31, 2009 and 2008, and the consolidated results of its operations and its cash flows for each of the three years in the period ended December 31, 2009, in conformity with U.S. generally accepted accounting principles.

As discussed in Note 1 to the consolidated financial statements, the Company adopted FASB No. 141(R) *Business Combinations*, codified in ASC 805, *Business Combinations*, effective January 1, 2009.

We also have audited, in accordance with the standards of the Public Company Accounting Oversight Board (United States), Amazon.com, Inc.'s internal control over financial reporting as of December 31, 2009, based on criteria established in Internal Control — Integrated Framework issued by the Committee of Sponsoring Organizations of the Treadway Commission and our report dated January 28, 2010 expressed an unqualified opinion thereon.

/s/ Ernst & Young LLP

Seattle, Washington
January 28, 2010

comprehensively reviewed all of the firm's activities. Even with audited financials, the actual preparation of financial statements remains the responsibility of management and is usually undertaken by CPAs and support staff. The auditor purports to have conducted the audit of those financial statements in accordance with the standards of the PCAOB. As explained in the report, the independent auditor simply spot-checked (i.e., "examin[ed], on a test basis") the company's internal procedures as well as the accounting standards and estimates used to compile the financial statements. These procedures are designed to provide the auditor with a "reasonable basis" for the opinion, as expressed in the third paragraph, that the financial statements are a materially fair presentation of the company's financial position in accordance with GAAP. This assurance may strike you as cramped and legalistic, but it is substantially more reassuring than what typically accompanies unaudited, internally generated financial statements.

3. Financial statements of public companies. The gold standard of financial disclosure in the United States can be seen in the financial statements of public corporations — firms subject to the SEC rules governing disclosure and financial statements. The details of SEC-mandated disclosure are well beyond our scope. But to get a sense of the kinds of additional financial information that public companies in the United States must provide, you should flip through the Amazon.com annual report (appended to this chapter). This document contains a number of interesting features that exemplify disclosure required by the SEC:

- The SEC mandates that all public firms have their financial statements audited by independent accounting firms in accordance with the standards of the PCAOB, with respect to financial statements maintained in accordance with GAAP. (Actually, the SEC accounting rules go beyond GAAP in several respects, but this subject is beyond the scope of our coverage.)
- The SEC requires public firms to disclose a great deal of information in addition to that in their audited financial statements. This information, much of which is financial, must be included in their SEC filings. For example, they include a textual description of a firm's financial

statements accompanied by a discussion of trends and future prospects, which financial analysts read with great care. Lawyers often have a role in drafting this kind of disclosure as well as related sections on cautionary statements. A list of the firm's major contracts and documents that can be retrieved from other sources may also appear in the SEC filing.

The legal regimen surrounding documents filed with the SEC is much more stringent than generally applicable legal rules or even the rules governing financial statements of nonpublic companies. This is especially true when the documents are used in connection with the public sale of securities. For this reason, companies, their accountants, and other advisers are extremely careful in preparing SEC disclosure documents. The quality of the information in these filings is thus typically quite high.

4. Qualified audit reports. At this stage, a note of warning is in order about another feature of auditors' reports: whether or not they contain qualifications. The report in Box 4-3 is what's known as an *unqualified report.* The auditor didn't find it necessary to include any qualifying statement. This is the kind of a report that a firm wants to get and analysts expect to see. On occasion, however, an auditor's report can be *qualified* in one or more respects. Any qualification should be evaluated carefully. Examples of qualifying language can be seen in the excerpts from audit letters in Boxes 4-4, 4-5, and 4-6.

Sometimes qualifications are fairly technical. For instance, in Box 4-4, we see that du Pont changed the way in which it accounted for certain kinds of retirement benefits during the period covered by the report. This change was, in fact, mandated by the release of a new FASB standard, but it had an impact at several places in the firm's statement, and the qualification was intended to alert readers to this fact.

The qualification in the report in Box 4-5 is the sort that often appears in audit reports prepared by foreign issuers — in this case, the Irish Telephone Company. The auditor includes the qualification that the financials were prepared in accordance with Irish GAAP, not U.S. GAAP. One of the principal differences — that Irish GAAP permits some assets

---

Box 4-4
Excerpt from the E. I. du Pont de Nemours
and Company Annual Report of 1994

. . . We believe that our audits provide a reasonable basis for our opinion.

As discussed in Note 1 to the consolidated financial statements, the company changed its method of accounting for postretirement benefits other than pensions and for income taxes in 1992.

Box 4-5
Excerpt from the Prospectus
of Telecom Eireann, July 7, 1999

. . . In our opinion, the consolidated financial statements referred to above present fairly, in all material respects, the consolidated financial position of Bord Telecom Eireann ple and subsidiaries as at 3 April 1997, 2 April 1998 and 1 April 1999, and the consolidated results of their operations, cash flows and changes in equity shareholders' funds for each of the three years in the period ended 1 April 1999, in conformity with *generally accepted accounting principles in Ireland* [italics added].

Generally accepted accounting principles in Ireland vary in certain significant respects from accounting principles generally accepted in the United States of America ("US GAAP"). The application of the latter would have affected the determination of consolidated results for each of the two years in the period ended 1 April 1999 and equity shareholders' funds as at 2 April 1998 and 1 April 1999 to the extent summarized in Note 33 to the consolidated financial statements. As described in Note 33, certain tangible assets were recorded at depreciated replacement cost at the start of business of Bord Telecom Eireann ple on 1 January 1984, in accordance with the Postal and Telecommunication Services Act, 1983, rather than their historical cost, as required by US GAAP.

Box 4-6
Excerpt from the Knudsen Corporation
Annual Report of 1995

The accompanying consolidated financial statements have been prepared assuming that the Corporation will continue as a going concern. As discussed in "Notes to Consolidated Financial Statements — Basis of Presentation and Management's Plans," the Corporation had substantial losses and negative cash flow from operations in 1994, which significantly reduced stockholders' equity and resulted in a substantial retained deficit and working capital deficit at December 31, 1994; was not in compliance with certain financial covenants of certain of its credit agreements at December 31, 1994 and subsequently failed to meet scheduled repayment terms; and will require additional funding to cover substantial expected negative cash flows in 1995. In addition, substantially all of the of the Corporation's short-term debt agreements expire on July 31, 1995. If the Corporation is unable to obtain adequate financing, it may be required to seek protection under the United States Bankruptcy Code in order to continue operating. *These conditions raise substantial doubt about the Corporation's ability to continue as a going concern* [italics added]. Management's plans in this regard are also described in the "Notes to Consolidated Financial Statements — Basis of Presentation and Management's Plans." The consolidated financial statements do not include any adjustments that might result from the outcome of this uncertainty.

As emphasized in "Notes to Consolidated Financial Statements — Estimated Losses on Uncompleted Contracts," the Corporation recorded significant provisions for losses during 1994 related to revised estimates of costs to be incurred to complete certain transit car contracts. *These management estimates are based on numerous assumptions which, if not ultimately achieved, could result in additional revisions of the estimates of costs to complete the transit car contracts and such revisions could be material* [italics added].

to be valued at depreciated replacement cost as opposed to depreciated historical cost — is explained, and readers are directed to note 33 for a more detailed explanation of the differences between the two accounting treatments. In essence, this type of qualification is a warning that the financials deviate from U.S. GAAP in a way that the SEC sometimes permits for certain foreign companies. In recent years, the SEC has become more willing to accept financial statements prepared in accordance with International Financial Reporting Standards (IFRS).

The most serious qualification appears in the report in Box 4-6. In the first paragraph, the accountant raises a "going concern" qualification. In light of the firm's current and pending financial commitments, the auditors raise substantial doubt about the firm's ability to continue operating. This doubt, in effect, precludes the issuance of a clean opinion because GAAP is based on the assumption that the reporting entity will continue operations — a point emphasized in the first sentence of the excerpt. A qualification of this sort is a flashing red light in the world of financial accounting. A second sort of qualification — one concerning the reasonableness of management's estimates of losses from outstanding contractual obligations — is raised in the second paragraph of Box 4-6. Most analysts would be concerned by this qualification and would want to investigate its implications.

6. The Analysis of Financial Statements

Knowing how to create financial statements is one thing. Being able to assess the information in them is yet another. Could an analyst have predicted from Amazon's early financial statements that it would become one of the world's most successful companies, or even that it would still be in existence today? Can analysts today determine how Amazon will fare in the future?

Evaluating financial statements is a discipline unto itself. In business schools, entire courses are devoted to the analysis of corporate financial reports, and financial analysts make their living helping investors decipher the periodic disclosures of public companies. Analysts have a wide variety of techniques (including many financial techniques that the next chapter addresses) at their disposal. *Ratio analysis* is an important one. It focuses attention on the relationship between various components of a firm's financial statements. Each ratio provides a certain kind of information when assessing a company. Analysts look at each ratio to determine whether it falls within a range appropriate for that firm. If it falls outside the benchmark range that has been established as the norm, additional investigation may be in order.

Applying ratio analysis necessitates revisiting the basic components of financial statements and reviewing the relationships among the components. Let's take a look at some basic financial ratios. The limitations of ratio analysis — dependent as it is on financial statements built on accounting conventions such as historical costs — offer an appropriate springboard for the more sophisticated methodologies of finance that are addressed in the next chapter.

The lawyer's perspective

When the line between legal and financial advice blurs, as it often does, lawyers are at an advantage if they understand financial ratios. But even an attorney working in an entirely legal context must occasionally make use of financial ratios. Loan covenants, for example, often include restrictions that require the borrower to maintain one or more of these ratios within a certain range. Failure to do so can constitute default — and is often defined as such in contracts — with economic consequences that can be dire for the borrower. To be able to draft such provisions or offer advice about them, an attorney must understand their significance.

A. Liquidity

Liquidity is the ability of an individual or entity to meet its short term financial responsibilities. One way to assess liquidity is to determine how much cash or cash reserves the individual or entity has on hand at a given time. You can obtain this information by looking at the entity's balance sheet. Alternatively, you could inspect the cash flow statement to see how cash reserves have changed over time. Taking yet another approach, you could look at the firm's current ratio, which is the ratio of its current assets (i.e., the sum of cash and assets likely to be converted into cash in the near future) to its current (or short-term) liabilities. Analysts track this ratio because, intuitively, current assets should always be greater than short-term liabilities. Indeed, as a rule of thumb, the current ratio should always be greater than 1.5 to 2.0 — that is, current assets should be at least one and a half to two times as large as current liabilities.

To test your understanding of how the current ratio is calculated, look at Amazon's 2009 balance sheet on page 173. Do you see why its current ratio is expressed by the following equation?

$$\text{current ratio} = \frac{\text{current assets}}{\text{current liabilities}}$$
$$= \frac{\$9,797,000,000}{\$7,364,000,000}$$
$$= 1.33$$

Note that the calculated current ratio is somewhat smaller than the benchmark (1.5 to 2.0) that was just mentioned. Might there be some fact about Amazon's business operation that explains why its current ratio would be below the norm? How might the firm improve its ratio, thereby making itself more attractive to short-term creditors?

B. Solvency

Solvency is a firm's ability to meet its long term obligations. Analysts approach solvency from two perspectives. One is by considering the ratio between a firm's liabilities and other components of its balance sheets. The measures most commonly looked at are the ratio of debt to equity and the related ratio of debt to total assets. The intuition here is that if a firm has too much debt (in financial parlance, is too highly leveraged), its solvency is imperiled: even a slight downturn in profitability could leave the firm incapable of repaying its creditors.

Criteria for evaluating leverage ratios vary considerably from industry to industry. The financial services industry tends to be highly leveraged, with debt equivalent to more than 90% of assets — that is, a debt-to-equity ratio of more than 9 to 1. The ratio tends to be much lower for manufacturing firms. For Amazon, its total liabilities at the end of 2009 were reported as $8,556,000,000 (current liabilities plus "Long-term debt" and "Other long-term liabilities") and its total owners' equity was $5,257,000,000. So its debt-to-equity ratio was 1.63, — in other words, its total liabilities were roughly equal to one-and-a-half times its total owners' equity. Measured against its total assets ($13,813,000,000), its debt was about 61.9%. One interpretation of this figure is that, for every dollar of assets, Amazon financed about 62 cents with debt and the other 38 cents with owners' money. Looking more closely, at the make-up of the liabilities, reveals a very large figure for accounts payable. A diligent analyst will certainly want to know why such a large outstanding bill has accumulated.

The second way that analysts quantify solvency is by comparing a firm's annual interest expenses to the earnings it has available to make these payments. By convention, this is a comparison of earnings before interest and tax (EBIT, rhymes with rivet) to annual interest expense.[1] (In the income statement in Figure 4-3, EBIT is called *operating earnings*.) This ratio is sometimes called *interest coverage*, and the larger this figure is, the more likely the firm is to be able to pay its future interest obligations as they come due. For example, if the ratio of EBIT to interest expense for a firm were 10 to 1, it could continue to make its interest payments even if its earnings declined by 90%. Do you see why? As an exercise, try to calculate the interest coverage ratio for Amazon 2009. (Answer: 33.21.)

C. Managerial Efficiency

A number of ratios relate to the efficiency of a firm's management. For example, sometimes analysts are interested in the relationship between a firm's accounts receivables and its gross revenues. The intuition here is that accounts receivable (i.e., the total amount of customer bills outstanding) should not be too great relative to the firm's annual sales. If too many customers aren't paying their bills, that's a bad sign. So, all other things being equal, when a firm's accounts receivable are more

---

1. The logic for using a measure of income that does not include interest or taxes is as follows: As to interest, because we are trying to figure out the earnings available to pay interest, interest should not already have been deducted from the amount of earnings available to pay interest. As to taxes, the theory is that taxes are due only on net income, so tax is paid only on the earnings remaining after interest has been paid. The obligation to pay interest, in this sense, has precedence over the obligation to pay taxes. In the extreme case, if EBIT equaled $100 and interest payments equaled $100, the firm would have no income for the period in question, and no taxes would be due.

than 15% of its annual revenues, eyebrows might rise, particularly if the ratio is higher than it had been in the past.

Looking back to the Amazon 2009 income statement, confirm that the ratio of accounts receivable to sales revenue would be roughly 4.0%:

$$\frac{\text{accounts receivable}}{\text{sales revenue}} = \frac{\$988,000,000}{\$24,509,000,000}$$
$$= .04$$

If we assumed that sales revenue had been generated evenly throughout the year, we would see that customers had been taking a little more than 2 weeks, on average, to pay off their accounts (i.e., 0.04 × 52 weeks = 2.08 weeks). This would usually be considered a very reasonable period.

Many other ratios are used to measure managerial performance. One of these is the *turnover ratio* — that is, the ratio of cost of goods sold to year-end inventory. It is an estimate of how many times a firm's inventory is sold during a year. The higher the turnover ratio, the more efficient the firm's inventory management is, or, in other words, the shorter the period of time items stay in inventory, the lower the firm's cost of maintaining inventory is. Among other useful ratios are those that relate interest payments to debt (providing a measure of a firm's interest costs) and after-tax income to pre-tax income (a measure of a firm's tax rate). Many other kinds of performance measures are possible. Measures of this sort are often used to evaluate the performance of individual employees, and they can even be used to calculate compensation packages.

D. Profitability

Another set of performance measures look to a firm's profitability. Again, this issue can be approached from a variety of perspectives, and relevant benchmarks vary considerably from industry to industry. For example, we could look at the ratio of a firm's operating earnings to its sales revenue, also referred to as the firm's *margin*. This ratio reflects the percentage of sales that remained after direct costs (costs of goods sold) and indirect costs (operating expenses) were deducted. If we look again at the Amazon 2009 income statement, and calculate the margin from information given there, we find that it's $1,129,000,000/24,509,000,000 =$ 4.6% (i.e., operating income/sales revenue). So, for Amazon 2009, every dollar of sales generated 4.6 cents of operating income. Supermarkets typically have much thinner (lower) margins, whereas high-tech firms like Microsoft have much higher ones.

   Another way to approach profitability is to compare earnings to the total amount of money invested in a firm. Ratios of this sort explore the relationship between income and balance sheet entries. By convention, the measure of income typically used is *net income* — that is, operating earnings minus interest expenses and taxes.[2] On the balance sheet side, total assets and total owners' equity are the entries used most often. The ratio of net income to total assets is the *return on assets* (ROA), which we can think of as the amount of income that each dollar of assets generated during the reporting period. Look at the Amazon financials and try to locate the components of the following equation:

$$\text{return on assets} = \frac{\text{net income}}{\text{total assets}}$$

$$= \frac{\$902,000,000}{\$13,813,000,000}$$

$$= 6.5\%$$

   The other common measure of profitability compares net income to owners' equity. This ratio, the *return on equity* (ROE), is, in effect, a measure of the return on the owners' investment in a firm. For Amazon 2009, it would be calculated as follows:

$$\text{return on equity} = \frac{\text{net income}}{\text{total owners' equity}}$$

$$= \frac{\$902,000,000}{\$5,257,000,000}$$

$$= 17\%$$

---

   2. The reason for using a more complete measure of earnings in this context is that the ratios at issue here — ROA and ROE — are intended to provide something of a bottom line on a firm's profitability. Net income is appropriate for such applications because it presents the fullest picture of a firm's earnings.

For Amazon 2009, the ROE (17%) is higher than its ROA (6.5%). Intuitively, this makes sense because owners' equity was less than total assets. And owners' equity was less than total assets because the firm had leveraged its equity with a certain amount of debt (in fact, about 62 cents of debt for every dollar of equity; see the discussion of solvency). For a firm that has no liabilities — that is, one that is fully funded with equity — ROA equals ROE. Do you see why?

E. Earnings per Share and Price-Earnings Ratios

This final category of measurements offers ways to relate accounting statement measures of profitability to a more ephemeral concept: market values. Recall that throughout our discussion of financial analysis we have been working with components of financial statements that, under GAAP, are principally based on historical costs. There is no guarantee that accounting entries on accounting statements will accord with market values. So, for example, if we were interested in estimating the market value of a company or a share of stock in a company (which constitutes a pro rata interest in the firm), turning to the firm's financial statements will be of only limited use. The component of the balance sheet that most closely accords with the value of the firm is total owners' equity ($5,257,000,000 for Amazon 2009). If this number is divided by the number of shares of stock outstanding, we can calculate a *book value* for a share of stock: $11.84 (i.e., total owners' equity/number of shares of common stock outstanding = $5,257,000,000/444,000,000 shares = $11.84 per share).

But a book value may or may not be a good estimate of the true market value of a firm or its shares. As we saw earlier, financial statements are built on historical costs, which do not reflect appreciation or deterioration in the value of certain long-lived assets. Moreover, the value of many intangible assets (e.g., reputation, employee morale, intellectual property) may not be reflected in financial statements. Finally, various contingencies that are difficult to place a value on (e.g., lawsuits) may not be reflected in the book value of owners' equity. In the case of Microsoft, for example, the government's antitrust suit wouldn't have appeared on its balance sheet (although it would presumably have been discussed in the notes to the company's financial statements.)

Many of these shortcomings are inherent in the nature of financial statements and cannot easily be avoided without resorting to wholly different valuation techniques (such as financial economics). But analysts do have one or two measures that may be more useful than simple calculations of book value per share.

One of these — *earnings per share* (EPS) — compares net income to number of shares outstanding. It is a measurement of the amount of earnings attributable to each share. Amazon 2009 reported a net income of $902,000,000 and 444,000,000 shares of common stock outstanding. Hence, its EPS was $2.03. This ratio is often used to evaluate the market price of a company's stock. For example, if you were trying to determine how much you would be willing to pay for a share of stock, you might ask yourself how much you would be willing to pay in order to receive $2.03 of income a year from a company like Amazon. If we thought this income stream would continue indefinitely and expected a 10% return on this sort of investment, we might be willing to pay $20.30 per share (i.e., $2.03 is 10% of $20.30). Note that this is almost twice as much as Amazon's book value per share ($11.84). Such discrepancy reinforces the point that market values may well deviate from book values.

A related ratio compares a firm's EPS to the actual market value of the firm's stock. Because this measure relies on market values, it can be calculated only for companies whose securities trade in the public markets or otherwise have a readily obtainable market price. In the United States, this information is generally available only for public firms that are subject to SEC regulations for disclosure, such as Amazon. The standard way of expressing the relationship of market value to EPS is by calculating the ratio of the price of a firm's common stock to the earnings per share of the stock. This ratio is the *price-earnings multiple,* sometimes referred to as the *PE ratio.* As we calculated above, Amazon's EPS in 2009 was $2.03. In the fourth quarter of 2009, its stock price ranged from $88.27 to $145.91 per share. Dividing the midpoint of this trading range ($117.09) by the 2009 EPS yields a PE ratio of 57.6. PE ratios vary by projected future company growth, with higher ratios indicating greater expected growth. For firms engaged in internet commerce, as of Jan. 2010, the average PE ratio was in the 50's.

7. Suggestions for Further Reading

If you're interested in learning more about accounting, you can find additional information in the publications listed below. A number of the topics addressed in the next chapter (Finance) build on the accounting principles and techniques that we have just worked through.

Robert N. Anthony, *Essentials of Accounting*, 10th ed. (Reading, MA: Addison-Wesley Publishing Company, 2002).

Lawrence A. Cunningham, *Introductory Accounting, Finance and Auditing for Lawyers*, 5th ed. (St. Paul, MN: West Group, 2009).

David R. Herwitz and Matthew J. Barrett, *Accounting for Lawyers*, 4th ed. (Westbury, NY: Foundation Press, 2006).

Gary John Previts and Barbara Dubis Merino, *A History of Accountancy in the United States: The Cultural Significance of Accounting* (Columbus, OH: Ohio State University Press, 1998).

Howard M. Schilit, *Financial Shenanigans: How to Detect Accounting Gimmicks and Fraud in Financial Reports*, 3rd ed. (Boston, MA: McGraw-Hill, 2010).

John A. Tracy, *How to Read a Financial Report: Wringing Vital Signs Out of the Numbers*, 5th ed. (New York, NY: John Wiley & Sons, Inc., 2009).

Gerald I. White et al., *The Analysis and Use of Financial Statements*, 3rd ed. (New York, NY: John Wiley & Sons, Inc., 2003).

2 0 0 9

A N N U A L   R E P O R T

Item 8.   *Financial Statements and Supplementary Data*

INDEX TO CONSOLIDATED FINANCIAL STATEMENTS

Report of Ernst & Young LLP, Independent Registered Public Accounting Firm

The Board of Directors and Stockholders
Amazon.com, Inc.

We have audited the accompanying consolidated balance sheets of Amazon.com, Inc. as of December 31, 2009 and 2008, and the related consolidated statements of operations, stockholders' equity, and cash flows for each of the three years in the period ended December 31, 2009. These financial statements are the responsibility of the Company's management. Our responsibility is to express an opinion on these financial statements based on our audits.

We conducted our audits in accordance with the standards of the Public Company Accounting Oversight Board (United States). Those standards require that we plan and perform the audit to obtain reasonable assurance about whether the financial statements are free of material misstatement. An audit includes examining, on a test basis, evidence supporting the amounts and disclosures in the financial statements. An audit also includes assessing the accounting principles used and significant estimates made by management, as well as evaluating the overall financial statement presentation. We believe that our audits provide a reasonable basis for our opinion.

In our opinion, the financial statements referred to above present fairly, in all material respects, the consolidated financial position of Amazon.com, Inc. at December 31, 2009 and 2008, and the consolidated results of its operations and its cash flows for each of the three years in the period ended December 31, 2009, in conformity with U.S. generally accepted accounting principles.

As discussed in Note 1 to the consolidated financial statements, the Company adopted FASB No. 141(R) *Business Combinations*, codified in ASC 805, *Business Combinations*, effective January 1, 2009.

We also have audited, in accordance with the standards of the Public Company Accounting Oversight Board (United States), Amazon.com, Inc.'s internal control over financial reporting as of December 31, 2009, based on criteria established in Internal Control—Integrated Framework issued by the Committee of Sponsoring Organizations of the Treadway Commission and our report dated January 28, 2010 expressed an unqualified opinion thereon.

/s/ Ernst & Young LLP

Seattle, Washington
January 28, 2010

AMAZON.COM, INC.

CONSOLIDATED STATEMENTS OF CASH FLOWS
(in millions)

	Year Ended December 31,		
	2009	**2008**	**2007**
CASH AND CASH EQUIVALENTS, BEGINNING OF PERIOD	$ 2,769	$ 2,539	$1,022
OPERATING ACTIVITIES:			
Net income	902	645	476
Adjustments to reconcile net income to net cash from operating activities:			
Depreciation of fixed assets, including internal-use software and website development, and other amortization	378	287	246
Stock-based compensation	341	275	185
Other operating expense (income), net	103	(24)	9
Losses (gains) on sales of marketable securities, net	(4)	(2)	1
Other expense (income), net	(15)	(34)	12
Deferred income taxes	81	(5)	(99)
Excess tax benefits from stock-based compensation	(105)	(159)	(257)
Changes in operating assets and liabilities:			
Inventories	(531)	(232)	(303)
Accounts receivable, net and other	(481)	(218)	(255)
Accounts payable	1,859	812	928
Accrued expenses and other	300	247	429
Additions to unearned revenue	1,054	449	244
Amortization of previously unearned revenue	(589)	(344)	(211)
Net cash provided by (used in) operating activities	3,293	1,697	1,405
INVESTING ACTIVITIES:			
Purchases of fixed assets, including internal-use software and website development	(373)	(333)	(224)
Acquisitions, net of cash acquired, and other	(40)	(494)	(75)
Sales and maturities of marketable securities and other investments	1,966	1,305	1,271
Purchases of marketable securities and other investments	(3,890)	(1,677)	(930)
Net cash provided by (used in) investing activities	(2,337)	(1,199)	42
FINANCING ACTIVITIES:			
Excess tax benefits from stock-based compensation	105	159	257
Common stock repurchased		(100)	(248)
Proceeds from long-term debt and other	87	98	115
Repayments of long-term debt and capital lease obligations	(472)	(355)	(74)
Net cash provided by (used in) financing activities	(280)	(198)	50
Foreign-currency effect on cash and cash equivalents	(1)	(70)	20
Net increase in cash and cash equivalents	675	230	1,517
CASH AND CASH EQUIVALENTS, END OF PERIOD	$ 3,444	$ 2,769	$2,539
SUPPLEMENTAL CASH FLOW INFORMATION:			
Cash paid for interest	$ 32	$ 64	$ 67
Cash paid for income taxes	48	53	24
Fixed assets acquired under capital leases and other financing arrangements	147	148	74
Fixed assets acquired under build-to-suit leases	188	72	15
Conversion of debt	—	605	1

See accompanying notes to consolidated financial statements.

AMAZON.COM, INC.

CONSOLIDATED STATEMENTS OF OPERATIONS
(in millions, except per share data)

	Year Ended December 31,		
	2009	2008	2007
Net sales	$24,509	$19,166	$14,835
Cost of sales	18,978	14,896	11,482
Gross profit	5,531	4,270	3,353
Operating expenses (1):			
Fulfillment	2,052	1,658	1,292
Marketing	680	482	344
Technology and content	1,240	1,033	818
General and administrative	328	279	235
Other operating expense (income), net	102	(24)	9
Total operating expenses	4,402	3,428	2,698
Income from operations	1,129	842	655
Interest income	37	83	90
Interest expense	(34)	(71)	(77)
Other income (expense), net	29	47	(8)
Total non-operating income (expense)	32	59	5
Income before income taxes	1,161	901	660
Provision for income taxes	(253)	(247)	(184)
Equity-method investment activity, net of tax	(6)	(9)	—
Net income	$ 902	$ 645	$ 476
Basic earnings per share	$ 2.08	$ 1.52	$ 1.15
Diluted earnings per share	$ 2.04	$ 1.49	$ 1.12
Weighted average shares used in computation of earnings per share:			
Basic	433	423	413
Diluted	442	432	424

(1) Includes stock-based compensation as follows:

Fulfillment	$ 79	$ 61	$ 39
Marketing	20	13	8
Technology and content	182	151	103
General and administrative	60	50	35

See accompanying notes to consolidated financial statements.

AMAZON.COM, INC.

CONSOLIDATED BALANCE SHEETS
(in millions, except per share data)

	December 31,	
	2009	2008
ASSETS		
Current assets:		
Cash and cash equivalents	$ 3,444	$2,769
Marketable securities	2,922	958
Inventories	2,171	1,399
Accounts receivable, net and other	988	827
Deferred tax assets	272	204
Total current assets	9,797	6,157
Fixed assets, net..	1,290	854
Deferred tax assets	18	145
Goodwill	1,234	438
Other assets	1,474	720
Total assets	$13,813	$8,314
LIABILITIES AND STOCKHOLDERS' EQUITY		
Current liabilities:		
Accounts payable	$ 5,605	$3,594
Accrued expenses and other	1,759	1,152
Total current liabilities	7,364	4,746
Long-term debt	109	409
Other long-term liabilities	1,083	487
Commitments and contingencies		
Stockholders' equity:		
Preferred stock, $0.01 par value:		
Authorized shares—500	—	—
Issued and outstanding shares—none		
Common stock, $0.01 par value:		
Authorized shares—5,000		
Issued shares—461 and 445	—	—
Outstanding shares—444 and 428	5	4
Treasury stock, at cost	(600)	(600)
Additional paid-in capital	5,736	4,121
Accumulated other comprehensive income (loss)	(56)	(123)
Retained earnings (accumulated deficit)	172	(730)
Total stockholders' equity	5,257	2,672
Total liabilities and stockholders' equity	$13,813	$8,314

See accompanying notes to consolidated financial statements.

AMAZON.COM, INC.
CONSOLIDATED STATEMENTS OF STOCKHOLDERS' EQUITY
(in millions)

	Common Stock Shares	Common Stock Amount	Treasury Stock	Additional Paid-In Capital	Accumulated Other Comprehensive Income (Loss)	Retained Earnings (Accumulated Deficit)	Total Stockholders' Equity
Balance at December 31, 2006	414	$ 4	$(252)	$2,517	$ (1)	$(1,837)	$ 431
Net income	—	—	—	—	—	476	476
Foreign currency translation losses, net of tax	—	—	—	—	(3)	—	(3)
Change in unrealized losses on available-for-sale securities, net of tax	—	—	—	—	8	—	8
Amortization of unrealized loss on terminated Euro Currency Swap, net of tax	—	—	—	—	1	—	1
Comprehensive income							482
Change in accounting principle	—	—	—	2	—	(14)	(12)
Unrecognized excess tax benefits from stock-based compensation	—	—	—	4	—	—	4
Exercise of common stock options and conversion of debt	8	—	—	92	—	—	92
Repurchase of common stock	(6)	—	(248)	—	—	—	(248)
Excess tax benefits from stock-based compensation	—	—	—	257	—	—	257
Stock-based compensation and issuance of employee benefit plan stock	—	—	—	191	—	—	191
Balance at December 31, 2007	416	4	(500)	3,063	5	(1,375)	1,197
Net income	—	—	—	—	—	645	645
Foreign currency translation losses, net of tax	—	—	—	—	(127)	—	(127)
Change in unrealized losses on available-for-sale securities, net of tax	—	—	—	—	(1)	—	(1)
Comprehensive income							517
Unrecognized excess tax benefits from stock-based compensation	—	—	—	(8)	—	—	(8)
Exercise of common stock options and conversion of debt	14	—	—	624	—	—	624
Repurchase of common stock	(2)	—	(100)	—	—	—	(100)
Excess tax benefits from stock-based compensation	—	—	—	154	—	—	154
Stock-based compensation and issuance of employee benefit plan stock	—	—	—	288	—	—	288
Balance at December 31, 2008	428	4	(600)	4,121	(123)	(730)	2,672
Net income	—	—	—	—	—	902	902
Foreign currency translation gains net of tax	—	—	—	—	62	—	62
Change in unrealized gains on available-for-sale securities, net of tax	—	—	—	—	4	—	4
Amortization of unrealized loss on terminated Euro Currency Swap, net of tax	—	—	—	—	1	—	1
Comprehensive income							969
Exercise of common stock options	7	—	—	19	—	—	19
Issuance of common stock for acquisition activity	9	1	—	1,144	—	—	1,145
Excess tax benefits from stock-based compensation	—	—	—	103	—	—	103
Stock-based compensation and issuance of employee benefit plan stock	—	—	—	349	—	—	349
Balance at December 31, 2009	444	$ 5	$(600)	$5,736	$ (56)	$ 172	$5,257

See accompanying notes to consolidated financial statements.

AMAZON.COM, INC.

NOTES TO CONSOLIDATED FINANCIAL STATEMENTS

Note 1—DESCRIPTION OF BUSINESS AND ACCOUNTING POLICIES

Description of Business

Amazon.com opened its virtual doors on the World Wide Web in July 1995 and offers Earth's Biggest Selection. We seek to be Earth's most customer-centric company for three primary customer sets: consumers, sellers, and developers. We serve consumers through our retail websites and focus on selection, price, and convenience. We also manufacture and sell the Kindle e-reader. We offer programs that enable sellers to sell their products on our websites and their own branded websites and to fulfill orders through us. We serve developers through Amazon Web Services, which provides access to technology infrastructure that developers can use to enable virtually any type of business. In addition, we generate revenue through co-branded credit card agreements and other marketing and promotional services, such as online advertising.

We have organized our operations into two principal segments: North America and International. See "Note 11—Segment Information."

Principles of Consolidation

The consolidated financial statements include the accounts of the Company, its wholly-owned subsidiaries, and those entities in which we have a variable interest and are the primary beneficiary. Intercompany balances and transactions have been eliminated.

Use of Estimates

The preparation of financial statements in conformity with U.S. GAAP requires estimates and assumptions that affect the reported amounts of assets and liabilities, revenues and expenses, and related disclosures of contingent liabilities in the consolidated financial statements and accompanying notes. Estimates are used for, but not limited to, valuation of investments, collectability of receivables, sales returns, incentive discount offers, valuation of inventory, depreciable lives of fixed assets and internally-developed software, valuation of acquired intangibles and goodwill, income taxes, stock-based compensation, and contingencies. Actual results could differ materially from those estimates.

Subsequent Events

We have evaluated subsequent events and transactions for potential recognition or disclosure in the financial statements through January 28, 2010, the day the financial statements were issued.

Earnings per Share

Basic earnings per share is calculated using our weighted-average outstanding common shares. Diluted earnings per share is calculated using our weighted-average outstanding common shares including the dilutive effect of stock awards as determined under the treasury stock method.

AMAZON.COM, INC.

NOTES TO CONSOLIDATED FINANCIAL STATEMENTS—(Continued)

The following table shows the calculation of diluted shares (in millions):

	Year Ended December 31,		
	2009	2008	2007
Shares used in computation of basic earnings per share	433	423	413
Total dilutive effect of outstanding stock awards (1)	9	9	11
Shares used in computation of diluted earnings per share	442	432	424

(1) Calculated using the treasury stock method, which assumes proceeds are used to reduce the dilutive effect of outstanding stock awards. Assumed proceeds include the unrecognized deferred compensation of stock awards, and assumed tax proceeds from excess stock-based compensation deductions.

Treasury Stock

We account for treasury stock under the cost method and include treasury stock as a component of stockholders' equity.

Cash and Cash Equivalents

We classify all highly liquid instruments, including money market funds that comply with Rule 2a-7 of the Investment Company Act of 1940, with an original maturity of three months or less at the time of purchase as cash equivalents.

Inventories

Inventories, consisting of products available for sale, are accounted for using primarily the FIFO method, and are valued at the lower of cost or market value. This valuation requires us to make judgments, based on currently-available information, about the likely method of disposition, such as through sales to individual customers, returns to product vendors, or liquidations, and expected recoverable values of each disposition category.

We provide fulfillment-related services in connection with certain of our sellers' programs. The third party seller maintains ownership of their inventory, regardless of whether fulfillment is provided by us or the third party seller, and therefore these products are not included in our inventories.

Accounts Receivable, Net, and Other

Included in "Accounts receivable, net, and other" on our consolidated balance sheets are amounts primarily related to vendor and customer receivables. At December 31, 2009 and 2008, vendor receivables, net, were $495 million and $400 million, and customer receivables, net, were $341 million and $311 million.

Allowance for Doubtful Accounts

We estimate losses on receivables based on known troubled accounts and historical experience of losses incurred. The allowance for doubtful customer and vendor receivables was $72 million and $81 million at December 31, 2009 and 2008.

AMAZON.COM, INC.

NOTES TO CONSOLIDATED FINANCIAL STATEMENTS—(Continued)

Internal-use Software and Website Development

Costs incurred to develop software for internal use and our websites are capitalized and amortized over the estimated useful life of the software. Costs related to design or maintenance of internal-use software and website development are expensed as incurred. For the years ended 2009, 2008, and 2007, we capitalized $187 million (including $35 million of stock-based compensation), $187 million (including $27 million of stock-based compensation), and $129 million (including $21 million of stock-based compensation) of costs associated with internal-use software and website development. Amortization of previously capitalized amounts was $172 million, $143 million, and $116 million for 2009, 2008, and 2007.

Depreciation of Fixed Assets

Fixed assets include assets such as furniture and fixtures, heavy equipment, technology infrastructure, internal-use software and website development. Depreciation is recorded on a straight-line basis over the estimated useful lives of the assets (generally two years for assets such as internal-use software, three years for our technology infrastructure, five years for furniture and fixtures, and ten years for heavy equipment). Depreciation expense is generally classified within the corresponding operating expense categories on our consolidated statements of operations.

Leases and Asset Retirement Obligations

We categorize leases at their inception as either operating or capital leases. On certain of our lease agreements, we may receive rent holidays and other incentives. We recognize lease costs on a straight-line basis without regard to deferred payment terms, such as rent holidays that defer the commencement date of required payments. Additionally, incentives we receive are treated as a reduction of our costs over the term of the agreement. Leasehold improvements are capitalized at cost and amortized over the lesser of their expected useful life or the life of the lease, excluding renewal periods. We establish assets and liabilities for the estimated construction costs incurred under build-to-suit lease arrangements to the extent we are involved in the construction of structural improvements or take some level of construction risk prior to commencement of a lease.

We establish assets and liabilities for the present value of estimated future costs to return certain of our leased facilities to their original condition. Such assets are depreciated over the lease period into operating expense, and the recorded liabilities are accreted to the future value of the estimated restoration costs.

Goodwill

We evaluate goodwill for impairment annually and when an event occurs or circumstances change that indicate that the carrying value may not be recoverable. We test goodwill for impairment by first comparing the book value of net assets to the fair value of the reporting units. If the fair value is determined to be less than the book value, a second step is performed to compute the amount of impairment as the difference between the estimated fair value of goodwill and the carrying value. We estimate the fair value of the reporting units using discounted cash flows. Forecasts of future cash flow are based on our best estimate of future net sales and operating expenses, based primarily on estimated category expansion, pricing, market segment penetration and general economic conditions.

We conduct our annual impairment test as of October 1 of each year, and have determined there to be no impairment for any of the periods presented. There were no events or circumstances from the date of our assessment through December 31, 2009 that would impact this conclusion.

AMAZON.COM, INC.

NOTES TO CONSOLIDATED FINANCIAL STATEMENTS—(Continued)

See "Note 4—Acquisitions, Goodwill, and Acquired Intangible Assets."

Other Assets

Included in "Other assets" on our consolidated balance sheets are amounts primarily related to marketable securities restricted for longer than one year, the majority of which are attributable to collateralization of bank guarantees and debt related to our international operations; acquired intangible assets, net of amortization; deferred costs; certain equity investments; and intellectual property rights, net of amortization.

Investments

We generally invest our excess cash in investment grade short to intermediate term fixed income securities and AAA-rated money market funds. Such investments are included in "Cash and cash equivalents," or "Marketable securities" on the accompanying consolidated balance sheets, classified as available-for-sale, and reported at fair value with unrealized gains and losses included in "Accumulated other comprehensive income (loss)."

Equity investments are accounted for using the equity method of accounting if the investment gives us the ability to exercise significant influence, but not control, over an investee. The total of these investments in equity-method investees, including identifiable intangible assets, deferred tax liabilities and goodwill, is classified on our consolidated balance sheets as "Other assets." Our share of the investees' earnings or losses and amortization of the related intangible assets, if any, is classified as "Equity-method investment activity, net of tax" on our consolidated statements of operations.

Equity investments without readily determinable fair values for which we do not have the ability to exercise significant influence are accounted for using the cost method of accounting. Under the cost method, investments are carried at cost and are adjusted only for other-than-temporary declines in fair value, distributions of earnings, and additional investments.

Equity investments that have readily determinable fair values are classified as available-for-sale and are recorded at fair value with unrealized gains and losses, net of tax, included in "Accumulated other comprehensive loss."

We periodically evaluate whether declines in fair values of our investments below their cost are other-than-temporary. This evaluation consists of several qualitative and quantitative factors regarding the severity and duration of the unrealized loss as well as our ability and intent to hold the investment until a forecasted recovery occurs. Additionally, we assess whether it is more likely than not we will be required to sell any investment before recovery of its amortized cost basis. Factors considered include quoted market prices; recent financial results and operating trends; other publicly available information; implied values from any recent transactions or offers of investee securities; other conditions that may affect the value of our investments; duration and severity of the decline in value; and our strategy and intentions for holding the investment.

Long-Lived Assets

Long-lived assets, other than goodwill, are reviewed for impairment whenever events or changes in circumstances indicate that the carrying amount of the assets might not be recoverable. Conditions that would necessitate an impairment assessment include a significant decline in the observable market value of an asset, a significant change in the extent or manner in which an asset is used, or any other significant adverse change that would indicate that the carrying amount of an asset or group of assets may not be recoverable.

AMAZON.COM, INC.

NOTES TO CONSOLIDATED FINANCIAL STATEMENTS—(Continued)

For long-lived assets used in operations, impairment losses are only recorded if the asset's carrying amount is not recoverable through its undiscounted, probability-weighted future cash flows. We measure the impairment loss based on the difference between the carrying amount and estimated fair value.

Long-lived assets are considered held for sale when certain criteria are met, including when management has committed to a plan to sell the asset, the asset is available for sale in its immediate condition, and the sale is probable within one year of the reporting date. Assets held for sale are reported at the lower of cost or fair value less costs to sell. Assets held for sale were not significant at December 31, 2009 or 2008.

Accrued Expenses and Other

Included in "Accrued expenses and other" at December 31, 2009 and 2008 were liabilities of $347 million and $270 million for unredeemed gift certificates. We reduce the liability for a gift certificate when it is applied to an order. If a gift certificate is not redeemed, we recognize revenue when it expires or, for a certificate without an expiration date, when the likelihood of its redemption becomes remote, generally two years from date of issuance.

Unearned Revenue

Unearned revenue is recorded when payments are received in advance of performing our service obligations and is recognized over the service period. Current unearned revenue is included in "Accrued expenses and other" and non-current unearned revenue is included in "Other long-term liabilities" on our consolidated balance sheets. Current unearned revenue was $511 million and $191 million at December 31, 2009 and 2008. Non-current unearned revenue was $201 million and $46 million at December 31, 2009 and 2008.

Income Taxes

Income tax expense includes U.S. and international income taxes. Except as required under U.S. tax law, we do not provide for U.S. taxes on our undistributed earnings of foreign subsidiaries that have not been previously taxed since we intend to invest such undistributed earnings indefinitely outside of the U.S. Undistributed earnings of foreign subsidiaries that are indefinitely invested outside of the U.S were $912 million at December 31, 2009. Determination of the unrecognized deferred tax liability that would be incurred if such amounts were repatriated is not practicable.

Deferred income tax balances reflect the effects of temporary differences between the carrying amounts of assets and liabilities and their tax bases and are stated at enacted tax rates expected to be in effect when taxes are actually paid or recovered.

Deferred tax assets are evaluated for future realization and reduced by a valuation allowance to the extent we believe a portion will not be realized. We consider many factors when assessing the likelihood of future realization of our deferred tax assets, including our recent cumulative earnings experience and expectations of future taxable income and capital gains by taxing jurisdiction, the carry-forward periods available to us for tax reporting purposes, and other relevant factors. We allocate our valuation allowance to current and long-term deferred tax assets on a pro-rata basis.

We utilize a two-step approach to recognizing and measuring uncertain tax positions (tax contingencies). The first step is to evaluate the tax position for recognition by determining if the weight of available evidence indicates it is more likely than not that the position will be sustained on audit, including resolution of related

46

AMAZON.COM, INC.

NOTES TO CONSOLIDATED FINANCIAL STATEMENTS—(Continued)

appeals or litigation processes. The second step is to measure the tax benefit as the largest amount which is more than 50% likely of being realized upon ultimate settlement. We consider many factors when evaluating and estimating our tax positions and tax benefits, which may require periodic adjustments and which may not accurately forecast actual outcomes. We include interest and penalties related to our tax contingencies in income tax expense.

Fair Value of Financial Instruments

Fair value is defined as the price that would be received to sell an asset or paid to transfer a liability in an orderly transaction between market participants at the measurement date. To increase the comparability of fair value measures, the following hierarchy prioritizes the inputs to valuation methodologies used to measure fair value:

Level 1—Valuations based on quoted prices for identical assets and liabilities in active markets.

Level 2—Valuations based on observable inputs other than quoted prices included in Level 1, such as quoted prices for similar assets and liabilities in active markets, quoted prices for identical or similar assets and liabilities in markets that are not active, or other inputs that are observable or can be corroborated by observable market data.

Level 3—Valuations based on unobservable inputs reflecting our own assumptions, consistent with reasonably available assumptions made by other market participants. These valuations require significant judgment.

We measure the fair value of money market funds based on quoted prices in active markets for identical assets or liabilities. All other financial instruments were valued based on quoted market prices of similar instruments and other significant inputs derived from or corroborated by observable market data.

Revenue

We recognize revenue from product sales or services rendered when the following four revenue recognition criteria are met: persuasive evidence of an arrangement exists, delivery has occurred or services have been rendered, the selling price is fixed or determinable, and collectability is reasonably assured. Revenue arrangements with multiple deliverables are divided into separate units of accounting if the deliverables in the arrangement meet the following criteria: there is standalone value to the delivered item; there is objective and reliable evidence of the fair value of the undelivered items; and delivery of any undelivered item is probable.

We evaluate whether it is appropriate to record the gross amount of product sales and related costs or the net amount earned as commissions. Generally, when we are primarily obligated in a transaction, are subject to inventory risk, have latitude in establishing prices and selecting suppliers, or have several but not all of these indicators, revenue is recorded gross. If we are not primarily obligated and amounts earned are determined using a fixed percentage, a fixed-payment schedule, or a combination of the two, we generally record the net amounts as commissions earned.

Product sales and shipping revenues, net of promotional discounts, rebates, and return allowances, are recorded when the products are shipped and title passes to customers. Retail sales to customers are made pursuant to a sales contract that provides for transfer of both title and risk of loss upon our delivery to the carrier. Return allowances, which reduce product revenue, are estimated using historical experience. Revenue from product sales and services rendered is recorded net of sales and consumption taxes. Amounts received in advance for subscription services, including amounts received for Amazon Prime and other membership programs, are

AMAZON.COM, INC.

NOTES TO CONSOLIDATED FINANCIAL STATEMENTS—(Continued)

deferred and recognized as revenue over the subscription term. For our products with multiple elements, where objective and reliable evidence of fair value for the undelivered elements cannot be established, we recognize the revenue and related cost over the expected life of the product.

We periodically provide incentive offers to our customers to encourage purchases. Such offers include current discount offers, such as percentage discounts off current purchases, inducement offers, such as offers for future discounts subject to a minimum current purchase, and other similar offers. Current discount offers, when accepted by our customers, are treated as a reduction to the purchase price of the related transaction, while inducement offers, when accepted by our customers, are treated as a reduction to purchase price based on estimated future redemption rates. Redemption rates are estimated using our historical experience for similar inducement offers. Current discount offers and inducement offers are presented as a net amount in "Net sales."

Commissions and per-unit fees received from sellers and similar amounts earned through other seller sites are recognized when the item is sold by seller and our collectability is reasonably assured. We record an allowance for estimated refunds on such commissions using historical experience.

Shipping Activities

Outbound shipping charges to customers are included in "Net sales" and were $924 million, $835 million, and $740 million for 2009, 2008, and 2007. Outbound shipping-related costs are included in "Cost of sales" and totaled $1.8 billion, $1.5 billion, and $1.2 billion for 2009, 2008, and 2007. The net cost to us of shipping activities was $849 million, $630 million, and $434 million for 2009, 2008 and 2007.

Cost of Sales

Cost of sales consists of the purchase price of consumer products and content sold by us, inbound and outbound shipping charges, packaging supplies, and costs incurred in operating and staffing our fulfillment and customer service centers on behalf of other businesses. Shipping charges to receive products from our suppliers are included in our inventory, and recognized as "Cost of sales" upon sale of products to our customers. Payment processing and related transaction costs, including those associated with seller transactions, are classified in "Fulfillment" on our consolidated statements of operations.

Vendor Agreements

We have agreements to receive cash consideration from certain of our vendors, including rebates and cooperative marketing reimbursements. We generally consider amounts received from our vendors as a reduction of the prices we pay for their products and, therefore, we record such amounts as either a reduction of "Cost of sales" on our consolidated statements of operations, or, if the product inventory is still on hand, as a reduction of the carrying value of inventory. Vendor rebates are typically dependent upon reaching minimum purchase thresholds. We evaluate the likelihood of reaching purchase thresholds using past experience and current year forecasts. When volume rebates can be reasonably estimated, we record a portion of the rebate as we make progress towards the purchase threshold.

When we receive direct reimbursements for costs incurred by us in advertising the vendor's product or service, the amount we receive is recorded as an offset to "Marketing" on our consolidated statements of operations.

AMAZON.COM, INC.

NOTES TO CONSOLIDATED FINANCIAL STATEMENTS—(Continued)

Fulfillment

Fulfillment costs represent those costs incurred in operating and staffing our fulfillment and customer service centers, including costs attributable to buying, receiving, inspecting, and warehousing inventories; picking, packaging, and preparing customer orders for shipment; payment processing and related transaction costs, including costs associated with our guarantee for certain seller transactions; and responding to inquiries from customers. Fulfillment costs also include amounts paid to third parties that assist us in fulfillment and customer service operations. Certain of our fulfillment-related costs that are incurred on behalf of other businesses are classified as cost of sales rather than fulfillment.

Marketing

Marketing costs consist primarily of online advertising, including through our Associates program, sponsored search, portal advertising, and other initiatives. We pay commissions to participants in our Associates program when their customer referrals result in product sales and classify such costs as "Marketing" on our consolidated statements of operations. We also participate in cooperative advertising arrangements with certain of our vendors, and other third parties.

Marketing expenses also consist of public relations expenditures; payroll and related expenses for personnel engaged in marketing, business development, and selling activities; and to a lesser extent, traditional advertising.

Advertising and other promotional costs, which consist primarily of online advertising, are expensed as incurred, and were $593 million, $420 million, and $306 million, in 2009, 2008, and 2007. Prepaid advertising costs were not significant at December 31, 2009 and 2008.

Technology and Content

Technology and content expenses consist principally of payroll and related expenses for employees involved in, application development, category expansion, editorial content, buying, merchandising selection, and systems support, as well as costs associated with the compute, storage and telecommunications infrastructure used internally and supporting Amazon Web Services.

Technology and content costs are expensed as incurred, except for certain costs relating to the development of internal-use software and website development, including software used to upgrade and enhance our websites and processes supporting our business, which are capitalized and amortized over two years.

General and Administrative

General and administrative expenses consist of payroll and related expenses for employees involved in general corporate functions, including accounting, finance, tax, legal, and human relations, among others; costs associated with use by these functions of facilities and equipment, such as depreciation expense and rent; professional fees and litigation costs; and other general corporate costs.

Stock-Based Compensation

Compensation cost for all stock-based awards is measured at fair value on date of grant and recognized over the service period for awards expected to vest. The fair value of restricted stock units is determined based on the number of shares granted and the quoted price of our common stock. Such value is recognized as expense over the service period, net of estimated forfeitures, using the accelerated method. The estimation of stock awards that

AMAZON.COM, INC.

NOTES TO CONSOLIDATED FINANCIAL STATEMENTS—(Continued)

will ultimately vest requires judgment, and to the extent actual results or updated estimates differ from our current estimates, such amounts will be recorded as a cumulative adjustment in the period estimates are revised. We consider many factors when estimating expected forfeitures, including types of awards, employee class, and historical experience.

Other Income (Expense), Net

Other income (expense), net, consists primarily of gains and losses on sales of marketable securities, foreign currency transaction gains and losses, and other losses.

Foreign Currency

We have internationally-focused websites for the United Kingdom, Germany, France, Japan, Canada, and China. Net sales generated from internationally-focused websites, as well as most of the related expenses directly incurred from those operations, are denominated in the functional currencies of the resident countries. The functional currency of our subsidiaries that either operate or support these international websites is the same as the local currency. Assets and liabilities of these subsidiaries are translated into U.S. Dollars at period-end exchange rates, and revenues and expenses are translated at average rates prevailing throughout the period. Translation adjustments are included in "Accumulated other comprehensive income (loss)," a separate component of stockholders' equity, and in the "Foreign currency effect on cash and cash equivalents," on our consolidated statements of cash flows. Transaction gains and losses arising from transactions denominated in a currency other than the functional currency of the entity involved are included in "Other income (expense), net" on our consolidated statements of operations.

Gains and losses arising from intercompany foreign currency transactions are included in net income. In connection with the remeasurement of intercompany balances, we recorded gains of $5 million, $23 million and $32 million in 2009, 2008 and 2007.

Recent Accounting Pronouncements

In December 2007, the Financial Accounting Standards Board ("FASB") issued Statements of Financial Accounting Standards ("SFAS") No. 141 (R), *Business Combinations*, codified as Accounting Standards Codification ("ASC") 805, *Business Combinations,* and SFAS No. 160, *Noncontrolling Interests in Consolidated Financial Statements*, codified as ASC 810, *Consolidations.* SFAS No. 141 (R) requires an acquirer to measure the identifiable assets acquired, the liabilities assumed, and any noncontrolling interest in the acquired entity at their fair values on the acquisition date, with goodwill being the excess value over the net identifiable assets acquired. SFAS No. 160 clarifies that a noncontrolling interest in a subsidiary should be reported as equity in the consolidated financial statements. The calculation of earnings per share will continue to be based on income amounts attributable to the parent. SFAS No. 141 (R) impacted acquisitions closed on or after January 1, 2009. Adoption did not have a material impact on our consolidated financial statements on the date of adoption.

In December 2009, the FASB issued Accounting Standards Update ("ASU") 2009-17, which codifies SFAS No. 167, *Amendments to FASB Interpretation No. 46(R)* issued in June 2009. ASU 2009-17 requires a qualitative approach to identifying a controlling financial interest in a variable interest entity ("VIE"), and requires ongoing assessment of whether an entity is a VIE and whether an interest in a VIE makes the holder the primary beneficiary of the VIE. ASU 2009-17 is effective for annual reporting periods beginning after November 15, 2009. We do not expect the adoption of ASU 2009-17 to have a material impact on our consolidated financial statements.

AMAZON.COM, INC.

NOTES TO CONSOLIDATED FINANCIAL STATEMENTS—(Continued)

In October 2009, the FASB issued ASU 2009-13, which amends ASC Topic 605, *Revenue Recognition.* Under this standard, management is no longer required to obtain vendor-specific objective evidence or third party evidence of fair value for each deliverable in an arrangement with multiple elements, and where evidence is not available we may now estimate the proportion of the selling price attributable to each deliverable. We have chosen to prospectively adopt this standard as of January 1, 2010.

Sales of our Kindle e-reader are considered arrangements with multiple elements which include the device, wireless access and delivery and software upgrades. The revenue related to the device, which is the substantial portion of the total sale price, and related costs will be recognized at time of delivery. Revenue for the wireless access and delivery and software upgrades will continue to be amortized over the life of the device, which remains estimated at two years.

We cannot reasonably estimate the effect of adopting this standard on future financial periods as the impact will vary based on actual volume of activity under these types of revenue arrangements.

For arrangements entered into prior to the adoption of the new accounting standard and for which revenue had been previously deferred, we will recognize $508 million throughout 2010 and 2011.

In January 2010, the FASB issued ASU 2010-6, *Improving Disclosures About Fair Value Measurements*, which requires reporting entities to make new disclosures about recurring or nonrecurring fair-value measurements including significant transfers into and out of Level 1 and Level 2 fair-value measurements and information on purchases, sales, issuances, and settlements on a gross basis in the reconciliation of Level 3 fair- value measurements. ASU 2010-6 is effective for annual reporting periods beginning after December 15, 2009, except for Level 3 reconciliation disclosures which are effective for annual periods beginning after December 15, 2010. We do not expect the adoption of ASU 2010-6 to have a material impact on our consolidated financial statements.

Note 2—CASH, CASH EQUIVALENTS, AND MARKETABLE SECURITIES

As of December 31, 2009 and 2008 our cash, cash equivalents, and marketable securities primarily consisted of cash, government and government agency securities, AAA-rated money market funds and other investment grade securities. Such amounts are recorded at fair value. The following table summarizes, by major security type, our cash, cash equivalents and marketable securities (in millions):

	December 31, 2009			
	Cost or Amortized Cost	Gross Unrealized Gains	Gross Unrealized Losses	Total Estimated Fair Value
Cash	$ 391	$—	$—	$ 391
Money market funds	2,750	—	—	2,750
Foreign government and agency securities	1,992	7	—	1,999
Corporate debt securities (1)	206	5	—	211
U.S. government and agency securities	1,268	5	(5)	1,268
Asset-backed securities	44	2	—	46
Other fixed income securities	6	—	—	6
Equity securities	2	—	(1)	1
	$6,659	$ 19	$ (6)	$6,672
Less: Long-term marketable securities (2)				(306)
Total cash, cash equivalents, and marketable securities				$6,366

51

AMAZON.COM, INC.

NOTES TO CONSOLIDATED FINANCIAL STATEMENTS—(Continued)

	December 31, 2008			
	Cost or Amortized Cost	Gross Unrealized Gains	Gross Unrealized Losses	Total Estimated Fair Value
Cash	$ 355	$—	$—	$ 355
Money market funds	1,682	—	—	1,682
Foreign government and agency securities	1,120	8	—	1,128
Corporate debt securities (1)	194	2	(2)	194
U.S. government and agency securities	589	5	—	594
Asset-backed securities	62	—	(4)	58
Other fixed income securities	23	—	—	23
Equity securities	2	—	(1)	1
	$4,027	$ 15	$ (7)	$4,035
Less: Long-term marketable securities (2)				(308)
Total cash, cash equivalents, and marketable securities				$3,727

(1) Corporate debt securities include investments in financial, insurance, and corporate institutions. No single issuer represents a significant portion of the total corporate debt securities portfolio.

(2) We are required to pledge or otherwise restrict a portion of our marketable securities as collateral for standby letters of credit, guarantees, debt, and real estate lease agreements. We classify cash and marketable securities with use restrictions of twelve months or longer as non-current "Other assets" on our consolidated balance sheets. See "Note 7—Commitments and Contingencies."

The following table summarizes gross gains and gross losses realized on sales of available-for-sale marketable securities (in millions):

	Year Ended December 31,		
	2009	2008	2007
Realized gains	$ 4	$9	$2
Realized losses	—	7	3

The following table summarizes contractual maturities of our cash equivalent and marketable fixed-income securities as of December 31, 2009 (in millions):

	Amortized Cost	Estimated Fair Value
Due within one year	$4,908	$4,909
Due after one year through five years	1,358	1,371
	$6,266	$6,280

AMAZON.COM, INC.

NOTES TO CONSOLIDATED FINANCIAL STATEMENTS—(Continued)

The following table summarizes, by major security type, our assets that are measured at fair value on a recurring basis and are categorized using the fair value hierarchy (in millions):

		December 31, 2009			
	Cash	Level 1 Estimated Fair Value	Level 2 Estimated Fair Value	Level 3 Estimated Fair Value	Total Estimated Fair Value
Cash	$391	$ —	$ —	$—	$ 391
Money market funds	—	2,750	—	—	2,750
Foreign government and agency securities	—	—	1,999	—	1,999
Corporate debt securities	—	—	211	—	211
U.S. government and agency securities	—	—	1,268	—	1,268
Asset-backed securities	—	—	46	—	46
Other fixed income securities	—	—	6	—	6
Equity securities	—	1	—	—	1
	$391	$2,751	$3,530	$—	$6,672

		December 31, 2008			
	Cash	Level 1 Estimated Fair Value	Level 2 Estimated Fair Value	Level 3 Estimated Fair Value	Total Estimated Fair Value
Cash	$355	$ —	$ —	$—	$ 355
Money market funds	—	1,682	—	—	1,682
Foreign government and agency securities	—	—	1,128	—	1,128
Corporate debt securities	—	—	194	—	194
U.S. government and agency securities	—	—	594	—	594
Asset-backed securities	—	—	58	—	58
Other fixed income securities	—	—	23	—	23
Equity securities	—	1	—	—	1
	$355	$1,683	$1,997	$—	$4,035

AMAZON.COM, INC.

NOTES TO CONSOLIDATED FINANCIAL STATEMENTS—(Continued)

Note 3—FIXED ASSETS

Fixed assets, at cost, consisted of the following (in millions):

	December 31,	
	2009	2008
Gross Fixed Assets:		
Fulfillment and customer service	$ 551	$ 564
Technology infrastructure	551	348
Internal-use software, content, and website development	398	331
Construction in progress (1)	278	87
Other corporate assets	137	79
Gross fixed assets	1,915	1,409
Accumulated Depreciation:		
Fulfillment and customer service	202	254
Technology infrastructure	178	82
Internal-use software, content, and website development	207	159
Other corporate assets	38	60
Total accumulated depreciation	625	555
Total fixed assets, net	$1,290	$ 854

---

(1) We capitalize construction in progress and record a corresponding long-term liability for certain lease agreements, including our Seattle, Washington corporate office space subject to leases scheduled to begin upon completion of development between 2010 and 2013. See "Note 6—Other Long-Term Liabilities" and "Note 7—Commitments and Contingencies" for further discussion.

Depreciation expense on fixed assets was $384 million, $311 million, and $258 million, which includes amortization of fixed assets acquired under capital lease obligations of $88 million, $50 million, and $40 million for 2009, 2008, and 2007. Gross assets remaining under capital leases were $430 million and $304 million at December 31, 2009 and 2008. Accumulated depreciation associated with capital leases was $184 million and $116 million at December 31, 2009 and 2008.

Note 4—ACQUISITIONS, GOODWILL, AND ACQUIRED INTANGIBLE ASSETS

2009 Acquisition Activity

On November 1, 2009, we acquired 100% of the outstanding equity of Zappos.com, Inc. ("Zappos"), in exchange for shares of our common stock, to expand our presence in softline retail categories, such as shoes and apparel.

The fair value of Zappos' stock options assumed was determined using the Black-Scholes model. The following table summarizes the consideration paid for Zappos (in millions):

Stock issued	$1,079
Assumed stock options, net	55
	$1,134

AMAZON.COM, INC.

NOTES TO CONSOLIDATED FINANCIAL STATEMENTS—(Continued)

The purchase price was allocated to the tangible assets and intangible assets acquired and liabilities assumed based on their estimated fair values on the acquisition date, with the remaining unallocated purchase price recorded as goodwill. The fair value assigned to identifiable intangible assets acquired has been determined primarily by using the income approach. Purchased identifiable intangible assets are amortized on a straight-line and accelerated basis over their respective useful lives.

The following summarizes the allocation of the Zappos purchase price (in millions):

Goodwill	$ 778
Other net assets acquired	83
Deferred tax liabilities net	(167)
Intangible assets (1):	
Marketing-related	223
Contract-based	103
Customer-related	114
	$1,134

_____

(1) Acquired intangible assets have estimated useful lives of between 1 and 10 years.

Zappos' financial results have been included in our consolidated statements of income as of November 1, 2009. The following pro forma financial information presents the results as if the Zappos acquisition had occurred at the beginning of each year presented (in millions):

	Year Ended December 31,	
	2009	**2008**
Net sales	$25,064	$19,801
Net income	853	606

We acquired certain additional companies during 2009 for an aggregate purchase price of $26 million, resulting in goodwill of $16 million and acquired intangible assets of $5 million. The results of operations of each of the businesses acquired have been included in our consolidated results from each transactions closing date forward. The effect of these acquisitions on consolidated net sales and operating income during 2009 was not significant.

2008 and 2007 Acquisition Activity

We acquired certain companies during 2008 for an aggregate purchase price of $432 million, resulting in goodwill of $210 million and acquired intangible assets of $162 million.

We acquired certain companies during 2007 for an aggregate purchase price of $33 million, resulting in goodwill of $21 million and acquired intangible assets of $18 million. We also made principal payments of $13 million on acquired debt in connection with one of these acquisitions.

The results of operations of each of the businesses acquired in 2008 and 2007 have been included in our consolidated results from each transaction closing date forward. The effect of these acquisitions on consolidated net sales and operating income during 2008 and 2007 was not significant.

AMAZON.COM, INC.

NOTES TO CONSOLIDATED FINANCIAL STATEMENTS—(Continued)

Goodwill

The following summarizes our goodwill activity in 2009 (in millions):

Goodwill—January 1, 2009	$ 438
New acquisitions	794
Other adjustments (1)	2
Goodwill—December 31, 2009	$1,234

(1) Primarily includes changes in foreign exchange for goodwill in our International segment.

At December 31, 2009 and December 31, 2008, approximately 9% and 22% of our acquired goodwill related to our International segment.

Intangible Assets

Acquired intangible assets, included within "Other assets" on our consolidated balance sheets, consist of the following:

	December 31,						
	2009				**2008**		
	Weighted Average Life Remaining	Acquired Intangibles, Gross (1)	Accumulated Amortization (1)	Acquired Intangibles, Net	Acquired Intangibles, Gross (1)	Accumulated Amortization (1)	Acquired Intangibles, Net
				(in millions)			
Marketing-related	9.5	$249	$(11)	$238	$ 23	$ (4)	$ 19
Contract-based	3	166	(20)	146	62	(8)	54
Technology and content	3.1	15	(7)	8	10	(5)	5
Customer-related	4.8	215	(40)	175	97	(15)	82
Acquired intangibles (2)	7.3	$645	$(78)	$567	$192	$(32)	$160

(1) Excludes the original cost and accumulated amortization of fully-amortized intangibles.
(2) Intangible assets have estimated useful lives of between 1 and 13 years.

Amortization expense for acquired intangibles was $48 million, $29 million, and $13 million in 2009, 2008, and 2007. Expected future amortization expense of acquired intangible assets as of December 31, 2009 is as follows (in millions):

Year Ended December 31,	
2010	$100
2011	90
2012	74
2013	69
2014	58
Thereafter	176
	$567

AMAZON.COM, INC.

NOTES TO CONSOLIDATED FINANCIAL STATEMENTS—(Continued)

Note 5—LONG-TERM DEBT

Our long-term debt is summarized as follows:

	December 31,	
	2009	**2008**
	(in millions)	
6.875% PEACS	$—	$335
Other long-term debt	131	133
	131	468
Less current portion of long-term debt	(22)	(59)
	$109	$409

In February 2008 our Board of Directors authorized a debt repurchase program, replacing our previous debt repurchase authorization in its entirety, and pursuant to which we redeemed for cash the remaining €240 million ($319 million based on the Euro to U.S. Dollar exchange rate on the date of redemption) in principal of our 6.875% PEACS in 2009, and we redeemed the remaining principal amount of $899 million of our outstanding 4.75% Convertible Subordinated Notes in 2008.

Other long-term debt relates to amounts borrowed to fund certain international operations.

Note 6—OTHER LONG-TERM LIABILITIES

Our other long-term liabilities are summarized as follows:

	December 31,	
	2009	**2008**
	(in millions)	
Tax contingencies	$ 202	$144
Long-term capital lease obligations	143	124
Construction liability	278	87
Other	460	132
	$1,083	$487

Tax Contingencies

As of December 31, 2009 and 2008, we have provided tax reserves for tax contingencies, inclusive of accrued interest and penalties, of approximately $202 million and $144 million for U.S. and foreign income taxes. These contingencies primarily relate to transfer pricing, state income taxes, and research and development credits. See "Note 10—Income Taxes" for discussion of tax contingencies.

AMAZON.COM, INC.

NOTES TO CONSOLIDATED FINANCIAL STATEMENTS—(Continued)

Capital Leases

Certain of our equipment fixed assets, primarily related to technology infrastructure, have been acquired under capital leases. Long-term capital lease obligations are as follows:

	December 31, 2009
	(in millions)
Gross capital lease obligations	$ 276
Less imputed interest	(14)
Present value of net minimum lease payments	262
Less current portion	(119)
Total long-term capital lease obligations	$ 143

Construction Liabilities

We capitalize construction in progress and record a corresponding long-term liability for certain lease agreements, including our Seattle, Washington corporate office space subject to leases scheduled to begin upon completion of development between 2010 and 2013.

For build-to-suit lease arrangements where we are involved in the construction of structural improvements prior to the commencement of the lease or take some level of construction risk, we are considered the owner of the assets during the construction period. Accordingly, as the landlord incurs the construction project costs, the assets and corresponding financial obligation are recorded in "Fixed assets, net" and "Other long-term liabilities" on our consolidated balance sheet. Once the construction is completed, if the lease meets certain "sale-leaseback" criteria, we will remove the asset and related financial obligation from the balance sheet and treat the building lease as an operating lease. If upon completion of construction, the project does not meet the "sale-leaseback" criteria, the leased property will be treated as a capital lease for financial reporting purposes.

The remainder of our other long-term liabilities primarily include deferred tax liabilities, unearned revenue, asset retirement obligations, and deferred rental liabilities.

Note 7—COMMITMENTS AND CONTINGENCIES

Commitments

We lease office, fulfillment center, and data center facilities and fixed assets under non-cancelable operating and capital leases. Rental expense under operating lease agreements was $171 million, $158 million, and $141 million for 2009, 2008, and 2007.

In December 2007, we entered into a series of leases and other agreements for the lease of corporate office space to be developed in Seattle, Washington with initial terms of up to 16 years commencing on completion of development between 2010 and 2013, with options to extend for two five-year periods. We expect to occupy approximately 1.7 million square feet of office space. We also have an option to lease up to an additional approximately 500,000 square feet at rates based on fair market values at the time the option is exercised, subject to certain conditions. In addition, if interest rates exceed a certain threshold, we have the option to provide financing for some of the buildings.

AMAZON.COM, INC.

NOTES TO CONSOLIDATED FINANCIAL STATEMENTS—(Continued)

The following summarizes our principal contractual commitments, excluding open orders for inventory purchases that support normal operations, as of December 31, 2009:

	Year Ended December 31,						
	2010	**2011**	**2012**	**2013**	**2014**	**Thereafter**	**Total**
				(in millions)			
Operating and capital commitments:							
Debt principal and interest	$ 31	$ 47	$ 36	$ 36	$—	$ —	$ 150
Capital leases, including interest	130	95	44	8	3	—	280
Operating leases	162	146	130	122	115	317	992
Other commitments (1)(2)	187	101	93	89	88	1,181	1,739
Total commitments	$510	$389	$303	$255	$206	$1,498	$3,161

(1) Includes the estimated timing and amounts of payments for rent, operating expenses, and tenant improvements associated with approximately 1.7 million square feet of corporate office space. The amount of space available and our financial and other obligations under the lease agreements are affected by various factors, including government approvals and permits, interest rates, development costs and other expenses and our exercise of certain rights under the lease agreements.

(2) Excludes $181 million of tax contingencies for which we cannot make a reasonably reliable estimate of the amount and period of payment, if any.

Pledged Securities

We have pledged or otherwise restricted a portion of our cash and marketable securities as collateral for standby letters of credit, guarantees, debt, and real estate leases. We classify cash and marketable securities with use restrictions of twelve months or longer as non-current "Other assets" on our consolidated balance sheets. The amount required to be pledged for certain real estate lease agreements changes over the life of our leases based on our credit rating and changes in our market capitalization. Information about collateral required to be pledged under these agreements is as follows:

	Standby and Trade Letters of Credit and Guarantees	**Debt (1)**	**Real Estate Leases (2)**	**Total**
		(in millions)		
Balance at December 31, 2008	$138	$160	$10	$308
Net change in collateral pledged	4	(3)	(6)	(5)
Balance at December 31, 2009	$142	$157	$ 4	$303

(1) Represents collateral for certain debt related to our international operations.

(2) At December 31, 2009, our market capitalization was $59.8 billion. The required amount of collateral to be pledged will increase by $1.5 million if our market capitalization is equal to or below $40 billion, an additional $5 million if our market capitalization is equal to or below $18 billion, and an additional $6 million if our market capitalization is equal to or below $13 billion.

Legal Proceedings

The Company is involved from time to time in claims, proceedings and litigation, including the following:

In June 2001, Audible, Inc., our subsidiary acquired in March 2008, was named as a defendant in a securities class-action filed in United States District Court for the Southern District of New York related to its

AMAZON.COM, INC.

NOTES TO CONSOLIDATED FINANCIAL STATEMENTS—(Continued)

initial public offering in July 1999. The lawsuit also named certain of the offering's underwriters, as well as Audible's officers and directors as defendants. Approximately 300 other issuers and their underwriters have had similar suits filed against them, all of which are included in a single coordinated proceeding in the Southern District of New York. The complaints allege that the prospectus and the registration statement for Audible's offering failed to disclose that the underwriters allegedly solicited and received "excessive" commissions from investors and that some investors allegedly agreed with the underwriters to buy additional shares in the aftermarket in order to inflate the price of Audible's stock. Audible and its officers and directors were named in the suits pursuant to Section 11 of the Securities Act of 1933, Section 10(b) of the Securities Exchange Act of 1934, and other related provisions. The complaints seek unspecified damages, attorney and expert fees, and other unspecified litigation costs. In March 2009, all parties, including Audible, reached a settlement of these class actions that would resolve this dispute entirely with no payment required from Audible. The settlement was approved by the Court in October 2009, and that settlement is currently under appeal to the Court of Appeals for the Second Circuit.

Beginning in March 2003, we were served with complaints filed in several different states, including Illinois, by a private litigant, Beeler, Schad & Diamond, P.C., purportedly on behalf of the state governments under various state False Claims Acts. The complaints allege that we (along with other companies with which we have commercial agreements) wrongfully failed to collect and remit sales and use taxes for sales of personal property to customers in those states and knowingly created records and statements falsely stating we were not required to collect or remit such taxes. In December 2006, we learned that one additional complaint was filed in the state of Illinois by a different private litigant, Matthew T. Hurst, alleging similar violations of the Illinois state law. All of the complaints seek injunctive relief, unpaid taxes, interest, attorneys' fees, civil penalties of up to $10,000 per violation, and treble or punitive damages under the various state False Claims Acts. It is possible that we have been or will be named in similar cases in other states as well. We dispute the allegations of wrongdoing in these complaints and intend to vigorously defend ourselves in these matters.

In December 2005, Registrar Systems LLC filed a complaint against us and Target Corporation for patent infringement in the United States District Court for the District of Colorado. The complaint alleges that our website technology, including the method by which Amazon.com enables customers to use Amazon.com account information on websites that Amazon.com operates for third parties, such as Target.com, infringes two patents obtained by Registrar Systems purporting to cover methods and apparatuses for a "World Wide Web Registration Information Processing System" (U.S. Patent Nos. 5,790,785 and 6,823,327) and seeks injunctive relief, monetary damages in an amount no less than a reasonable royalty, prejudgment interest, costs, and attorneys' fees. In September 2006, the Court entered an order staying the lawsuit pending the outcome of the Patent and Trademark Office's re-examination of the patents in suit. We dispute the allegations of wrongdoing in this complaint and intend to vigorously defend ourselves in this matter.

In August 2006, Cordance Corporation filed a complaint against us for patent infringement in the United States District Court for the District of Delaware. The complaint alleges that our website technology, including our 1-Click ordering system, infringes a patent obtained by Cordance purporting to cover an "Object-Based Online Transaction Infrastructure" (U.S. Patent No. 6,757,710) and seeks injunctive relief, monetary damages in an amount no less than a reasonable royalty, treble damages for alleged willful infringement, prejudgment interest, costs, and attorneys' fees. In response, we asserted a declaratory judgment counterclaim in the same action alleging that a service that Cordance has advertised its intent to launch infringes a patent owned by us entitled "Networked Personal Contact Manager" (U.S. Patent No. 6,269,369). In August 2009, the case was tried and the jury ruled that Amazon was not liable on Cordance's claims. An appeal is expected.

In October 2007, Digital Reg of Texas, LLC filed a complaint against our subsidiary, Audible, Inc., and several other defendants in the United States District Court for the Eastern District of Texas. The complaint

AMAZON.COM, INC.

NOTES TO CONSOLIDATED FINANCIAL STATEMENTS—(Continued)

alleges that Audible's digital rights management technology infringes a patent obtained by Digital Reg purporting to cover a system for "Regulating Access to Digital Content" (U.S. Patent No. 6,389,541) and seeks injunctive relief, monetary damages, enhanced damages for alleged willful infringement, prejudgment and post-judgment interest, costs and attorneys' fees. In November 2009, we obtained a license to the patent in suit and were dismissed from the lawsuit with prejudice.

In January 2009, we learned that the United States Postal Service, including the Postal Service Office of Inspector General, is investigating our compliance with Postal Service rules, and we are cooperating.

In March 2009, Discovery Communications, Inc. filed a complaint against us for patent infringement in the United States District Court for the District of Delaware. The complaint alleges that our Kindle and Kindle 2 wireless reading devices infringe a patent owned by Discovery purporting to cover an "Electronic Book Security and Copyright Protection System" (U.S. Patent No. 7,298,851) and seeks monetary damages, a continuing royalty sufficient to compensate Discovery for any future infringement, treble damages, costs and attorneys fees. In May 2009, we filed counterclaims and an additional lawsuit in the United States District Court for the Western District of Washington against Discovery alleging infringement of several patents owned by Amazon and requesting a declaration that several Discovery patents, including the one listed above, are invalid and unenforceable. We dispute the allegations of wrongdoing and intend to vigorously defend ourselves in this matter.

In March 2009, the Tobin Family Education and Health Foundation filed a complaint against us for patent infringement in the United States District Court for the Middle District of Florida. The complaint alleges, among other things, that the technology underlying the Amazon Associates program infringes a patent owned by Tobin purporting to cover a "Method and System for Customizing Marketing Services on Networks Communication with Hypertext Tagging Conventions" (U.S. Patent No. 7,505,913) and seeks injunctive relief, monetary damages, costs and attorneys fees. We dispute the allegations of wrongdoing and intend to vigorously defend ourselves in this matter.

In April 2009, Parallel Networks, LLC filed a complaint against us for patent infringement in the United States District Court for the Eastern District of Texas. The complaint alleges, among other things, that our website technology infringes a patent owned by Parallel Networks purporting to cover a "Method And Apparatus For Client-Server Communication Using a Limited Capability Client Over A Low-Speed Communications Link" (U.S. Patent No. 6,446,111) and seeks injunctive relief, monetary damages, costs and attorneys fees. We dispute the allegations of wrongdoing and intend to vigorously defend ourselves in this matter.

In May 2009, Big Baboon, Inc. filed a complaint against us for patent infringement in the United States District Court for the Central District of California. The complaint alleges, among other things, that our third-party selling and payments technology infringes a patent owned by Big Baboon, Inc. purporting to cover an "Integrated Business-to-Business Web Commerce and Business Automation System" (U.S. Patent No. 6,115,690) and seeks injunctive relief, monetary damages, treble damages, costs and attorneys fees. We dispute the allegations of wrongdoing and intend to vigorously defend ourselves in this matter.

In June 2009, Bedrock Computer Technologies LLC filed a complaint against us for patent infringement in the United States District Court for the Eastern District of Texas. The complaint alleges, among other things, that our website technology infringes a patent owned by Bedrock purporting to cover a "Method And Apparatus For Information Storage and Retrieval Using a Hashing Technique with External Chaining and On-the-Fly Removal of Expired Data" (U.S. Patent Nos. 5,893,120) and seeks injunctive relief, monetary damages, enhanced damages, a compulsory future royalty, costs and attorneys fees. We dispute the allegations of wrongdoing and intend to vigorously defend ourselves in this matter.

AMAZON.COM, INC.

NOTES TO CONSOLIDATED FINANCIAL STATEMENTS—(Continued)

In September 2009, SpeedTrack, Inc. filed a complaint against us for patent infringement in the United States District Court for the Northern District of California. The complaint alleges, among other things, that our website technology infringes a patent owned by SpeedTrack purporting to cover a "Method For Accessing Computer Files and Data, Using Linked Categories Assigned to Each Data File Record on Entry of the Data File Record" (U.S. Patent Nos. 5,544,360) and seeks injunctive relief, monetary damages, enhanced damages, costs and attorneys fees. In November 2009, the Court entered an order staying the lawsuit pending the outcome of the Patent and Trademark Office's re-examination of the patent in suit and the resolution of similar litigation against another party. We dispute the allegations of wrongdoing and intend to vigorously defend ourselves in this matter.

In September 2009, Alcatel-Lucent USA Inc. filed a complaint against us for patent infringement in the United States District Court for the Eastern District of Texas. The complaint alleges that our website technology and digital content distribution systems infringe six of Alcatel-Lucent's patents and seeks injunctive relief, monetary damages, a continuing royalty sufficient to compensate Alcatel-Lucent for any future infringement, treble damages, costs and attorneys fees. In January 2010, we filed counterclaims against Alcatel-Lucent alleging infringement of a patent owned by Amazon and that the patents asserted by Alcatel-Lucent are invalid and unenforceable. We dispute the allegations of wrongdoing and intend to vigorously defend ourselves in this matter.

In October 2009, Eolas Technologies Incorporated filed a complaint against us for patent infringement in the United States District Court for the Eastern District of Texas. The complaint alleges, among other things, that our website technology infringes two patents owned by Eolas purporting to cover "Distributed Hypermedia Method for Automatically Invoking External Application Providing Interaction and Display of Embedded Objects within a Hypermedia Document" (U.S. Patent No. 5,838,906) and "Distributed Hypermedia Method and System for Automatically Invoking External Application Providing Interaction and Display of Embedded Objects within a Hypermedia Document" (U.S. Patent No. 7,599,985) and seeks injunctive relief, monetary damages, costs and attorneys fees. We dispute the allegations of wrongdoing and intend to vigorously defend ourselves in this matter.

In October 2009, Leon Stambler filed a complaint against us for patent infringement in the United States District Court for the Eastern District of Texas. The complaint alleges, among other things, that our use of secure online payments systems and services infringes two patents owned by Stambler purporting to cover a "Method for Securing Information Relevant to a Transaction" (U.S. Patent Nos. 5,793,302 and 5,974,148) and seeks monetary damages, costs and attorneys fees. We dispute the allegations of wrongdoing and intend to vigorously defend ourselves in this matter.

In December 2009, Nazomi Communications, Inc. filed a complaint against us for patent infringement in the United States District Court for the Eastern District of Texas. The complaint alleges, among other things, that the processor core in our Kindle 2 device infringes two patents owned by Nazomi purporting to cover "Java virtual machine hardware for RISC and CISC processors" and "Java hardware accelerator using microcode engine" (U.S. Patent Nos. 7,080,362 and 7,225,436) and seeks monetary damages, injunctive relief, costs and attorneys fees. We dispute the allegations of wrongdoing and intend to vigorously defend ourselves in this matter.

Depending on the amount and the timing, an unfavorable resolution of some or all of these matters could materially affect our business, results of operations, financial position, or cash flows.

See also "Note 10—Income Taxes."

AMAZON.COM, INC.

NOTES TO CONSOLIDATED FINANCIAL STATEMENTS—(Continued)

Inventory Suppliers

During 2009, no vendor accounted for 10% or more of our inventory purchases. We generally do not have long-term contracts or arrangements with our vendors to guarantee the availability of merchandise, particular payment terms, or the extension of credit limits.

Note 8—STOCKHOLDERS' EQUITY

Preferred Stock

We have authorized 500 million shares of $0.01 par value Preferred Stock. No preferred stock was outstanding for any period presented.

Common Stock

Common shares outstanding plus shares underlying outstanding stock awards totaled 461 million, 446 million, and 435 million at December 31, 2009, 2008 and 2007. These totals include all stock-based awards outstanding, without regard for estimated forfeitures, consisting of vested and unvested awards. Common shares outstanding increased in 2009 due primarily to issuance of stock to acquire Zappos and vesting of restricted stock units.

Stock Repurchase Activity

We did not repurchase any of our common stock in 2009. We repurchased 2.2 million shares of common stock for $100 million in 2008 under the $1 billion repurchase program authorized by our Board of Directors in February 2008. We repurchased 6.3 million shares of common stock for $248 million in 2007 under the $500 million repurchase program authorized by our Board of Directors in August 2006.

In January 2010, our Board of Directors authorized a program to repurchase up to $2 billion of our common stock which replaces the Board's prior authorization.

Stock Award Plans

Employees vest in restricted stock unit awards over the corresponding service term, generally between two and five years.

Stock Award Activity

We granted restricted stock units representing 6.0 million, 7.3 million, 7.6 million shares of common stock during 2009, 2008, and 2007 with a per share weighted average fair value of $79.24, $72.21, and $47.04.

AMAZON.COM, INC.

NOTES TO CONSOLIDATED FINANCIAL STATEMENTS—(Continued)

The following summarizes our restricted stock unit activity (in millions):

	Number of Units
Outstanding at January 1, 2007	14.5
Units granted	7.6
Units vested	(3.3)
Units forfeited	(2.5)
Outstanding at December 31, 2007	16.3
Units granted	7.3
Units vested	(5.5)
Units forfeited	(1.4)
Outstanding at December 31, 2008	16.7
Units granted	6.0
Units vested	(6.0)
Units forfeited	(1.0)
Outstanding at December 31, 2009	15.7

Scheduled vesting for outstanding restricted stock units at December 31, 2009 is as follows (in millions):

| | Year Ended December 31, | | | | | | |
	2010	2011	2012	2013	2014	Thereafter	Total
Scheduled vesting—restricted stock units	5.9	5.5	2.6	1.4	0.2	0.1	15.7

As of December 31, 2009, there was $415 million of net unrecognized compensation cost related to unvested stock-based compensation arrangements. This compensation is recognized on an accelerated basis resulting in approximately half of the compensation expected to be expensed in the next twelve months, and has a weighted average recognition period of 1.2 years.

During 2009 and 2008, the fair value of restricted stock units that vested was $551 million and $362 million.

As matching contributions under our 401(k) savings plan, we granted 0.1 million shares of common stock in both 2009 and 2008. Shares granted as matching contributions under our 401(k) plan are included in outstanding common stock when issued.

Common Stock Available for Future Issuance

At December 31, 2009, common stock available for future issuance to employees is 149 million shares.

AMAZON.COM, INC.

NOTES TO CONSOLIDATED FINANCIAL STATEMENTS—(Continued)

Note 9—OTHER COMPREHENSIVE INCOME (LOSS)

The components of other comprehensive income (loss) are as follows:

	Year Ended December 31,		
	2009	**2008**	**2007**
	(in millions)		
Net income	$902	$ 645	$476
Net change in unrealized gains/losses on available-for-sale securities:			
Unrealized gains (losses), net of tax of $(2), $0, and $(4)	7	—	8
Reclassification adjustment for losses (gains) included in net income, net of tax effect of $1, $1, and $0	(3)	(1)	—
Net unrealized gains (losses) on available for sale securities	4	(1)	8
Foreign currency translation adjustment, net of tax effect of $0, $3, and $6	62	(127)	(3)
Amortization of net unrealized losses on terminated Euro Currency Swap, net of tax effect of $0, $0, and $0	1	—	1
Other comprehensive income (loss)	67	(128)	6
Comprehensive income	$969	$ 517	$482

Balances within accumulated other comprehensive income (loss) are as follows:

	December 31,	
	2009	**2008**
	(in millions)	
Net unrealized losses on foreign currency translation, net of tax	$ (66)	$(128)
Net unrealized gains on available-for-sale securities, net of tax	10	6
Net unrealized losses on terminated Euro Currency Swap, net of tax	—	(1)
Total accumulated other comprehensive income (loss)	$ (56)	$(123)

AMAZON.COM, INC.

NOTES TO CONSOLIDATED FINANCIAL STATEMENTS—(Continued)

Note 10—INCOME TAXES

In 2009, 2008 and 2007 we recorded net tax provisions of $253 million, $247 million, and $184 million. A majority of this provision is non-cash. We have current tax benefits and net operating losses relating to excess stock-based compensation that are being utilized to reduce our U.S. taxable income. As such, cash taxes paid, net of refunds, were $48 million, $53 million, and $24 million for 2009, 2008, and 2007.

The components of the provision for income taxes, net are as follows:

	Year Ended December 31,		
	2009	2008	2007
	(in millions)		
Current taxes:			
U.S. and state	$149	$227	$ 275
International	23	25	8
Current taxes	172	252	283
Deferred taxes:			
U.S. and state	89	3	(109)
International	(8)	(8)	10
Deferred taxes	81	(5)	(99)
Provision for income taxes, net	$253	$247	$ 184

U.S. and international components of income before income taxes are as follows:

	Year Ended December 31,		
	2009	2008	2007
	(in millions)		
U.S.	$ 529	$436	$360
International (1)	632	465	300
Income before income taxes	$1,161	$901	$660

(1) Included in 2008 is the impact of the $53 million non-cash gain associated with the sale of our European DVD rental assets. This gain was taxed at rates substantially below the 35% U.S. federal statutory rate.

The items accounting for differences between income taxes computed at the federal statutory rate and the provision recorded for income taxes are as follows:

	Year Ended December 31,		
	2009	2008	2007
Federal statutory rate	35.0%	35.0%	35.0%
Effect of:			
Impact of foreign tax differential	(16.9)	(13.8)	(11.7)
State taxes, net of federal benefits	1.1	2.8	2.1
Tax credits	(0.4)	(2.2)	(1.1)
Nondeductible stock-based compensation	1.7	1.7	1.4
Valuation allowance	0.4	2.6	(1.2)
Other, net	1.0	1.3	3.4
Total	21.9%	27.4%	27.9%

AMAZON.COM, INC.

NOTES TO CONSOLIDATED FINANCIAL STATEMENTS—(Continued)

The effective tax rate in 2009, 2008, and 2007 was lower than the 35% U.S. federal statutory rate primarily due to earnings of our subsidiaries outside of the U.S. in jurisdictions where our effective tax rate is lower than in the U.S. Included in the total tax provision as a discrete item during 2008 is the impact related to the $53 million noncash gain associated with the sale of our European DVD rental assets. This gain was taxed at rates substantially below the 35% U.S. federal statutory rate.

Deferred income tax assets and liabilities are as follows:

	December 31,	
	2009	**2008**
	(in millions)	
Deferred tax assets:		
Net operating losses—stock-based compensation (1)	$ 120	$ 120
Net operating losses—other	50	31
Net operating losses—obtained through acquisitions (2)	7	14
Stock-based compensation	118	73
Assets held for investment	125	152
Revenue items	58	53
Expense items	172	155
Other items	42	40
Net tax credits (3)	6	2
Total gross deferred tax assets	698	640
Less valuation allowance (4)	(173)	(199)
Deferred tax assets, net of valuation allowance	525	441
Deferred tax liabilities:		
Basis difference in intangible assets	(218)	(80)
Expense items	(168)	(12)
Deferred tax assets, net of valuation allowance and deferred tax liabilities	$ 139	$ 349

(1) Excludes unrecognized federal net operating loss carryforward deferred tax assets of $40 million and $73 million at December 31, 2009 and 2008. The total gross deferred tax assets relating to our federal excess stock-based compensation net operating loss carryforwards at December 31, 2009 and 2008 were $160 million and $193 million (relating to approximately $456 million and $550 million of our federal net operating loss carryforwards). The majority of our net operating loss carryforwards begin to expire in 2021 and thereafter.
(2) The utilization of some of these net operating loss carryforwards is subject to an annual limitation under applicable provisions of the Internal Revenue Code.
(3) Presented net of fully reserved deferred tax assets associated with tax credits of $193 million and $130 million at December 31, 2009 and 2008. Total tax credits available to be claimed in future years are approximately $199 million and $171 million as of December 31, 2009 and 2008, and begin to expire in 2017.
(4) Relates primarily to deferred tax assets that would only be realizable upon the generation of future capital gains and net income in certain foreign taxing jurisdictions.

Tax Contingencies

We are subject to income taxes in the U.S. and numerous foreign jurisdictions. Significant judgment is required in evaluating our tax positions and determining our provision for income taxes. During the ordinary

AMAZON.COM, INC.

NOTES TO CONSOLIDATED FINANCIAL STATEMENTS—(Continued)

course of business, there are many transactions and calculations for which the ultimate tax determination is uncertain. We establish reserves for tax-related uncertainties based on estimates of whether, and the extent to which, additional taxes will be due. These reserves are established when we believe that certain positions might be challenged despite our belief that our tax return positions are fully supportable. We adjust these reserves in light of changing facts and circumstances, such as the outcome of tax audits. The provision for income taxes includes the impact of reserve provisions and changes to reserves that are considered appropriate.

The reconciliation of our tax contingencies is as follows (in millions):

	December 31,	
	2009	**2008**
	(in millions)	
Gross tax contingencies—January 1, 2009	$166	$112
Gross increases to tax positions in prior periods	15	39
Gross decreases to tax positions in prior periods	—	(4)
Gross increases to current period tax positions	1	22
Audit settlements paid during 2008	—	(3)
Foreign exchange gain (loss) on tax contingencies	(1)	—
Gross tax contingencies—December 31, 2009 (1)	$181	$166

(1)   As of December 31, 2009, we had $181 million of tax contingencies of which $180 million, if fully recognized, would decrease our effective tax rate and increase additional paid-in capital by $1 million to reflect the tax benefits of excess stock-based compensation deductions.

Due to the nature of our business operations we expect the total amount of tax contingencies for prior period tax positions will grow in 2010 in comparable amounts to 2009. We do not believe it is reasonably possible that the total amount of unrecognized tax benefits will significantly decrease in 2010. The increase to current period tax positions in 2008 resulted primarily from acquisition-related activity and new regulations.

As of December 31, 2009 and 2008, we had accrued interest and penalties, net of federal income tax benefit, related to tax contingencies of $17 million and $14 million. Interest and penalties, net of federal income tax benefit, recognized for the year ended December 31, 2009 and 2008 was $3 million and $5 million.

We are under examination, or may be subject to examination, by the Internal Revenue Service ("IRS") for calendar years 2005 through 2009. Additionally, any net operating losses that were generated in prior years and utilized in 2005 through 2009 may also be subject to examination by the IRS. We are under examination, or may be subject to examination, in the following major jurisdictions for the years specified: Kentucky for 2005 through 2009, France for 2006 through 2009, Germany for 2003 through 2009, Luxembourg for 2004 through 2009, and the United Kingdom for 2003 through 2009. In addition, in 2007, Japanese tax authorities assessed income tax, including penalties and interest, of approximately $120 million against one of our U.S. subsidiaries for the years 2003 through 2005. We believe that these claims are without merit and are disputing the assessment. Further proceedings on the assessment have been stayed during negotiations between U.S. and Japanese authorities over the double taxation issues the assessment raises, and we have provided bank guarantees to suspend enforcement of the assessment. We also may be subject to income tax examination by Japanese tax authorities for 2006 through 2009.

AMAZON.COM, INC.

NOTES TO CONSOLIDATED FINANCIAL STATEMENTS—(Continued)

Note 11—SEGMENT INFORMATION

We have organized our operations into two principal segments: North America and International. We present our segment information along the same lines that our chief executive reviews our operating results in assessing performance and allocating resources.

We allocate to segment results the operating expenses "Fulfillment," "Marketing," "Technology and content," and "General and administrative," but exclude from our allocations the portions of these expense lines attributable to stock-based compensation. We do not allocate the line item "Other operating expense (income), net" to our segment operating results. A significant majority of our costs for "Technology and content" are incurred in the United States and most of these costs are allocated to our North America segment. There are no internal revenue transactions between our reporting segments.

North America

The North America segment consists of amounts earned from retail sales of consumer products (including from sellers) and subscriptions through North America-focused websites such as *www.amazon.com* and *www.amazon.ca*. This segment includes export sales from *www.amazon.com* and *www.amazon.ca*.

International

The International segment consists of amounts earned from retail sales of consumer products (including from sellers) and subscriptions through internationally focused websites such as *www.amazon.co.uk*, *www.amazon.de*, *www.amazon.co.jp*, *www.amazon.fr*, and *www.amazon.cn*. This segment includes export sales from these internationally based sites (including export sales from these sites to customers in the U.S. and Canada), but excludes export sales from *www.amazon.com* and *www.amazon.ca*.

AMAZON.COM, INC.

NOTES TO CONSOLIDATED FINANCIAL STATEMENTS—(Continued)

Information on reportable segments and reconciliation to consolidated net income is as follows:

	Year Ended December 31,		
	2009	2008	2007
	(in millions)		
North America			
Net sales	$12,828	$10,228	$ 8,095
Cost of sales	9,538	7,733	6,064
Gross profit	3,290	2,495	2,031
Direct segment operating expenses	2,581	2,050	1,631
Segment operating income	$ 709	$ 445	$ 400
International			
Net sales	$11,681	$ 8,938	$ 6,740
Cost of sales	9,440	7,163	5,418
Gross profit	2,241	1,775	1,322
Direct segment operating expenses	1,378	1,127	873
Segment operating income	$ 863	$ 648	$ 449
Consolidated			
Net sales	$24,509	$19,166	$14,835
Cost of sales	18,978	14,896	11,482
Gross profit	5,531	4,270	3,353
Direct segment operating expenses	3,959	3,177	2,504
Segment operating income	1,572	1,093	849
Stock-based compensation	(341)	(275)	(185)
Other operating expense, net	(102)	24	(9)
Income from operations	1,129	842	655
Total non-operating income (expense), net	32	59	5
Provision for income taxes	(253)	(247)	(184)
Equity-method investment activity, net of tax	(6)	(9)	—
Net income	$ 902	$ 645	$ 476

Net sales shipped to customers outside of the U.S. represented approximately half of net sales for 2009, 2008, and 2007. Net sales from *www.amazon.de*, *www.amazon.co.jp,* and *www.amazon.co.uk* each represented 13% to 17% of consolidated net sales in 2009, 2008 and 2007.

Total assets, by segment, reconciled to consolidated amounts were (in millions):

	December 31,	
	2009	2008
North America	$ 9,252	$5,266
International	4,561	3,048
Consolidated	$13,813	$8,314

AMAZON.COM, INC.

NOTES TO CONSOLIDATED FINANCIAL STATEMENTS—(Continued)

Fixed assets, net, by segment, reconciled to consolidated amounts were (in millions):

	December 31,	
	2009	2008
North America	$1,059	$666
International	231	188
Consolidated	$1,290	$854

Depreciation expense, by segment, is as follows (in millions):

	Year Ended December 31,		
	2009	2008	2007
North America	$327	$262	$212
International	57	49	46
Consolidated	$384	$311	$258

Note 12—QUARTERLY RESULTS (UNAUDITED)

The following tables contain selected unaudited statement of operations information for each quarter of 2009 and 2008. The following information reflects all normal recurring adjustments necessary for a fair presentation of the information for the periods presented. The operating results for any quarter are not necessarily indicative of results for any future period. Our business is affected by seasonality, which historically has resulted in higher sales volume during our fourth quarter.

Unaudited quarterly results are as follows (in millions, except per share data):

	Year Ended December 31, 2009 (1)			
	Fourth Quarter	Third Quarter	Second Quarter	First Quarter
Net sales	$9,519	$5,449	$4,651	$4,889
Gross profit	1,976	1,273	1,133	1,148
Income before income taxes	471	262	179	248
Provision for income taxes	85	60	39	69
Net income	384	199	142	177
Basic earnings per share	$ 0.87	$ 0.46	$ 0.33	$ 0.41
Diluted earnings per share	$ 0.85	$ 0.45	$ 0.32	$ 0.41
Shares used in computation of earnings per share:				
Basic	440	432	431	429
Diluted	450	441	440	437

AMAZON.COM, INC.

NOTES TO CONSOLIDATED FINANCIAL STATEMENTS—(Continued)

	Year Ended December 31, 2008 (1)			
	Fourth Quarter	Third Quarter	Second Quarter	First Quarter
Net sales (2)	$6,704	$4,264	$4,063	$4,135
Gross profit	1,348	999	967	956
Income before income taxes	302	182	208	207
Provision for income taxes	79	59	46	62
Net income	225	118	158	143
Basic earnings per share	$ 0.52	$ 0.28	$ 0.38	$ 0.34
Diluted earnings per share	$ 0.52	$ 0.27	$ 0.37	$ 0.34
Shares used in computation of earnings per share:				
Basic	428	427	420	417
Diluted	436	436	430	426

(1) The sum of quarterly amounts, including per share amounts, may not equal amounts reported for year-to-date periods. This is due to the effects of rounding and changes in the number of weighted-average shares outstanding for each period.

(2) Our year-over-year revenue growth was 36% for the first three quarters of 2008. For Q4 2008, our quarterly revenue growth rates declined to 18%, driven primarily by decreased consumer demand following disruptions in the global financial markets and changes in foreign exchange rates (excluding the $320 million unfavorable impact from year-over-year changes in foreign exchange rates throughout the fourth quarter, net sales would have grown 24% compared with Q4 2007).

Item 9.   *Changes in and Disagreements with Accountants On Accounting and Financial Disclosure*

None.

Item 9A.   *Controls and Procedures*

Evaluation of Disclosure Controls and Procedures

We carried out an evaluation required by the 1934 Act, under the supervision and with the participation of our principal executive officer and principal financial officer, of the effectiveness of the design and operation of our disclosure controls and procedures, as defined in Rule 13a-15(e) of the 1934 Act, as of December 31, 2009. Based on this evaluation, our principal executive officer and principal financial officer concluded that, as of December 31, 2009, our disclosure controls and procedures were effective to provide reasonable assurance that information required to be disclosed by us in the reports that we file or submit under the 1934 Act is recorded, processed, summarized, and reported within the time periods specified in the SEC's rules and forms and to provide reasonable assurance that such information is accumulated and communicated to our management, including our principal executive officer and principal financial officer, as appropriate to allow timely decisions regarding required disclosures.

Management's Report on Internal Control over Financial Reporting

Management is responsible for establishing and maintaining adequate internal control over financial reporting, as defined in Rule 13a-15(f) of the 1934 Act. Management has assessed the effectiveness of our internal control over financial reporting as of December 31, 2009 based on criteria established in Internal Control—Integrated Framework issued by the Committee of Sponsoring Organizations of the Treadway Commission. As a result of this assessment, management concluded that, as of December 31, 2009, our internal control over financial reporting was effective in providing reasonable assurance regarding the reliability of financial reporting and the preparation of financial statements for external purposes in accordance with generally accepted accounting principles. Ernst & Young has independently assessed the effectiveness of our internal control over financial reporting and its report is included below.

Changes in Internal Control Over Financial Reporting

There were no changes in our internal control over financial reporting during the quarter ended December 31, 2009 that materially affected, or are reasonably likely to materially affect, our internal control over financial reporting.

Limitations on Controls

Our disclosure controls and procedures and internal control over financial reporting are designed to provide reasonable assurance of achieving their objectives as specified above. Management does not expect, however, that our disclosure controls and procedures or our internal control over financial reporting will prevent or detect all error and fraud. Any control system, no matter how well designed and operated, is based upon certain assumptions and can provide only reasonable, not absolute, assurance that its objectives will be met. Further, no evaluation of controls can provide absolute assurance that misstatements due to error or fraud will not occur or that all control issues and instances of fraud, if any, within the Company have been detected.

Report of Ernst & Young LLP, Independent Registered Public Accounting Firm

The Board of Directors and Stockholders
Amazon.com, Inc.

We have audited Amazon.com, Inc.'s internal control over financial reporting as of December 31, 2009, based on criteria established in Internal Control—Integrated Framework issued by the Committee of Sponsoring Organizations of the Treadway Commission (the COSO criteria). Amazon.com, Inc.'s management is responsible for maintaining effective internal control over financial reporting and for its assessment of the effectiveness of internal control over financial reporting included in the accompanying Management's Report on Internal Control over Financial Reporting. Our responsibility is to express an opinion on the Company's internal control over financial reporting based on our audit.

We conducted our audit in accordance with the standards of the Public Company Accounting Oversight Board (United States). Those standards require that we plan and perform the audit to obtain reasonable assurance about whether effective internal control over financial reporting was maintained in all material respects. Our audit included obtaining an understanding of internal control over financial reporting, assessing the risk that a material weakness exists, testing and evaluating the design and operating effectiveness of internal control based on the assessed risk, and performing such other procedures as we considered necessary in the circumstances. We believe that our audit provides a reasonable basis for our opinion.

A company's internal control over financial reporting is a process designed to provide reasonable assurance regarding the reliability of financial reporting and the preparation of financial statements for external purposes in accordance with generally accepted accounting principles. A company's internal control over financial reporting includes those policies and procedures that (1) pertain to the maintenance of records that, in reasonable detail, accurately and fairly reflect the transactions and dispositions of the assets of the company; (2) provide reasonable assurance that transactions are recorded as necessary to permit preparation of financial statements in accordance with generally accepted accounting principles, and that receipts and expenditures of the company are being made only in accordance with authorizations of management and directors of the company; and (3) provide reasonable assurance regarding prevention or timely detection of unauthorized acquisition, use, or disposition of the company's assets that could have a material effect on the financial statements.

Because of its inherent limitations, internal control over financial reporting may not prevent or detect misstatements. Also, projections of any evaluation of effectiveness to future periods are subject to the risk that controls may become inadequate because of changes in conditions, or that the degree of compliance with the policies or procedures may deteriorate.

In our opinion, Amazon.com, Inc. maintained, in all material respects, effective internal control over financial reporting as of December 31, 2009, based on the COSO criteria.

We have also audited, in accordance with the standards of the Public Company Accounting Oversight Board (United States), the consolidated balance sheets of Amazon.com, Inc. as of December 31, 2009 and 2008, and the related consolidated statements of operations, stockholders' equity, and cash flows for each of the three years in the period ended December 31, 2009 of Amazon.com, Inc. and our report dated January 28, 2010 expressed an unqualified opinion thereon.

/s/   Ernst & Young LLP

Seattle, Washington
January 28, 2010

5
Finance

1. Introduction

What is finance? To many, the term conjures up phalanxes of well-heeled investment bankers and gargantuan sums of money whizzing back and forth across international borders. To be sure, these caricatures reflect facets of the world of finance. But finance is also an academic discipline — less glamorous than the Wall Street of Hollywood imaginations, but a field of study with its own logic and organizing principles. The contours of the field are not always clear, but one leading text offers the following definition:

> Finance is the study of how people allocate scarce resources over time. Two features that distinguish financial decisions from other resource allocation decisions are that the costs and benefits of financial decisions are (1) spread out over time and (2) usually not known with certainty in advance by either the decision maker or anybody else.[1]

---

1. Zvi Bodie & Robert C. Merton, *Finance* (2000).

As a rough cut, this synopsis is quite helpful. First, it highlights the inter-temporal dimension of the subject. The techniques we will be studying in this chapter are designed to balance the costs of taking some action today — making an investment or entering into a contract — with benefits that will accrue from that action at some time in the future — as a stream of dividends or some other form of return. Second, the definition emphasizes a critical dimension of financial analysis: problems of finance almost always involve uncertainty. When deciding whether to purchase shares in a particular company, an investor does not know — is uncertain — whether the firm will turn out to be a dud or the next Microsoft. When a university is offered the opportunity to purchase a piece of land, it cannot know for certain whether another, more attractive piece of land might become available tomorrow. Finance provides a set of tools for evaluating these uncertainties.

Another important preliminary point to recognize about the field of finance is its recent pedigree. Unlike accounting, whose roots can be traced back over five hundred years, the study of finance is comparatively new. Although the foundations of financial theory were laid in a smattering of academic papers in the 1930s, real progress in the field did not begin until the post–World War II era. Works that now stand as seminal contributions date back only to the 1950s and early 1960s, and the first Nobel Prizes for work in the field were not awarded until the 1990s.[2] So the field of finance is still new and evolving rapidly.

Finally, the field of finance can be extraordinarily complex. The theoretical arguments upon which modern finance is based are often elaborate and multifaceted. Moreover, much of the debate over financial theory turns upon the interpretation of empirical evidence accumu-

---

2. The first prize, awarded in 1990, went to Harry Markowitz (for work on portfolio theory), William Sharpe (for developing the capital asset pricing model), and Merton Miller (for contributions to the theory of corporate finance). The 1997 Nobel Prize was shared by Robert C. Merton and Myron Scholes for their contribution to options pricing theory. By the end of this chapter, you should have at least a general sense of the nature of the academic achievements of these individuals. Two other authors whose work is excerpted in this chapter also won Nobel Prizes in economics but not for work that would ordinarily be characterized as pure finance: Franco Modigliani in 1985 for his work on the analysis of savings and of financial markets and Ronald Coase in 1991 for his work on transaction costs and property rights.

lated and presented through the use of econometric analysis (akin to the techniques that we will introduce in the chapters on statistics and regression analysis). Unlike issues of accounting, which often can be reduced to addition, subtraction, multiplication, and occasionally division, financial arguments routinely employ calculus and other sorts of higher-level mathematics. With finance, sooner or later everyone is in over his or her head.

Nevertheless, finance is a field with which attorneys must have some familiarity. Most obviously, corporate counsel must comprehend the logic of finance because many business transactions are designed to advance financial goals and because associated documentation and negotiations must comport with the transactions' purposes. But financial considerations are relevant to a much broader category of lawyers. Attorneys practicing family law spend much of their time on estate planning and marital disputes, areas where uncertain costs and benefits must be balanced over time — that is, areas well suited to financial analysis. Indeed, one could plausibly argue that in every area of law in which decision analysis might be applied (and, you'll recall from the decision analysis chapter, this includes litigation, negotiations, and many other areas of legal practice), a lawyer might make use of financial techniques to establish appropriate endpoint values. For example, when considering the value of going to trial, an attorney is evaluating the likelihood of success (an uncertainty) at the end of a trial (a point in the future). In fact, one could think of finance as a specialized extension of decision analysis, where the mechanical elements of the decision trees are superseded by more efficient (but less transparent) analytical tools.

Within the confines of this chapter, we will not be able to address the tools of finance in any detail, but we will attempt to give an overview of a number of analytical methods that make use of financial theory and that a broad range of attorneys routinely encounter or employ. We will begin with several qualitative — as opposed to technical — financial arguments employed in legal analysis and featured prominently in upper-level law school courses, including Corporations and Taxation. Next we will present a number of important financial techniques and theories: the time value of money, the basic principles of portfolio diversification, the risk-return trade-off, the efficient market hypothesis, and the capital asset pricing model. We will complete the chapter with an introduction of valuation techniques that financial analysts and other business people typically use to appraise financial assets and investment opportunities.

2. The Foundations of Financial Theory

To introduce the subject of finance, we begin with a selection of excerpts from important academic papers in the field. Our goal in presenting these readings is twofold. First, these excerpts illustrate the intellectual underpinnings of the discipline, both illuminating the kinds of problems financial analysis was developed to solve and suggesting the basic logic of finance. Second, this section introduces students to several of the most prominent thinkers in the field. In upper-level law school courses and sometimes even in the world of practice, reference will be made to *Coasean analysis* or a *Berle and Means corporation* or the *Modigliani and Miller theorem*. Well-trained lawyers should have at least a passing familiarity with these intellectual landmarks.

A. The Theory of the Firm

The theory of the firm was one of the first problems that attracted the attention of financial theorists. In this area, economists strive to understand the economic function of firms. We start with what may be the most famous and frequently cited article on the subject. Here, Nobel laureate Ronald Coase (to whom you may have been introduced in other first-year courses) addresses the question of why some economic activities are located within a firm while other activities are organized through transactions executed at prices determined by the market — that is, through contracts. The answer offered in this excerpt has had a major impact on the field of finance as well as other areas of economic study.

R. H. Coase
The Nature of the Firm
4 *Economica* 386, 389–93 (1937)

[T]he distinguishing mark of the firm is the supersession of the price mechanism. . . .

Our task is to attempt to discover why a firm emerges at all in a specialized exchange economy. . . .

The main reason why it is profitable to establish a firm would seem to be that there is a cost of using the price mechanism. The most obvious cost of "organizing" production through the price mechanism is that of discovering what relevant prices are. This cost may be reduced but it will not be eliminated by the emergence of specialists who will sell this information. The costs of negotiating and concluding a separate contract for each exchange transaction which takes place on a market must also be taken into account . . . It is true that contracts are not eliminated when there is a firm but they are greatly reduced. A factor of production (or the owner thereof) does not have to make a series of contracts with the factors with whom he is co-operating within the firm, as would be necessary, of course, if this co-operation were as a direct result of the working of the price mechanism. For this series of contracts is substituted one. At this stage, it is important to note the character of the contract into which a factor enters that is employed within a firm. The contract is one whereby the factor, for a certain remuneration (which can be fixed or fluctuating) agrees to obey the directions of an entrepreneur *within certain limits.* The essence of the contract is that it should only state the limits to the powers of the entrepreneur. Within these limits, he can therefore direct the other factors of production.

There are, however, other disadvantages — or costs — of using the price mechanism. It may be desired to make a long-term contract for the supply of some article or service. This may be due to the fact that if one contract is made for a longer period, instead of several shorter ones, then certain costs of making each contract will be avoided. Or, owing to the risk attitude of the people concerned, they may prefer to make a long rather than a short-term contract. Now, owing to the difficulty of forecasting, the longer the period of the contract is for the supply of the commodity or service, the less possible, and indeed, the less desirable it is for the person purchasing to specify what the other contracting party is expected to do. It may well be a matter of indifference to the person supplying the service or commodity which of several courses of action is taken, but not to the purchaser of that service or commodity. But the purchaser will not know which of these several courses he will want the supplier to take. Therefore the service which is being provided is expressed in general terms, the exact details being left until a later date. All that is stated in the contract is the limits to what the persons supplying the commodity or service is expected to do. The details of what the supplier is expected to do is not stated in the contract but is decided later by the purchaser. When the direction of resources (within the limits of the contract) becomes dependent on the buyer in this way, that relationship which I term a "firm" may be obtained. A firm is therefore likely to emerge in those cases where a very short term contract would be unsatisfactory. . . .

We may sum up this section of the argument by saying that the operation of a market costs something and by forming an organization and allowing some authority (an "entrepreneur") to direct the resources, certain marketing costs are saved. The entrepreneur has to carry out his function at less cost, taking into account the fact that he may get factors of production at a lower price than the market transactions which he supersedes, because it is always possible to revert to the open market if he fails to do this.

The question of uncertainty is one which is often considered to be very relevant to the study of the equilibrium of the firm. It seems improbable that a firm would emerge without the existence of uncertainty. . . .

Another factor that should be noted is that the exchange transactions on a market and the same transactions organized within a firm are often treated differently by Governments or other bodies with regulatory powers. . . .

These, then, are the reasons why organizations such as firms exist in a specialized exchange economy in which it is generally assumed that the distribution of resources is "organized" by the price mechanism. A firm, therefore, consists of the system of relationships which comes into existence when the direction of resources is dependent on an entrepreneur.

This excerpt may strike some students as familiar. The question it considers — under what circumstances is economic activity located within the firm? — is really the inverse of one of the principal questions we were considering in the chapter on Contracting: When should a party (including a firm) use contractual arrangements to farm out a project?

Indeed, Professor Coase's definition of a firm is an organization within which economic activity is centralized under the discretionary authority of an entrepreneur. Professor Coase's paper has had a major influence on the way we now think and talk about the organization of economic activity.

But there is also an important practical legacy of Professor Coase's *Nature of the Firm:* the notion that corporate managers and owners must constantly be on the lookout for opportunities to reduce costs and increase efficiencies by moving certain economic activities into or outside a particular firm. Mergers and acquisitions (the aggregation of economic functions) and corporate downsizing (the divestiture of activities) are staples of corporate finance. One way of understanding the role of the phalanxes of investment bankers and management consultants deployed across the American economic landscape is that these individuals are in the business of rationalizing the structure of American business in precisely the manner Professor Coase outlined above. And, of course, the ranks of lawyers who service these financial professionals are also playing an important role in this enterprise.

Another important point to note about the excerpt from Professor Coase's article is the role he assigns to entrepreneurial discretion. One of the reasons it makes sense to move economic activity into the firm is the value of allowing the firm's managers the latitude to organize firm resources as opportunities arise — to assign workers to different tasks or deploy equipment in new ways. This discretion, according to Coase, is what distinguishes the firm from market transactions.[3] As you will see when you study corporate law, the preservation of managerial

3. Having studied contracting, some students may recognize that Professor Coase's distinction between inflexible contractual arrangements and discretionary allocations of resources within the structure of a firm is over-stated. As we saw in Chapter 3, there are many ways to write contracts to give additional discretion to particular parties, that is, to make the contractual relationship more firmlike. Conversely, modern corporate law scholars increasingly discuss corporate law in contractarian terms, emphasizing that corporate charters can best be understood as specialized forms of contracts. These developments in legal thinking in no way diminish the importance of Professor Coase's original insight. By articulating fundamental distinctions between firms and market transactions, he contributed to intellectual developments that changed the way we think about both fields.

discretion is one of the hallmarks of American corporate law. Practicing lawyers must also be constantly mindful of the problems created when contractual commitments or legislative reforms threaten to infringe upon managerial discretion. Oftentimes, lawyers must take on the role of explaining why it is important for managers to retain the freedom to manage. Advocacy in this vein often draws upon the contributions of Professor Coase and his successors.

With discretion, however, comes the potential for abuse. This was true in the context of contracting, and it is also true with respect to the theory of the firm. The classic treatment of the less savory side of managerial discretion was published just a few years before Professor Coase's article in a famous book written by two Columbia University professors, Adolf Berle of Columbia Law School and Gardiner Means of the Columbia Economics Department.

Adolf A. Berle and Gardiner C. Means
The Modern Corporation and Private Property
Chapter 1 (1932)

Corporations have ceased to be merely legal devices through which the private business transactions of individuals may be carried on. Though still much used for this purpose, the corporate form has acquired a larger significance. The corporation has, in fact, become both a method of property tenure and a means of organizing economic life. Grown to tremendous proportions, there may be said to have evolved a "corporate system" — as there was once a feudal system — which has attracted to itself a combination of attributes and powers, and has attained a degree of prominence entitling it to be dealt with as a major social institution. . . .

In its new aspect the corporation is a means whereby the wealth of innumerable individuals has been concentrated into huge aggregates and whereby control over this wealth has been surrendered to a unified direction. The power attendant upon such concentration has brought forth princes of industry, whose position in the community is yet to be defined. The surrender of control over their wealth by investors has effectively broken the old property relationships and has raised the problem of defining these relationships anew. The direction of industry by persons other than those who have ventured their wealth has raised the question of the motive force back of such direction and the effective distribution of the returns from business enterprise. . . .

Such organization of economic activity rests on two developments, each of which has made possible an extension of the area under unified control. The factory system, the basis of the industrial revolution, brought an increasingly large number of workers directly under a single management. Then, the modern corporation, equally revolutionary in its effect, placed the wealth of innumerable individuals under the same central control. By each of these changes the power of those in control was immensely enlarged and the status of those involved, worker or property owner, was radically changed. The independent worker who entered the factory became a wage laborer surrendering the direction of his labor to his industrial master. The property owner who invests in a modern corporation so far surrenders his wealth to those in control of the corporation that he has exchanged the position of independent owner for one in which he may become merely recipient of the wages of capital.

In and of itself, the corporate device does not necessarily bring about this change. It has long been possible for an individual to incorporate his business even though it still represents his own investment, his own activities, and his own business transactions; he has in fact merely created a legal alter ego by setting up a corporation as the nominal vehicle. If the corporate form had done nothing more than this, we should have only an interesting custom according to which business was carried on by individuals adopting for that purpose certain legal clothing. It would involve no radical shift in property tenure or in the organization of economic activity; it would inaugurate no "system" compared to the institutions of feudalism.

The corporate system appears only when this type of private or "close" corporation has given way to an essentially different form, the quasi-public corporation: a corporation in which a large measure of separation of ownership and control has taken place through the multiplication of owners. . . .

Though the American law makes no distinction between the private corporation and the quasi-public, the economics of the two are essentially different. The separation of ownership from control produces a condition where the interests of owner and ultimate manager may, and often do, diverge, and where many of the checks which formerly operated to limit the use of power disappear. Size alone tends to give these giant corporations a social significance not attached to the smaller units of private enterprise. By the use of the open market for securities, each of these corporations assumes obligations towards the investing public which transform it from a legal method clothing the rule of a few individuals into an institution at least nominally serving investors who have embarked their funds in its enterprise. New responsibilities towards owners, the workers, the consumers, and the State thus rest upon the shoulders of those in control. In creating these new relationships, the quasi-public corporation may fairly be said to work a revolution. It has destroyed the unity that we commonly call property — has divided ownership into nominal ownership and the power formerly joined to it. Thereby the corporation has changed the nature of the profit-seeking enterprise. This revolution forms the subject of the present study. . . .

The dissolution of the atom of property destroys the very foundation on which the economic order of the past three hundred years has rested. Private enterprise, which has molded economic life since the close of the middle ages, has been rooted in the institution of private property. . . . Whereas the organization of feudal economic life rested upon an elaborate system of binding customs, the organization under the system of private enterprise has rested upon the self-interest of the property owner — a self-interest held in check only by competition and the conditions of supply and demand. Such self-interest has long been regarded as the best guarantee of economic efficiency. It has been assumed that, if the individual is protected in the right both to use his own property as he sees fit and to receive the full fruits of its use, his desire for personal gain, for profits, can be relied upon as an effective incentive to his efficient use of any industrial property he may possess.

In the quasi-public corporation, such an assumption no longer holds. As we have seen, it is no longer the individual himself who uses his wealth. Those in control of that wealth, and therefore in a position to secure industrial efficiency and product profits, are no longer, as owners, entitled to the bulk of such profits. Those who control the destinies of the typical modern corporation own so insignificant a fraction of the company's stock that the returns from running the corporation profitably accrue to them in only a very minor degree. The stockholders, on the other hand, to whom the profits of the corporation go, cannot be motivated by those profits to a more efficient use of the property, since they have surrendered all disposition of it to those in control of the enterprise. The explosion of the atom of property destroys the basis of the old assumption that the quest for profits will spur the owner of industrial property to its effective use. It consequently challenges the fundamental economic principle of individual initiative in industrial enterprise. It raises for reexamination the question of the motive force back of industry, and the ends for which the modern corporation can be or will be run.

The problem of the so-called Berle-Means corporation — that is, a corporation with centralized management and dispersed shareholders — is another centerpiece of corporate law and corporate finance in the United States. Indeed, the tension between the value of retaining managerial discretion (to promote efficiencies in the corporate form, as outlined in Coase's *Nature of the Firm*) and the dangers of unchecked managerial discretion (as outlined in the Berle-Means excerpt) is *the* central issue in corporate law. Much of the Corporations course at law school is devoted to understanding mechanisms of managerial control that protect investors without unduly constraining the business judgment of managers. Maintaining this balance in a sensible manner is an important role of corporate counsel.

As a matter of intellectual history, the interesting point is to recognize when the problem of managerial discretion in the public corporation was first identified: 1932, in the depths of the Great Depression and on the eve of the New Deal. Large corporations with widely dispersed shareholders gained prominence in the United States only after the First World War. Previously, the major industrial firms tended to be owned by a small number of extremely wealthy families (such as the Carnegies, Rockefellers, and Mellons). Only with the boom of the stock

market in the 1920s and the emergence of a large body of retail investors did dispersed public ownership of corporations become common.
So what Professors Berle and Means articulated in their famous book
was a relatively new phenomenon. The acuity of their analysis was,
however, quickly recognized, and it generated support for a number of
President Roosevelt's legislative proposals, most notably the principal
federal securities laws — the Securities Act of 1933 and the Securities
Exchange Act of 1934 — which attempt to tilt the balance of power away
from managers and back toward shareholders.

Corporate lawyers in the United States are all intimately familiar with
the problem of the Berle-Means corporation. And a host of common corporate activities — from tender offers to proxy fights — are understood
as important mechanisms for controlling managerial discretion. (Tender
offers and proxy fights are mechanisms that shareholders can use to seize
control from managers.) As you will see when you study corporate law,
there remains an active debate as to whether these and other mechanisms
of control adequately police potential managerial abuses or whether
other legal developments (such as poison pills and other takeover de-
fenses) have tipped the balance back in management's favor. We leave
the details of these interesting and important issues to another day. For
current purposes, what you should recognize is that what Berle and
Means identified in their book was a form of the principal-agent problem
inherent in the corporate structure. Many of the legal developments that
have occurred since their book was written are attempts to resolve this
conflict. Analytically, they are similar to the solutions we discussed in
the Contracting chapter: legal requirements designed to make the agent
(in this context, the manager) behave in a way that is consistent with the
interest of the principal (here, the shareholder).[4]

---

4. Although the Berle-Means corporation has become a shorthand for conflicts between shareholders and managers of public corporations, the excerpt above (as well
as the full book) was also concerned about the expanding power of managers over
other parties, particularly workers. And Professors Berle and Means favored public
interventions to protect these other parties, sometimes even at the expense of shareholder interests. Modern invocations of the Berle-Means thesis do not usually pick up
this strain of the original argument, at least not in the United States.

B. The Roots of Modern Finance

Most academic writing in modern finance is much too technical for an introductory treatment. To give students a sense of the general tenor of this literature, we have provided in this section short excerpts from two seminal works, both of which you are likely to encounter again in upper-level law school courses.

The first is from the initial article of a two-part series in which Professors Modigliani and Miller explored a question that has fascinated financial theorists for many years: how should a firm finance its operations in order to maximize the firm's value? Should firms borrow money (i.e., take out loans) or raise equity (i.e., sell stock)? Or do some combination of the two? Which approach gives the firm the best financing (or the lowest *cost of capital*)? After making a series of simplifying assumptions, the professors reached a startling conclusion: the capital structure of a firm (that is, the proportion of its financing that comes from debt or equity) has *no* impact on its overall value.

Franco Modigliani and Merton H. Miller
The Cost of Capital, Corporation Finance,
and the Theory of Investment
3 *Am. Econ. Rev.* 261, 261–71 (1958)

What is the "cost of capital" to a firm in a world in which funds are used to acquire assets whose yields are uncertain; and in which capital can be obtained by many different media, ranging from pure debt instruments, representing money-fixed claims, to pure equity issues, giving holders only the right to a pro-rata share in the uncertain venture? . . .

In much of his formal analysis, the economic theorist at least has tended to side-step the essence of the cost-of-capital problem by proceeding as though physical assets [e.g., plants and equipment] could be regarded as yielding known, sure streams. Given this assumption, the theorist has concluded that the cost of capital to the owners of a firm is simply the rate of interest on bonds; and has derived the familiar proposition that the firm, acting rationally, will tend to push investment to the point where marginal yield on physical assets is equal to the market rate of interest. . . .

Considered as a convenient approximation, the model of the firm constructed via this certainty — or certainty-equivalent — approach has admittedly been useful in dealing with some of the grosser aspects of the process of capital accumulation. . . . Yet few would maintain that this approximation is adequate. . . .

. . . [A]n alternative approach, based on market value maximization, can provide the basis for an operational definition of the cost of capital and a workable theory of investment. Under this approach any investment project and its concomitant financing plan must pass only the following test: Will the project, as financed, raise the market value of the firm's shares? If so, it is worth undertaking; if not, its return is less than the marginal cost of capital to the firm. . . .

The potential advantages of the market-value approach have long been appreciated; yet analytical results have been meager. What appears to be keeping this line of development from achieving its promise is largely the lack of an adequate theory of the effect of financial structure on market valuations, and of how the effects can be inferred from objective market data. It is with the development of such a theory and of its implications for the cost-of-capital problem that we shall be concerned in this paper.

Our procedure will be to develop . . . the basic theory itself and give some brief account of its empirical relevance. [Then], we show how the theory can be used to answer the cost-of-capital question and how it permits us to develop a theory of investment of the firm under conditions of uncertainty. . . .

[After making a number of simplifying assumptions regarding, among other things, perfect information, frictionless contracting, and the absence of taxation, the paper then begins its formal analysis of the relationship between a firm's financial structure and its market value, and proceeds to defend the following two provocative and influential propositions:]

Proposition I: . . . *[T]he market value of any firm is independent of its capital structure and is given by capitalizing its expected [stream of profits from its physical assets] at the rate . . . appropriate to its class. . . . That is, the average cost of capital to any firm is completely independent of its capital structure. . . .*

> Proposition II. *[T]he expected yield of a share of stock is equal to the appropriate capitalization rate . . . for a pure equity stream in the class, plus a premium related to the financial risk [associated with the firm's] debt-to-equity ratio.*

At first reading, the language of this excerpt may seem a bit dense, but the essence of the Modigliani and Miller propositions can be easily summarized. In brief, their insight is that the more a firm relies on debt to finance its activities, the more risky and less valuable its equity will become. In the past, financial analysts had assumed that because the interest rate paid on debt is usually cheaper than the cost of a firm's equity, a firm could lower its average cost of capital by financing its activities with more debt and less equity. Modigliani and Miller challenge this once-conventional wisdom by pointing out that the issuance of debt reduces the value of a firm's remaining equity by increasing its riskiness. Through technical analysis that goes beyond the scope of this precis, Modigliani and Miller's article demonstrates that however much a firm saves by issuing new debt, that savings are exactly offset by the reduction in the value of its equity. Thus, a firm's capital structure cannot, in theory, affect a firm's overall value.

What you should also recognize at the outset is that even the authors never believed the propositions summarized above were an accurate reflection of the real world. Rather the propositions were important because they forced financial analysts and academic theorists to think more carefully and systematically about why the choice of capital structures does, in the real word, seem to have an effect on the value of firms. In brief, what subsequent writers (including Modigliani and Miller themselves) have argued is that the choice of capital structure makes a difference in firm value because a number of the simplifying assumptions in the original article are not true in reality. In particular, for certain companies, taxes favor borrowing as compared to the issuance of equity. In addition, costs associated with financial distress and bankruptcy will influence a firm's choice of capital structures.

For a practicing attorney, the importance of this debate is the effect that it has on the activities of corporate clients and their financial advisers. Much of what goes on in the everyday world of corporate finance can be understood as efforts to adjust the capital structure of firms in order to enhance their overall value. For example, when a company issues new stock or retires outstanding debt, the firm is altering its capital structure and (ideally) improving the firm's overall value. Under the stylized assumptions of Modigliani and Miller's original article, these sorts of transactions wouldn't make any sense. But in the real world, they are a staple of everyday corporate practice.

Another important dimension of the choice of capital structure is its effect on the principal-agent problem identified in the Berle-Means excerpt presented above: the tendency of managers in public corporations (agents) not to abide by the interests of their shareholders (principals). In the following famous article, Professors Jensen and Meckling explore how changes in capital structure can be used to resolve that conflict.

Michael C. Jensen and William H. Meckling
Theory of the Firm: Managerial Behavior
3 *J. Fin. Econ.* 35, 36–43 (1976)

Many problems associated with the inadequacy of the current theory of the firm can be viewed as special cases of the theory of agency relationships in which there is a growing literature. . . .

We define an agency relationship as a contract under which one or more persons (the principal(s)) engage another person (the agent) to perform some service on their behalf which involves delegating some decision-making authority to the agent. If both parties to the relationship are utility maximizers there is good reason to believe that the agent will not always act in the best interests of the principal. The *principal* can limit divergences from his interest by establishing appropriate incentives for the agent and by incurring monitoring costs designed to limit the aberrant activities of the agent. In addition in some situations it will pay the *agent* to expend resources (bonding costs) to guarantee that he will not take certain actions which would harm the principal or to ensure that the principal will be compensated if he does take such actions. However, it is generally impossible for the principal or the agent at zero cost to ensure that the agent will make optimal decisions from the principal's viewpoint. In most agency relationships the principal and the agent will incur positive monitoring and bonding costs (non-pecuniary as well as pecuniary), and in addition there will be some divergence between the agent's decisions and those decisions which would maximize the welfare of the principal. The dollar equivalent of the reduction in welfare experienced by the principal due to this divergence is also a cost of the agency relationship, and we refer to this latter cost as the "residual loss." We define agency costs as the sum of:

(1) the monitoring expenditures by the principal,
(2) the bonding expenditures by the agent,
(3) the residual loss . . . (actions by agent not made in best interest of principal)

Since the relationship between the stockholders and manager of a corporation fit the definition of a pure agency relationship it should be no surprise to discover that the issues associated with the "separation of ownership and control" in the modern diffuse ownership corporation are intimately associated with the general problem of agency. We show below that an explanation of why and how agency costs generated by the corporate form are born[e] leads to a theory of the ownership (or capital) structure of the firm. . . .

In this section we analyze the effect of outside equity on agency costs by comparing the behavior of a manager when he owns 100 percent of the residual claims on a firm to his behavior when he sells off a portion of those claims to outsiders. If a wholly owned firm is managed by the owner, he will make operating decisions which maximize his utility. These decisions will involve not only the benefits he derives from pecuniary returns but also the utility generated by various non-pecuniary aspects of his entrepreneurial activities such as the physical appointments of the office, the attractiveness of the secretarial staff, the level of employee discipline, the kind and amount of charitable contributions, personal relations ("love", "respect", etc.) with employees, a larger than optimal computer to play with, purchase of production inputs from friends, etc. The optimum mix (in the absence of taxes) of the various pecuniary and non-pecuniary benefits is achieved when the marginal utility derived from an additional dollar of expenditure (measured net of any productive effects) is equal for each non-pecuniary item and equal to the marginal utility derived from an additional dollar of after tax purchasing power (wealth).

If the owner-manager sells equity claims on the corporation which are identical to his (i.e., share proportionately in the profits of the firm and have limited liability)[,] agency costs will be generated by the divergence between his interest and those of the outside shareholders, since he will then bear only a fraction of the costs of any non-pecuniary benefits he takes out in maximizing his own utility. If the manager owns only 95 percent of the stock, he will expend resources to the point where the marginal utility derived from a dollar's expenditure of the firm's resources on such items equals the marginal utility of an additional 95 cents in general purchasing power (i.e., *his* share of the wealth reduction) and not one dollar. Such activities, on his part, can be limited (but probably not eliminated) by the expenditure of resources on monitoring activities by the outside stockholders. But as we show below, the owner will bear the entire wealth effects of these expected costs so long as the equity market anticipates these effects. Prospective minority shareholders will realize that the owner-manager's interests will diverge somewhat from theirs, hence the price which they will pay for shares will reflect the monitoring costs and the effect of the divergence between the manager's interest and theirs. Nevertheless, ignoring for the moment the possibility of borrowing against his wealth, the owner will find it desirable to bear these costs as long as the welfare increment he experiences from converting his claims on the firm into general purchasing power is large enough to offset them.

As the owner-manager's fraction of the equity falls, his fractional claim on the outcomes falls and this will tend to encourage him to appropriate larger amounts of the corporate resources in the form of perquisites. This also makes it desirable for the minority shareholders to expend more resources in monitoring his behavior. Thus, the wealth costs to the owner of obtaining additional cash in the equity markets rise as his fractional ownership falls.

We shall continue to characterize the agency conflict between the owner-manager and outside shareholders as deriving from the manager's tendency to appropriate perquisites out of the firm's resources for his own consumption. However, we do not mean to leave the impression that this is the only or even the most important source of conflict. Indeed, it is likely that the most important conflict arises from the fact that as the manager's ownership claim falls, his incentive to devote significant effort to creative activities such as searching out new profitable ventures falls. He may in fact avoid such ventures simply because it requires too much trouble or effort on his part to manage or to learn about new technologies. Avoidance of these personal costs and the anxieties that go with them also represent a source of on the job utility to him and it can result in the value of the firm being substantially lower than it otherwise could be. . . .

The agency costs of debt

In general if the agency costs engendered by the existence of outside owners are positive it will pay the absentee owner (i.e., shareholders) to sell out to an owner-manager who can avoid these costs. This could be accomplished in principle by having the manager become the sole equity holder by repurchasing all of the outside equity claims with funds obtained through the issued of limited liability debt claims and the sum of his own personal wealth. This single owner corporation would not suffer the agency costs associated with outside equity. Therefore there must be some compelling reasons why we find the diffuse-owner corporate firm financed by equity claims so prevalent as an organizational form.

An ingenious entrepreneur eager to expand, has open to him the opportunity to design a whole hierarchy of fixed claims on assets and earnings, with premiums paid for different levels of risk. Why don't we observe large corporations individually owned with a tiny fraction of the capital supplied by the entrepreneur in return for 100 percent of the equity and the rest simply borrowed? We believe there are a number of reasons: (1) incentive effects associated with highly leveraged firms, (2) monitoring costs these incentive effects engender, and (3) bankruptcy costs. Furthermore, all of these costs are simply particular aspects of the agency costs associated with the existence of debt claims on the firm. . . .

A theory of the corporate ownership structure

In the previous sections we discussed the nature of agency costs associated with outside claims on the firm — both debt and equity. Our purpose here is to integrate these concepts into the beginnings of a theory of the corporate ownership structure. We use the term "ownership structure" rather than "capital structure" to highlight the fact that the crucial variables to be determined are not just the relative amounts of debt and equity but also the fraction of the equity held by the manager. . . .

This Jensen and Meckling excerpt combines elements of our three previous readings in this section. Its title invokes Professor Coase's *Nature of the Firm*, and the Jensen and Meckling article represents a continuation of the Coasean project of attempting to define the optimal set of economic relationships to be organized within the structure of a firm. Jensen and Meckling are arguing that the firm is best structured when equity ownership and managerial control are aligned in the same party. Viewed from this perspective, the Jensen and Meckling excerpt also speaks directly to the problem of the Berle-Means corporation: one way to eliminate the problems of unbridled managerial discretion inherent in public corporations is to encourage managers to become (once again) the owners of their own firms — that is, to privatize the public corporation. Finally, Jensen and Meckling are writing in the Modigliani and Miller tradition because, at root, Jensen and Meckling are addressing the optimal capital structure of the firm. In advancing their argument, Jensen and Meckling are balancing the value-enhancing properties of aligning management and ownership against the costs of maintaining high levels of debt.

The Jensen and Meckling thesis also has real-world applications. Since this article was written in 1976, corporate takeovers have become increasingly common. In some of these transactions, a small group of investors backed with large quantities of debt (a.k.a. junk bonds) acquire a public firm. These investor groups are pursuing precisely the strategy that Jensen and Meckling have advocated. By substituting themselves for a large group of public shareholders, these investor groups hope to improve control over corporate management (i.e., restrain unbridled discretion) and thereby enhance corporate value. The debate over the propriety and efficacy of these transactions is fascinating and as yet unresolved, but there is no question that their intellectual foundations can be traced back to Professors Jensen and Meckling and the academic traditions upon which their article is based.

C. The Goals of Finance

The foregoing excerpts suggest some of the critical questions that financial theory seeks to address. How much economic activity should be located within a particular firm? How can we make sure that the managers of firms remain faithful to the interests of their principals (traditionally understood to be their shareholders)? What is the best capital structure for a particular firm? Should it have more or less debt? Should its shares of common stock be distributed broadly to many shareholders, or should they be concentrated in the hands of a small number of individuals who can more easily keep track of the firm's activities?

To answer these questions, financial theorists have developed a number of techniques, several of which are introduced in the balance of this chapter. Many of these techniques provide tools for analysts to estimate the value of business activities (such as the construction of a new plant) that will generate benefits over extended periods of time. Others techniques look to the performance of a firm's stock in the capital markets as a means of measuring the company's riskiness and also the quality of its managers' performance. Armed with these and related tools, the financial analyst can offer guidance as to whether a firm should launch a new product or make an adjustment in its capital structure or even replace existing management with new blood.

In the following section, we summarize several basic financial techniques that are characteristic of the field and also of particular relevance to practicing attorneys. We begin in the next section with one of the most fundamental financial concepts: the time value of money. Then we turn to several more complex but equally important tenets of modern finance.

3. The Time Value of Money

One basic financial principle that all lawyers should understand is the relationship between the value of money received today and the value of

money received in the future. This relationship is sometimes described as the *time value of money*. This section introduces the concept and illustrates its relevance to the practice of law.

A. Comparing Current Dollars to Future Dollars

A choice that attorneys often face is helping clients decide whether to accept a payment immediately or to get a somewhat larger payment at some point in the future. Suppose, for example, you were representing a plaintiff with a wrongful discharge claim against his former employer. And suppose further that the employer offered your client a $1,000 payment to settle the dispute but that you were confident that, if litigated, the claim would generate $1,100 for your client (net of attorney's fees and all other expenses). The only fact you didn't know was how long it would take for the suit to be litigated. How can you help your client decide whether to accept the $1,000 settlement offer today or reject the offer and litigate the claim?[5]

One way of approaching this problem would be to calculate how much money your client would have if he accepted the settlement offer, put the funds into a bank account, and kept the funds there until the litigation was completed. Comparing the future balance of such a hypothetical bank account with the expected subsequent court award offers a good initial illustration of the time value of money. To complete the analysis, you need to know (or estimate) the rate of interest your client could earn on a bank deposit. Let's say, after investigation, that interest paid on a bank account turns out to be 5% a year. So, if the settlement payment stayed in the bank account for 1 year, it would grow to $1,050, which is

---

5. Thinking back to the decision analysis section of the course, some students may recognize that this presentation omits various potential complexities. In most cases there will be uncertainty as to the amount of a litigated award, and so multiple possible awards might have to be analyzed or, perhaps, analysis of an expected award would be more appropriate. In addition, one might want to consider the possibility that the defendant will raise its settlement offer if you choose to proceed to trial. Also, there is a possibility that the award of pre-judgment interest might increase the amount of an award the longer the trial is delayed. We omit these and other complexities here in order to focus on the time-value-of-money issue.

$1,000 plus 5% of $1,000. In mathematical notation, you would typically write this as

$$\$1{,}000 + 0.05 \times \$1{,}000 = \$1{,}000\,(1 + 0.05)$$
$$= \$1{,}050$$

(Remember that the term *percent* means *for every one hundred*; thus, 5% is 5 divided by 100, or 0.05.)

So, if you knew the litigation would be over at the end of 1 year, you would know that the litigated value of the case — $1,100 — is a bit greater than the value of putting the settlement offer into a bank account for 1 year — $1,050. But what if the litigation would take 2 years to complete? At this point, one might be tempted to say that since we got $50 of interest on the account in the first year, then we'll get another $50 the second year, giving us exactly $1,100 in the account at the end of 2 years. This simplistic approach is, however, wrong. In year 2, interest is being paid on $1,050 (the original amount plus interest earned during the first year) and not on $1,000 (just the original amount). In other words, the simplistic approach fails to take account of the interest paid in year 2 on interest earned the first year. Properly calculated, by the end of year 2, the balance in the account would be equal to $1,050 plus 5% of $1,050, or $1,102.50:

$$5\% \text{ of } \$1{,}050 = 0.05 \times \$1{,}050$$
$$= \$52.50$$

so

$$\$1{,}050 \times (1.05) = \$1{,}050 + \$52.50$$
$$= \$1{,}102.50$$

Thus, your client would be slightly better off accepting the settlement offer and leaving it in a bank account earning 5% interest for 2 years than going to trial and receiving a net settlement of $1,100 at the of 2 years. What's more, the longer the trial took to complete, the more attractive the immediate settlement offer would become. In the language of decision

$$PV = A \cdot (1 + R)^{Y}$$

(handwritten annotations: "← initial deposit", "← rate of interest", "Y ← years")

analysis, the crossover point for choosing the immediate settlement offer or going to trial is a bit less than 2 years.

To abstract a bit from the foregoing illustration, one can see the basic structure of the time value of money. After 1 year, the bank account is worth $1,000 × (1 + 0.05). After 2 years, the account is worth $1,050 × (1 + 0.05), which can be rewritten as $1,000 × (1 + 0.05) × (1 + 0.05). (Do you see why?) Getting a bit more mathematical, this last expression can be written in the following shorthand: $1,000 × (1 + 0.05)^2. If the money stayed in the account for 5 years, it would have a value of $1,000 × (1 + 0.05)^5, which is $1,276.28. If the money stayed in the account for 10 years, it would have a value of $1,000 × (1 + 0.05)^{10}, or $1,628.89. And so on.[6]

B. Simple versus Compound Interest

Let's return a moment to the simplistic, but erroneous, method of calculating interest mentioned in the preceding subsection. Projecting the interest to be paid in future years based on the interest generated in year 1 has a certain appeal. It is easy to do, and for short periods of time, the use of this method (known as simple interest) is not that much different from the more accurate technique described above (known as compound interest). In our example, using interest of $50 per year yielded a value at the end of year 2 of $1,100, only slightly off from the correct value of $1,102.50. Over longer periods, however, the differences can be large, and before too long astronomical. In the example given above, after 10 years the amount in the bank account under compound interest was $1,628.89. That means the accrued interest ($628.89) was $128.89 more than what would have been projected with simple interest ($500.00, or 10 × $50).

The power of compound interest is one of the enduring miracles of finance, and its effect on the time value of money is often much larger than one's intuitions would suggest, particularly with higher interest rates. One heuristic that is worth remembering is the Rule of 72 — which provides a rough estimate of the number of years it takes for a sum of

---

6. More generally, the future value (FV) of a sum of money (PV) deposited into a bank account yielding a given rate of interest (r) over a specified number of years (n) can be described by this equation: $FV = PV \times (1 + r)^n$.

Figure 5-1
How Fast Does Your Money Grow?
(Actual Years to Double)

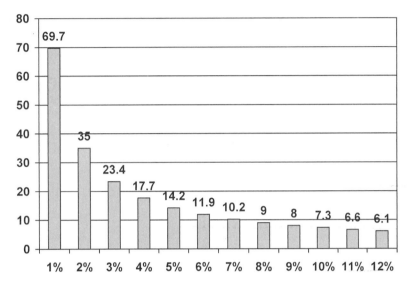

money to double under compound interest at a given interest rate. If you divide 72 by the annual rate of interest, the answer is a fairly accurate estimate of the number of years it takes money to increase by 100% — that is, to double. So money deposited into a bank account paying 5% will double in roughly 14.4 years (72/5). You can check this prediction using our example above. If you left your immediate settlement of $1,000 in the bank for 14 years, it would equal $1,000 × (1 + 0.05)^{14}, or $1,979.93, just shy of $2,000. Figure 5-1 summarizes the actual doubling period for a sum growing at a compound interest rate for a range of interest rates.

C. Finding the Present Value of a Single Future Payment

Another common problem that arises in many legal contexts is trying to calculate the current value of a payment to be made at some point in the future. For example, suppose a client of yours wins a lottery entitling the client to a payment of $1 million at the end of 1 year. Suppose further that the state lottery commission offers to make a somewhat smaller payment — say $940,000 — but will make that payment immediately. How should you advise your client?

$$PV = \frac{FV}{(1+R)^Y}$$

Clearly, this problem is quite similar to the problems we discussed above — choosing between an immediate settlement offer and a somewhat larger expected award after trial. There, we were calculating the future value of a sum received now. Here, we are asking about the present value of a sum to be received in the future. The way lawyers (and financial analysts) solve these two sorts of problems is also quite similar. If we can figure out what sum of money placed in a bank account with the appropriate interest rate would grow to $1 million at the end of a year, then we would know the present value of that $1 million lottery payment. Restated more formally — and assuming that 5% is still the right rate of interest — we are trying to calculate a sum of money that, if multiplied by (1 + 0.05), equals 1,000,000:

$$\text{present value} \times (1 + 0.05) = \$1 \text{ million}$$

And, dividing both sides of the equation by (1 + 0.05), you find

$$\text{present value} = \$1 \text{ million} / (1 + 0.05)$$
$$= \$952,380.95$$

So the lottery commission's offer of $940,000 is a bit lower than the present value of $1 million in a year's time. While there may be other reasons for your client to take the money right now — who wants to wait a year to be a millionaire? — our financial analysis would counsel otherwise.

With this basic approach, one can evaluate the present value of payments to be made much further in the future. Suppose the lottery commission were not required to make its $1 million payment until 4 years had passed. What would the present value be under those circumstances? Intuitively, you may sense that the further in the future the payment is, the lower the present value must be, and that's exactly right. Again, a helpful way to frame the problem is to consider how much money you would have to put in the bank today in order to have $1 million in 4 years. Following the analysis presented above:

$$\text{present value} \times (1 + 0.05) \times (1 + 0.05) \times (1 + 0.05) \times (1 + 0.05) = \$1 \text{ million}$$

And, dividing both sides of the equation by $(1 + 0.05)^4$, you find

$$\text{present value} = \$1 \text{ million} / (1 + 0.05)^4$$
$$= \$822{,}702.47$$

Just as the power of compound interest increases the size of a bank account over time, similar factors enhance the discount of payments that will not be made until far in the future.[7]

D. Valuing a Stream of Future Payments

A variant on the foregoing problem involves the calculation of the present value of a series (or stream) of future payments. Lawyers face this problem when they receive settlement offers in the form of a proposal to make 10 payments of $50,000 annually for 10 years. Such a settlement might be plausible in a tort case where a 55-year-old plaintiff had been incapacitated in such a way that it was no longer possible for the plaintiff to work. A series of $50,000 payments could be viewed as replacing wages for the rest of the plaintiff's working life. The question a lawyer would have to consider is whether it would be better to accept this structured settlement or a lump-sum settlement of, say, $400,000.

In practice, most lawyers (and even most financial analysts) would use a calculator or computer program to answer questions of this sort. But we have already developed sufficient analytical tools to figure out the answer ourselves. You can simply break up the settlement proposal into 10 separate payments of $50,000. (See Figure 5-2, Option A.) You already know how to figure out the present value of the first payment, which is received at the end of the first year. As long as the 5% interest rate is still appropriate, the present value is $50,000/(1 + 0.05), or $47,619.05. (Note: this is the same calculation we did above for the $1 million lottery

---

7. The general formula for the present value (PV) of a payment to be received a specified number of years (n) in the future (FV) is $PV = FV / (1 + r)^n$, where r is the appropriate interest rate. Notice that this equation is simply a restatement of the formula given in the previous footnote, after dividing both sides by $(1 + r)^n$.

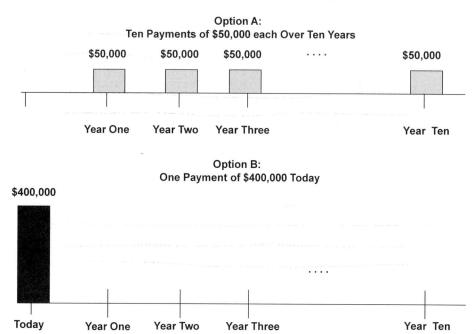

Figure 5-2
Periodic Payments v. Lump Sum Payment

Option A:
Ten Payments of $50,000 each Over Ten Years

payment at the end of a year.) And you could make a similar calculation for the 9 other payments:

$$\text{present value} = \$50,000/(1+.05)+$$
$$\$50,000/(1+.05)^2+$$
$$\$50,000/(1+.05)^3+$$
$$\dots$$
$$\$50,000/(1+.05)^{10}$$

$$= \$47,619+$$
$$\$45,351+$$
$$\$43,192+$$
$$\dots$$
$$\$30,696$$

$$= \$386,087$$

So $400,000 looks pretty good by comparison. (Another way of thinking about this analysis is to recognize that if you put $400,000 into a bank

---

Box 5-1
Present Value or Future Value

When comparing present payments and future payments, you can either convert the present values into future values (as we did in section A) or convert future values into present values (as we did in section C). Both approaches work. The key is to express the payments to be compared in the values associated with the same time period. You want to compare apples with apples and oranges with oranges.

In practice, analysts almost always use the latter technique: converting future values into present values. There are a number of reasons for this convention. Most notably, most people find it easier to understand payments expressed in terms of present values. The dollars in your wallet right now are "present value" dollars. If we determine that a future payment has a present value of $100, what we mean is that the future payment has the same value as $100 in your wallet.

---

account yielding 5% interest and took out $50,000 a year for 10 years, there would be something left in the account at the end of 10 years.)

Streams of payments are surprisingly common in legal settings. Oftentimes, the payments will be made for the remainder of a person's life. In that context, the payment is known as a life annuity, and many retirement benefits as well as some tort settlements are made in this manner. In order to value payment streams of this sort, one must estimate life expectancies as well as appropriate interest rates. Financial textbooks devote considerable attention to the valuation of life annuities and derive a number of helpful formulas for calculating their present value.[8]

---

8. For example, the present value (PV) of a perpetual (i.e., continuing forever) annual annuity (P) discounted at an interest rate (r) has a quite simple formula: $PV = P/r$. The present value (PV) of a perpetual annuity that grows at a given annual rate (g) has this formula: $PV = P/(r - g)$. If you're interested in reviewing the derivation of these and similar formulas, you should consult Ross, et al., *Corporate Finance* (2010).

E. Internal Rates of Return

So far in this section, we have been trying to figure the present or future value of cash payments. To make these valuations, we have had to make certain assumptions about the appropriate interest rate to use. And, for simplicity's sake, we have been using a 5% rate of interest. Sometimes, however, financial problems arise the other way around: we know the present and future values of a transaction, and what we need to figure out is the interest rate implicit in the cash stream. In financial argot, this is called the *internal rate of return.* Suppose you have a 55 year-old client who wants to deposit $30,000 in a bank account to use for the client's retirement that will begin in ten years. Suppose further the bank offers your client the following two choices: either the deposit can earn 10 percent per year on the deposit, compounded annually, over the ten year period or your client can receive a single payment of $100,000 at the end of the ten year period. Which option should you recommend?

You could approach this problem in several ways. One approach would be to calculate the value of the bank account after ten years, growing at a compounded interest rate of 10 percent per year. From our prior discussions, we know how to do this calculation of future values:

$$\text{Future Value} = \text{initial deposit} \times (1 + \text{annual interest rate})^{(\text{number of years})}$$

$$= \$30,000 \times (1 + 0.10)^{10}$$
$$= \$30,000 \times (2.59)$$
$$= \$77,812$$

Based on this analysis, you can tell that it's better for your client to take the second choice, which promises a $100,000 payment at the end of ten years (in contrast to the $77,812 payment implicit in a 10 percent rate of interest on a bank deposit).

But what if you wanted to know exactly how high the bank's stated rate of interest on a ten-year deposit would have to be in order to offer your client a better return than the second option? This might be a relevant question if you were shopping around at other banks that offered a range of different interest rates.

One somewhat clunky method is trial and error, whereby you would experiment with a number of possible interest rates and see which one does the best job of making $30,000 grow into $100,000 at the end of 10 years. We already know that a 10% interest rate is too low (it generates only $77,812 after 10 years).

So 10% is too low, how about 15%?

$$\$30,000 \times (1+0.15)^{10} = \$30,000 \times 4,046$$
$$= \$121,366.70$$

That's closer to the mark ($100,000) but a bit too high. Perhaps something on the order of 12% would be more appropriate:

$$\$30,000 \times (1+0.12)^{10} = \$30,000 \times 3,106$$
$$= \$93,175.40$$

Better, but still not quite right. But you can see how we might proceed with this methodology.

Another approach is to resort to a financial calculator, which will perform essentially the same iterative operations (but much more quickly) and then tell you that the exact interest rate needed to grow $30,000 into $100,000 at the end of ten years is 12.7945%. In other words,

$$\$30,000 \times (1+0.127945)^{10} = \$30,000 \times 3.33$$
$$= \$100,000$$

What this calculation suggests is that the second option presented to your client — a promise of $100,000 at the end of ten years on an initial deposit of $30,000 — carries an implicit interest rate of 12.79% per year compounded annually. With this analysis you could advise your client that it would make sense to choose the bank's second option unless another bank were offering to pay an interest rate of more than 12.79% on a 10-year deposit. Internal rates of return are also used in various other legal and financial contexts, such as the evaluation of investment opportunities.

F. What Interest Rate Should You Use?

So far in our discussion, we've skipped over one of the most difficult and important aspects of time-value-of-money techniques: selecting an appropriate interest rate. Because of the properties of compound interest, changes in interest rate assumptions can make a huge difference in valuations. Just looking back to the preceding section, we saw that $30,000 invested at 10% grows to less than $78,000 at the end of 10 years, but at 12.79% grows to a full $100,000. Particularly when dealing with longer periods of time, present and future value calculations are highly sensitive to interest rate assumptions.

In practice, the role of selecting the correct interest rate assumptions will usually fall to financial professionals. Investment bankers typically do this sort of analysis in major transactions, and oftentimes clients will have considerable in-house expertise in the area. Even in these contexts, however, attorneys should have a general idea of what is going on. Moreover, for smaller corporate clients and individual clients, the lawyer will often be the most financially sophisticated participant in a transaction. In these contexts, the lawyer's advice may be crucial. In the land of the blind, the one-eyed man (or woman) is king (or queen).

Crudely speaking, there are three different ways to think about selecting an interest rate. The second has the greatest analytical purity — and is the one most analogous to the approach that financial analysts typically follow — but the first and the third offer practical guidance that may have considerable salience in certain contexts.

1. **Current return on your own savings.** In the initial illustrations discussed in this section of the chapter, we made reference to the rate of interest paid by your client's bank. In some contexts, this may be a wholly sensible way of proceeding. For a tort victim who is going to use a settlement payment to pay future expenses — cover lost wages and costs associated with rehabilitation — there is a certain appeal to using an interest rate that describes what the client will earn on the funds. There are, however, certain problems with this approach. For one thing, this approach implicitly equates funds deposited in a bank with payments due from other parties who may well be substantially less creditworthy than a regulated financial institution and almost certainly not covered

Assumes payers are creditworthy → look at risk of payer

by federal deposit insurance. Depending on the context, this difference may have more or less significance. If the future payment is to come in a year or two and the payer is Microsoft, then maybe the difference in risk is not that important. On the other hand, if the future payment is not due for 5 years and is coming from a start-up enterprise that may well go bankrupt in the meantime, then the risk differential would be highly relevant, and using a bank interest rate to discount future payments would be problematic in that it would overvalue future payments.

2. **A rate based on the characteristics of the payer.** A second, alternative approach is to peg interest rates to the risk characteristics of the entity or individual who is going to be making the payment. With this approach, the interest rate used to value a future payment would be relatively low if the payment were to come from the federal government (which is generally thought to be the payer least likely to default on its obligation), somewhat higher for Microsoft, and higher still for high-technology companies and most individual payers. While the intuitive appeal of this risk-adjusted approach is clear, exactly how you should go about determining the precise interest rates to use for different payers is not. Indeed, a large proportion of financial theory deals with adjusting rates of return to account for the varying degrees of risk of different payers. Later on in this chapter — when we introduce the so-called Capital Asset Pricing Model — we will explore the most common technique for estimating the riskiness of firms with publicly traded common stock. And, if you were helping a client to select an interest rate for discounting future promises of some firms, you would likely employ the Capital Asset Pricing Model and similarly spirited techniques.

Crudely speaking, what these financial techniques attempt to do is estimate how much particular firms have to pay to raise funds in the capital market. Once you know what the market is charging a firm for funds, that information gives you a benchmark for determining how much your client should discount future payments from the firm. So, let's go back. Imagine, for example, you had a client who was offered a $100,000 payment in ten years as settlement for a contract dispute. But, suppose this offer is not coming from a bank, but rather from a building contractor. Based on calculations we did in the preceding section, we know the present value of $100,000 in ten years discounted at 12.79% is $30,000. (Do you remember why?) But what if we knew that other creditors were charging the building contractor interest rates of 20% to borrow money? That would suggest that a promise from the contractor to pay $100,000 in ten years has less than a $30,0000 present value. Indeed, $100,000 discounted at a 20% interest rate over ten years has a present value of only $16,151.

As the foregoing illustration suggests, moving from an interest rate based on the rate of return on your client's savings account to a rate of return based on the payer's cost of borrowing can have a profound effect on your present value calculations. With an interest rate of 5%, the present value of $100,000 at the end of 10 years is $61,391.33 ($100,000 divided by $[1 + 0.05]^{10}$), which is more than twice as much as the value of $30,000 that was based on a 12.79% interest rate. Similarly, raising the discount rate to 20% reduces the present value of $100,000 in ten years by nearly half again, to only $16,151.

3. Your own costs of borrowing funds. While conceptually attractive, it may not always be practical or even appropriate to use the payer's cost of funds to calculate present values. Imagine, for example, that your client's delicatessen had been destroyed as a result of flooding from a broken water main. To get the store open again, your client needs to spend $50,000 immediately. Your client's only way to get the money right now is to run up her personal credit cards, which charge an annual interest rate of 20%. The water company, which has an AAA (i.e., very good) credit rating, offers you the choice of either $48,000 right now or $56,000 at the end of a year. Which offer should your client accept? Well, if you employed a discount rate based on the water company's credit rating, you would probably opt for the later payment. A payment of $56,000 is 16.67% greater than $48,000 ($56,000 is $8,000 more than $48,000, and $8,000 is 16.67% of $48,000). So, as long as the water company's cost of borrowing was less than 16.67%, the present value of $56,000 discounted at the payer's cost of borrowing will be greater than $48,000. Your client, however, would be worse off taking the later payment, because your client is forced to borrow at 20% on high-cost credit cards. Another way of making this point is to note that, discounted at your client's cost of borrowing (20%), $56,000 has a net present value of $46,666.67 ($56,000 divided by [1 + 0.20]), which is less than the immediate settlement offer of $48,000.[9]

4. Risk aversion, again. Before leaving the issue of selecting interest rates, we should note that issues of risk aversion also arise in this context. Just because you have adjusted a future payment into a present value does not mean that you have addressed the issue of risk aversion. You still need to consider whether the various outcomes being evaluated might have an especially bad consequence for your client — for example, small future payouts in some situations where your clients will have large needs.

In addition, when employing interest rates based on the payer's cost of borrowing derived from market-based prices, one must be aware that the market has a unique way of evaluating risks. We will deal with this issue in more detail in the next section of this chapter, but the important point to recognize is that the market tends not to factor in risks that can be eliminated through diversification, but rather includes only nondiversifiable risks. In many legal contexts, your clients will not have a diversified portfolio of claims against a sufficiently large group of payers. So in these contexts, unconsidered reliance on a market-derived cost of funds may be inappropriate.

G. Take-Home Lessons on the Time Value of Money

Although it takes some time and practice to get comfortable with the time value of money, the rudiments of this analytical method are fairly straightforward. As a general rule, money in the future is worth less than the same amount of money today. Exactly how much less depends on both how far in the future the future payment is to be made and which

---

9. Figuring out when it is appropriate to use the payer's cost of funds as opposed to the recipient's opportunity costs can be tricky. As mentioned above, financial analysts prefer to use a payer's-cost-of-funds approach. This will be appropriate in situations in which the recipient can sell the payer's obligation into some sort of market. So, in the case described above, if your client could sell the water company's commitment to make a $56,000 payment at the end of the year, the market would presumably value the claim based on the water company's cost of funds, and then that rate would be the appropriate discount rate for your client. In practice, however, not all future claims can be liquidated in this manner. Accordingly, in some contexts, relying upon your client's cost of borrowing will be appropriate.

interest rate you use to discount the future payment. The further in the future, the lower the present value, and the higher the discount rate, the lower the present value. If you keep these basic principles in mind, you are well on the way to understanding the time value of money.

4. Key Concepts in Corporate Finance

We turn now from the time value of money, which is an analytical tool with a broad range of applications, to a more specialized set of concepts developed for use in the field of corporate finance. Our discussion will cover four fundamental and related topics: efficient market hypotheses, the relationship between risk and return; the benefits of diversification; and the capital asset pricing model.

A. The Efficient Market Hypotheses

Oftentimes, both in law school classrooms and in legal practice, reference will be made to the *efficiency* of the stock market. When used in this context, efficiency means more than operating in a cost-effective manner. It implies something about the prices of securities traded on the markets. In casual usage, people sometimes equate stock market efficiency with the fundamental correctness of stock market prices. For example, you might hear someone say, "I know IBM stock is really worth $150 a share because that's what it's trading at on the stock market and the market is efficient." Formally speaking, however, market efficiency has a narrower meaning or, more accurately, a narrower set of meanings. The following excerpt from a well-known law review article explains.

Ronald J. Gilson and Reinier H. Kraakman
The Mechanisms of Market Efficiency
70 *Va. L. Rev.* 549 (1984)

Of all recent developments in financial economics, the efficient capital market hypothesis ("ECMH") has achieved the widest acceptance by the legal culture. It now commonly informs the academic literature on a variety of topics; it is addressed by major law school casebooks and textbooks on business law; it structures debate over the future of securities regulation both within and without the Securities and Exchange Commission; it has served as the intellectual premise for a major revision of the disclosure system administered by the Commission; and it has even begun to influence judicial decisions and the actual practice of law. In short, the ECMH is now the context in which serious discussion of the regulation of financial markets takes place. . . .

The fixation on the fact of market efficiency has also characterized much of the financial economics literature on the ECMH. Professor Jensen has stated that "there is no other proposition in economics which has more empirical evidence supporting it than the efficient market hypothesis." Despite certain anomalies, numerous studies demonstrate that the capital market responds efficiently to an extraordinary variety of information. Indeed in the single area of financial accounting data, even the number of surveys of empirical studies of capital market efficiency is substantial. . . .[12]

The language of efficient capital market theory reveals its origins as a vocabulary of empirical description. The common definition of market efficiency, that "prices at any time 'fully reflect' all available information," is really a shorthand for the empirical claim that "available information" does not support profitable trading strategies or arbitrage opportunities. Similarly, Eugene Fama's landmark 1970 review article first proposed the now-familiar division of the ECMH into "weak," "semi-strong," and "strong" forms as a device for classifying empirical tests of price behavior.[24]

- Weak tests examined the claim that the histories of securities prices could not yield lucrative trading opportunities.[25]

12. See, e.g., . . . P. Griffin, *Usefulness to Investors and Creditors of Information Provided by Financial Reporting: A Review of Empirical Accounting Research* (1981). . . .

24. [Eugene Fama, Efficient Capital Markets: A Review of Theory and Empirical Work, 25 *J. Fin.* 383, 388 (1970)]. Fama credited Harry Roberts with distinguishing weak and strong form tests. Id. at 383 n.1.

25. Id. at 389–96 (review of tests). Numerous weak form tests support the hypothesis that the history of securities prices does not yield exploitable trading opportunities. . . . Generally, these tests take two forms: serial correlation analyses, which establish little or no relationship between changes in securities prices over successive periods. . . .; and analyses of "filter rule" trading strategies, which reject the possibility that trading on complex patterns of price movements of the sort employed by "chartists" can yield abnormal returns.

- Semi-strong form tests probed the same prediction about categories of publicly available information of obvious information to investors.[26]
- Finally, strong form tests examined the extension of the hypothesis to information that was available only to particular groups of privileged investors [e.g., corporate insiders].[27]

In this usage, the weak, semi-strong, and strong form categories have proved both useful and precise. The hypothesized dearth of arbitrage opportunities, whatever its explanation, clearly grows in strength with each successive genre of test. The more private the information, the more intuitively reasonable the proposition that one might profit by trading on it, and so the stronger the opposing claim that such profitable trading is impossible.

Over time, however, scholars have pressed the weak, semi-strong, and strong form categories beyond their original service as a classification of empirical tests into more general duty as a

---

26. [Id.] at 404–09 (reviewing empirical tests). Studies of semi-strong form efficiency are tests of how long market prices require to adjust to price-relevant information that is released to the public. These studies typically ask whether trading activity that follows the release of such information can earn investors abnormally high returns and focus on the security's price history before and after the trading period. . . . The discovery of abnormal returns indicates trading opportunities and, therefore, possible market inefficiency. The results thus far indicate efficient price responses to a wide variety of publicly released information, ranging from earning reports and dividend announcements to accounting changes, stock splits, press evaluations, and even changes in Federal Reserve policy. . . . Not all semi-strong form tests indicate market efficiency, however.

27. [Id.] at 409–13 (reviewing strong form tests). Unlike weak and semi-strong form tests, which probe trading opportunities that might arise from particular kinds of information . . . strong form studies cannot test for analogous opportunities arising from the generation of non-public information because investigators are unlikely to learn about such information (or if they do, they are unlikely to employ it for research purposes). For this reason, strong form tests must probe indirectly for trading opportunities arising from non-public information. Such tests seek to identify investors who are likely to possess non-public information and to determine whether these traders consistently earn net returns higher than the market average. The results have been mixed. Corporate insiders, such as officers, directors and affiliated bankers, systematically outperform the market. So do specialists on the major stock exchanges who posses non-public information about unexecuted orders. . . . Mutual funds, however, appear to outperform the market only enough to cover administrative and trading costs.

classification of market responses to particular kinds of information. For example, prices might be said to incorporate efficiently
one genre of information that is semi-strong or public, but fail to
reflect another that is strong form, or non-public. Indeed, taken
a step further, scholars sometimes describe markets themselves
as weak, semi-strong, or strong form efficient. Without ever being quite explicit, this powerful shorthand implies that different
market dynamics are involved in the reflection of different kinds
of information into price, and that varying degrees of market efficiency might well be the consequence.

As the Gilson and Kraakman excerpt indicates, the various permutations
of the efficient market hypothesis all deal with *informational* efficiency.
Technically speaking, the hypotheses simply predict that investors cannot
use certain kinds of information (whether past price movements in the
weak form, all public information in the semi-strong form, or public and
private information in the strong form) to achieve better-than-average
profits from stock market investments. The hypotheses postulate that
market prices already take these categories of information into account.
Importantly, the efficient market hypotheses do not speak directly to
the fundamental correctness of stock market prices. For example, many
internet companies with high stock market valuations in the late 1990s
ended up in bankruptcy a few years later, and — in retrospect — their
previous valuations turned out to be wrong. These outcomes, however,
do not undermine the efficient market hypotheses because the hypotheses do not concern long term or ultimate values. Moreover, the fact that
the value of the entire stock market declined dramatically in 2000-2002
and again in 2008-2009 does not refute the efficient market hypotheses
unless the declines could have been predicted based on one of the sets
of information that market prices were to have impounded.[10]

---

10. Most of the empirical evidence supporting the efficient market hypothesis is
drawn from studies of large U.S. markets, principally the New York Stock Exchange
and the NASDAQ market, where large quantities of securities are traded and many
analysts are following each class of security. In markets where there is less trading or
where prices are determined in different ways, informational efficiency may not be
present. In the extreme, imagine that a company offered to sell you some stock for $100
a share in a private transaction to which you and the company were the only parties.

Box 5-2
Market Efficiency and Behavioral Finance

Even before the marked decline in the US stock market in the past few years, some financial theorists were reconsidering the validity of prior claims about stock market efficiency. In part, this reconsideration was based on additional empirical studies suggesting a variety of "anomalies" in stock market performance that appeared to contradict the efficient market hypothesis. For example, one set of studies suggested that investors might be able to use certain kinds of historical information (like the ratio of a company's market value to its book value) to predict the future performance of common stock. Other theorists speculated that "irrational exuberance" and other psychological factors may cause financial and other markets to suffer from fads and trends, in the extreme culminating in bubbles, during which prices rise to what subsequently appear to be unreasonable levels. Think tulip bulbs in the first half of the 17th century or the U.S. real estate market 1997-2005. While market efficiency remains an important landmark of financial theory, the scope of its domain is likely to remain contested for some time. For a sympathetic and informative introduction to this critique of market efficiency, see Andrei Shleifer, *Inefficient Markets: An Introduction to Behavioral Finance* (2000). For an up-to-date textbook presentation of the state of behavioral finance, which is accessible to the non-specialist reader, see Lucy F. Ackert and Richard Deaves, *Behavioral Finance: Psychology, Decision-Making, and Markets* (2010).

The efficient capital market hypotheses have had an extraordinary influence on legal developments over the past few decades. Their impact is

---

The market would have no role in setting the price of that stock, and so there would be no reason to believe the $100 proposed price was, in any meaningful sense, efficient. Accordingly, one needs to be careful not to extend the lessons of the ECMH literature to other kinds of markets in which its applicability has not been demonstrated.

most pronounced, naturally enough, in the field of securities regulation. Consider, for example, the plaintiff's burden of proof in a securities fraud case. Traditionally, to prove fraud a plaintiff would have to introduce evidence that the plaintiff relied on a defendant's fraudulent statement, typically by showing that the plaintiff had heard or read the fraudulent statement and then purchased the defendant's securities as a result of that information. In light of the ECMH, courts for the past twenty years have generally waived this traditional showing of reliance for shares of stock purchased in stock market transactions on the ground that the stock market price of the securities would have impounded the defendant's fraudulent statement and so when a plaintiff purchases securities at the market price the plaintiff indirectly relied on the defendant's fraudulent statement. This innovation in legal doctrine — known as the fraud-on-the-market theory — has greatly facilitated the prosecution of securities claims and is a direct result of the ECMH.

The efficient capital market hypothesis has also been influential in other legal settings. Consider, for example, compensation arrangements for corporate managers. In the Accounting chapter, we talked a bit about how compensation might be tied to various accounting measures, such as return on assets or return on equity. As we saw, however, financial statements are an imperfect reflection of economic reality. If a company developed an extremely valuable new patent, its economic value might increase substantially, but there would be no accounting impact (because of the accounting treatment of intangible assets). So, if the chief executive officer's compensation were based on an accounting measure of profitability, the impact of the new patent would not be reflected. If, on the other hand, compensation were tied to the performance of the company's stock, then (as a result of the market's informational efficiency) the impact of the new patent would be taken into account.[11] For this and other reasons, managerial compensation of top executives in public companies is increasingly tied to stock market performance.

---

11. If the relevant market were efficient in only the semi-strong sense, news of the patent would need to be disclosed to the public for the information to be reflected in the company's stock price. If the market were strong-form efficient — a more debatable proposition — then the discovery would be impounded into stock prices even without public disclosure.

B. Risk and Return

A second fundamental financial concept of importance to lawyers is the trade-off between risk and return. In finance, "risk" and "return" are terms of art and warrant careful consideration.

The return on a financial asset is the total economic benefit that an asset generates over a certain period of time, typically a year. Economic benefit can come in the form of periodic payments, such as interest on bonds or dividends on stock, or in the form of appreciation in value. So, if a share of common stock increased in value from $100 dollars at the beginning of the year to $110 at the end of the year, the value of the stock would have appreciated 10% ($10 appreciation divided by $100 beginning price per share) over the course of the year. If the common stock also paid a $5 dividend at the end of the year, its total annual return would be 15% ($10 appreciation plus $5 dividend divided by $100 beginning price per share).

Risk, in contrast, is a measure of expected variation in return. In other words, risk relates to the amount of uncertainty regarding the return that a financial asset will achieve over some period of time. Let's return to the share of common stock discussed in the previous paragraph. Let's suppose we are considering that share of stock at the beginning of the year when its price was $100 per share. And suppose further that we thought the stock probably would appreciate $10 over the course of the year and pay a $5 dividend. Based on these assumptions, the stock's most likely economic return in the coming year would be 15%. However, let's say we were uncertain as to this outcome. There was a chance (let's say a one in four chance) that the stock would perform worse, appreciating only $5 in value during the year and paying no dividend, and also a chance (again, say one in four) that the stock would appreciate by $15 dollars in the coming year and pay a $10 dividend. Figure 5-3 presents a graphic representation of the financial risk of this hypothetical security: the predicted dispersion of possible economic returns on that security. The graph reveals the risk-return characteristics of this particular financial asset. The security has an expected return of 15% in the coming year, but its actual return could be as high as 25% or as low as 5%.

An important goal of financial analysis has been to document the risk-return characteristics of different kinds of financial assets — essentially

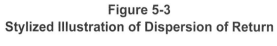

Figure 5-3
Stylized Illustration of Dispersion of Return

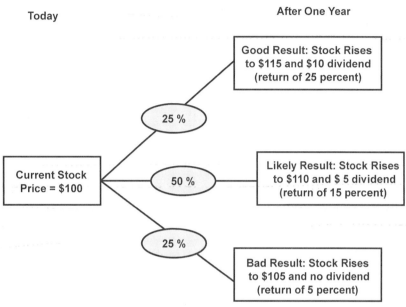

trying to develop more realistic information about actual dispersions in economic returns that financial assets have achieved in the past. What empirical investigation of financial markets has discovered is that there is a strong and consistent relationship between the return on various classes of assets and the variation in the return (a.k.a. riskiness) of those assets. Government debt tends to have lower returns and lower risk (that is, variations in returns) than does corporate debt. Corporate debt, in turn, has lower returns and lower risk than corporate stock. And the stocks of larger, established corporations have lower returns and lower risk than the stocks of smaller, start-up firms. At least within the context of the U.S. capital markets in the last century, a wealth of empirical data supports these relationships. Figure 5-4, which is drawn from data collected by Ibbotson Associates for the 1926-2009 period, summarizes the kind of analysis that financial economists have used to demonstrate the risk-return trade-off.

The first column of Figure 5-4 reports the average annual returns on various classes of financial assets during the 83 years between 1926 and 2009. As suggested above, stocks show the highest average returns, with

Figure 5-4
Historical Performance of U.S. Financial Assets: 1926-2009

Asset Class	Average Annual Returns	Risk premium (relative to U.S. Treasury bills)	Standard Deviation of Annual Returns	Distribution of Annual Returns
Large-company stocks	11.8 %	8.1 %	20.5 %	
Small-company stocks	16.6 %	12.9 %	32.8 %	
Long-term corporate bonds	6.2 %	2.5 %	8.3 %	
Long-term government bonds	5.8 %	2.1 %	9.6 %	
Intermediate-term government bonds	5.5 %	1.8 %	5.7 %	
U.S. Treasury bills	3.7 %		3.1 %	
Inflation	3.1 %		4.2 %	-90 0 90

Modified from *Stocks, Bonds, Bills and Inflation: 2009 Yearbook* (Chicago: Ibbotson Associates, 2010).

large company stocks reporting average annual returns of 11.8% and small-company stocks showing an average annual return of 16.6%. The average returns are lower for long-term corporate bonds (6.2%), long-term government bonds (5.8%), intermediate-term government bonds (5.5%), and the U.S. Treasury bills (3.7%), which represent short-term government obligations.[12] U.S. Treasury bills represent an important

---

12. The last row in Figure 5-4 reports the average level of inflation in the United States during the 83 year period. This is an important number to bear in mind. The average rates of return for the other asset classes are reported in what's known as "nominal" terms, which includes both a "real" rate of return plus inflation. If a stock goes up in value by 10% in a year but inflation is 2%, then the real rate of return on the stock is approximately 8%. Although we tend to experience financial returns in nominal terms ("My stock portfolio went up twenty five percent last year!"), it is often more appropriate to focus on the real rate of return: an asset's expected rate of nominal return minus the expected rate of inflation. For example, if you wanted to know low long it would take for the real purchasing power of your portfolio to double, you would want to make that calculation based on the expected real rate of return of your

benchmark in financial analysis, because they are considered to be a risk-free form of investment. Other financial assets are sometimes described in terms of the amount by which their returns exceed a risk-free rate of return. The second column in Figure 5-4, denominated risk premium, shows how much the average annual return on each asset class exceeded the average return on U.S. Treasury bills during the 1926-2009 period.

The next two columns of Figure 5-4 offer two different perspectives on the financial risk — that is, variation in return — associated with each asset class. On the far right is a histogram plotting the distribution of annual returns for the asset class during the 83 year period of analysis. Notice that the returns on stocks are much more spread out than the returns on other asset classes, and that there have been a reasonably large number of years in which returns on stocks were negative. The column directly to the left of the histograms — "Standard Deviation of Average Annual Returns" — is a summary statistic that measures variation in annual returns. You'll learn more about standard deviations and how they are calculated in the Fundamentals of Statistical Analysis chapter, but for current purposes what is important to note is that the higher an asset class's average annual returns, the higher the variation in its annual returns. This fact is consistent with a basic premise of finance: that risk and return are positively correlated. The greater the return on an asset class, the greater the risk.

Practicing attorneys need not become experts in the intricacy of empirical studies into the historical performance of financial assets. But lawyers should know about the basic findings of this work, and also appreciate the way in which financial analysts employ this information to make predictions about the future and also to value investment opportunities today. A major premise of financial analysis is that the future performance of financial assets will, to some degree, be comparable to their past performance. Government securities are generally expected to yield lower returns than common stocks, but are also expected to generate less variation in return. The financial past is thus assumed to be prologue to the financial future. (But see Box 5-3.) Often times, it will

---

portfolio. Using the Rule of 72, discussed above, if you thought the real rate of return on your portfolio were going to be 6%, then you would expect the purchasing value of that portfolio to double in 12 years.

Box 5-3
Is the Past Really Prologue?

As explained in the text, financial analyses often proceed on the assumption that the past performance of financial assets — particularly the performance of common stock — is a good basis for predicting future returns, at least over extended periods of time such as ten years or more. Within the academic community, however, there are growing concerns that traditional presentations of the risk-return trade-off may overstate the size of the equity premium (that is, amount by which average returns on common stock are expected to exceed average returns on other classes of financial assets). Some skeptics have expressed concern about drawing inferences about future stock market returns based solely on performance in the U.S. stock markets in the twentieth century. Arguably, our stock markets during this period were the most profitable of all time. Stock market returns in few if any other markets during the twentieth century performed as well, and many stock markets failed during the century. (How well over the long run do you think the average Russian investor did in the St. Petersburg stock market of 1900? Answer: very badly.) Another concern of those critical of the use of historical returns is that even if one stays with U.S. data only, predicted future returns will be very different depending on how far back one chooses to go. Do U.S stock markets today resemble the stock markets of the 1930's and 1940's enough, so that predictions of future performance will be improved by incorporating data from those decades? Should one use 50, 60, 70 years of data, or are better predictions likely to result from using only "recent" data? If you believe, as some experts do, that the 2007-2008 downturn in global stock markets resulted from changes in global economic conditions that are likely to persist into the foreseeable future, even data from the last 10 years may produce overoptimistic forecasts.

fall to the attorney to remind his or her clients of the risk-return trade-off, and also to make sure that the client considers the implications of potential losses on assets, like investments in common stock, that have historically been associated with higher rates of return.

The Lawyer's Perspective

An important way in which lawyers make use of the risk-return trade-off is in helping clients avoid — or at least be adequately compensated for — potentially risky transactions. For example, suppose you represented a small bakery that was going to enter into a long-term contract to supply bread to a manufacturing firm and that the contract was going to require your client to make significant up-front investments (such as buying expensive new ovens). In addition to inspecting the counter-party's financial statements, you might also want to find out the interest rate that the manufacturing firm was paying on any bank loans or other outstanding debt. A high rate of interest would suggest that the firm was at above average risk of defaulting on its obligations. Accordingly, you might recommend that your client insist on an up-front payment to cover the cost of the new ovens, or at least a higher payment to compensate for the risks associated with entering into a long-term contract with the firm.

C. The Value of Diversification

The value of diversification is another lesson from financial theory that lawyers should understand. This subject was first explored in Harry Markowitz, *Portfolio Selection* (1959). In essence, diversification offers investors a way of reducing the risk associated with particular investments without sacrificing return.

At root, the insight underlying diversification is that each individual investment has its own unique risks. Since these risks are unique, investors can offset the downside of some investments with the upside of other investments. This point can be illustrated if you think of the risks facing Suntan Lotion Co., a company that sells only suntan lotion, as compared with the risks facing Umbrellas Inc., a firm that manufactures only umbrellas. Sunny years are good for the former and bad for the latter, whereas rainy years are bad for the former and good for the latter.

Figure 5-5
Profitability of Two Hypothetical Firms

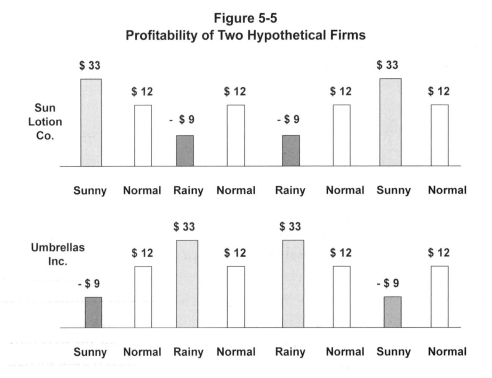

Normal weather means normal profitability for both firms. Figure 5-5 illustrates the hypothetical profits and losses that these two firms would earn across a series of years. When Suntan Lotion Co. does well, Umbrellas Inc. does poorly and vice versa.

An investment solely in either Suntan Co. or Umbrellas Inc. will have a considerable amount of "weather" risk. For each firm, profits will vary from a $33 profit in good years to a $9 loss in bad years with an average $12 profit when the weather is normal. But imagine what would happen if you divided your investment evenly between the two firms — that is, if you diversified your investment across both firms. A portfolio divided evenly between the two investments will have no weather risk. In years with sunny weather, the extra profitability of Suntan Co. would exactly offset the losses on Umbrellas Inc. In years with rainy weather, the net effect would be the same but work in the other direction. With equal investments in both firms, you would obtain a consistent return in all years. In other words, you would have eliminated the expected variation in your return (a.k.a. risk).

Following up on the line of research inspired by Markowitz's early writings, financial analysts now tend to distinguish between diversifiable risk — that is, expected variations in return that can be eliminated through diversification — and nondiversifiable risk. The latter category of risks — nondiversifiable risk — is also sometimes called market risk or systematic risk. As these alternative formulations suggest, some financial risks are related to general market conditions or fluctuations in the larger economic system. Because variations in returns from these broader forces affect all investments (research suggests), these market risks cannot be eliminated through diversification.[13]

Again, lots of empirical evidence underlies portfolio theory, most of which is beyond the scope of this introductory coverage. To give readers a taste of the literature, we include Figure 5-6, which summarizes the variation in return of different-sized portfolios of U.S. common stocks, as calculated in a study published in 1987. As this figure indicates, if your portfolio consisted of just 1 stock — that is, had no diversification — then the average annual variation in your return would be nearly 50%. If your portfolio were evenly divided between just 2 securities, the average variation of return for such a portfolio would decline to 37%, and with a diversified portfolio of 10 securities, the expected variation would come down to 23%. Following the curve down to a diversified portfolio of 30 securities, one finds expected variation would decline to under 21%, which is fairly close to the levels of expected variation in fully diversified portfolios. (With 1,000 securities, expected variation declines only a little bit further to 19.21%.) For this reason, money managers are often satisfied that they have achieved most of the gains from

---

13. Portfolio theory was largely developed through the analysis of U.S. financial markets. In the past decade, as financial markets have become more global, there has been considerable attention to the question of whether some U.S. market risk — hitherto thought to be nondiversifiable — might be reduced through diversification across national boundaries. Preliminary research suggests that this might be possible, at least to a limited degree; hence, our original understanding of nondiversifiable risk is beginning to change.

Figure 5-6
Gains from Diversification

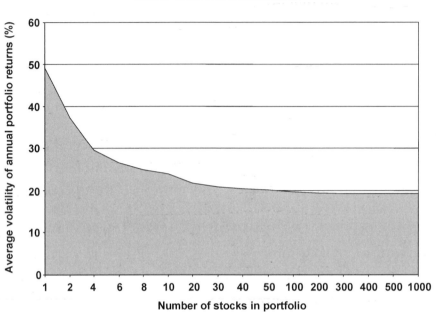

Source: Meir Statman, How Many Stocks Make a Diversified Portfolio, 22 J. Fin. & Quant. Anal. 353 (1987)

diversification if they divide their portfolios among at least 30 different investments.[14]

For practicing lawyers, portfolio diversification offers several important lessons. Most importantly, in many contexts, lawyers assist their clients in making investment decisions. Individual clients will need to allocate retirement savings. Charities will have endowments to invest. Fiduciaries will be responsible for the management of trust assets. Regardless of the particular client's preference for balancing risk and return, the client's lawyer should be prepared to advise the client on the benefits of maintaining a diversified portfolio. The alternative — holding a nondiversified portfolio — exposes the client to unnecessary risks.

Understanding the value of diversification is also important if you represent a business enterprise that has a large amount of business

---

14. One need be a bit careful about following this rule of thumb, as the full benefits of diversification will not be achieved if all 30 investments are from a single sector of the economy — say, the shrimp-fishing industry — because the unique risks of each firm will be closely associated with other firms in the portfolio. Also, some more recent research has suggested that additional diversification may have significant benefits.

risk — such as a start-up technology firm. When trying to attract potential investors for such clients, lawyers often find themselves trying to persuade these investors that, as long as they are diversified, the investors shouldn't worry about the unique risks of a particular firm — only its market risk.[15] The force of arguments of this sort explains why institutional investors in the United States have become increasingly willing to invest in start-up companies; as long as these investors put funds in a large enough number of start-ups, the unique risks of particular firms should wash out as a result of diversification. Similarly, regulatory officials have slowly come to appreciate the benefits of diversification. Thirty years ago, many financial intermediaries, from pension plans to trust funds, were largely restricted to investing in lower-risk assets, such as investment-grade bonds and blue-chip stocks. Now these entities are often allowed to invest in a much broader category of assets, provided their holdings are fully diversified. Within the academic world, this development is generally thought to be desirable because it has increased the expected returns of financial intermediaries (do you see why?) and because it has brought new sources of capital to certain segments of the economy.

D. The Capital Asset Pricing Model

As explored in the previous section, the risk — that is, expected variation in return — associated with individual securities can be divided into diversifiable and nondiversifiable risk. For financial economists and well-advised investors, the critical component of a security's risk is its nondiversifiable risk. In many areas of finance, including the valuation of financial assets discussed later in this chapter, analysts need to estimate the non-diversifiable risk of a particular security, for example, the common stock of a company like GE or Intel. Financial economists have developed a number of different methods to provide such estimates, the most familiar of which is the Capital Asset Pricing Model or CAPM.

First proposed in a pair of articles by John Lintner and William Sharpe in the mid-1960s, CAPM is another important and useful financial theory

---

15. The possible range of returns for a start-up company are not irrelevant to investors as the range of returns determines a company's expected return. As we will see when we get to the valuation section of this chapter, expected returns have a substantial impact on the valuation of companies.

that builds upon the concepts discussed above. The CAPM is, at root, an explanation of how capital markets establish the price of financial assets, most importantly common stocks. The CAPM accepts the premise that diversifiable risk is unimportant because it can (by definition) be eliminated through diversification. The model then predicts that the return on a particular stock depends to a substantial degree on the extent to which the stock's return varies with respect to general market movements. The model then postulates that, by looking to the manner in which a particular company's stock has varied in relationship to the general market in the past, analysts can determine how capital markets will value the stock now and in the future.

A formal presentation of CAPM is beyond the scope of this text. For practicing attorneys, what's important to know about the CAPM is that this model is the means whereby financial analysts derive a measure — known as beta — that summarizes the relationship between an individual stock's movements and general market fluctuations. The stock of a company with a beta of 1.0 has had an average market risk. A stock with a beta of more than 1.0 has been more volatile than the market average — that is, its price has tended to go up more in strong markets and go down more in bad markets. Finally, a stock with a beta of less than 1.0 has been less volatile than the market average.[16] Within the financial world, beta is often used as a shorthand way of describing a company's market risk.

A detailed presentation of the theoretical dimensions of beta and the CAPM more generally is not possible here. Nor do we have time to explore a recent debate over whether the historical price movement of a company stock as compared to market fluctuations is an accurate predictor of future price movements, an implicit premise of the CAPM. (In

---

16. More precisely, CAPM beta measures the relationship between the amount by which returns on particular security exceed a risk-free rate of return (for example, the return on Treasury bills) and the amount by which the overall market return exceeds the risk-free rate or return. Once a security's beta is calculated, an analyst can estimate the expected return on the security. For the quantitatively inclined, the formula for deriving the expected returns on a particular security with CAPM is:

$$\text{Expected Returns} = \text{Risk-Free Return} + \text{Beta} \times (\text{Market Return} - \text{Risk-Free Return}).$$

brief, questions have been raised about the stability of this relationship, but the weight of authority still seems to support some relationship and hence the usefulness of betas derived from historical price movements.) In addition, there is the complexity of determining which market's fluctuations should be used to determine a security's beta. Traditionally, betas have been derived by comparing individual stock prices to general movements of U.S. stock markets; however, it may be more appropriate to make the comparisons with respect to global stock markets or perhaps even some aggregate market of financial assets. Finally, a number of alternative asset pricing models have emerged in recent years that arguably do a better job of explaining the risk and return of particular securities. These and other related issues are explored in upper-level courses on corporate finance, particularly when taught in business school or economics department curricula.

What lawyers need to know is that the CAPM remains a popular technique for estimating the nondiversifiable risk (a.k.a. market risk) of individual stocks. Depending on the nature of their practice, lawyers will have varying degrees of exposure to the CAPM and its use in deriving betas. Lawyers working on Wall Street and in other financial centers might encounter the techniques on a daily basis. Others will deal with the concepts less frequently. Many lawyers do, however, get involved in advising clients who are making investment decisions. How should a client invest a 401(k) pension plan? What should a charitable organization do with its cash reserves? What is an appropriate investment strategy for a school endowment? To help clients make decisions of this sort, lawyers need to have a basic appreciation of the risk-return trade-off and also the principles underlying CAPM and other models for estimating the risk-return characteristics of individual securities.

5. The Valuation of Assets

The valuation of assets is not, typically, the responsibility of attorneys (at least not attorneys acting as legal advisers). Lawyers are, however, often involved in transactions where other parties — whether financial analysts or investment bankers (an increasing number of whom have legal training) — are engaged in valuation exercises. Sometimes these transactions are purely business transactions, such as deciding how much to offer to purchase a firm in a takeover transaction or merger. But valuation can also be important in family law (in determining a fair division of marital property for a divorce settlement), in litigation (in calculating the amount of damages caused by wrongful disruption of business activities), or in a host of other legal contexts. Accordingly, lawyers will often find it useful to understand how valuation techniques work, at least in a general sense.

A. Contemporaneous Transactions Involving Substantially Similar Assets

Perhaps the simplest way to estimate the value of an asset is by reference to a recently established market price for an identical or substantially similar asset. For example, in establishing the value of 100 shares of IBM common stock contributed to a charity, a donor would typically look at the price at which the common stock traded on the New York Stock Exchange on the date of the donation. Since shares of IBM common stock are essentially fungible, the market price of IBM shares is generally accepted as a good estimate of the value of other shares of the security at the time the market price was established.

In other contexts, where similar but not identical assets have recently been sold, a comparable approach can be used. A good example arises in the underwriting procedures for residential mortgages — the loans that most Americans use to purchase their homes. Typically, lending institutions will have underwriting standards that specify that the value of the loan may not exceed a certain percentage — say 80% or 95% — of the market value of the property the loan is used to finance. To demonstrate compliance with these requirements, licensed appraisers typically estimate the value of particular properties by comparing the property in question to similar properties that have recently been sold. So, to determine the value of a three-bedroom ranch house in Smallville, an appraiser would typically look at the price of comparable houses in the same community. Adjustments are made to reflect differences in the comparables upon which the appraiser has relied (for example, in the number of bedrooms or quality of construction), and an estimated market value of the property of interest is thereby derived. Real estate attorneys often work closely with appraisers in such procedures and might even suggest comparable properties to corroborate the proposed valuation of their client's property.

B. Market Valuation Estimates Derived from Financial Statements

When the asset to be valued is an enterprise for which financial statements are available, there are a number of valuation techniques that derive valuation estimates from elements of those statements. Such approaches might be useful if the asset to be valued were a business that was wholly-owned by two partners, and one of the partners wanted to buy out the other partner's interests, perhaps because the second partner wanted to retire or perhaps because the two had had a falling out. Since such a partnership would typically be privately held, there would be no public market in partnership interests from which a market price could be readily estimated. However, the firm might well have audited financial statements, from which financial analysts could estimate the firm's market value.

The most common techniques of this sort consist of identifying one element of the firm's financial statement and then ascertaining the relationship between that element and the market value of the entity. One example of this approach is based on the value of a firm's owners' equity as reported on the firm's balance sheet, sometimes referred to as the firm's "book value."[17] If it can be ascertained that within a particular industry a typical ratio of market value of a firm to its book value is 2 to 1, then an analyst can estimate the firm's market value once the analyst knows the book value of the firm. Another similarly motivated approach looks to the entity's income statement and draws inferences based on an assessment of price earnings multiples within the relevant industry.[18]

---

17. Owners' equity consists of contributed capital plus retained earnings. See page 124 above. As discussed in the Accounting chapter, there are a variety of reasons why accounting measures of owners' equity will not equal market value, including the reliance on historical values in accounting statements and the omission of many intangible assets and contingent liabilities.

18. Price earnings multiples or PE ratios are explained earlier on pages 172-173. In brief, the PE ratio is the ratio of the price of a company's shares of common stock to the company's earnings per share in the most recent accounting period.

With this information and an estimate of a company's current earnings, it is also possible to estimate the company's current market value.

Both of these approaches proceed on an assumption that there is a reasonably consistent relationship between market values and financial statement measures, at least within similar industries. So, for example, if the two-person partnership mentioned above consisted of a national chain of fast-food restaurants similar to those operated by McDonald's, then an analyst might look to information about the market-to-book value and price earnings multiples for McDonald's and other comparable public firms (Burger King et al.) in order to make estimates of the market value of the firm being appraised.

C. Discounted Cash Flow Analysis

Discounted cash flow analysis is another, more flexible technique for valuing assets. At root, this approach is similar to the way we valued periodic payments on a lottery ticket earlier in this chapter. The analyst first figures out how much cash a proposed investment will generate in the future and then calculates the present value of those cash payments using an appropriate discount rate. If the cost of making the investment is less than the present value of projected cash payments, then the investment is said to have a positive net present value and may be worth undertaking.

Discounted cash flow analysis is commonly used to value companies — either to estimate an appropriate price of the company's common stock or to value the entire company in the context of a takeover transaction or merger. In valuations of this sort, the analyst would typically begin by examining the firm's financial statements and, in particular, its cash flow statement in order to determine the amount of cash that the firm has generated in recent years. Then, the analyst would have to make some predictions about how that level of cash flow is likely to increase (or decrease) in future years. Finally, the analyst would have to determine an appropriate discount rate to calculate a present value of these cash payments.

Often times, analysts would use CAPM or some comparable asset pricing model to derive this discount rate. Thus, for a firm in an industry with betas of 1.5 or higher, the analyst would use a relatively large

Figure 5-7
Projected Cash Flow for Hypothetical Firm

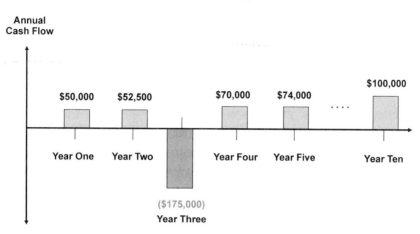

discount rate, whereas for a firm in an industry with betas of less than 1, the analyst would use a lower discount rate. Within the logic of finance, this approach has intuitive appeal because a stream of cash flows from a risky industry (one with a high beta) should have a lower present value than a comparable stream of cash flows from a less risky industry (one with a lower beta). Do you understand why?

Figure 5-7 presents a schematic view of the hypothetical cash flows of the sort that an investment banker might project for a potential takeover target. Initially, the analyst predicts, the firm is projected to generate $50,000 of cash in year one and slightly more in year two. In year three, the firm is expected to be shut down for renovations, and as a result will require a cash infusion (negative cash flow) of $175,000 to cover renovation costs. Thereafter, the firm's cash flows are projected to jump up to $70,000 and continue to grow at a healthy rate, reaching $100,000 in year ten. Armed with these projections the analyst would then determine an appropriate discount rate of return for investments of this sort — perhaps relying on CAPM or some similar methodology — and then calculate a present value of these cash flows. That present value would suggest a plausible price for the take-over target. Obviously, projections and calculations of this sort require considerable expertise, if not clairvoyance, about industry trends and a host of other considerations, but for

Box 5-4
Real Options and Valuation

An interesting recent extension of financial analysis is an approach known as real options. The approach combines aspects of decision analysis and traditional valuation techniques. Rather than valuing investment opportunities on the assumption that they will be undertaken on an all or nothing basis, real options analysis focuses on decision points in the future where decision-makers will have an option to abandon or continue the undertaking. In certain contexts — for example, when expensive investments can be postponed until the likelihood of a project's success will be clearer — real options analysis can uncover valuable investment opportunities where traditional discounted cash flow analysis would indicate an investment with low or even negative net present value. Real options might be useful to evaluate an investment in a new drug that would entail both an initial research phase and subsequent investment in expensive processing equipment. Particularly if the ultimate chances of success were low, expected returns on the drug might not warrant immediate investment in both the research and equipment. However, if the project were re-evaluated with a recognition that the decision to purchase processing equipment could be postponed until the research stage indicated whether there was a high likelihood that the drug would be successful, then the financial assessment of the project might well turn positive. Rather than valuing the overall project, the real option approach encourages analysts to consider whether the initial research is likely to generate a sufficiently valuable "option" to continue the project to the manufacturing phase.

our purposes what is important to appreciate is the underlying logic of the valuation technique.

Once basic discounted cash flow analysis is completed along the line outlined above, analysts would commonly consider a wide range of alternative scenarios. For example, following up on the intuition of Coase's *Nature of the Firm* article, the analyst might see if the value of the firm could be increased by selling off some assets or perhaps by making some additional investments in plant and equipment. The resulting change in cash flows for each new scenario would then be examined to determine if it enhanced firm value.

Similar attention would be given to the financial structure of the target firm. Notwithstanding Modigliani & Miller's theoretical insights, financial analysts have long appreciated the tax advantages of debt financing. Accordingly, analysis might consider whether additional borrowings might lower the overall cost of capital for the firm, thereby decreasing the appropriate discount rate used to value the firm's cash flows and increasing the present value of the firm's projected cash flows.

While the details of discounted cash flow analysis are beyond the scope of this chapter, the basic principles of this foundational technique should be accessible to readers now. It is, in essence, simply a fancy application of the time value of money. There are three key questions: how much cash will the project in question produce in the future, when will that cash be generated, and what discount rate should be used to determine the present value of those cash flows. Everything else is detail.

For those who wish to pursue the concept of valuation further, we have appended to this chapter a Harvard Business School case study on the Eskimo Pie Corporation. In the case, the managers are trying to figure out how much the company is worth — that is, they are making a decision about valuation. The case includes much of the information necessary to apply many of the valuation methods described in this section. How much do you think this company is worth?

6. Suggestions for Further Reading

Students interested in the topics covered in this chapter can learn more about financial theory in the basic course on corporations as well as upper-level offerings in corporate finance, mergers and acquisitions, and securities regulation. Time-value-of-money issues are also treated in taxation courses, especially those focusing on the tax treatment of new financial instruments. More general questions of valuation are presented in a number of additional law school courses, such as family and employment law, although not always explicitly.

For those interested in exploring more technical aspects of finance, there are a number of good texts available. Stephen A. Ross, Randolph W. Westerfield, and Jeffery Jaffee, *Corporate Finance*, 9th ed. (New York, NY: McGraw Hill/Irwin, 2010), offers a particularly clear presentation of the fundamentals of corporate finance. Another standard and slightly more challenging text is Richard A. Brealey, Stewart C. Meyers, and Franklin Allen, *Principles of Corporate Finance*, 10th ed. (New York, NY: McGraw Hill/Irwin, 2011). For those interested in a treatment that emphasizes option pricing theory, try Zvi Bodie and Robert C. Merton, *Finance* (Upper Saddle River, NJ: Prentice Hall, 2000). For a less technical treatment of the subject but a good overall introduction to the field, see Robert C. Higgins, *Analysis for Financial Management*, 6th ed. (Boston, MA: McGraw Hill/Irwin, 2001). For a standard, highly influential presentation and defense of efficient markets theory, see Burton Malkiel, *A Random Walk Down Wall Street*, 9th ed. (New York, NY: W.W. Norton & Company, 2007). For a critical overview of research on market efficiency, see Andrei Shleifer, *Inefficient Markets: An Introduction to Behavioral Finance* (Oxford, UK: Oxford University Press, 2000). Lucy F. Ackert and Richard Deaves, *Behavioral Finance* (Mason, OH: Southwestern, 2010) is an excellent presentation, at an introductory level, of the current state of behavioral finance.

H A R V A R D | B U S I N E S S | S C H O O L

9-293-084
REV: AUGUST 30, 2001

RICHARD S. RUBACK

Eskimo Pie Corporation

In early 1991, Reynolds Metals, the makers of Aluminum Foil and other aluminum products, decided to sell its holding of Eskimo Pie, a marketer of branded frozen novelties. Reynolds had few interests outside its aluminum and packaging business, and the Eskimo Pie Corporation, with roughly $47 million in sales, accounted for less than 1% of Reynolds revenues. Reynolds planned to use the proceeds from the sale of Eskimo Pie to fund investments in its core aluminum business. Eskimo Pie was 84% owned by Reynolds Metals, and 4% owned by the Reynolds Foundation. The remaining 12% of the Eskimo Pie was held by various Reynolds family members and a small group of outside investors.

Goldman Sachs, a New York investment banking firm, was retained to assist with the sale of Eskimo Pie. Goldman estimated that the sale price of Eskimo Pie would be about 1.2 times 1990 sales, or about $57 million. Nestle Foods paid a comparable multiple for Drumstick, another ice cream novelty company, in 1990. Goldman organized an auction for Eskimo Pie, and Nestle was the highest of six bidders with a price of $61 million.

Mr. David Clark, President of Eskimo Pie Corporation, recognized that the sale of Eskimo Pie to Nestle would mean the end of its independence. Nestle was likely to consolidate its ice cream novelty businesses by eliminating Eskimo Pie's headquarters and management staff. He had struggled to find a way to keep the company independent since he first learned of the sale. But Clark had been unable to raise sufficient funds to purchase Eskimo Pie in a leveraged buyout, and the sale to Nestle seemed inevitable.

The Eskimo Pie Corporation

Background

Eskimo Pie, a chocolate covered bar of vanilla ice cream, was the first ice cream novelty. Its history appears on the Eskimo Pie box:

> *Genuine Eskimo Pie . . .*

293-084   Eskimo Pie Corporation

One day working in a confectionery store to supplement his teaching income, Christian K. Nelson became puzzled by a little boy's indecision between a chocolate candy bar and a scoop of ice cream. When questioned, the freckle-faced boy replied, "I want 'em both but I only got a nickel."

With a clever hunch and a little ingenuity, Mr. Nelson found a way to combine the two ingredients in what would become America's first chocolate-covered ice cream bar. The little boy got his wish and Mr. Nelson founded a corporation on the success of the Eskimo Pie product.

Christian Nelson, age 27, began trying to make chocolate stick to ice cream in 1920 while operating an ice cream and confectionery store in Iowa. After months of experimentation, Nelson discovered that cocoa butter made the chocolate adhere to the ice cream. He introduced his product as the "I-Scream-Bar" in 1921. One year later, Mr. Nelson formed a partnership with Russell Stover and the product was renamed Eskimo Pie.

Because the lack of refrigeration made centralized production and distribution impossible, Eskimo Pie licensed rights to make and distribute the Eskimo Pie bar according to Mr. Nelson's recipe. By the spring of 1922, licenses had been sold to 2,700 manufacturers across the country. Sales were averaging one million Eskimo Pies a day and soared to two million a day by early summer. Russell Stover, Nelson's business partner, designed a tin foil wrapper which added to the product's glamour and provided a mechanism to collect royalties. U.S. Foil Company (which was later renamed Reynolds Metal Company) manufactured the printed wrappers around the clock to satisfy demand.

In spite of the popularity of Eskimo Pies, the Eskimo Pie Corporation was not financially successful. Eskimo Pie had difficulty collecting royalties both because the company lacked a reliable accounting system and because of patent infringers. By the summer of 1923, it was estimated that over a billion Eskimo Pies had been sold and yet the firm could not pay its debt of $100,000. Nelson sold Eskimo Pie to the U.S. Foil Company, and in 1924 Eskimo Pie Corporation became a subsidiary of U.S. Foil Company.[1] Nelson was paid a small fraction of a cent in royalties on every Eskimo Pie sold thereafter.

1991 Operations

Eskimo Pie had two lines of business in 1991. The first was the licensing of the Eskimo Pie brand products and the sublicensing of Welch's and Heath brand products. The second was a manufacturing operation that produced and distributed ingredients and packaging for the dairy industry. **Table A** presents the sales breakdown of these businesses. The company was also engaged in intensive research and product development efforts to extend its product lines. Eskimo Pie had a total of 130 employees.

---

[1] Stover sold his share for $30,000 in 1923. Stover went on to develop a nationwide candy business. After the sale of Eskimo Pie to U.S. Foil, Nelson was employed by Eskimo Pie and retired as a vice president in 1961. His significant inventions include the use of dry ice to store ice cream and machinery that automated the production of ice cream novelties. Mr. Nelson died on March 8, 1992 at the age of 98.

Table A   Sales by Business Line

	Year Ended December 31,		
Business	**1989**	**1990**	**1991**
Licensing			
Eskimo Pie	58%	59%	56%
Welch's and Heath[a]	14	14	24
Flavors, packaging and other	28	27	20

[a]Heath products included only in 1991.

     Exhibit 1 presents Historical Financial Information for Eskimo Pie from 1987 to 1990, and **Exhibit 2** contains summary of Cash Flows from 1989 and 1990.

Licensing

     Eskimo Pie granted exclusive territorial licenses for the manufacture, distribution, and sale of Eskimo Pie brand products through a national network of about 20 dairy product manufacturers. Eskimo's licensees agreed to maintain the strict quality standards, and Eskimo maintained the right to inspect all premises used for the manufacture and handling of Eskimo products. The licensees are Eskimo Pie's direct customers, and the top 10 licensees account for over 75% of revenues. Carnation was Eskimo Pie's largest licensee and manufacturer with territorial licenses to 11 western states.

     Payment to Eskimo Pie by licensees was embedded in the price paid for ingredients and packaging supplied by Eskimo Pie rather than as a royalty payment based on units sold. If a licensee elected to use outside parties for certain ingredients and packaging, the licensee then paid Eskimo Pie a trademark license fee.

     Eskimo Pie also sublicensed the manufacture and distribution of frozen novelties under established brand names of other food companies. Sublicensing had been an important component of Eskimo Pies strategy since 1975 when it developed the Nestle Crunch Bar and sublicensed its manufacture and distribution. Shortly after it acquired Carnation, Nestle terminated the sublicensing arrangement in 1986.

     In 1991 Eskimo Pie licensed frozen novelties for Welch's and Leaf Incorporated, who owns the Heath brand name. Under the arrangements, Eskimo Pie had the exclusive authority to grant sublicenses for the manufacture and sale of these products similar to the way it did for its own Eskimo Pie brand products. Eskimo Pie purchased the base ingredients from the food companies and re-sold them, along with packaging, to sublicensees. Approximately 80% of the Eskimo Pie brand licensees were also licensees for Welch's and/or Heath products.

     Eskimo Pie provided centralized marketing for Eskimo Pie, Welch's, and Heath brand products. The majority of marketing expenses were spent on retail advertising and promotions; the balance went to regional consumer promotions using television and coupon campaigns. One or more of the Company's Eskimo Pie brand products were found in 98% of all U.S. grocery stores, and Eskimo Pie enjoyed one of the highest consumer brand name recognition levels in the industry. **Exhibit 3** shows the distribution and market share of Eskimo Pie products (including Heath and Welch's) during the 1987-1991 period.

Manufacturing

Eskimo Pie operated three plants in the United States. These plants manufactured key ingredients and packaging used by licensees, such as the proprietary chocolate coating, *Midnite Sun*, that gave Eskimo Pie products their distinctive flavor. The plants also produced generic ingredients and packaging sold both to licensees and non-licensees in the dairy industry. The plants employ a total of 46 hourly workers at an average hourly wage of $10.06. The plants also employed 18 salaried employees.

Product Innovation

Eskimo Pie's new product program was successful: ten products introduced since 1987 were being actively marketed and sold in 1991. Eskimo Pie was the first to market a sugar free frozen dairy novelty bar made with NutraSweet and held a patent on that product's coating. The introduction of *Sugar Freedom Eskimo Pie* products in 1987 was largely responsible for the growth of Eskimo Pie's unit market share from 2.3% in 1987 to 5.3% in 1991. As of 1991, the *Sugar Freedom Eskimo Pie* products were leading the Eskimo Pie line. The company was also the first to introduce a fat-free frozen novelty product made with Simplesse, a patented fat substitute. By the end of 1991, Eskimo Pie was test marketing a fat free ice cream sandwich and expected to introduce a *Fat Freedom Eskimo Pie* line in the spring of 1992.

The Frozen Novelty Industry

The frozen novelty industry in 1991 was highly fragmented with over 400 brands representing sales of $1.3 billion. During the 1980's, major food companies such as General Foods, Mars, and Coca Cola entered the frozen novelties business. This transformed the industry's structure of low growth, little advertising, and few participants into a rapidly growing industry. Industry revenues went from $590 million in 1980 to $1.5 billion by 1987. The number of ice cream novelty brands, 100 in 1980, expanded to over 500 by 1987. Advertising expenditures increased from less than $2 million to $75 million per year during this period. **Exhibit 4** presents the frozen novelties sales trends.

By the late 1980's, the industry began to consolidate, with many of the larger companies exiting or significantly reducing their commitment to the frozen novelty business. By 1991, advertising expenditures had been reduced to about $25 million, and the market growth had slowed significantly. **Table B** shows the top five frozen novelties as ranked by unit market share in 1991.

Table B   1991 Leading Frozen Novelty Brands

Brand	Company	Unit Share
Popsicle	Unilever	7.6%
Klondike	Empire of Carolina	5.4
Eskimo Pie	Eskimo Pie	5.3
Snickers	Mars	4.8
Weight Watchers	H.J. Heinz	4.3

Nestle's Offer

Reynolds retained Goldman Sachs to sell Eskimo Pie because of its long-standing relationship with Reynolds and because it represented Nestle in its Drumstick acquisition. David Clark was directed to work with the Goldman Sachs team that arrived in April 1991 to prepare a sales strategy and the documentation required by buyers. Clark and his staff cooperated reluctantly, recognizing that Eskimo Pie would be unlikely to continue its 70 year history of operating as a stand-alone company in Richmond and that its corporate staff would be unlikely to retain their positions. **Exhibit 6** presents the projected income statements that Goldman collected.

Eskimo Pie's management and Wheat First Securities, a Richmond, Va. investment banking firm, formed a group to attempt a private buyout. This group obtained $20 million in credit and contributed another $15 million in equity, but the bid was rejected early on when higher offers came in. The buyout proposal could not secure additional financing because of the generally tight credit environment and the unpopularity of high yield debt financed LBOs. Also, Eskimo Pie could not use secured borrowing because the business was not asset intensive.

Goldman contacted several potential buyers. Many expressed interest but were concerned that Eskimo Pie's licensing approach to the business diverged from the more traditional integrated manufacturing and marketing approach. Reynolds received six offers for Eskimo Pie. Nestle Foods was the highest bidder at $61 million, and Reynolds began negotiating the specifics of the sale in mid-1991.

Negotiations between Reynolds and Nestle progressed slowly because of two complications. First, Nestle, a Swiss company, wanted to tailor the transaction to take advantage of its tax conditions. Second, Eskimo Pie discovered in the third quarter of 1991 that a small quantity of cleanup solvents, inks and oils were disposed of at its New Jersey plant. The company contacted the regulatory authorities, and conducted testing to determine the extent of any contamination. Although Eskimo Pie did not expect cleanup costs to exceed $300,000, Nestle remained cautious.

The Proposed Initial Public Offering

As the end of fiscal year 1991 approached, it was becoming apparent that Eskimo Pie was going to have a record year. Sales were higher than anticipated and operating margins had improved. In addition, Eskimo had also accumulated a $13 million cash reserve. David Clark contacted Wheat First again, searching for an alternative to the Nestle acquisition that would keep Eskimo Pie independent. Any solution would have to provide Reynolds with as much cash as the proposed acquisition.

Wheat First proposed the initial public offering of Reynolds' shares. Reynolds had dismissed this possibility early on, at the advice of Goldman Sachs. Goldman argued that a public offering would be worth less than a private sale because of the potential for synergies with an acquiring firm. The fact that Nestle, with its potential synergies in its Carnation and Drumstick units, had submitted the highest bid seem to confirm Goldman's reasoning. Wheat First, however, had two reasons to think that its initial public offering might yield more than the sale to Nestle. First, as **Exhibit 5** shows, the new issues market was hot, and the number of new issues and their dollar value soared. Second, Wheat First was working with an updated forecast, and it projected a more promising outlook. The forecasted 1991 net income in **Exhibit 6** is $2,893,000; actual results were going to be closer to $4,000,000. And forecasted sales in 1991 were projected at about $57 million; actual sales would be about $61 million. Capital expenditures were expected to be less than $1 million in 1992.

Wheat First proposed a two-step transaction. First, Eskimo Pie would pay out a $15 million or $4.52 per share special dividend. The $15 million dividend would be funded by the $13 million in cash that Eskimo Pie had accumulated and another $2 million in debt. The second step of the transaction was an initial public offering of up to 100% of the existing Eskimo Pie common shares. Wheat First suggested offering 3.3 million secondary shares with the option to offer 10-15% more shares. This "Green Shoe"[2] clause would provide cash to payoff the $2 million loan and provide over $2 million in working capital.

Wheat First estimated that the offering price would be between $14 and $16 a share. **Exhibit 7** shows the proceeds from the initial public offerings at the two offering prices. At $16 a share, the firm and Reynolds obtained more from the IPO than from the Nestle bid of $61 million. Furthermore, even at an offering price of $14, the IPO equalled the Nestle offer, without the complications and conditions that Nestle wanted to attach to its purchase of Eskimo Pie. **Exhibit 8** shows that price earnings ratios for comparable companies such as Ben & Jerry's and Dreyer's Grand Ice Cream were about 30x. The S&P 500 was trading at 25 X earning at the time.

Wheat First had not done business with Reynolds, and Goldman Sachs advised Reynolds Metals against the initial public offering. Goldman argued a deal with Nestle was more certain, and they remained skeptical that an initial offering could yield as much as the private sale. The sale to Nestle was likely to be closed soon, especially in light of the potential public offering. An initial public offering would take several months to complete, and Reynolds would risk changes in market conditions that would cool off the IPO market. Furthermore, an offering the size of the proposed Eskimo Pie deal would be one of Wheat First's largest. Wheat First and the management of Eskimo Pie stressed that with a public offering, the sale of Eskimo Pie by Reynolds would be made much easier, without complicated negotiations and compromises. In addition, an independent Eskimo Pie would stay in Richmond which allowed Reynolds to get liquidity while saving a local company and local jobs.

---

[2] A "Green Shoe" clause in an underwriting agreement provides the issuer the opportunity to issue additional shares for distribution.

Eskimo Pie Corporation   293-084

Exhibit 1   Historical Financial Information

	Year Ended December 31,			
	1987	1988	1989	1990
Income Statement Data (in thousands):				
Net sales[a]	$30,769	$36,695	$46,709	$47,198
Cost of goods sold	21,650	25,635	31,957	31,780
Gross profit[a]	9,119	11,060	14,752	15,418
Advertising and sales promotions	4,742	4,241	5,030	5,130
General and administrative	6,068	5,403	6,394	7,063
Operating income (loss)	(1,691)	1,416	3,328	3,225
Interest income	308	550	801	1,004
Interest expense	(88)	(107)	(88)	(67)
Other income (expense)-net[b]	1,738	(77)	(108)	(20)
Income taxes	96	729	1,511	1,616
Net income	$ 171	$ 1,053	$ 2,422	$ 2,526
Balance Sheet Data (in thousands):				
Cash	$ 5,550	$ 8,109	$10,723	$13,191
Working capital	9,342	11,107	10,830	$ 11,735
Total assets	20,857	23,006	26,159	29,518
Long-term debt	1,269	1,094	919	744
Stockholders' equity	16,162	17,215	18,215	19,496
Per Share Data:				
Weighted average number				
of common shares outstanding	3,316	3,316	3,316	3,316
Net income per share	$ 0.05	$ 0.32	$ 0.73	$ 0.76
Cash dividend per share	-	-	$ 0.40	$ 0.40

Source: Eskimo Pie Prospectus, p. 10.

[a]Beginning in 1991 the Company increased prices for products and assumed responsibility for advertising and sales promotion costs previously shared with licensees. This change in business practice accounts for approximately one-half of the increase in net sales for 1991 with a similar impact on 1991 gross profit.

[b]Includes the gain on sale of building of approximately $1,700,000 in 1987.

Exhibit 2 Cash Flow Summary

	Year Ended December 31,	
	1989	1990
Operating activities:		
Net income	$2,422	$2,526
Depreciation	1,006	1,352
Amortization	175	118
Deferred income taxes	250	(58)
Pension liability and other	(154)	(156)
Decrease (increase) in receivables	1,212	(734)
Decrease (increase) in inventories and prepaid expenses	(524)	(51)
Increase (decrease) in payables to parent	2,054	(621)
Increase (decrease) in accounts payable and accrued expenses	143	3,006
Net cash provided by operating activities	6,595	5,382
Investing activities		
Capital expenditures[a]	(2,358)	(1,311)
Other	(121)	(101
Net cash used in investing activities	(2,479)	(1,412)
Financing activities		
Cash dividends	(1,327)	(1,327)
Principal payments on long-term debt	(175)	(175)
Net cash used in financing activities	(1,502)	(1,502)
Increase (decrease) in cash and cash equivalents	2,614	2,468
Cash and cash equivalents at beginning of year	8,109	10,723
Cash and cash equivalents at end of year	$10,723	$13,191

Source: Eskimo Pie Prospectus, p. F-4.

[a]Capital expenditures in 1989 are principally related to equipment acquired for use by licensees and, in 1990, an expansion of an ingredients manufacturing facility.

Eskimo Pie Corporation 293-084

Exhibit 3 Distribution and Market Share of Eskimo Pie, Heath, and Welch's Frozen Novelties

	1987	1988	1989	1990	1991
Distribution of at least one Eskimo product at U.S. Grocery Stores	76.3%	78.1%	91.2%	95.6%	97.9%
Unit Market Share of Eskimo products	3.3	3.9	5.7	6.8	7.5

Source: Eskimo Pie Prospectus

Exhibit 4 Industry Information for Frozen Novelties

Year	Industry Revenues (millions)	Units Sold (millions)	% Change in Sales	Average Price	Advertising Spending (millions)
1980	$590	N/A	N/A	N/A	$ 2
1981	680	N/A	15.3%	N/A	4
1982	770	457	13.2	$1.69	17
1983	940	525	22.1	1.79	23
1984	1,100	577	17.0	1.90	32
1985	1,300	643	18.2	2.02	44
1986	1,400	681	7.7	2.06	77
1987	1,500	717	7.1	2.09	38
1988	1,355	637	-9.7	2.13	26
1989	1,332	623	-1.7	2.19	40
1990	1,321	590	-0.8	2.24	21

Source: 1980-87 Nieldsen; 1988-90 IRI

Exhibit 5   Initial Public Offerings, Volume in $ billions, by Quarter

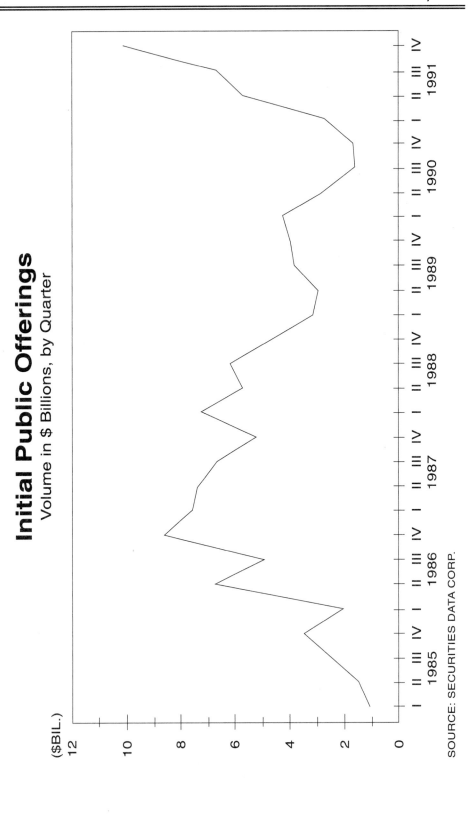

Initial Public Offerings
Volume in $ Billions, by Quarter

SOURCE: SECURITIES DATA CORP.

Exhibit 6   Goldman Sachs Projected Income Statements[a]

		Year Ended December 31,	
	1991	1992	1993
Net Sales	$56,655	$59,228	$59,961
Operating expenses	52,610	54,755	55,337
Operating income	4,045	4,473	4,624
Interest income	828	890	1,058
Interest expense	52.5	38.5	24.5
Pretax income	4,821	5,324	5,657
Income taxes	1,928	2,130	2,263
Tax rate	40.00%	40.00%	40.00%
Net income	$2,893	$3,195	$3,394
Margin	5.1%	5.4%	5.7%
Earning per share	$0.87	$0.96	$1.02
Average shares outstanding	3316	3316	3316

Source: Goldman Sachs

[a]Adjusted for 2.5 to 1.0 stock split in March 1992.

Exhibit 7   Hypothetical Proceeds from an Initial Public Offering

Total for firm:		
Offer Price	14.00	16.00
Special dividend	4.52	4.52
Total per share	18.52	20.52
Shares outstanding	3,316	3,316
Total	61,421	68,054
1991 Net Income	3,749	3,749
Implied P/E Multiple	12.38	14.15
Reynolds' Proceeds:		
Shares owned	2,789	2,789
Per share proceeds:		
Stock price	14.00	16.00
Special dividend	4.52	4.52
Total per share	18.52	20.52
Total for holdings	51,645	57,222

Source: Casewriter estimates

Exhibit 8   Information about Comparable Companies

293-084   -12-

Company	Sales	Cash Flow	Operating Income[a]	Net Income	Book Value of Equity	Market Value of Equity	Total Debt	Beta
Ben & Jerry's	97.0	6.7	10.2	3.7	26.3	110.1	2.8	1.2
Dreyer's Grand Ice Cream	354.9	24.1	37.0	15.9	113.1	534.0	44.3	1.4
Empire of Carolina, Inc.	243.1	16.8	37.4	8.8	45.1	51.4	89.8	0.3
Steve's Homemade Ice Cream	35.1	2.7	3.9	1.8	11.1	37.4	3.1	2.5
Hershey Foods Corp.	2,899.2	292.3	463.0	219.5	1,335.3	4,002.5	282.9	1.0
Tootsie Roll Inds.	207.9	32.5	47.2	25.5	152.8	728.8	0.0	1.0

Source: Standard & Poor's, Compustat, and casewriter estimates.

[a]Before extraordinary items.

Exhibit 9   Selected Financial Market Data, November 1991

I. Treasury Yields	
90 day	4.56%
Six months	4.61
One year	4.64
Five years	6.62
Ten years	7.42
Thirty years	7.92
II. Corporate Borrowing Rates	
Long-term Bond Yields	
AA	8.74%
A	9.27
BBB	9.56
BB	11.44
B	14.68
Floating Rates	
Prime rate	7.50%
Prime commercial paper (6 months)	4.76

Source: Federal Reserve Bulletin, S&P Bond Guide.

6
Microeconomics

1. Introduction

Microeconomics is the branch of economics that focuses on the behavior of individual actors and that deals with individual markets. In contrast, *macroeconomics* analyzes broad economic phenomena — the overall level of economic activity, unemployment, interest rates, inflation, and the like. Our survey of microeconomics will begin with the classical theory of a competitive market. Then we'll move on to imperfect consumer information, monopoly and imperfect competition, externalities, public goods, and welfare economics. In doing so, we'll cover much of what is traditionally addressed in a course on microeconomics, although more compactly.

The subject of microeconomics is relevant for lawyers in a wide variety of areas of practice. It's of obvious importance in business-related subjects, such as antitrust law, securities regulation, bankruptcy, commercial law, product liability, and intellectual property law. But microeconomics is also helpful in understanding issues in other types of law, such as healthcare law, family law, and environmental law. In one way or another, legal issues in many, if not most, areas of law involve markets or issues of market failure; furthermore, damage assessment frequently requires consideration of markets. Additionally, an appreciation of microeconomics is of value to lawyers in their roles as citizens and as policymakers (especially as judges, civil servants, or legislators), for social policy issues generally have economic aspects.

2. The Theory of the Competitive Market

How are the price and the quantity of goods sold on a market determined? In what sense can the price and the quantity be evaluated as socially good or bad? These are classic questions, and we will consider them in this section assuming that markets are competitive.

There are various ways of describing what is meant by a *competitive market*. A rough description is simply this: each consumer and each seller essentially take the prevailing price as given, because each individual is a small actor in the market in the sense that each person's transactions are a tiny fraction of all transactions. This is a good approximation to the truth in many markets, such as those for generic commodities like wheat and steel, and it is nearly true for a host of goods that aren't quite generic, like pizza and refrigerators. Even sellers of many branded products, like Starbucks coffee, can't sell very much if they deviate too greatly from the prevailing price for their type of product; thus, for some purposes, we can regard these products as being sold in a more or less competitive market. One way of describing a firm in a competitive market is to say that it is a price *taker*, as opposed to a price *maker*.

Price and total quantity sold in a competitive market are determined through the interaction of two forces: supply and demand. These twin forces are encapsulated in the notions of supply curves and demand curves. We will focus on each type of curve individually, and then we'll look at how, together, they can be used to find the price of an item and the quantity sold in a market.

A. Demand Curves

A *demand curve* for strawberries is shown in Figure 6-1. It records the total quantity of strawberries that people would want to purchase, depending on the price. The demand curve doesn't indicate the quantity of strawberries that people actually want to purchase. Rather, it is a

Figure 6-1
Demand Curve

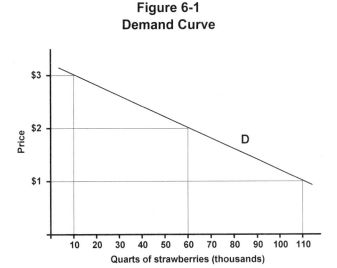

Quarts of strawberries (thousands)

hypothetical registering of the total quantity that they would want to buy at different possible prices. We can see from the curve that, at the price of $1.00 per quart, the total quantity of strawberries that people would wish to buy is 110,000 quarts; at $2.00 per quart, 60,000 quarts; at $3.00 per quart, 10,000 quarts; and so forth.

The total demand for a good falls as its price rises because, of course, people often decide to do without it, buy less of it, or perhaps substitute another good for it. When the price of strawberries rises, people may decide to skip putting fruit in their breakfast cereal, put fewer strawberries in their cereal, or substitute bananas or raisins for strawberries in their cereal. This, then, is why the total amount that people want to buy goes down as the price goes up, or, equivalently, why the total amount that people want to buy goes up as the price goes down. The graphical implication of this point is that demand curves generally slope downward.

The demand curve can be conceived of as reflecting the demand for a good by a named, relevant population of individuals — for example, all the people in a city, state, or country, or everybody in the world — or by single individual. Usually, what the demand curve is representing is stated or is clear from context.

It's worth noting that the graph of demand is drawn with quantity represented on the horizontal axis and price on the vertical axis. This is

---

Box 6-1
Where Do Demand Curves Come From?

Economists have a wealth of data that they use to estimate demand curves. The general way this is done is to look at how the demand for a good varies as its price has actually varied. Prices for most goods change over time, and economists can see how the total amount purchased has fluctuated with changes in price. Also, prices tend to vary somewhat at any given time, depending on location of sale. Of course, there are many reasons that quantity purchased will change other than that the price changed. For instance, suppose that incomes of people go up at the same time that the price of foreign travel falls, and that the amount of foreign travel increases. Might this increase in travel be due more to the income increase than to the fall in price? Fortunately, given enough data and statistical tools, the effects of factors like income on amount purchased can be disentangled from the effect of price, and a demand curve can be obtained.

---

merely a convention; there is no logical reason why it has to be drawn this way.

1. Shift in the demand curve. When something affects the entire relationship between price and total quantity demanded, the demand curve shifts. Suppose, for example, that there's a scare about strawberries raised, perhaps by news reports that some strawberries are contaminated with a bacterium that can cause illness. We would expect the total quantity demanded to go down: at any given price, people would want to buy fewer strawberries — perhaps far fewer. As can be seen in Figure 6-2, the result would be a leftward shift in the curve. At any given price, the total amount demanded would be lower than it was originally — for example, at $2.00 per quart, instead of being 60,000 quarts, it would be only 30,000 quarts.

Such a *shift* in the demand curve is sometimes distinguished from a movement *along* a *given* demand curve, which is to say, a movement

Figure 6-2
Leftward Shift in the Demand Curve

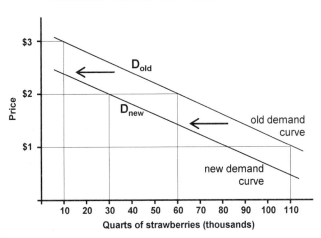

from one quantity demanded at a particular price to another quantity demanded at another price. Let's look again at the old demand curve in Figure 6-1 (the demand curve for strawberries before the news about bacterial contamination). At a price of $2.00, the demand for strawberries is 60,000 quarts, and at a price of $3.00, it's 10,000 quarts. The change in demand from 60,000 quarts to 10,000 quarts would be described as a movement along the demand curve due to a price change.

Figure 6-3 shows the consequence of something that would increase the total quantity of strawberries demanded — for example, a report from the National Institutes of Health that strawberries increase longevity and reduce the risk of cancer. The demand curve to the right of the original one shows that, at any price, the total amount that people would demand is higher than it had been initially.

Demand curves can shift when any factor affecting the amount that people would want to buy comes into play. One such factor is individual income. (What would you expect to happen to the demand curve for strawberries if incomes rose?) Another general factor affecting the demand curve for a good is the price of substitute goods. (What would you expect to happen to the demand curve for strawberries if the price of bananas increased?) A related factor is the price of complementary goods. (What would you expect to happen to the demand curve for strawberries if the price of breakfast cereal fell?)

Figure 6-3
Rightward Shift in the Demand Curve

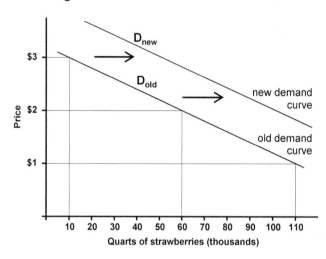

2. The demand curve and the concept of price elasticity. The slope of a demand curve reflects the responsiveness of quantity demanded to price. From Figure 6-4A, we can see that a demand curve that slopes very steeply signifies that the amount people would buy is *not* much affected by a change in price. When price doubles from $1.00 to $2.00, for instance, the quantity that people would want to purchase falls only from 100 to 90. Contrast this with the less steep demand curve in Figure 6-4B, which shows that a doubling in price from $1.00 to $2.00 would result in a large decrease in quantity demanded, from 180 down to 40.

Economists use a special number — the *price elasticity of demand* — to capture the degree of responsiveness of total quantity demanded to changes in the price of a good. It is defined this way:

$$\text{price elasticity of demand} = \frac{\text{\% change in quantity demanded}}{\text{\% change in price}}$$

To illustrate, let's return to the steep demand curve of Figure 6-4A we just looked at. According to this curve, when the price goes from $1.00 to $2.00, the quantity demanded falls from 100 to 90. Thus, the percent change in price is 100% (from $1.00 to $2.00), and the percent change in

Figure 6-4
Steeply and Gently Sloping Demand Curves

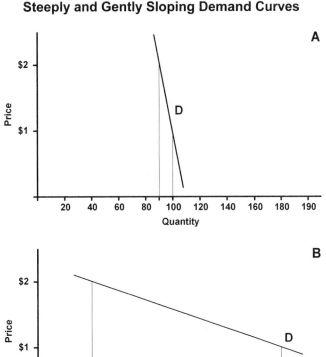

quantity is 10% (from 100 to 90), so the price elasticity is 10%/100%, or .1.[1] In the case of the less steep demand curve in Figure 6-4B, when the price goes from $1.00 to $2.00, the quantity demanded falls from 180 to 40. Thus, the percent change in price is 100%, and the percent change in quantity is 78% (i.e., 140/180), so the price elasticity is 78%/100%, which equals 0.78. Let's work through just one more example. Suppose that the price of some good falls from $5.00 to $4.00 and the total quantity

---

1. In computing the percent change, one convention — which will be ours — is to use the beginning number as the base. Thus, when the price changes from $1.00 to $2.00, we use $1.00 as the base, and since the change is $1.00, the percent change is $1.00/$1.00, or 100%.

Table 6-1
Common Demand Elasticities

Product	Price elasticity of demand
Coffee	0.3
Cigarettes	0.3
Shoes	0.7
Automobiles	1.2
Foreign travel	1.8
Restaurant meals	2.3
Motion pictures	3.7

Source: Arthur O'Sullivan and Steven M. Sheffrin, *Microeconomics* (Prentice Hall, 1998), page 84.

demanded rises from 200 units to 300 units. In this case, the percent change in price is 20%, and the percent change in quantity is 50%, so the elasticity is 2.5 (i.e., 50%/20% = 2.5). Evidently, then, higher elasticity numbers correspond to greater responsiveness of quantity to price. If the elasticity is greater than 1.0, the demand relationship is said to be elastic, and if the elasticity is less than 1.0, the demand relationship is said to be *inelastic*.[2] Some elasticities of demand are shown in Table 6-1.

With elasticity figures like this, which economists have estimated statistically, the effect of price changes on the amount sold can be readily calculated. For example, what would you predict to be the effect on cigarette purchases of a doubling in price (perhaps as a result of a hefty increase in cigarette taxes)? The percent change in price would be 100%, and, according to the table, the elasticity of demand for cigarettes is 0.3. Given that 0.3 would be the percent change in quantity divided by 100%,

---

2. You might ask yourself why economists defined elasticity as they did. In particular, why don't economists simply use the slope of a demand curve as a measure of the responsiveness of quantity demanded to price and call this the elasticity? The reason is that tricks can be played with the slope of a curve. For example, the slope of a curve can always be made to be steep by choosing to use large quantity units (e.g., by measuring strawberries in tons instead of quarts). In contrast, if elasticity is defined as economists have chosen, the elasticity for a price change remains the same regardless of the units in which quantities and prices are measured.

the percent change in quantity would be 30%. Hence, cigarette demand should fall by 30%.

Optional material

Technical points. Two technical points should be noted about price elasticity of demand. First, because an *increase* in price results in a *decline* in quantity demanded, one percentage is positive and the other is negative, so their ratio is literally a *negative* number. Although price elasticities are sometimes reported as negative numbers, more often the convention of ignoring the minus sign is followed, and that's what we do here. This is confusing, admittedly, but it's something you should be aware of.

Second, although we have spoken of *the* price elasticity, it is not necessarily a fixed value. Its value may well depend on the prices and quantities at which we begin and end on the demand curve, as becomes apparent when we do some calculations. If we begin and end on a fairly flat region of a demand curve, the calculated elasticity would tend to be high, whereas if both points are on a steep region of the curve, elasticity would be low. Hence, elasticity is really not a fixed number, and it's often treated and spoken of as an approximation.

Price elasticity and revenue. There is a relationship between elasticity and the responsiveness of revenue (i.e., price × quantity) to price. First, if the elasticity is greater than 1.0, then an increase in price reduces revenue. Let's suppose that the elasticity is 2.0 and that, when the price is $2.00, the quantity sold is 300. In this case, revenue is $600.00. Then let's suppose that the price goes up to $2.20, which is a 10% increase. Because the elasticity is 2.0, we know that quantity must fall by 20%, to 240 (because 20% × 300 = 60). Hence, revenue is $2.20 × 240.00, or $528.00. That is, revenue falls. This makes sense intuitively: if quantity is very responsive to price, then when price goes up, the fall in quantity will be more important than the increase in price, and the quantity reaction will drag down revenue. Likewise, a decrease in price will raise revenue.

Similar logic (which we won't go into here) shows that when elasticity is less than 1.0, an increase in price will raise revenue, and a decrease in price will lower revenue.

Other types of elasticities of demand. There are other concepts of elasticity. The *cross elasticity of demand* for a good is the responsiveness of the demand for the good to a change in the price of *another* good. For instance, the cross elasticity of demand for strawberries with respect to bananas is the responsiveness of the quantity demanded of strawberries to a change in the price of bananas. If bananas become more expensive, we would expect some people to switch from bananas to strawberries and thus the demand for strawberries to increase. Formally, cross elasticity is defined as follows:

$$\text{cross elasticity of demand} = \frac{\%\ \text{change in quantity demanded}}{\%\ \text{change in price of another good}}$$

So, if the cross elasticity of demand for strawberries with respect to bananas is 0.2 and the price of bananas goes up by 50% for some reason, the quantity of strawberries demanded should rise by 10% (i.e., 0.2 × 50% = 10%). A high cross elasticity signifies that goods are pretty substitutable in consumers' eyes. If we want to know how substitutable two different branded products are — say, BMWs and Mercedes — we would look at the cross elasticity of demand between them. (Do you think that the cross elasticity of demand for BMWs with respect to the price of Mercedes is higher or lower than the cross elasticity of demand for BMWs with respect to the price of the Ford Taurus?)

Income elasticity is a measure of the responsiveness of quantity demanded to changes in individuals' income (rather than to the price of a good). Specifically,

$$\text{cross elasticity of demand} = \frac{\%\ \text{change in quantity demanded}}{\%\ \text{change in income}}$$

For example, if the income elasticity of demand for laptop computers is 1.5 and we learn that incomes have risen by 6%, we would expect the demand for laptops to go up by 9% (i.e., 1.5 × 6% = 9%).

Figure 6-5
Supply Curve

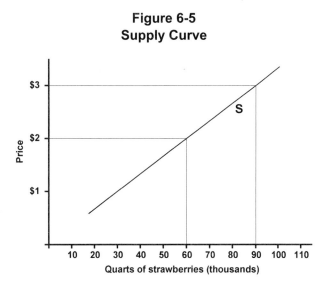

B. Supply Curves

The *supply curve* is a graph of the total quantity that firms in an industry would be willing to sell at different possible prices. According to the supply curve for strawberries in Figure 6-5, when the price rises from $2.00 to $3.00, the quantity of strawberries that firms want to sell increases from 60,000 quarts to 90,000 quarts.

Why should firms want to sell more strawberries when the price goes up? There are two basic reasons: (1) Existing firms in the strawberry industry will tend to produce more strawberries if they can sell them at a higher price. They will do so because they will invest in equipment that will more efficiently handle strawberries, thereby reducing crushing and wastage; because they will plant more land with strawberries; and so forth. (2) Over time, new firms will enter the industry. For example, farms that had devoted their efforts to other crops may switch to strawberries, and perhaps some individuals who are not growing any crops will enter the strawberry industry.[3]

———————

3. Note that, if the price of strawberries falls, existing firms may exit from the industry.

Figure 6-6
Leftward Shift in the Supply Curve

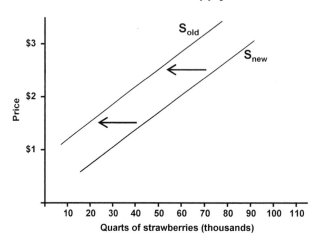

Quarts of strawberries (thousands)

How much the supply of strawberries will rise when the price increases will depend on the joint effects on existing firms and new entrants.

A point that deserves to be emphasized is that the effect that a change in price has on the quantity supplied by an industry depends, importantly, on the length of time in question. Economists often speak of the *short run* — by which they mean a period too short for new firms to be able to enter the market and too short also for existing firms to be to able make major changes in capital and equipment. Over the *long run*, however, both of these things can happen. Thus, the short-run supply curve is steeper than the long-run supply curve. (Can you explain why?)

1. Shift in the supply curve. A shift in the supply curve is analogous to a shift in the demand curve. It occurs when something affects the relationship between price and quantity supplied. Suppose that a fungus attacks strawberries and that, as a result, they become harder to grow to maturity. The quantity of strawberries produced at any given price will tend to fall, as illustrated in Figure 6-6 by the leftward shift in the supply curve. Or suppose that a genetically engineered strawberry resistant to disease and rot is developed. In this case, the quantity of strawberries that firms supply at any given price will be likely to rise, and the supply curve will shift to the right, as depicted in Figure 6-7.

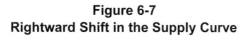

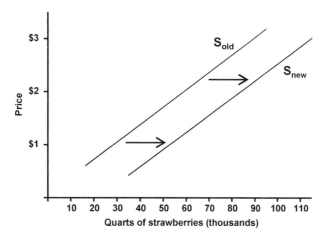

2. The supply curve and elasticity of supply. The concept of elasticity of supply is similar to that of elasticity of demand, so the discussion can be brief here. Observe first that a steeply rising supply curve, as in Figure 6-8A, corresponds to a good for which an increase in price results in only a small change in quantity produced. The interpretation, therefore, is that existing firms won't produce much more when price goes up because they can't profitably do so and also that new firms won't enter the market in significant numbers. Indeed, an almost vertical supply curve signifies that, for the good in question, an increase in price would result in virtually no increase in quantity produced. An example of such a good is land: when the price goes up, more cannot be produced (short of draining swamps and the like).

Second, note that a fairly flat demand curve, such as the one in Figure 6-8B, corresponds to a good for which a small increase in price results in a large increase in quantity supplied. One interpretation is that existing firms will produce much more when price goes up by a little. This would be the case when a lot more of a good can be produced if only a modest amount more would need to be spent per unit — for instance, by spending slightly more on labor or materials. Another interpretation is that, if the price goes up slightly, many new firms will enter the industry. This could happen if the production technology is

Figure 6-8
Steeply and Gently Sloping Supply Curves

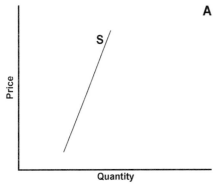

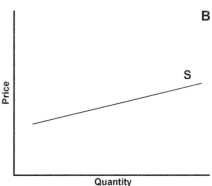

fairly widely known and access to material inputs and labor is nearly equal.

Supply elasticity is formally defined this way:

$$\text{elasticity of supply} = \frac{\% \text{ change in quantity supplied}}{\% \text{ change in price}}$$

To illustrate, suppose that the supply elasticity is 2.0 and that the price rises by 10%. The amount supplied by the industry would increase by 20%.

C. Determination of Market Price and Quantity

1. Intersection of /supply and demand curves determines equilibrium price and quantity. We can predict what will occur in a competitive market — what the price and the quantity will be — by using supply and demand curves. *The price and the quantity would be expected to gravitate toward the price and quantity at which the supply and demand curves intersect.*

Consider Figure 6-9, in which the demand and supply curves for strawberries intersect where the price is $2.00 per quart and the quantity supplied is 60,000 quarts. Let's analyze why the point of intersection of these two curves determines the price and quantity that we expect to observe.

Figure 6-9
Demand and Supply Curves and Market Equilibrium

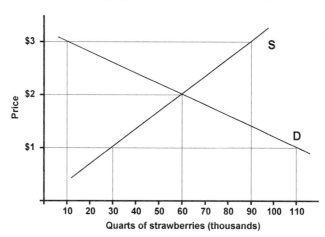

When the price of strawberries is $2.00 per quart, people want to buy 60,000 quarts, and industry also wants to produce 60,000 quarts. In other words, the total quantity that people want to buy *matches* the total quantity that industry wants to produce. Thus, the situation is one in which there is a balance, or an *equilibrium,* between consumers' desire to purchase and industry's willingness to produce.

Moreover, any price different from $2.00 per quart (the price at which the demand and supply curves intersect) cannot persist. To explain: Suppose that the price is above $2.00 for some reason — say, at $3.00 per quart. We can see from the supply curve that, for the price to remain at this higher-than-equilibrium level, industry would supply a larger quantity, namely, 90,000 quarts rather than 60,000 quarts. But the demand curve tells us that, at $3.00 per quart, people would purchase only 10,000 quarts. Hence, the quantity of strawberries brought to stores and put onto shelves — 90,000 quarts — would far exceed the quantity that people would buy — 10,000 quarts. Such a situation is often referred to as one of excess supply. Obviously, it cannot persist — because when stores find that they have strawberries on hand that aren't selling, they *lower the price* in order to sell more strawberries. (This would be so even if strawberries weren't perishable, for stores wouldn't want to store a commodity forever.) The foregoing argument applies whenever price exceeds

$2.00, because at any such price the quantity supplied would be above 60,000 quarts and the quantity demanded would be below 60,000 quarts; thus, there would always be an excess supply and a downward pressure on price. Our conclusion, therefore, is that no price exceeding $2.00 can persist and that price must fall if it exceeds $2.00.

Now suppose that the price is below $2.00 per quart — say, at $1.00 per quart. Industry would produce 30,000 quarts, whereas people would want to purchase 110,000 quarts. In this situation the quantity demanded would outstrip the quantity produced. It is a situation of *excess demand,* and it would result in an *upward movement of price.* In particular, sellers would notice that they were running short of strawberries and would, naturally, start raising prices. Hence, a situation in which the price is $1.00 could not persist. In fact, any price below $2.00 would lead to an upward pressure on price.

Obviously, if at any price above $2.00 the price would fall and if at any price below $2.00 the price would rise, the price would gravitate toward $2.00. Moreover, we would expect the price to stick at $2.00 once it got there. Recall that at $2.00 per quart the total quantity that people would want to buy is 60,000 quarts, which is also the quantity that industry would want to produce. Hence, there would neither be a shortage of strawberries, resulting in an upward pressure on price, nor a surfeit of strawberries, resulting in a downward pressure on price. Hence, the price of $2.00 per quart would indeed be stable. This is another reason why it is called the equilibrium price.

Corresponding to the $2.00 equilibrium price, where the supply and demand curves intersect, is a quantity that is both produced and de-manded — namely, 60,000 quarts. This is the *equilibrium quantity.*

2. Changes in equilibrium with changes in demand and supply curves. If the demand curve or the supply curve changes, the equilibrium price and quantity generally change as well. For example, let's say that strawberries are found to have previously unknown health benefits and that, in response to this good health news, the demand curve shifts to the right. As we can see from Figure 6-10, the point of intersection of the supply and demand curves would change from point A to point B. In other words, the equilibrium price and the quantity sold would increase: the price would rise from $2.00 to $2.50, and the quantity sold would go

Figure 6-10
Effect of a Shift in the Demand Curve on Equilibrium

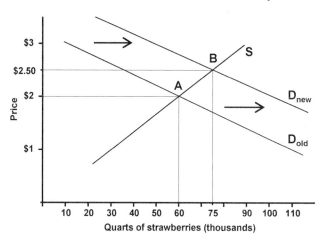

from 60,000 quarts to 75,000 quarts. A story can be told to explain how this would happen: As we can see in Figure 6-10, if stores didn't react to the good news about strawberries and didn't raise the price, there would be a shortage of strawberries. The total quantity demanded would increase from 60,000 quarts at a price of $2.00 to about 100,000 quarts. (Make sure you can see from the graph that, according to the new demand curve, approximately 100,000 quarts would be demanded at the price of $2.00.) This shortage of strawberries would lead to an increase in the price. An increase in price from $2.00 would have two effects. On one hand, the quantity of strawberries demanded by consumers would fall from the 100,000-quart level to a lower level (moving along the new demand curve). On the other hand, the quantity of strawberries produced would rise from the 60,000-quart level. When the price reached $2.50, the amount demanded would have shrunk from 100,000 quarts to 75,000 quarts, and the amount supplied would have grown from 60,000 quarts to 75,000 quarts. In other words, there would be a new equilibrium at the higher price and higher quantity.

Figure 6-11 illustrates the effect of an increase, a rightward shift, in the supply curve following, say, a decrease in the cost of producing strawberries due to lower labor costs. Can you tell a story explaining why the new equilibrium price would be $1.50 per quart and the new quantity sold would be 85,000 quarts?

Figure 6-11
Effect of a Shift in the Supply Curve on Equilibrium

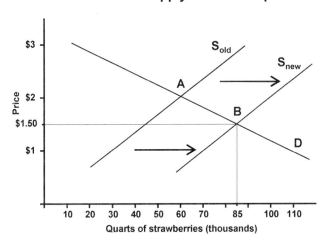

D. Government Intervention in Markets

We can use demand and supply curves to understand various kinds of government policies involving market intervention. Let's consider three.

1. Price floors. A classic government policy is to place a floor — that is, a minimum — on the price of a good, such as a floor on the price of milk to help dairy farmers. The effect of a price floor can be seen in Figure 6-12.

As illustrated, were there no price floor, milk would sell at an equilibrium price of $2.00 per gallon, and 10,000 gallons would be produced and sold. Given a price floor of $3.00 per gallon, the quantity demanded would fall to 5,000 gallons, and this is all that would be sold. However, at a price of $3.00 per gallon, the dairy industry would be willing to produce 15,000 gallons, even though they would learn that only 5,000 gallons would be purchased. This situation, in which industry would want to produce more milk than people would want to buy could not result in a decline in the price of milk, because the assumption is that government has set a floor of $3.00 per gallon. Hence, some mechanism has to be devised, by government or by dairy farmers, to determine which farmers enjoy the privilege of selling milk at $3.00 per gallon. The mechanism might be an allocation system, whereby each dairy farmer

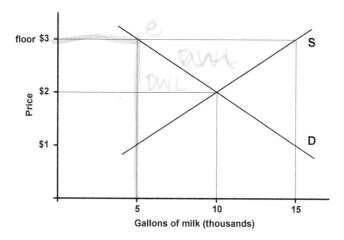

Figure 6-12
Price Floor

Box 6-2
Subsidies

Government can help producers like dairy farmers not by setting a price floor, but instead by *subsidizing* milk production. That is, the government can pay dairy farmers some amount per gallon of milk the farmers sell on the market. How would you represent a subsidy using demand and supply curves? (Hint: look a bit ahead at a commodity tax and note that a subsidy is like a tax, except it's in the opposite direction.) Verify that the effect of a subsidy would be to increase the quantity of milk produced. What would the effect of it be on the market price? How does it compare to a price floor?

---

is allowed to sell a certain number of gallons of milk (perhaps based on past sales).

2. Price ceilings. Now let's consider a government policy of the opposite type, in which a ceiling — a maximum — is placed on a price, say, to protect consumers against high prices. Suppose, for instance, that a ceiling were imposed on the price of heating oil. Consider the graphical

Figure 6-13
Price Ceiling

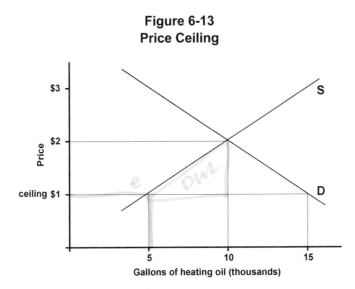

Gallons of heating oil (thousands)

representation of such a price control in Figure 6-13, where the equilibrium price of heating oil is $2.00 per gallon and the number of gallons supplied is 10,000. If a price ceiling were put into effect to limit the price to $1.00 per gallon, the demand for heating oil would be 15,000 gallons, whereas the number of gallons supplied by industry would be lower, only 5,000 gallons. This is a situation of excess demand: the amount of heating oil that people would want to buy would exceed by 10,000 gallons the amount that industry supplies. Somehow, the 5,000 gallons of heating oil supplied has to be distributed among people, perhaps by means of an allocation based on size of buildings, perhaps by some other means.

3. Commodity taxes. Now let's consider a classic commodity tax, such as a tax of $1.00 per bottle of perfume. When people have to pay an extra dollar for a bottle of perfume, the demand at any given market price should fall, and the demand curve should shift to the left. The price, then, should fall, and so should the quantity. Such a scenario is illustrated in Figure 6-14: the equilibrium price decreases from $3.00 per bottle to $2.50 per bottle (but the after-tax price is $3.50 per bottle), and the equilibrium quantity goes from 6,000 bottles down to 5,000 bottles. Note that the after-tax demand curve is vertically below the old demand curve by a distance of exactly $1.00. We can understand why by considering any price and the corresponding quantity on the old demand curve in Figure 6-14 — let's say $5.00 and 2,000 bottles. If people had to pay

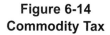

Figure 6-14
Commodity Tax

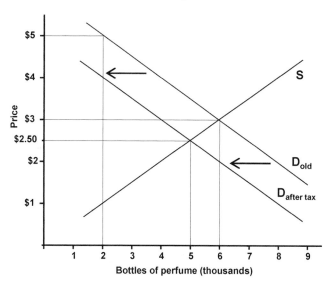

Bottles of perfume (thousands)

$5.00, they would buy 2,000 bottles. However, at a market price of $4.00 ($1.00 less than the original) *plus* a tax of $1.00, the after-tax, total price of a bottle would be $5.00. So people would be expected to buy precisely 2,000 bottles if the market price were $4.00 and a tax of $1.00 were levied. Additionally, we can tell from the geometry of the supply and demand curves — again, see Figure 6-14 — that the market price can't fall by as much as the $1.00 tax; it must fall by less. (Can you explain why this is so in intuitive terms?)

E. Social Welfare and the Market

We have seen how price and quantity are determined in competitive markets and how various policies affect price and quantity, but we haven't yet evaluated the social desirability of price and quantity outcomes. Although we won't focus on the general topic of social welfare until later, we should be familiar with one measure of social welfare, a simple and intuitively appealing one, at this point: *the value that parties obtain from consuming goods minus the cost of producing them.* This quantity is sometimes called *total surplus,* or just surplus, because it's the excess of the value placed on things over the cost of making them. The appeal of surplus as a social goal or measuring rod is that it reflects in

Table 6-2
Valuations of Individuals

Individual	Value placed on 1 quart of strawberries
Amy	$5.00
Bob	$4.00
Ralph	$3.00
Jill	$2.00

a positive way the value that we assign to things and in a negative way the resources needed to produce them. Despite the drawbacks associated with measuring social welfare in this way (we'll discuss them later), it is a very useful tool for thinking, and economists frequently employ it as a benchmark for evaluating policies.

1. Value of consumption. The value an individual obtains from consumption is conventionally measured as the maximum a person is willing to pay for the item consumed. For example, if I'm willing to pay as much as $5.00 for a quart of strawberries, then $5.00 is the measure of my valuation. In fact, it measures my valuation in at least two senses: (1) My valuation is not greater than $5.00 — say, for example, $6.00 — because if it were, then this higher amount — $6.00 — would be the maximum I am willing to pay for the strawberries, but in fact I'm not willing to pay more than $5.00. (2) My valuation is not less than $5.00 — say, $4.00 — because if it were, then this lower amount — $4.00 — would be the maximum I'm willing to pay, whereas I'm actually willing to pay as much as $5.00 for the strawberries.

Similarly, *total value* reflects the sum of valuations assigned by all of the individuals in a group. Suppose, for example, that four individuals assign four different values to a quart of strawberries (see Table 6-2), and assume, for the sake of simplicity, that none of them wants more than a quart. If 4 quarts are consumed, 1 quart by each person, the total value enjoyed is $5.00 + $4.00 + $3.00 + $2.00 = $14.00.

To see how we can use a demand curve to get information about total value placed on consumption, let's look at Figure 6-15, the demand curve for strawberries representing the same four individuals as above. Note that, at a price of $5.00 per quart, only Amy would buy strawberries, so

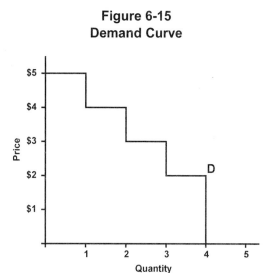

Figure 6-15
Demand Curve

the quantity demanded would be 1 quart. At $4.00 per quart, both Amy and Bob would purchase a quart, so the quantity demanded would be 2 quarts. And so forth. If we look closely at the curve, a very important point becomes apparent: at any price at which strawberries are sold, *the total value placed on the quantity purchased equals the area under the demand curve* up to that quantity.

For example, at a price of $5.00, at which just Amy purchases a quart of strawberries, the area under the demand curve is $5.00 (i.e., 1 × $5.00 = $5.00), which is Amy's willingness to pay for a quart. If the price is $4.00, the demand is for 2 quarts, so the area under the demand curve up to 2 quarts is $9.00 (i.e., 1 × $5.00 + 1 × $4.00 = $9.00). This is the total value placed by the two people, Amy and Bob, who would purchase the 2 quarts. We could continue in like manner to calculate total value at other prices. Clearly, the area under the demand curve, up to the quantity demanded at any given price, equals the total value assigned by all the people who would make purchases at that price. To look at one more example, the area under the demand curve up to 3 quarts (as designated by the shaded region in Figure 6-16) is the total value placed by Amy, Bob, and Ralph if strawberries sold at $3.00 per quart: 1 × $5.00 + 1 × $4.00 + 1 × $3.00 = $12.00.

Although the preceding examples involved purchases of the same quantity, 1 quart, by each of several people, the approach is the same

Figure 6-16
Area under the Demand Curve

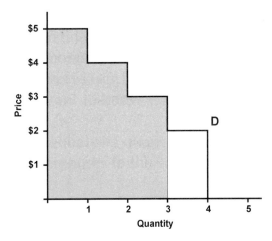

when one person buys different quantities, depending on the price. Suppose, for instance, that Lucy places a value of $5.00 on having 1 quart of strawberries, an additional value of $4.00 on having a second quart, an additional value of $3.00 on having a third quart, and yet an additional value of $2.00 on having a fourth quart. The demand curve representing the total value placed on strawberries by Lucy alone — that is, one person — would be identical to the demand curve in Figure 6-15. To look at this situation from a slightly different perspective: at a price of $4.00, Lucy would buy 2 quarts, because the first and second quarts would each be worth at least $4.00 to her, but she wouldn't buy a third quart at $4.00, because its value to her would be only $3.00. Also, by the same logic given above, the area under the demand curve at any given quantity of strawberries would equal the total value that Lucy places on that quantity.

   2. Consumer surplus. The difference between the value consumers place on what they buy and the price they actually pay is referred to as *consumer surplus.* For instance, if the price of strawberries is $3.00, and Amy buys a quart that she values at $5.00, her consumer surplus is $2.00 (i.e., $5.00 – $3.00 = $2.00). It is a measure of her benefit after she has paid for the quart of strawberries. Like total valuation, total consumer surplus can be easily seen from the demand curve. Let's consider again the demand curve for strawberries that we've been working with. At a price

Figure 6-17
Consumer Surplus

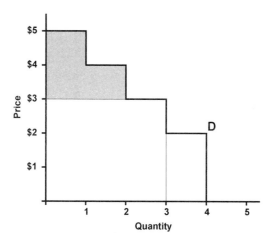

of $3.00, Amy, Bob, and Ralph purchase a quart each. Amy's consumer surplus is $2.00 (i.e., $5.00 – $3.00 = $2.00), which corresponds to the area between the demand curve and the $3.00 price line (see Figure 6-17). Bob's consumer surplus is $1.00 (i.e., $4.00 – $3.00 = $1.00), again the area between the demand curve and the price line. Ralph's consumer surplus is zero, as the amount he pays is exactly equal to the value he places on strawberries. The total surplus for these three people is, therefore, $3.00 (i.e., $2.00 + $1.00 = $3.00). In this example, then, and in general, *total consumer surplus corresponds to the area between the price line and the demand curve.* To put it differently: the area under the entire demand curve is the total value (as we already know), and the area under the price line is the total amount paid by consumers for the quantity they purchase, so the difference must be the surplus they enjoy.

Obviously, for many of the things that we buy, we enjoy substantial consumer surplus, for the prices we pay for them are much lower than what we would be willing to pay.

3. Production cost. Before we can determine total surplus, we have to consider the cost of producing goods. As it turns out, total production costs equal the *area under the supply curve.* The reason why this is so is analogous to the reason why the area under the demand curve equals total consumer valuation. We can see this by extending our hypothetical strawberry scenario. Let's say that four firms produce strawberries

Table 6-3
Production Costs of Firms

Firm	Production cost for 1 quart of strawberries
Alpha	$1.00
Beta	$2.00
Gamma	$3.00
Delta	$4.00

and that each produces exactly 1 quart. (Admittedly, no firm would produce just 1 quart, but we make this assumption for expositional convenience.) Let's also say that each firm faces a different production cost (see Table 6-3). With this information at hand, we can construct the supply curve (see Figure 6-18): At a price of $1.00 per quart, only one firm, Alpha, would produce strawberries, so the total quantity produced would be 1 quart. If strawberries sold for $2.00 per quart, 2 quarts would be produced, because two firms, Alpha and Beta, would produce 1 quart each. And so forth for prices of $3.00 and $4.00. Now it's easy to verify that the area under the supply curve up to the quantity produced is a measure of the total production cost: at a price of $2.00, the area under the curve (i.e., the shaded area in Figure 6-18) is $3.00 (i.e., $1.00 + $2.00 = $3.00), which is Alpha's and Beta's combined costs of production.

4. Profit, or producer surplus. In a similar way, we can determine a firm's profit from its supply curve. If the price is $2.00, Alpha makes a profit of $2.00 – $1.00, which is $1.00, and Beta a profit of $2.00 – $2.00, or $0.00 (i.e., Beta doesn't make a profit). Thus, *profit equals the area between the price line and the supply curve,* as represented by the shaded area in Figure 6-19. This makes sense, as the area under the price line is total revenue and the area under the supply curve measures total production cost. Sometimes profit is called *producer surplus.*

5. Surplus. Total surplus is, as we know, defined to be the difference between consumer valuation and production cost. With the aid of the demand and supply curves, we can figure it out for any quantity produced. Let's look at the demand and supply curves for strawberries in Figure 6-20. (We're now imagining many individuals and firms, whereas, for convenience, the preceding examples involved only a few.) For a

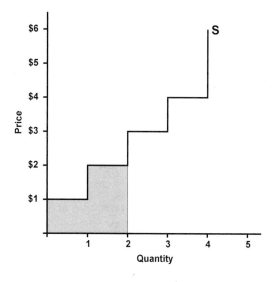

Figure 6-18
Area under the Supply Curve

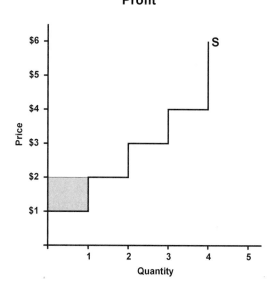

Figure 6-19
Profit

quantity of 40,000 quarts, the value of the strawberries to consumers is the area under the demand curve up to 40,000 quarts, and the cost of producing them is the area under the supply curve up to 40,000 quarts. Hence, the surplus is the shaded area in between. More generally, then,

---

Box 6-3
Ticket Scalping and Surplus

Some people — so-called scalpers — buy tickets to events, like baseball games, and then sell them to people who come to the events. This would appear to increase surplus: people who buy tickets from scalpers benefit — they save the time they'd have to spend waiting in line, or they get better tickets than they otherwise would — and the scalpers make money from the transactions. Yet ticket scalping is often illegal. Why should that be?

Figure 6-20
Total Surplus

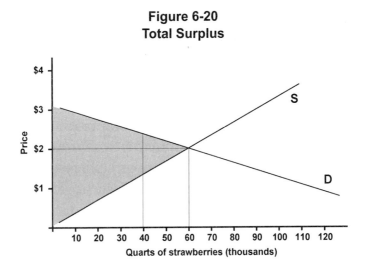

for any given quantity, surplus is the area between the demand and supply curves up to that quantity.

6. Maximum surplus. It follows from what we've said that surplus can increase — that is, it is not at the maximum possible level — as long as quantity is less than the equilibrium quantity. Let's look again at the demand and supply curves for strawberries in Figure 6-20. When the quantity is to the left of the intersection of these two curves at 60,000 quarts, the demand curve is higher than the supply curve. This means that, if quantity is increased, the area between the two curves increases, so surplus rises. More directly, the value placed by some person on one additional quart of strawberries, as measured by the height of the demand curve, exceeds the cost of producing this quart; the quart should, therefore, be produced. When quantity reaches the equilibrium quantity, increasing production is no longer socially beneficial.

Similarly, surplus can always be increased if quantity exceeds the equilibrium quantity. As we can see from Figure 6-20, for any quantity to the right of 60,000 quarts, the supply curve is higher than the demand curve. In other words, beyond 60,000 quarts, production cost is higher than the value people place on strawberries; as a result, producing those quarts would reduce the surplus. By limiting production to 60,000 quarts, the savings from not producing the additional quarts is greater than the amount by which people's valuations diminish; hence, surplus rises.

The conclusion, then, is that *surplus is maximized when quantity produced is the competitive equilibrium quantity.* In plain terms, the market will result in production of every unit whose cost is less than its value, but the market will not lead to production of any unit whose cost is greater than its value.

Graphically, the maximum surplus is reached when the market establishes the equilibrium price and the corresponding quantity is sold. At this price, the surplus is the shaded area in Figure 6-21. The upper shaded triangle is consumer surplus, and the lower shaded triangle is profit, or producer surplus. This should be geometrically obvious.[4]

We haven't yet explicitly noted the reason, as it is expressed in ordinary discourse, why competitive markets are good: through vigorous competition and unimpeded entry into an industry, prices fall and buyers are thereby made better off. This point can also be expressed in terms of surplus: lower prices resulting from competition and entry into an industry raise consumer surplus and thus surplus.[5]

---

4. The explanation may be expressed algebraically as well: Let v be the value of a unit of the good, c the production cost of that unit, and p the price of the good. Then the surplus created by production of that unit of the good is $v - c$, consumer surplus is $v - p$, and profit is $p - c$. But $v - c = (v - p) + (p - c)$; that is, surplus equals consumer surplus plus profit.

5. A more detailed explanation for why entry and competition raises surplus is that entry moves the supply curve to the right. Do you see why this must raise surplus,

Figure 6-21
Consumer Surplus and Profit

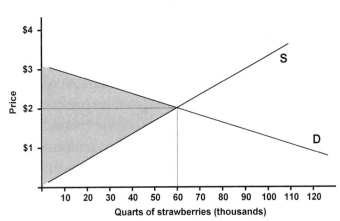

Quarts of strawberries (thousands)

7. Limitations of surplus as a measure of social welfare. Although surplus can be a useful measure of social welfare, it does have its limitations.

First, surplus represents an aggregate and doesn't reflect distributional factors. For example, surplus might be large overall but enjoyed mainly by rich individuals or, in the form of high profits, primarily by firms (though, ultimately, firms' profits are returned to the individuals who own the firms).

Second, surplus depends on the allocation of wealth in the population, because a person's willingness to pay for something (i.e., the measure of value used to calculate surplus) obviously depends on how much wealth the person has. For example, a larger surplus may be created by production of a sweater for a rich lady's poodle that she is more than willing to pay for than by production of a jar of peanut butter for a poor mother's hungry children that she is hesitant to pay for because of her lack of means.

Third, surplus as a measure of social welfare is based on the assumption that consumers properly appreciate the benefits of what they purchase. If they overestimate the value of goods, the willingness-to-pay measure exaggerates the real benefits of consumption; if they underestimate the

assuming that the quantity produced is the quantity at which the supply and demand curves intersect?

value of goods, the willingness-to-pay measure understates the benefits of consumption. For example, if a good is of poor quality (such as a drug touted to prevent male-pattern baldness that doesn't do so) but people don't know this, they may be willing to pay a lot for it even though it won't actually produce the benefits they expect.

Despite these limitations — which can be addressed, however, as we will soon see — the notion of surplus is very useful, mainly because surplus is a rough proxy for social welfare. It corresponds to some sort of total "pie" that is society's to enjoy.

F. Social Welfare Evaluation of Government Intervention in Competitive Markets

We now have the tools and knowledge we need to be able to evaluate the reduction in social welfare, in terms of a decline in surplus, that accompanies certain government interventions in competitive markets. Let's look at two specific ones: price ceilings and taxes.

1. Price ceilings. The heating oil scenario we looked at earlier provides a good example. The graph from Figure 6-13 is reproduced, in slightly modified form (one area has been shaded), in Figure 6-22.

Because the price ceiling of $1.00 a gallon results in production and sale of only 5,000 gallons, whereas 10,000 gallons would be produced and sold at the equilibrium price of $2.00 per gallon, there is a loss in surplus relative to the maximum surplus. This loss is represented by the triangular area between the demand and supply curves from 5,000 gallons to 10,000 gallons. It is the forgone surplus due to the extra 5,000 gallons not being supplied. This can be seen in a mechanical way: if 5,000 gallons are produced, surplus is the area between the demand and supply curves up to the quantity of 5,000 gallons; and if the quantity is 10,000 gallons instead of 5,000 gallons, the area representing surplus expands to include the shaded area.

Intuitively, the price ceiling limits the surplus by effectively reducing the number of gallons supplied that cost less to produce than people would be willing to pay for them. For instance, the first 100 gallons or so beyond the 5,000th gallon would cost a bit over $1.00 per gallon to produce (because the height of the supply curve is just over $1.00 in this region), yet people value these gallons at roughly $3.00 (because the

Figure 6-22
Price Ceiling

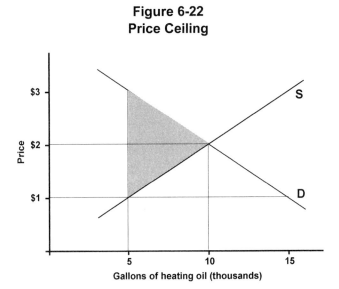

Gallons of heating oil (thousands)

height of the demand curve is about at this level). Hence, because of the price ceiling, the people who value the heating oil at almost $2.00 per gallon more than production cost can't get it. (Note that although the price ceiling lowers surplus, it benefits consumers who do buy heating oil by keeping the price down; in this way, it transfers surplus from sellers of heating oil to buyers. We'll explore a little later the idea of using surplus-lowering policy to effect distributional goals.)

2. Commodity taxes. The effect of a $1.00 a bottle tax on perfume is represented by the shaded area in Figure 6-23 (a slightly modified version of Figure 6-14). Here, surplus drops relative to the maximum surplus that could be attained in a competitive market, and the forgone surplus is equal to the shaded area. The reason is similar to the one given above for the effect of a price ceiling. Namely, because of the tax, perfume that would cost less to make than the value placed on it isn't supplied, so surplus that could have been enjoyed isn't available to be enjoyed. For the 1,000 bottles of perfume not produced because of the tax, the cost of production would be less than the value placed on them. The bottles just over the 5,000th would cost about $2.50 each to produce and would be worth about $3.50 each to consumers, but they won't be produced, because their after-tax price would be $3.50 a bottle. Hence, people are basing their purchase decisions, not on the true, lower cost of produc-

Figure 6-23
Commodity Tax

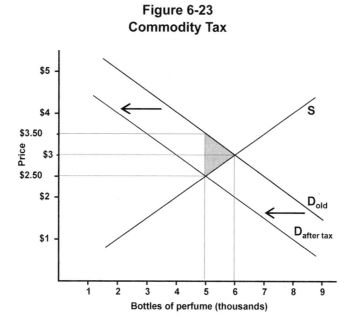

tion — $2.50 — but on the higher, tax-included figure. The surplus triangle representing the loss attributable to taxation is the *deadweight loss due to taxation.*

3. Imperfect Consumer Information

It is a commonplace that consumer information is often imperfect: we can't judge the quality of many goods and services on the basis of their outward appearance.

A. Importance

How important is the problem of imperfect information? It depends. For someone buying a hammer or an apple, the informational problem would probably not be great. We all pretty much know what hammers are used for and how apples taste, and our ability to make a judgment about a particular hammer or a particular apple, while not perfect, is not bad. We can tell a lot by looking at it. For someone buying newly created computer software, on the other hand, not very much may be known about its utility. The information that a person has also depends on the type of consumer that the individual is. For example, a repeat customer or a business customer who buys in large quantities would be likely to know a lot more than a one-time purchaser of a modest quantity would. Notable sources that consumers can turn to for information are advertising, reputation, and publications like *Consumer Reports.* In all, the significance of imperfect information is a function of context.

B. Problems: Inappropriate Purchases and Distorted Product Quality

Consumers make purchases on the basis of price and perceived characteristics of products and services. Thus, if the information they have is imperfect, they may make errors in their purchase decisions.

On one hand, consumers may mistakenly buy a good because they overestimate its value. A family may buy bottled water, for instance, in the belief that it's more healthful than tap water, whereas their tap water may actually be much cleaner than they think. Or a person may decide to go to see a particular movie because it has received good reviews, only to discover that it has been greatly overrated. When people mistakenly buy goods, there may be a loss in surplus, because the value they obtain may be less than the production cost.

On the other hand, consumers may mistakenly refrain from purchasing a good or service because they underestimate its true value. For example, I may not buy eggs because I think that the cholesterol in them will do me grave harm, yet the truth may be quite different. Here, surplus would be lost, because I don't eat eggs even though I really like them and would, if I knew the truth about them, value them more highly than their cost.

Another problem caused by lack of consumer information is that the quality of products supplied by firms may be distorted. Suppose that an automobile manufacturer knows that reinforced doors would significantly reduce injury in accidents, and suppose also that these doors would add an extra $100.00 to the price of the cars. Perhaps consumers would gladly pay the additional $100.00 if they understood the value of the doors. But if consumers lack this information and think that the doors have little value, they won't be willing to pay the $100.00. In this case, the car maker will not opt for the stronger doors: if it does, it will lose profits, because it can't charge the additional amount for the reinforced doors. Thus, as a result of consumer misperception, the quality of the product — the cars — will be lower than need be. The opposite side of the coin is that consumer misperception can lead to the addition of product features that lack any real intrinsic value. If consumers erroneously believe that the new features have a value that warrants the additional cost, these features will be incorporated into the product.

C. Policy Responses

There are several basic ways in which government can alleviate problems arising from imperfect consumer information.

1. Provide consumers with information. By providing consumers with information, government enables them to base their purchase decisions on correct information and thereby to avoid mistakes. For instance, consumers will not erroneously buy bottled water if they have been informed that it is no better than tap water. In addition, when government provides information to consumers, producers will produce goods of the quality that consumers really want, because consumers will recognize the true value of product characteristics and pay for good ones and not pay for bad ones. For example, a car maker will install reinforced doors if government crash tests show that such doors improve vehicle safety and government conveys this information about the value of reinforced doors to consumers.

Government can provide information to consumers, not only directly, but also indirectly, through grading and licensing of goods and services. When we see that milk is grade A or that a physician has graduated from a good medical school, we know that the milk or the physician meets certain quality standards.

Despite the importance of direct and indirect government provision of information to consumers, this mechanism for solving problems stemming from imperfect consumer information is not free from problems. First, the government must ascertain the quality of products and services. This isn't an easy task, especially in light of the complexity and changing nature of so many of our products and services. Second, transmitting information to consumers isn't necessarily cheap. As an example, television advertising about the risks of cigarette smoking isn't free. Third, the ability of consumers to absorb and understand information is limited. We are assaulted by all kinds of information in our daily lives and can't take anywhere near all of it into account. Thus, provision of information by government is a costly and imperfect process that inevitably leaves us somewhat ignorant about many products and services.

2. Regulate purchases. Another way in which government can attempt to solve problems associated with imperfect consumer information is by regulating purchases. On one hand, government can discourage the purchase of goods or services that it believes would not be in consumers' interests. One way that government can do this is simply by banning purchases — for example, by making it illegal for minors to buy cigarettes, on the premise that minors don't properly evaluate the hazards of smoking, or forbidding the sale of certain drugs over the counter, on the theory that the general population doesn't fully appreciate their usefulness and dangers. Government can prohibit individuals from providing a service unless they are licensed — for instance, it can prohibit nonphysicians from performing certain medical-care tasks. Yet another method is for government to impose taxes to discourage the purchase of goods, such as cigarettes.

In a similar vein, government can encourage the purchase of goods and services whose value consumers underestimate. It can do this by providing or subsidizing goods and services that are generally not fully appreciated. Although people who undervalue fire extinguishers might not ordinarily buy them, for example, they may do so if government subsidized the purchase.

What drawbacks are associated with regulation as a means of addressing the problems resulting from imperfect consumer information? And how does regulation compare with government provision of information? For one thing, administrative expense goes hand in hand with regulation of purchases, and it's hard to determine a priori how this expense compares to the cost of providing information. Another important factor is that regulation of purchases can be effective only if government has accurate information about consumer desires. For example, government may incorrectly believe that consumers want reinforced car doors. But perhaps people don't like the weight of the doors and their clunkiness, and perhaps they feel that money is better spent on side airbags as a way of improving safety in side-impact collisions. If so, and if government subsidized reinforced car doors, it would be erring. Or government may incorrectly believe that consumers would be harmed if they are allowed

---

Box 6-4
Should the Practice of Medicine
Be Limited to Doctors?

It has been proposed by well-known economists that any person be able to practice medicine. The role of the government would be mainly to *certify* how much medical education a person has, but the government would not require that a person have this or that amount of medical education to do what we now call practicing medicine. The main arguments in favor of this policy are that there are many medical care tasks that could be carried out fairly well by nonphysicians at far lower cost than now, when the tasks can only be performed by physicians. Hence, among other things, many people who now don't get medical care due to its high cost would get medical care, because it would be cheaper. The drawbacks to the policy include a concern that people would get inferior care from nonphysicians when they have serious illness. How do you react to this criticism, given the ability of government not only to certify medical practitioners, but also to advise people on which practitioners are capable of giving which kind of medical care?

---

to decide for themselves whether to take a particular drug. If so, and if government makes the drug a prescription drug, it would be erring. In contrast, when government provides information about products to consumers, individuals can decide on the basis of their desires after considering the information whether to purchase those products. Hence, purchase decisions tend to be socially desirable.

3. Regulate product quality. Government can regulate product quality to address directly the problem of producers supplying inadequate quality because consumers lack information. In the case of car doors that manufacturers wouldn't strengthen even though doing so would be worth the $100.00 additional cost, government could mandate that cars have reinforced doors.

In comparing regulation of product quality with provision of consumer information as a remedy, the points that can be made are similar to those just made about regulation of purchases. Notably, the effectiveness of regulation of product quality depends on the quality of information government has about consumer desires. Providing information, if successful, would generally lead to better results.

4. Do nothing. The possibility that the best course is to do nothing should not be overlooked. Given the cost of providing information and the expense of and possible consumer harm from regulation, sometimes it's best for government to do nothing, especially when government information about consumer desires is only tolerably good.

4. Monopoly and Related Market Behavior

A monopoly is a market in which there is a single seller of a good or service. For instance, there may be just one movie theater in a small town. Some markets, though not monopolies, are far from perfectly competitive. These are markets where there is more than a single seller but not enough sellers to approximate perfect competition. An example is the market for burgers at fast-food chains like McDonald's, Burger King, and Wendy's.

A. Why Monopoly Arises

Monopoly arises in several ways. A single owner may purchase a crucial input to production, thereby preventing other firms from competing with it. This is nearly the case with De Beers, which owns a substantial fraction of the world's diamond-mining capacity.

Monopoly may also arise when a party has invented a new product and is given patent protection or has authored a work and is given copyright protection. The inventor enjoys a monopoly because the government has forbidden other companies to sell the product. Thus, the inventor of a drug, such as Viagra, will be a monopolist in that drug during the life of the patent.

In some circumstances, it is substantially cheaper for just one company to produce a good in large quantity than for many companies to produce it in smaller quantities. The result is what is referred to as a *natural monopoly*. This is the case, for example, with natural gas, which is cheaper to supply through a single network of gas lines owned by one company than through multiple networks owned by different companies. With just one network, the cost of the network can be spread over all the buyers of gas. If cost is significantly lower when a single company sells, that company is often able to maintain a monopoly position. A competitor's cost per customer would probably be high. Thus, competing with the established monopoly would be difficult, and the competitor's profit would likely not be sufficient to cover the cost of building another network. Moreover, in such natural monopoly situations, the government may grant an exclusive right to a single company to operate.

B. How a Monopolist Sets Price

The price that a monopolist sets is the one that maximizes its profits. To determine what this price is, the monopolist has to know how both its costs and its revenues change as its level of production changes. The goal is to adjust production to the level at which profits are at their maximum. The information that the monopolist needs can be derived from a variety of graphs. The best way for us to understand these graphs, or curves, is by working through them one by one.

The *total cost curve* is a graph of total production costs as a function of quantity produced (see Figure 6-24). Obviously, total costs go up as quantity produced increases.

The *marginal cost curve* shows how much more it costs to produce one additional unit. For the good represented in Figure 6-25, we can see that the marginal cost at a quantity of 120 is $5.00, meaning that to produce the 120th unit costs $5.00 more than it costs to produce the first 119 units. The marginal cost curve is often U-shaped, as it is in Figure 6-25. This is the case when the first units are expensive to produce because efficient techniques (e.g., involving division of labor, machines and equipment for mass production, and so forth) can't be employed. As more units are produced, however, the use of efficient techniques becomes feasible, and marginal cost declines. But at some point, marginal cost often begins to rise again, perhaps because capacity constraints necessitate the use of additional plant and equipment or because the company has to pay overtime or hire and train less-experienced employees.

Figure 6-24
Total Cost Curve

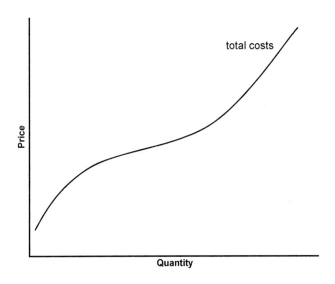

Figure 6-25
Marginal and Average Cost Curves

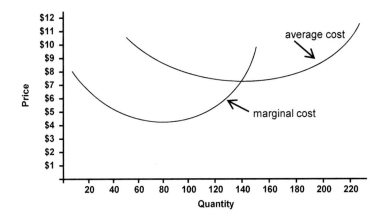

The marginal cost curve is sometimes a flat line, when the added cost of producing each additional unit is the same, because capacity constraints and so forth are not relevant. For example, the marginal cost of producing a product like chairs might be constant because the cost of materials and labor used to make chairs remains essentially the same over a wide range of production levels.

Figure 6-26
Demand Curve

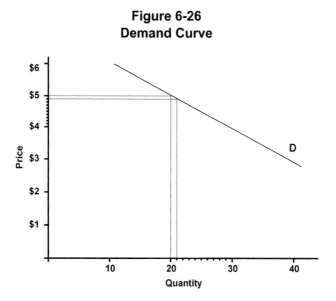

Another curve of interest is the *average cost curve*. As the name implies, it's the graph of the average per-unit cost as a function of number of units produced. The average cost curve is often U-shaped, as the marginal cost curve is, and for similar reasons. Average cost is high if a small number of units are produced, because various fixed costs are incurred (e.g., a plant has to be built or leased, basic machinery for production has to be purchased) regardless of the number of units produced. Then, as fixed costs are spread over a larger number of units and efficient production techniques become feasible, average cost falls. But ultimately, average cost rises again when capacity constraints are encountered.

Now let's turn our focus from the monopolist's costs to its revenue and ask how its revenue changes when it increases production. The change in revenue when one more unit is sold — that is, the amount of extra revenue obtained from the sale of an additional unit — is the *marginal revenue*. Consider the demand curve in Figure 6-26. If the monopolist is going to sell 20 units, it can charge $5.00 for each unit, and it will charge that amount. (If it charges more than $5.00, it will sell fewer than 20 units; if it charges less, it will receive less than it could have, and it wouldn't want to do this.) Therefore, the revenue will be $100.00 (i.e., 20 × $5.00 = $100.00). Now suppose that the monopolist decides to sell one more unit. Would its revenue increase by $5.00, the per-unit price it would charge

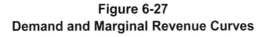

Figure 6-27
Demand and Marginal Revenue Curves

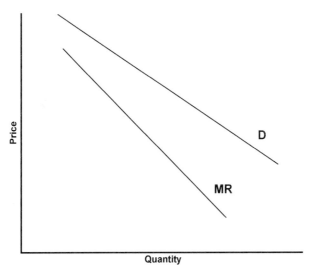

if it were selling 20 units? The answer is no: in order to sell 21 units, the monopolist would have to lower the price slightly so as to induce the purchase of one more unit. It's evident from the demand curve that, to sell 21 units, the price must be lowered to $4.90 (see Figure 6-26). Therefore, the revenue from selling 21 units would be $102.90, whereas the revenue from selling 20 units is $100. The difference of $2.90 is the marginal revenue from selling the 21st unit. Note that the marginal revenue of $2.90 would be less than the $5.00 per-unit price at which 20 units could have been sold and also less than the $4.90 price at which the 21st unit would be sold. The reason is that the per-unit price would have been lowered by $.10 to induce the purchase of the 21st unit, so each of the 20 units that could have been sold at $5.00 (if only 20 units were going to be sold) would be sold for $.10 less. (More exactly, marginal revenue would be the $4.90 obtained from the 21st unit minus the $.10 decrease on each of the first 20 units — that is, minus $2.00 — which is $2.90.) Because, then, marginal revenue is generally less than price, the graph of marginal revenue is drawn below the demand curve, as in Figure 6-27.

If the marginal cost curve and the demand and marginal revenue curves are put together on the same graph, the quantity that would

Figure 6-28
Demand Curve and Cost Curves

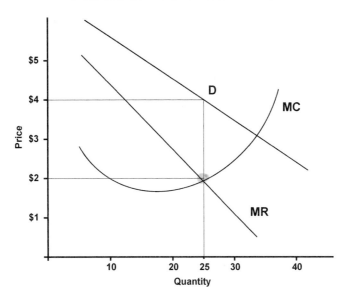

maximize the monopolist's profits can be determined (see Figure 6-28).[6] It can be helpful to think of the process that the monopolist goes through in making this determination as a sequence of choices: produce the first unit if the revenue from selling it would exceed the cost of producing it; go on to produce the second unit if the marginal revenue it would yield exceeds the marginal cost of producing it; then produce the third unit if the marginal revenue would be greater than the marginal cost; and so on. Increasing production as long as marginal revenue exceeds marginal cost would make sense; doing so would enhance profit. In fact, profit is greatest at the level of production where marginal revenue exactly equals marginal cost. In Figure 6-28, marginal revenue matches marginal cost — $2.00 — at a quantity of 25. Hence, a quantity of 25 would yield maximum profit for the monopolist, and the price would

---

6. Alternatively, we could determine the *price* that would yield the greatest profit for the monopolist. However, the quantity approach turns out to be more helpful. (Of course, if we know the quantity that would maximize the monopolist's profit, in effect we know the price that would do the same: we can tell from the demand curve the price that can be charged for this quantity.)

be $4.00 per unit. Note that, were the monopolist to produce more than 25 units, marginal cost would exceed marginal revenue, and the profit would be less.

A point worth noting about the profit-maximizing behavior of the monopolist: the price it charges exceeds the marginal cost, as can be seen in Figure 6-28. That this is generally so follows from the geometry of the curves: the monopolist would produce the quantity at which marginal cost equals marginal revenue, and the marginal revenue curve must lie underneath the demand curve. This shouldn't come as a surprise. After all, charging a price that is higher than the marginal cost would be profitable.[7]

Optional material

> We can graphically describe the profit that the monopolist makes by adding to Figure 6-28 the average cost curve, as shown in Figure 6-29. The monopolist's profit is represented by the shaded area. The reason for this is that the average profit per unit is the price minus the average cost, which corresponds to the height of the shaded rectangle. If the average profit per unit is multiplied by the number of units sold, the result is total profit, which corresponds to the area of the shaded rectangle.

C. The Principal Economic Arguments Against Monopoly

The main disadvantage of monopoly, according to the classic economic argument, is that *the quantity sold is too low,* where "too low" means that *surplus would increase if the monopolist sold more units.* Look again at Figure 6-28 and recall that the monopolist maximizes profit when the price is $4.00 and the marginal cost is $2.00, which is lower than the price. The implication is that surplus would go up if another unit were produced: the value placed on this unit by the buyer would be approximately $4.00 and the marginal cost of production about $2.00, so $2.00 of additional surplus would be created. The reason the unit is

---

7. A closely related explanation emerges if we consider the quantity where marginal cost equals price — that is, where the marginal cost curve intersects the demand curve. Can you see why raising price would always enhance profit for the monopolist, meaning that price must exceed marginal cost?

Figure 6-29
Demand Curve, Cost Curves, and Monopoly Profit

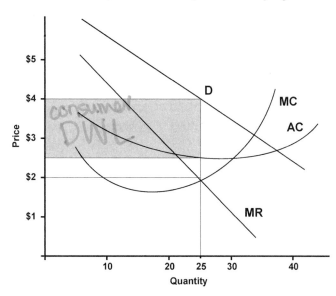

not produced, of course, is that the monopolist has set the price at $4.00, which discourages another person from purchasing the good.

This forgone surplus can be represented graphically. In Figure 6-30, the shaded area corresponds to the unrealized surplus from all the units that the monopolist doesn't produce but for which marginal cost curve would be below the demand curve. This shaded triangle of forgone surplus is called the *deadweight loss due to monopoly.*

To understand the reality of the deadweight loss due to monopoly, think of a monopoly price and the implication of the price exceeding marginal cost. For example, a cable TV company charges $30.00 a month for service, but its marginal cost of service per household is much less — say, $5.00. Any person who values service between $5.00 and $30.00 will not purchase it, so the surplus that could be derived from that person is forgone. Someone who values service at $20.00 a month will not purchase it, and $15.00 of surplus will be forgone as a result. There may be many such people, in which case the deadweight loss would be large.

The potential profit that a monopolist can earn might motivate a firm to spend significantly, but socially wastefully, to secure a monopoly position. This, too, is a social cost of monopoly. For example, a cable

Figure 6-30
Deadweight Loss Due to Monopoly

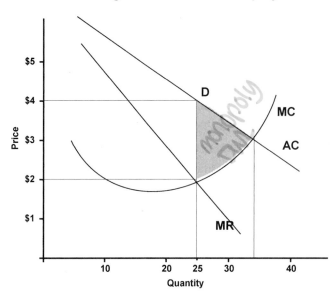

TV company might spend on lobbying to obtain an exclusive license to provide cable service in a city. The name given to efforts that a company makes to obtain or to maintain a monopoly position is *rent-seeking behavior,* for the company is seeking to capture the "rents" — that is, the profits — from being a monopolist. Rent-seeking expenditures are often unproductive and, to this extent, constitute a social cost associated with monopoly. Lobbying, for example, is not of direct value to consumers.

The monopolist makes a profit at the expense of buyers, and this is often viewed as a social cost, at least by the public at large. In other words, monopoly results in a distributional effect that favors the monopolist and harms consumers. We will discuss distributional issues a bit later, but for the present, it's sufficient to keep in mind that distributional effects don't influence surplus, as surplus is an aggregate number and is not altered by who enjoys it.

D. Price Discrimination

Although we assumed in the last section that the monopolist charges a single price for its product, in some circumstances a monopolist is able to, and wants to, charge different prices to different types of buyers — in other words, to engage in *price discrimination*. Some typical examples: airline travelers who book in advance are charged less than those who do not; children and the elderly are charged less than others for some goods and services; residential customers are charged less than businesses for telephone service; students are charged less for computers and software under educational discount programs than nonstudents who have to pay through typical retail channels.

1. Why and how price discrimination occurs. Monopolists engage in price discrimination because doing so allows them to match the prices they charge to the demand curve for particular groups of customers and thereby to enhance their profits. For example, children generally have a lower willingness to pay for movie tickets than adults do, so a movie theater may reap higher profits if it charges children less than adults, such as $4.00 rather than $8.00. If the theater must charge a single price, its profit won't be as great. By keeping the price high, at $8.00, for all individuals, it would lose many of its young customers, and thus its profits would fall, yet if it lowered the price to $4.00 for all customers, it would sacrifice substantial profits from its adult customers willing to pay $8.00.

To engage in price discrimination, a monopolist has to be able to do two things. First, it has to be able to distinguish different customers according to their willingness to pay. This is sometimes relatively easy, as in the case of a movie theater determining who is a child and who is not. Second, the monopolist must be able to prevent consumers from circumventing high prices. In the case of movie tickets, the theater has to be able to prevent adults from having children buy tickets for them. This, however, is probably not a serious problem. In the case of educational discounts on computers, the monopolist has to be able to prevent students from reselling purchased equipment to nonstudents; this can be difficult.

2. Is price discrimination socially undesirable? Price discrimination may be socially *desirable,* according to the surplus criterion, because it may increase the amount sold from the too-low level under monopoly with a single price. Equivalently, price discrimination may reduce the forgone surplus by allowing a monopolist both to charge high prices to those who are willing to pay a lot and to charge low prices to those who aren't willing to pay a lot, whereas the latter individuals would be unwilling to pay the high price if that were the only price the monopolist charged. For example, a movie theater fills more seats by allowing children to purchase tickets at a reduced price, like $4.00. If it charged the single price of $8.00, fewer children would buy tickets, and the empty seats would represent forgone surplus.

Price discrimination may also be socially desirable because the extra profit it generates may be what allows the monopolist to operate. Perhaps a movie theater would close if it weren't able to make the additional profit by selling children tickets for $4.00.

However, price discrimination is not necessarily socially desirable. One reason is that price discrimination might not increase sales. For example, it's possible that the prices a monopolist would charge to two subgroups of customers would result in lower total sales than a single price would. Another reason why price discrimination may not be socially desirable is that the effort expended to price discriminate — such as the effort that it takes for airlines to separate advance purchasers from others — is costly but not directly beneficial to consumers. Finally, the distributional effect of price discrimination (the higher profits that it results in for monopolists) is sometimes considered socially undesirable. However, as noted earlier, this is not a factor that affects its evaluation according to the surplus criterion.

E. Government Policy and Monopoly

The best type of government policy response to monopoly depends on the context and, notably, on the reasons for the monopoly's existence.

1. Monopoly and antitrust law. In the case of a monopoly that exists because the company has somehow established a monopoly position for itself and erected barriers to entry, the social costs of monopoly — the deadweight losses due to high prices and inadequate sales, and possibly the waste due to rent-seeking behavior — justify government intervention, at least in principle. Antitrust law would be an appropriate way to deal with this type of situation. In general, it addresses the problem of monopoly by *preventing the formation or continued existence of monopoly.* For example, if one company tried to buy all the movie theaters in the United States, antitrust law could prevent it from doing so. Or if the main burger chains — McDonald's, Burger King, and so forth — attempted to merge, the merger might not be allowed on the ground that it would create a monopoly. Additionally, antitrust law allows government to divide companies considered to be monopolies, as happened in 1911, when Standard Oil was broken up. However, antitrust law does not enable the government to force a monopoly to lower its price. A possible justification for this is that the government would face a huge difficulty in obtaining the information required to determine the correct price.[8]

2. Monopoly and intellectual property. In the case of a monopoly that exists because of a patent or copyright granted by the government, the policy response is quite different. It's true, of course, that monopolies in patented drugs and copyrighted computer software and books cause deadweight losses. However, monopolies of these types are thought to have redeeming social benefits: they induce innovation and authorship. Indeed, the main purpose of the patent and copyright systems is to spur innovation and authorship by rewarding creators with monopoly profits. Society has made a judgment, in other words, that the social benefits of new creations engendered by the intellectual property rights system are worth the social cost of monopoly during the life of patents and copyrights. Hence, this kind of monopoly is not one that society wants to undermine. This is not to say that government shouldn't oversee particular aspects of the behavior of patent and copyright holders. For example, it should ensure that pharmaceutical firms holding patents on drugs don't obtain larger, broader protection than the law sets out. But it is to say that these monopolies are ones that we want to exist.

3. Natural monopoly and regulation. Another type of monopoly that society shouldn't seek to eliminate is the natural monopoly, such as one consisting of ownership of a network of gas lines. Doing so would mean losing cost savings, like those associated with having a single network of gas lines. However, it *would* be desirable to prevent the monopolist from charging the high monopoly price that it would want to charge, a price that would result in too little being sold and thus in deadweight

---

8. However, as we'll see in a moment, in our discussion of natural monopoly, government does sometimes control the price that a monopoly charges.

losses. So, in the context of natural monopoly, there is a justifiable reason to subject the monopolist to *price regulation*.

What is the best form of price regulation? In the ideal, the allowed price should equal the marginal cost of production. Let's say that the marginal cost of gas is $.25 per unit. Anyone who values a unit of gas at more than $.25 would buy it, and this would lead to maximization of surplus. But in practice there are several problems with this kind of pricing scheme.

One shortcoming of marginal cost pricing is that, even though the revenue received would cover the gas company's marginal cost of production (i.e., the cost of securing the gas and maintaining the network), it wouldn't be sufficient to cover the high cost of constructing the network. Thus, to stay in business, the monopolist would need extra funds.

The problem of insufficient funds under marginal cost pricing can be solved in several ways. The government could give the gas company a subsidy. Alternatively, the price could be allowed to be higher than marginal cost, sufficiently high to cover the cost of network construction. In other words, the gas company could be allowed to charge a price equal to average cost. This approach, however, partially defeats the purpose of price regulation. If average cost is much higher than marginal cost — say, $1.00 per unit of gas — some people would be discouraged from making purchases even if the value they placed on a unit exceeded the marginal cost of $.25. (However, the monopoly price that an unregulated monopolist gas company would charge might be a lot higher than $1.00 per unit.)

Several other problems inherent in all regulated pricing schemes deserve mention. One is the difficulty that government regulators face in obtaining accurate information from the regulated monopolist. The monopolist has an incentive to skew what it reports to the regulator: it would be allowed to charge a higher price if it exaggerated its costs. A second problem is that the monopolist has little motive to hold costs down if the price it's allowed to charge is based on these costs. A third problem is that regulators may be "captured" by industry — for example, regulators may leave government service and work for industry — and end up serving industry's interests rather than the public's.

An alternative to regulation would be for government itself to own and operate the monopoly, such as the network of gas lines. Gas could then be priced at marginal cost. But some people question government's ability to operate business efficiently because of various constraints it faces.

F. Oligopoly and Monopolistic Competition

As mentioned earlier, sometimes there is more than one seller but not so many that the situation would be described as highly competitive. Situations of this type are often referred to generically as ones of *imperfect competition*. The sellers may be offering identical products — such as gas stations that sell the same type of gasoline — or fairly closely related products, such as the burgers sold by McDonald's and Burger King. Imperfect competition is complicated to describe because of the number of types of interactions that may exist among a small number of sellers, who are aware of each other's existence and who compete strategically.

To understand the range of possibilities and some of the issues, let's consider the example of two gas stations, Bill's and Sue's, located near each other and selling essentially identical gasoline. Let's assume that the two stations have to sell at the same price — otherwise, customers would flock to the cheaper station. If the cost of a gallon of gasoline for each station is $1.00, what price would we expect the stations to charge consumers?

One possibility is that the price would be driven by competition between the two stations down to $1.00, with neither station making a profit. At a higher price, say $1.20, one station, say Bill's, would cut its price to $1.19 in order to steal all customers from Sue's. So, if Bill and Sue had been dividing the market when the price was $1.20 and making a $.20 profit on each gallon, Bill would now make a profit of $.19 per gallon from the *entire* market and thus do much better. (It's much more profitable to sell 200 gallons and get a $.19 profit per gallon than to sell 100 gallons and get a $.20 profit per gallon.) Sue, however, would immediately notice Bill's price reduction and the disappearance of her customers, and she would lower her price. She might match Bill's price of $1.19, so they would again share the market, but in this case each would make only a $.19 profit per gallon. Alternatively, Sue might undercut Bill and charge $1.18, stealing the entire market from him but making only $.18 per gallon. In either case, Bill might retaliate, and the process might go on until each is charging $1.00, at which point neither would undercut the other, for doing so would only result in losses.

Because lowering the price to $1.00, equal to cost, would lead to the elimination of their profits, it might seem unlikely that they would go this route. We might expect them to realize or to have learned from experience that price wars spell ruin in the end. An attractive approach would be for Bill and Sue to make an explicit agreement — that is, collude — to set a high price. By acting as a unit, they could set the single monopoly price, perhaps $1.20 or more, that maximizes their joint profits. Thus, they have an incentive to collude. However, collusive agreements about price violate the antitrust laws and are penalized. If Bill and Sue conspire to set price and are found out, they will suffer sanctions. An additional possibility is that Bill and Sue might come to a tacit accommodation not to undercut each other.

The issues that we have been looking at arise in many settings, and traditionally they are ascribed mainly to oligopoly. *Oligopoly* usually refers to markets in which the number of firms is between two and some not very large number, say 10, and in which these firms consciously take into account how the other firms will react to what they do as well as how the firms might collude.

The term *monopolistic competition* applies to markets where the number of firms is larger than in oligopoly (say, all the barbershops in a city), where each firm has a somewhat different product from the others (each barbershop has a unique location and perhaps a unique style of haircutting), and where the firms don't really take into account how the others will react to what they do individually. A point about monopolistic competition that is emphasized concerns entry into the industry: firms join the market until supernormal profits are competed away. Thus, although each firm is a mini-monopolist in a sense, it doesn't make substantial profits, because entry lowers its demand curve (e.g., barbershops enter into business in the city until most of them aren't making very large profits, even though each has a somewhat unique product).

5. Externalities

A. What Are Externalities?

One party's action is said to create an *externality* if it influences the well-being of another person. To give you an idea of the generality of externalities, consider the following examples:

- *Nuisance.* When a person disturbs his neighbors by making noise, producing foul odors, allowing a misbehaving pet to roam free, and the like, he is commonly said to be creating a nuisance.
- *Pollution.* When a firm discharges an undesirable substance into a body of water or into the air, it reduces the utility of others who use the water or breathe the air.
- *Dangerous, risk-creating behavior.* When somebody speeds on the road, he or she is creating the risk of an accident; when a construction firm fails to take the precaution of fencing off its work site, it's creating the risk of an accident if children wander by.
- *Use of a common resource.* One person's use of a resource, such as a beach or a pasture, may harm others: the user of the beach may litter, the user of the pasture may overgraze his animals, causing erosion of the pastureland.
- *Salutary behavior.* A person's actions may occasionally help not only him but others as well, as where an apiarist's bees help to pollinate a nearby farmer's fruit trees, or where a person beautifies his land, to the advantage of others who will see it as well.
- *Behavior that has a psychological effect on others.* My actions may have ramifications for others even though there is no physical effect on them; the influence may be purely psychological. The very fact that others know that I am praying to a strange God may affect them and thus may constitute an externality.

As these examples show, externalities are many and varied in nature, they may be beneficial for, or detrimental to, the affected party, may have effects contemporaneously or in the future, and may be probabilistic in character.

B. The Problem of Externalities: Private Behavior Is Not Socially Desirable

A socially desirable act, given the social goal of maximizing surplus, is one for which the benefits exceed the costs, where the benefits and costs should include all externalities. The problem that externalities create is that those who make decisions about acts with externalities do not naturally take into account the external effects — because they are not experienced by the decision makers. Hence, decisions will tend to be inappropriate, and in two possible ways.

The first problem is that there will be too much activity that causes external harms. For example, a factory might burn waste and derive a $1,000 benefit from this (because it does not have to haul the wastes to a dump), even though the cost to neighbors who dislike smoke is $5,000. In general, we would expect nuisances, pollution, dangerous behavior, and the whole range of actions that create detrimental externalities to be observed more often than is socially desirable, unless something happens to correct the problem.

The second problem created by externalities is the converse of what we just mentioned, namely, that there will be too little activity that generates external benefits. A person might decide not to landscape his or her yard at a cost of $1,000 because the value he or she personally would derive is only $500, whereas those living in the neighborhood would together place a value of $900 on the landscaping, so the total value of $1,400 would make landscaping socially desirable.

C. Resolution of Externality Problems Through Bargaining

Externality problems can sometimes be resolved through bargaining. However, obstacles can get in the way of bargaining.

1. Frictionless bargaining and the desirable resolution of externality problems. Suppose that bargaining between the creator of an externality and the parties affected by it is frictionless: bargaining will take place, and a mutually beneficial agreement about externalities will be concluded whenever such an agreement exists in principle. This means that any externality problem that is desirable to eliminate will be eliminated — because any undesirable action will be forestalled by bargaining and agreement. In the example of the burning of waste by the factory, an agreement in which the neighbors who would suffer harm of $5,000 pay an amount between $1,000 and $5,000 — say $3,000 — for waste not to be burned will be mutually desirable. For receiving $3,000 and not burning waste is preferable to the factory to burning waste, which saves it only $1,000; and paying $3,000 is preferable to the neighbors to suffering harm of $5,000.[9] In the example of the landscaping that ought to be carried out, the neighbors will be willing to pay an amount between $500 and $900, such as $700, for the person to undertake the landscaping. If he is paid $700, then after paying $1,000 for the landscaping, he will enjoy a benefit of $500, so his net benefit is $200 and he will be better off than if he had not landscaped; also, the neighbors will have paid $700 for a $900 benefit, so they too will be better off.

   2. Asymmetric information may stymie bargaining. We have been assuming that when mutually beneficial agreements exist, such agreements will be made. But experience tells us that success in making agreements is not guaranteed, and as economists emphasize generally, an explanation involves asymmetric information between parties that leads to miscalculations in bargaining. Suppose that the neighbors who would be disturbed by smoke think that the benefit to the factory of burning waste is probably only $100 (rather than the true $1,000), and they offer only $200 to induce the factory not to burn the waste. The factory would refuse this offer, and there might be an impasse in bargaining. Such misgauging of the other side's true situation can easily lead to failures to agree, even though both sides are acting rationally given their information.

---

9. Note as well that if the neighbors have the right to prevent smoke, the factory would not be willing to pay enough to secure permission to generate smoke, for that would require at least $5,000. Hence, the outcome would be the same. This point, that the allocation of legal rights does not affect the outcome when there is bargaining, and that the outcome maximizes surplus, is known as the Coase Theorem. It was emphasized in an influential article by Ronald Coase (The Problem of Social Cost, *Journal of Law and Economics*, 1960, vol. 3, 1–44).

Box 6-5
Reluctance to Bargain

Many people who are disturbed by someone else, such as by a noisy neighbor, are quite reluctant to discuss the matter with them, and it's not because of the time it would take. Rather, it's due to a psychological aversion to bargaining, to the unpleasantness of having to confront openly a person in a situation of conflicting interests. This can be a quite powerful "cost" that stands in the way of bargaining as a means of resolving externality problems. Another factor that often prevents bargaining as a resolution is that people are hesitant to make payments to resolve problems like noise. If you were to offer your neighbor $50 to have his noisy party end by midnight, this might make you seem mercenary and might somehow insult the neighbor (people are supposed to be considerate of each other because this is right, not because they are paid to behave that way).

---

3. Bargaining may not even occur. Not only may bargaining not succeed, due to problems of asymmetric information. It may not even get off the ground, for any of several important reasons.

a. Distance between parties. If the potentially concerned parties aren't physically proximate, bargaining may be difficult to arrange. For example, a driver who is contemplating speeding in an automobile can hardly bargain with potential victims of accidents, for they aren't nearby (and are unknown) when the driver puts his foot to the gas pedal. Or a person who is at the point of deciding whether to erect a fence that the neighbor might regard as objectionable may find that the neighbor is on vacation at an unknown location, so can't be contacted about an alternative, possibly superior agreement (such as sharing the higher cost of planting a screen of trees instead of installing the fence).

b. Number of parties. If the number of involved parties is large, the likelihood that all can come together to bargain may be small, because of coordination difficulties, which tend to increase with the number of parties. In addition, the motivation to bargain may diminish as the number of parties increases. If, for example, each individual in a neighborhood believes that the others can be depended on to engage in bargaining for an agreement that will benefit the individual, such as for a factory to stop blowing its whistle early in the morning, then no one, or too few people, will participate in bargaining with the factory to obtain the agreement. This problem of free-riding on others' efforts may be acute if the benefits that would be gained from bargaining are individually small.

   c. Lack of knowledge of external effects. Clearly, someone who isn't aware that a future loss or benefit is at stake is unlikely to engage in bargaining. If I live near a factory and don't know that I'm at risk of developing cancer from its discharges, then I will hardly bargain for a change in its behavior.

D. Resolution of Externality Problems Through Markets

Another way in which externality problems may be resolved is through the operation of certain markets. One example is marketable pollution rights, which are rights that firms may purchase that allow them to generate pollution. Because firms have to pay for the right to generate pollution, they will not pollute unless the benefit they derive from doing so exceeds the cost. Another example is the market for the pollination services of bees. Farmers who want to improve their fields purchase the services of bees (which are transported to their farms) in a well-organized market. From the perspective of the beekeepers, hiring out their bees provides an additional source of income. Thus, beekeepers will tend to raise bees when they should — that is, when the total benefits from the honey produced and the pollination services outweigh the cost of raising the bees. Such instances of externalities being resolved by organized markets are, however, unusual. (Can you explain why the problem of a factory whose smoke bothers just the immediate neighbors can't be resolved by an organized market?)

E. Resolution of Externality Problems Through Legal Rules

Just as some externality problems may be resolved through bargaining or markets, others may be addressed through legal rules of various types. We'll focus on just several of the important types.

1. Types of rule. Under direct *regulation,* the state directly constrains behavior to reduce externality problems. For example, a factory may be prevented from generating pollution that may present a health hazard; a fishing vessel may be required to limit its catch to help reverse depletion of a fishery; or a person may be prevented by a zoning ordinance from opening a business establishment in a residential area in order to preserve its ambience.

Closely related to regulation is assignment of property rights and their protection at the request of parties who hold the rights. Assuming that people have the right to clean air, for example, they can prevent a firm from polluting by asking the state to intervene. The complaining party obtains an *injunction* against the injurer, and the police powers of the state are then brought to bear to enforce the injunction.

Society can also make use of financial incentives to reduce harmful externalities. Under *tort liability,* parties who suffer harm can bring suit against injurers and obtain compensation for their losses. Having to pay for the harm they inflict will motivate injurers to reduce the amount of harm they cause.[10]

Another financial incentive to reduce harm is the corrective tax (sometimes called the *Pigouvian tax,* after the economist Pigou, who was the first to study externalities). Under it, a party makes a payment to the state equal to the harm the party is expected to cause — for example, a firm pays for the harm that discharge of a pollutant into a lake is likely to cause. The corrective tax is similar to tort liability in that it creates a financial incentive to reduce harm, for an injuring party will reduce harm in an effort to avoid having to pay a tax equal to expected harm. However, there are differences between the corrective tax and tort liability. A corrective tax reflects anticipated harm (the harm the pollution is expected to cause), whereas tort liability is liability for harm actually done. Another difference is that the corrective tax is paid to the state, whereas tort liability payments are made to victims.

---

10. The assumption here is that the injurer must pay for any harm caused and thus that the rule is strict liability. We do not consider the negligence rule, under which the injurer pays for harm caused only if the injurer was negligent.

2. Comparison of rules. Let's sketch the comparison of the foregoing legal rules for controlling externalities, focusing one at a time on a list of factors that are relevant to the operation of the rules.

a. Information of the state. If the state has complete information about acts, that is, knows the injurer's benefit and the victim's harm, then each of the rules leads to optimality. To amplify in terms of the example of pollution, suppose that the state can ascertain whether the cost of the smoke arrestor is less than the harm from pollution and thus determine whether it is best to prevent pollution. If that is so, the state can accomplish its purpose by regulation: it can forbid pollution. The state can also achieve optimality by giving the property right to clean air to the victim. The state can also employ tort liability. This will lead the injurer not to cause harm because he would have to pay for it, and harm exceeds his benefit. Similarly, under the corrective tax he would not pollute.

If the state doesn't have complete information about harm and benefit, however, it can't determine with certainty whether or not an action like polluting should take place. Hence, the state can't necessarily achieve optimality through regulation or assignment of property rights, for to do so, it would have to know what action is optimal. For instance, under regulation, if the harm from pollution would be 100 and the state doesn't know whether the cost of an arrestor would be 75 or 150, it doesn't know whether or not to require installation of the arrestor.

Yet as long as the state has information about the magnitude of harm, it can achieve optimality under tort liability or the corrective tax. Under these approaches, the injurer compares the cost of installing the arrestor to liability or the tax for harm: the injurer will cause pollution if and only if the cost of the arrestor exceeds the harm, which is optimal. The virtue of tort liability and the corrective tax is that they harness the information that injurers have about the cost of reducing harm or the benefit they would obtain from acting, by making them compare the cost or benefit to the harm.

b. Information of victims. Information of victims is relevant to the functioning of the rules requiring victims to play a role in enforcement. Namely, for victims to bring injunctions to prevent harmful acts and protect their property rights, they have to know who might harm them, such as who might pollute, and what the harm would be if it occurred.

If the pollution is colorless and odorless and inflicts harm only over time, they might be totally unaware of the pollution and its long-range effects and thus wouldn't have the knowledge they would need to bring an injunction. Similarly, for tort liability to function, victims must know both that harm occurred and who caused it. For regulation or corrective taxation to function, victims don't need such information. The state imposes corrective taxes or regulates regardless of whether victims know who is causing them harm or understand its nature.

c. Administrative costs. Administrative costs are the costs borne by the state and the parties in association with the use of a legal rule. Tort liability has a general administrative cost advantage over the other rules in that the legal system becomes involved only if harm is done, whereas under the other approaches, the legal system is involved whether or not harm occurs. This advantage may be significant, especially when the likelihood of harm is small. Nevertheless, administrative costs are sometimes low under the non-liability approaches. For example, determining whether a party is in compliance with regulation is easy in some circumstances (e.g., determining whether factory smokestacks are sufficiently high would be) and may be done through random monitoring, saving resources. Also, levying a corrective tax can be inexpensive if, for instance, it's paid at the time a product is purchased (e.g., a firm could be made to pay the tax when it buys the fuel that causes pollution). In the end, the particulars of the situation at hand have to be examined in order to determine which type of rule is superior on grounds of administrative cost.

d. Ameliorative behavior of victims. Victims can often take steps to reduce harm (e.g., they can purchase clothes dryers rather than hang laundry outdoors, where it can be soiled by smoke). This is a desirable approach when taking these steps is sufficiently cheap and effective (accounting, of course, for the injurer's opportunity to reduce harm). Under regulation, corrective taxation, and other approaches that don't compensate victims for the harm they experience, victims have a natural incentive to take optimal precautions because they bear their own losses. Under tort liability, however, this incentive would be lacking to the extent that victims will be compensated for the losses they suffer.

Box 6-6
If Taxes Are So Good,
Why Are They So Rarely Used?

Economists have traditionally favored taxes as the best cure for harmful externalities, like pollution. Yet taxes are rarely used to prevent harmful effects. The main tools that all societies employ to combat harmful effects are regulation and liability. To understand why, think about the mundane problem of people leaving their sidewalks icy, which can lead to accidents. How would a tax work to correct this? Would it be based on measurements of the amount of ice that is left on the sidewalks? On the foot traffic on the sidewalks? Wouldn't this be very expensive to administer? By contrast, what would be the nature of administrative costs under regulation? Under liability for actual harm that occurs due to icy sidewalks?

---

e. Ability of injurers to pay. For tort liability to induce potential injurers to behave appropriately, they must have assets sufficient to make the required payments. Otherwise, they would have inadequate incentives to reduce harm. This is especially relevant in settings where the potential harm is sufficiently large to exceed the assets of the potential injurer (e.g., a fire could cause a harm that exceeds the assets of the owner of the property; an explosion at a factory or a leak of toxic material could cause much more harm than the company's assets are worth). Inability to pay is likely to be less of a problem for the corrective tax, which equals the expected harm, an amount generally less than the actual harm. In situations where inability to pay is a problem, regulation and the other approaches become more appealing.

f. Conclusion. This review of factors bearing on the effectiveness of the rules suggests that their relative strengths depend very much on the context. Let 's consider the classic problem of pollution caused by the burning of fuel at factories. Liability might be expected not to work well because the victims might have difficulty ascertaining that they were harmed and determining who was responsible. The injunction might not function well for similar reasons. Regulating the amount of fuel burned would be unappealing, because doing so would require the state to determine the optimal amount, meaning that it would have to determine the value of production or the cost of alternative fuels, either of which would depend on many particulars that would be expensive, if not impractical, for the state to learn. Thus, the corrective tax, relying only on the state's knowledge of the harm that the pollution tends to cause, becomes appealing.

6. Public Goods

A. Definition

Goods (or services) that are nonexcludable and nonrival are called *public goods* by economists. Goods are *nonexcludable* if people can't be prevented from enjoying them. Two examples are national defense and fireworks displays: we can't be prevented from benefitting from national defense, and we can't be prevented from viewing a nearby fireworks display. Goods are *nonrival* if one person's use doesn't diminish another person's. This, too, is true of both national defense and fireworks displays: my benefitting from national defense doesn't reduce your benefitting from it, and my viewing of a fireworks display doesn't diminish your viewing of it. Other stock examples of public goods include lighthouses, city streets, radio programs, and basic research. (Can you say why each of these is nonexcludable and nonrival?) Let's note that sometimes one person's use of a public good will, in a limited way, detract from another person's use. This may be the result of congestion: if many people are at a fireworks display, the views of children and short people will be blocked; if many people are using the city streets, traffic will be impeded. For now, however, we'll set this matter aside.

B. Ideal Supply

In principle, society often wants public goods to be supplied. In terms of the surplus criterion, society wants a public good supplied if its value to the individuals who would enjoy it exceeds the cost of supplying it. Thus, a lighthouse ought to be built if its value to all the ships that would benefit from its beacon outweighs the cost of its construction and operation.

C. Inadequate Supply by the Private Sector

It is apparent that public goods will not be adequately supplied by the private sector. The reason is plain: because people can't be excluded from using public goods, they can't be charged money for using them, so a private supplier can't make money from providing them. For instance, no ship would pay for the services of a lighthouse, because it could benefit from the lighthouse even if it didn't pay. Hence, no entrepreneur would build a lighthouse. Likewise, no company could make money selling national defense to individuals, because all individuals would benefit from national defense even if they didn't pay for it. Thus, national defense wouldn't be privately supplied. Even though many public goods are eminently socially worthwhile, they will not be supplied by the private sector.

Box 6-7
Lighthouses

Lighthouses have been very important to the safety of shipping, especially in antiquity. One of the greatest construction projects in ancient history was of the giant lighthouse Pharos in Alexandria, Egypt. Although economic theory predicts that lighthouses have to be built by the state, Ronald Coase wrote an article critical of economic theorizing, for he discovered that for over a century most lighthouses in Britain were built and operated by private individuals for profit! But how could the lighthouse owners have collected fees from ships? Later investigation revealed the answer: the state *forced* ships to pay lighthouses, for instance, by not letting ships leave port without making payment. So the lighthouses weren't really supplied in the usual way by the private sector after all, and the message of economic theory about lighthouses remains intact.

D. Public Provision

Because public goods are generally not adequately supplied by the private sector, they have to be supplied by the public sector. Thus, a lighthouse that is desirable to supply, because its benefits to all users outweigh its costs, can be built by the state. The same holds true for streets, national defense, basic research, and so forth. This is the basic argument for public supply of public goods (and the reason why they are referred to as public goods).

Several problems are associated with the public provision of public goods, however. One is the need for the government to obtain information about the benefits and costs of the goods, in order to determine whether they are worth supplying. A notable difficulty is that people have an incentive to distort the truth when questioned about the value they place on public goods. When asked whether they want a fireworks display (or a street extended), those who want this would have an incentive to report a very high number as their valuation: exaggerating the truth would cost them nothing. For this and other reasons, government faces a problem in deciding which public goods are worthwhile supplying. Other problems with public provision of public goods stem from the imperfections of the political process and the cost of raising funds through taxation for the purchase of public goods.

E. Qualifications

One qualification to the general argument that public goods have to be publicly provided is that, in some contexts, private parties can convert a public good into an excludable good and, being able to charge for it, might supply it. For instance, a company that wants to make money from a fireworks display could erect a tall fence around the display area and charge for entry; a company that wants to profit from constructing a road could erect and operate toll booths at all entrances to the road. Thus, some fireworks displays and some roads would be supplied by the private sector. However, note that the private supplier would be able to act as a monopolist and charge a monopoly price, causing deadweight losses. Moreover, private supply of public goods involves the expense of excluding nonpayers — the cost of fencing off the area around the fireworks display and the cost of constructing and staffing toll booths at entrances to the road. Such expenses need not be borne by the state under public provision, so the expenses constitute a disadvantage of private provision.

The other qualification concerns the possibility noted earlier, that a public good may not be entirely nonrival, principally because its use leads to congestion. Congestion effects (e.g., those resulting from too many people viewing a fireworks display or using a road) make it socially desirable to limit use of a public good to those who place a higher value on using it than they contribute to its congestion. If each person who uses a road imposes a cost of $5.00 on others in terms of congestion, only those individuals who value using the road at more than $5.00 should use it. Hence, it may be best for the road, if publicly provided, to be a toll road for which $5.00 is the toll.[11]

F. Direct Versus Indirect Public Provision

Although the private market would not be expected to supply various public goods, the public need not provide them directly. Rather than providing a good itself — for example, building roads, erecting a lighthouse, or conducting basic research — the government can pay a private company to provide it.

7. Welfare Economics

A. What Is Welfare Economics?

The term *welfare economics* refers to the organizing framework that economists have for analyzing so-called *normative* questions, those of the form, What policy *should* we adopt? Questions of this type are to be distinguished from *descriptive* questions, which are of the form, What will the *effect* of a policy be? Descriptive questions are concerned with identifying the results of a policy, not with evaluating the social goodness or badness of the results. The task of *evaluation* is that of welfare economics.

---

11. Whether it's best for a public provider of the road to charge for use depends on the cost of erecting toll booths and collecting tolls. If the congestion effect would be small, allowing congestion would be better than incurring the cost of charging tolls for use of the road.

B. Individual Well-Being

An important factor to consider in evaluating policies is, of course, the well-being of individuals. Economists use the notion of an individual's *utility* to refer to the person's well-being. The concept of utility is completely general and thus encompasses not only conventional elements of a person's happiness — the material comforts of life and the things that a person selfishly cares about — but also any aesthetic pleasures and any satisfaction derived from helping relatives, friends, and mankind in general or from doing one's duty in any sense that the individual conceives to be important. *Anything* that pleases a person is, by definition, something that augments that person's utility.

C. Social Welfare

Economists evaluate social well-being by referring to a measure of social welfare. This measure is typically built up from things that matter to individuals in some way.

For example, in this chapter we've been using surplus (aggregate benefits to people minus costs of production) as the measure of social welfare. We've said that market outcomes are socially desirable because they maximize this measure of social welfare, and we've said that monopoly is socially undesirable because it does not. We have focused on the surplus measure because it has two important properties that we presume most ways of measuring social welfare would have in common: (1) that when individuals' benefits rise and people become happier, social welfare rises, and (2) that when costs go up and people who bear the costs become less happy, social welfare falls.

Even though we've emphasized the surplus measure of social welfare, as is conventional, we've done so mainly because of its analytical convenience. In general, *economists do not assume that any specific measure of social welfare is objectively correct.* Different measures appeal to different people. Whatever measure is used, however, the objective for the person who endorses it is to maximize it. Measures of social welfare include the following:

- *Classical utilitarianism:* The utilities of individuals are added together and maximized.

- *Other functions of individuals' utilities:* Many measures of social welfare are different from utilitarianism yet depend on the utilities of individuals. For example, consider a function equal to the sum of utilities minus a "penalty" that depends on the variability of utilities in the population. This measure of social welfare depends on the distribution of utilities, because the more disparate the distribution is, the higher the penalty is, and thus the lower social welfare is. Another example is the so-called maximin criterion associated with the philosophical position of Rawls: social welfare is assumed to equal the utility of the least well off person in the population; hence, the social goal is to maximize the well-being of the least well off person (thus, the term maximin).

- *Factors other than individuals' utilities:* Many measures of social welfare depend on factors that are distinct from individuals' utilities. For instance, social welfare might be a function of individuals' utilities and, in addition,

---

Box 6-8
Rawlsian "Maximin" Social Objective

According to the Rawlsian criterion, social welfare is taken to equal the utility of the least well off person, so the social objective is to maximize the utility of this least fortunate person — the entire focus is on this person. Thus, for example, suppose that there are 99 people in a hospital who can be greatly helped by getting medical attention but who won't die without it, and 1 virtually comatose person on the edge of death whose life can be prolonged slightly by getting lavish attention. Then to promote the Rawlsian criterion, *all* the medical resources would go to making the virtually comatose person live a bit longer, none would go to the 99 who would be made substantially better off by receiving medical attention.

it might decline whenever some notion of fairness is violated (such as the notion that wrongdoers should be punished in proportion to the gravity of their bad acts), regardless of the effect of maintaining the notion of fairness on individuals' utilities.[12]

Because *any* notion of the social good can be cast as a measure of social welfare, the social welfare framework, from the perspective of economists, is more a language or organizing tool for analysis than it is a system of thinking that embodies restrictions on what constitutes the social good. As an analytical aid, it has proved to be very powerful.

Economists typically restrict their attention to measures of social welfare that depend *solely* on individuals' utilities. They usually don't consider ones of the third type described above (i.e., ones depending on factors other than individuals' utilities). Such measures tend to lack appeal because, by hypothesis, they depend on something that *no* person cares about. In fact, it can be demonstrated that any measure of social welfare that depends, even in part, on a factor that no one cares about leads to the following possibility: policy A, which promotes the factor that no one cares about, may be ranked higher than policy B, even though *all* individuals prefer policy B. This fact — that any measure of social welfare that depends at all on an element that no one cares about leads in some situations to contravention of the unanimous preferences of individuals — makes such a measure of social welfare unappealing.

Although we'll assume that measures of social welfare depend solely on individuals' utilities, we're left with a very wide scope for consideration, from utilitarianism to any type that deems the distribution of well-being important. The economic view of desirable social choice is this: *given* a measure of social welfare, what social policy is best? The question of what measure of social welfare should be considered is often not part of the economist's inquiry, so the inquiry about social choice is of a conditional nature.

---

12. Thus, even if punishment doesn't affect anyone's well-being by, for example, encouraging deterrence, incapacitation, or reform, it should be imposed in order to promote the notion of fair punishment and the measure of social welfare depending upon it.

D. Social Welfare Maximum: Efficiency and Distribution

We can ask the hypothetical question, given the natural and human resources available to us, and our technology, what would truly maximize social welfare? Although the particular answer will depend on the measure of social welfare, we can usefully describe the answer as being composed of two steps: first produce goods and services in the most *efficient* manner, and then *distribute* them so as to maximize the measure of social welfare. Consider a simple world with just one produced good, pie, that everybody wants more of. Then what is socially optimal under any measure of social welfare is for the net amount of pie produced to be as large as possible — this is efficiency — and then for the pie to be sliced up and distributed in a way that is best according to the particular measure of social welfare under consideration. If the measure is highest when people have equal shares, then that is how the pie would be divided, for instance.

E. Social Welfare and the Market

There is a connection between the market and the hypothetical social welfare maximum just discussed. Suppose that society can costlessly redistribute wealth. Then the following is true: Regardless of the measure of social welfare, the social welfare maximum can be achieved by redistributing wealth and allowing competitive markets to function.[13] The idea behind this *central theorem* of welfare economics is that markets will lead to efficient production of goods and services, and that appropriately designed redistribution of wealth will accomplish the desired allocation of utilities among individuals. To maximize a measure of social welfare that favors equality, for instance, wealth would be redistributed so as to achieve equality.

F. Answers to Questions and Common Criticisms

A number of questions and criticisms are frequently raised about welfare economics.

---

13. This statement presumes that there are no problems of consumer information, no harmful externalities, or other factors impeding market functioning.

1. How does the fact that redistribution is not costless — notably, that income taxation dilutes work effort — affect the statement just made about social welfare maximization and the market? It's generally thought that the income tax system dulls work incentives; certainly if one faced a 90 percent income tax rate, the incentive to work overtime, to work extra years before retirement, or to start a business rather than work for salary, would be reduced. Thus, the attempt to redistribute via the income tax system turns out to reduce the amount of income that there is redistribute. In other words, the act of slicing up the pie — the redistributive step represented by income taxation and transfers — shrinks the size of the pie.

The implications of this important point are several. First, the hypothetical social optimum of the central theorem of welfare economics cannot be achieved. Second, the practically achievable social welfare optimum in general involves a tradeoff between the reduction in output caused by redistribution — the so-called efficiency loss due to income taxation — and the benefits of redistribution in terms of raising social welfare. Thus, there will be less redistribution than in the ideal. How much less will depend on how much efficiency is lost as a result of the attempt to redistribute. If the social welfare function endorsed would, in the ideal, result in an equal distribution of income, the optimal distribution, given the effect of income taxation on work effort, might allow considerable inequality of income.

2. Should policy evaluation be influenced by distributional concerns, given the existence of an income tax and a transfer system that can be used to redistribute? Both efficiency and distributional factors are generally of importance to social welfare and thus would seem to matter in the evaluation of social policy. However, the existence of an income tax and transfer system that can be used to redistribute suggests that policies should be judged solely in terms of their efficiency effects. The kernel of the argument behind this claim is that, if a policy results in undesirable distributional effects, they can be remedied by the income tax (and transfer) system. For example, consider policies like price ceilings on drugs that are intended to benefit poor people but that may retard incentives of drug companies to develop new drugs. If society feels that drug prices have too great an impact on the poor, the problem can be remedied by adjusting the income tax system (e.g., by reducing taxes on the poor, by giving them credits for drug purchases, and the like). Compromising incentives to develop drugs in order to help the poor is socially unwise because they can be aided without diminishing incentives.[14]

3. Do economists believe that the market is best? The short answer is that it depends. Although the central theorem of welfare economics constitutes a powerful argument in favor of the market, it is only a benchmark for thinking and is subject to many important exceptions and qualifications. Earlier in this chapter we discussed categories of problems with the functioning of the market: lack of consumer information, monopoly, externalities, and public goods. In each of these cases, intervention in the market may advance social welfare.

Another point should be mentioned that we haven't remarked upon: use of the market involves transaction costs of various types, and in some domains it may be better to avoid them with other regimes. One important example is the vast amount of activity that takes place *within* firms and other organizations. Typically, this activity takes place because of commands and orders, not through the medium of a market. When an employee performs a particular task, it isn't because he or she is paid something for doing that task; rather, it's because this is what was ordered; when one division of a company produces a part of a machine and supplies it to another division of the company for further work, it is generally not paid to make the transfer but is, rather, working according to overall production plans. The reason that all this activity occurs without the market mediating it has to do with the simplicity of using orders, especially when the party issuing the orders has the information

---

14. The argument that policies should be evaluated solely on efficiency grounds and that redistribution should be pursued through the income tax system is sometimes thought not to hold because the income tax may result in dilution of incentives to work. To illustrate: It might be asserted that drug prices should be controlled to help the poor, because using the tax system to help them would further reduce their incentive to work. This line of argument is fallacious, however, because controlling drug prices would also dilute the incentive to work. Space doesn't allow the matter to be pursued further here, except for reiteration of a point: the conclusion remains that, even when the influence of the income tax on work effort is recognized, it is still best to choose policies *only* on the basis of their effect on efficiency and to pursue distributional objectives only through the income tax.

needed to determine the proper action. Economists are actively studying the functioning of organizations, and the theme of their work is hardly that a mini-market, a market in the small, should guide the activity that is observed. It is, rather, that the market is not the best way to undertake this activity.

4. Does economics leave out soft variables, hard-to-measure things, and thus overlook important factors? There is no principle of economics that would lead to exclusion of any factor that matters to individuals. Practitioners of economics, however, might have a tendency to give short shrift to factors of importance if they are difficult to evaluate. For example, an economist evaluating a policy for preserving wilderness areas might fail to take into proper account subtle but important benefits of such preservation to our population (e.g., perhaps we would be made happier because our visits to wilderness areas or even our awareness of their continued existence enhances our ability to appreciate nature). Obviously, such a failure to include appropriately a relevant factor in a social welfare evaluation should not be considered an intrinsic drawback of welfare economics, but, rather, of how it might be applied.

5. Does economic thinking not give due weight to notions of fairness? The term *fairness* is used in multiple senses. One sense in which it is employed concerns the fairness of the distribution of income. This aspect of fairness, we have already said, may be taken into account in a measure of social welfare. Notably, we emphasized that the measure may be such that social welfare is raised the more equal the distribution of income.[15] Thus, fairness in the *income distributional sense* is definitely accommodated within the framework of welfare economics.

Another very general category of use of the term fairness is that in many contexts, we have beliefs about proper outcomes and treatment

---

15. There are two reasons why social welfare may increase if the distribution of income is made more nearly equal. (1) As mentioned already, equalizing incomes tends to make the utilities of different individuals more nearly equal, and social welfare may increase the more equal are peoples' utilities. (2) The marginal utility that individuals derive from income may fall the more income they have. If this is so, then shifting a dollar of income from rich to poor raises the poor person's utility by more than it lowers the rich person's utility. Hence, total utility tends to increase as a result of the redistribution, and thus social welfare often rises as well.

of individuals. For instance, we have ideas of what proper punishment is for wrongdoing, of the circumstances in which we ought to honor contracts, of whether individuals in many situations should be benefitted or penalized, as the case may be, in a manner that is independent of their race or gender. These particularistic notions of fairness (which have no direct connection to the distribution of income or wealth) are many and varied, and they relate to welfare economics in several ways. First, individuals may care about the satisfaction of notions of fairness per se (a person may care whether punishment is in proportion to wrongdoing, about keeping contracts, about not discriminating). To this extent, individuals' utility, and thus social welfare, is affected by adherence to the notions of fairness. Second, satisfaction of the notions of fairness may lead to changes in behavior and outcomes that increase social welfare (if we punish in proportion to wrongdoing, we may often turn out to deter appropriately; if we usually honor contracts, we may promote trust and joint enterprise; if we do not discriminate, we may advance production and create beneficial incentives). Third, we may want to invest social resources in inculcating beliefs in notions of fairness (by parents, teachers, religious authorities), because such beliefs lead to increases in social welfare, as just noted. Hence, the connections between welfare economics and the study of morality and ethics are significant.[16]

8. Suggestions for Further Reading

Two recommendations for an introductory treatment of microeconomics are N. Gregory Mankiw, *Principles of Economics,* 5th ed. (Mason, OH: South-Western, 2008), and Michael Parkin, *Microeconomics,* 9th ed. (Upper Saddle River, NJ: Prentice-Hall, 2009). A good intermediate text is Robert Pindyck and Daniel Rubinfeld, *Microeconomics,* 7th ed. (Upper Saddle River, NJ: Prentice-Hall, 2008).

---

16. The relationship between morality and social welfare was studied by economically oriented writers such as Bentham and Sidgwick in the nineteenth century, and is today undergoing a resurgence.

7
Economic Analysis of Law

---

1. Introduction

A. The Economic Approach

The economic approach to the analysis of law seeks to answer two basic questions about legal rules. One type of question is *descriptive*, concerning the effects of legal rules on behavior and outcomes. For example, will liability for causing car accidents result in fewer accidents? The other type of question is *normative*, concerning the social desirability of legal rules. Thus, we might ask whether liability for car accidents is socially desirable, given its effect on the incidence of accidents, the compensation of accident victims, and the costs of the legal system.

In answering the two types of questions under the economic approach, we usually focus our attention on stylized models of individual behavior and the legal system. The advantage of studying models is that they allow predictive and normative questions to be answered in an unambiguous way and that they may clarify understanding of the actual influence of legal rules on behavior and help to make actual legal policy decisions.

357

To answer the descriptive questions, we will generally take the view that actors are forward-looking and "rational." Given the characterization of individuals' behavior as rational, the influence of legal rules on behavior can be ascertained. This can be done with definitude in the world of the models, because all relevant factors about individuals' desires, knowledge, and the environment will have been made explicit. For example, whether a person will drive carefully will be determinable, for it will have been stated whether the person will himself be injured in an accident, what the rule of liability is, under what circumstances suit will occur, whether he owns first-party and liability insurance, and so forth.

Of course it is realized that individuals in fact behave in ways that deviate from what is predicted in most models. Notably, individuals are influenced by many psychological factors resulting in "biases" in their decision making. Nevertheless, because the standard assumptions of rationality usually explain the central tendencies of human behavior, it is useful to focus on models relying on these assumptions.

The evaluation of social policies, and thus of legal rules, will be with reference to a stated measure of *social welfare:* a legal rule will be said to be superior to a second if the first rule results in higher social welfare, given the stated measure. (We discussed social welfare in general in Chapter 6, Microeconomics.) Mainly for analytical convenience, it is standard for economic analysts to restrict attention to fairly simple measures of social welfare, and we will do that here.

Two types of simplification that we will make should be noted at the outset. One is that the measure of social welfare will usually not accord importance to the distribution of income, meaning that the effect of legal rules on the distribution of income will not be relevant to their evaluation. The reason for so doing is certainly not that the distribution of income is felt to be unimportant (again, recall our discussion of welfare economics in Microeconomics). It is, rather, that taking into account the effect of legal rules on income distribution would complicate our analysis but would not in the end alter our conclusions. Why would taking into account income distribution not alter our conclusions, given its importance? The answer is (as explained in Microeconomics) that we have an income tax and transfer system that society can employ to redistribute income.

The other type of simplification that we want to note now concerns notions of fairness and morality. Consider, for example, the notion of corrective justice that demands that a wrongdoer compensate his victim for harm sustained. Ideas of corrective justice may be important to individuals and thus ought to enter into the determination of social welfare. We will exclude them, however, from the analysis proper, in the interests of simplicity. But we will take up the general issue of integration of morality and notions of fairness into normative analysis later in this chapter.

B. What Distinguishes Economic from Other Analysis of Law?

One might ask whether there is any qualitative difference between economic analysis of law, as it has been defined, and other approaches. Is it not of interest to any legal analyst to determine how legal rules affect behavior and to evaluate the rules with reference to some criterion of goodness? The answer would seem to be yes, and thus in this general sense, one cannot distinguish economic analysis from other analysis of law.

What does seem to mark economic analysis are three characteristics. First, emphasis is generally placed on the use of stylized models and on empirical tests of theory. Second, in descriptive analysis, the view that actors are rational is given much greater weight than by other types of analysts. And third, in normative analysis, the measure of social welfare is made explicit, whereas other analysts are often unclear about the criterion they are studying or leave it implicit.

C. History of the Economic Approach

One might say that the economic approach had its beginnings in writing on crime by Beccaria (1770) and Bentham (1789). Bentham, especially, developed in fairly significant detail the idea that both the probability and the magnitude of sanctions affect deterrence of crime and that sanctions should be used when they can effectively deter but not be used when they cannot deter (as with the insane). Curiously, however, after Bentham, the economic approach to law lay largely dormant until the 1960s and 1970s. In that period, Coase (1960) wrote a provocative article on the incentives to reduce harm to neighbors engendered by property rights assignments; Calabresi (1970) published an extended treatment of liability rules and the accident problem; Becker (1968) authored an influential article on crime, updating and extending Bentham's earlier

---

Box 7-1
The Growing Importance of Law and Economics

Law and economics is a field of increasing importance. In legal practice, you'll frequently find that you
and your opponent will be using economic arguments
and perhaps hiring economic experts. One sign of this
is the emergence of a number of highly successful firms
supplying economic analysis and advice for litigation.
In legal academia, the success of law and economics
is marked by the growth of courses in the field, faculty
who identify themselves with it, and law review articles
as well as journals dedicated to it. In economics, interest is increasing as well, and the award of two recent
Nobel Prizes in economics were strongly influenced by
law and economics: to Gary Becker, in part for his work
on crime, and to Ronald Coase, in part for his work on
law, bargaining, and legal rules.

---

contributions; and Posner wrote a comprehensive textbook (1972) and
a number of articles and established the *Journal of Legal Studies,* where
scholarship in economic analysis of law could be regularly published.
Since that time, economic analysis of law has grown rapidly.

2. Property Law

In this part, we will discuss the justifications for property rights, instances
of their emergence, and then a number of topics including the division
of property rights, the acquisition and transfer of property, and takings. Finally, we will discuss the somewhat special topic of intellectual
property.

A. Definition of Property Rights

We will use the term *property rights* to refer broadly to possessory rights
and rights of transfer. *Possessory rights* allow individuals to use things
and to prevent others from using them. *Rights of transfer* refer to the
option of individuals who hold possessory rights to sell them or give
them to others.

B. Justifications for Property Rights

A time-honored and fundamental question is, Why should there be any property rights? That is, in what respects do the protection of possessory interests in things and the ability to transfer them promote social welfare, broadly construed? One factor is incentives to work, and another, related factor is incentives to maintain and improve things. For example, if a person owns land, he will have an incentive to grow crops on it, to prevent erosion on the land, and the like.

Another factor is the fostering of the beneficial transfer of things. Given property rights, individuals will tend to transfer them when this is mutually advantageous, such as when someone is too old to farm his land or wants to move away. In addition, trade enhances social welfare indirectly because it allows the use of efficient methods of production, which require that agglomerations of individuals devote themselves to making just one or several related goods. But this means that the allocation of goods immediately after they are produced is far from what is best for purposes of consumption — for example, the individuals at a factory who produce thousands of units of some good cannot consume that good alone. Yet the transfer and trade of produced goods allows ultimately for each individual to consume many different types of good.

A fourth factor is avoidance of dispute and avoidance of efforts to protect or to take things. Disputes, which may involve physical conflict, and efforts devoted to protecting things or to taking things from others are socially undesirable in themselves, because they may result in harm and because they do not result in the production of things, only in their possible reallocation. Two final advantages of property rights are protection against risk and achievement of a desired distribution of wealth. The protection of property rights obviously gives individuals protection against the risk of theft, and it also makes possible achievement of desired distribution of wealth rather than a distribution determined by force.

It should be noted that, although the foregoing factors help to explain why property rights may be socially valuable, they do not support a specific form of property rights and, notably, do not constitute an argument for *private property,* wherein things generally are owned (and can be sold) by private parties rather than by the state. The benefits of property rights may often be enjoyed under different property rights regimes. For example, in a socialist state, just as in a capitalist state, the protection of possessory rights will result in avoidance of dispute and avoidance of wasteful effort to take or to safeguard things. Further, incentives to work in a socialist enterprise — or, for that matter, in a firm in a capitalist setting — are obviously possible to engender even though individuals do not own their output, through observation of their behavior by supervisors and use of an appropriate salary structure. The question of the circumstances in which a private property regime versus a socialist or other property rights regime is superior is significantly more complex than that of the justification for property rights per se and is beyond our scope.

C. Emergence of Property Rights

We would expect property rights to emerge from a background of no, or poorly established, rights when the various advantages of property rights outweigh the costs of instituting and maintaining the rights. A number of examples of the establishment of property rights illustrate their advantages.

One famous instance concerns rights in land during the California Gold Rush. When gold was discovered in California in 1848, property rights in land and minerals were largely undetermined, as the territory was being acquired from Mexico. But after a short time, the gold-bearing area of California found itself divided into districts. In each district, goldseekers made explicit agreements governing property rights, stating in some detail how land was to be assigned and how theft and other infractions of rules were to be sanctioned. Evidently, the reason was that, in order to obtain gold, effort had to be expended and investments of one type or another had to be made. For instance, excavations had to be undertaken, and sluices had to be constructed in which to separate gold from dirt. These things would not have been done and relatively little gold would have been collected if individuals could not be reasonably confident that their gold would not be stolen and that the land on which they had dug a ditch or built a sluice would not subsequently be taken over and benefit others.

Another example concerns rights in land on the Labrador Peninsula during the days of the French and Indian fur trade. At the time of the development of the fur trade on the Labrador Peninsula in North America, certain Indian tribes established a system of property rights in land, where none had existed before. An owner's territory was often marked off by identifiable blazes on trees, and proprietorship included retaliation against trespass. The explanation for the system of rights that has been suggested is that, without the rights, overly intensive hunting of fur bearing animals (especially beaver) would have taken place, and the stock of animals would have been depleted. With property rights, owners of land had incentives to husband their animal resources (e.g., by sparing the young, by rotating the area of their land on which they trapped animals, and so forth), because they would later be able to enjoy the benefits of having a larger stock.

Another example involves rights to the resources of the sea: fisheries, oil, and minerals from the seabed. For most of history, there were no property rights in the ocean's fisheries, because fish were in inexhaustible supply for all practical purposes. However, certain fisheries came under strain with the introduction of trawler fleets in the late nineteenth century, and fish populations are under significantly greater pressure today because of the increased scale of and the modern methods employed in fishing (e.g., factory fleets, miles-long nets, and electronic detection of fish). In response to the need to preserve the fisheries, countries have developed, through a series of treaties, property rights in the fish found

---

Box 7-2
Mysteries about Beavers and Indians

One mystery about the explanation for land rights on the Labrador Peninsula is how a person could have prevented theft of beavers from his land. He couldn't have expended the effort to guard the beavers night and day. So what do we think the Indians did to prevent poaching?

Another mystery is why the Indians didn't just make an agreement not to hunt too many beavers. Wouldn't this have been simpler than creating a system of property in land?

in their coastal waters. At present, a country enjoys such rights in an Exclusive Economic Zone (EEZ), extending 200 miles from its coastline. This gives a country a natural incentive not to deplete its fisheries, because it will then enjoy a greater catch in the future, provided that the fish in question do not tend to swim outside the EEZ. Likewise, there were no property rights established for oil and minerals from the seabed until it became apparent, around the end of the Second World War, that extraction might be commercially viable. Coastal countries today have property rights to the resources of the seabed within the EEZ, which gives them (or, more precisely, gives companies that they license) a motive to explore, to develop technology for extraction, and then to exploit oil and mineral resources (to date, principally manganese nodules).

D. Division of Property Rights

Having considered the general reasons for the existence of property rights, we now discuss briefly their division. The division of rights can occur in a variety of ways: into different contemporaneous rights (e.g., where someone enjoys an easement, giving him the right of passage upon another person's land); according to the contingency that turns out to occur (e.g., a right to extract oil from land if it is discovered); or measured by time (e.g., as in a rental arrangement). Further, possessory rights and rights to transfer them may be separated from each other — for example, consider a trusteeship relationship, where the trustee has the right to sell the property but does not own it or receive the payment for it.

The general advantage of division of possessory rights is that some rights are more valuable to one party than to the original holder of the rights. Thus, trade in these particular rights will often be mutually advantageous, raising the well-being of each. For example, if A owns a home but will not be using it for a period during which B would want to use it, a rental arrangement will benefit both. An advantage pertaining to division of possessory rights from rights to transfer is that the holder of possessory rights may not have the information to make decisions about transfer. Thus, for instance, a child may have an adult act as trustee.

The main disadvantages of division of possessory rights are that conflicts may arise over the terms of the division (e.g., individuals may disagree about where on an owner's land another person with an easement has a right to walk). Also, division of rights may cause harm to other parties (e.g., a person with an easement may trample the owner's crops, or a renter may mistreat the home in which he is living). Moreover, division may entail certain fixed costs (e.g., renting property may involve expenses for both the owner and the renter, such as the cost to the owner of storing articles and the cost to the renter of moving them).

E. Acquisition and Transfer of Property

Here we consider a number of topics concerning the acquisition and transfer of property.

1. Previously unowned property. Wild animals and fish, long-lost treasure, certain mineral and oil deposits, and, historically, unclaimed land constitute primary examples of unowned property that individuals may acquire. The law has to determine under what conditions a person will become a legal owner of such previously unowned property.

A general legal rule is that anyone who finds or takes into his possession unowned property becomes its owner. Under this *finders-keepers rule,* incentives to invest in capture (such as to hunt for animals or explore for oil) are optimal if only one person is making the effort, for that person will be motivated to invest in effort if and only if the cost is less than the expected value of the property that might be found.

However, if, as is typical, many individuals seek unowned property, they will tend to invest socially excessively in search. The essential reason is that one person's investment or effort usually will not simply increase the total probability of success but, rather, will come at least partly at the expense of *other* persons' likelihood of finding unowned property. A stock example illustrating this general point is as follows: Suppose that the number of people fishing in a lake is such that they will definitely catch all the fish in it. Thus, it is not socially desirable for another person to fish, as all the fish are going to be caught without him. However, he might well want to fish because, by doing so, he will be likely to catch a certain number of fish. The fish that he catches are benefits to him, and he does not take into account the fact that all the fish he catches are fish that others will not catch because he is present to find them first.

Various aspects of the law governing the acquisition of property may be regarded as ameliorating the problem of excessive search effort under the finders-keepers rule. Notable instances are regulations limiting the quantities of fish and wild animals that can be taken, auctioning the right to search for minerals, and unitization of oil-extraction rights.

2. Validity of title. A basic difficulty associated with sale of property that a legal system must solve is establishing validity of ownership, or *title*. How does the buyer know whether the seller has good title, and how does the buyer obtain good title? If these questions are not readily answered, sales transactions are impeded, and theft may be encouraged.

One route that legal systems may take involves the use of *registration systems:* lists of items and their owners. Important examples are registries of land, ships, motor vehicles, and many financial instruments. Assuming that an item is recorded in a registry, it will be easy for a buyer to check whether the seller holds good title to it, and the buyer will obtain title by having his name recorded in the registry as the new owner. Also, a thief obviously cannot claim that something he has stolen is his if someone else's name is listed as the owner in the registry.

For most goods, however, registries do not exist because of the expense of establishing and maintaining them relative to the value of the goods and of the deterrence of theft. Two legal rules for determination of title are available in the absence of registries. Under the *original ownership rule,* the buyer does not obtain good title if the seller did not have it; the original owner can always claim title to the item if he can establish his prior ownership. Under the *bona fide purchaser rule,* a buyer acquires good title as long as he had reason to think that the sale was bona fide (i.e., that the seller had good title) — even if the item sold was previously stolen or otherwise wrongfully obtained. These rules have different effects on incentives for theft. Notably, under the bona fide purchaser rule, theft is made attractive because thieves will often be able to sell their property to buyers (who will be motivated to "believe" that the sale is bona fide) and because the buyers can use the now validly held property or resell it. Another social cost of the bona fide purchaser rule is that original owners will spend more to protect their property against theft because theft will be more frequent and, when it occurs, owners will be less likely to recover their property. Finally, under the bona fide purchaser rule, buyers will not have an incentive to expend effort determining whether there exists a third-party original owner. This is an advantage in the

---

Box 7-3
What Might be Wrong with Selling Babies?

Some economically-oriented commentators, such as Judge Richard Posner, have considered the notion of a market for babies. The benefit of this would include the standard one that the market would allow people who want to adopt and those who want to give up babies for adoption to transact, making each better off. But might there be troublesome externalities at work in such a market? What about the babies involved in the transactions? What about other people? If there are detrimental externalities, would the best solution be to regulate the market for babies or to ban it?

---

direct sense that it reduces transaction costs, but it also compromises deterrence of theft.

3. Legal constraints on sale. Although sale of property is normally socially desirable to facilitate, as it benefits both parties engaging in the transaction, it may be advantageous for two important reasons to impose legal restrictions on the sale of goods and services, including taxation and the outright banning of sale. One standard justification for such policies is externalities. For example, the sale of handguns may be made illegal because of the externality their ownership creates (namely, crime), and a tax may be imposed on the sale of a fuel because its use pollutes the air. The other standard justification for legal restrictions on sale is lack of consumer information. For instance, a drug may not be sold without a prescription because of fear that buyers would not use it appropriately. Here, though, one must compare the alternative of the government supplying relevant information to consumers (explaining that the drug has dangerous side effects or that it should be taken only on the advice of a medical expert).

4. Gifts. The major way in which property changes hands, other than by sale, is by the making of gifts, including bequests. Gifts are, as one would expect, rather freely permitted because, like sales, they typically make both parties better off (the donor must be made better off;

otherwise, why would the donor make a gift?). It should be observed that, in the absence of a state subsidy, the level of giving may well fall short of the socially optimal level because a donor's private incentive to make a gift typically will not take into full account the donee's benefit. In addition, some gifts, particularly to charities, may support public goods or accomplish redistribution, which may provide a further ground for subsidy. In fact, the law does favor certain types of giving by conferring tax advantages on donees (and, in the case of charities, on donors). On the other hand, heavy gift and estate taxes are levied on large donative transfers to individuals.

F. Conflicts in the Use of Property: Externalities

When individuals use property, they may cause externalities — namely, harm or benefit to others. This subject was covered earlier, in Chapter 6, Microeconomics.

G. Public Property

The justifications for public property were discussed generally in Chapter 6, Microeconomics.

H. Acquisition of Public Property

The state will need to acquire property for public use from time to time, and it may acquire property in two principal ways: through purchase or through exercise of its power of *eminent domain*, which is to say, by *taking* the property. In the latter case, the law typically provides that the state must compensate property owners for the value of what has been taken from them (for the moment, we will assume that this is so).

The difference between purchases and compensated takings is that the amount owners receive is determined by negotiation in the former case but unilaterally by the state in the latter situation. Because of possible errors in governmental determinations as well as concerns about abuse of its authority and other factors bearing on the behavior of government officials, purchase would ordinarily be superior to compensated takings. An exception, however, arises when the state is concerned about holdouts by parties who might delay or stymie worthwhile government projects. This is especially likely where the government needs to assemble many contiguous parcels, as for a road. Here, it does often seem likely that acquisition by purchase might be prevented by holdout problems, making the power to take socially advantageous.

The actual pattern of governmental acquisition of property largely reflects these simple observations. Most state acquisition of real estate and virtually all acquisition of movable property are through purchase. Governmental takings are restricted mainly to situations where there is a need for roads, dams, and parks, and where certain private rights-of-way, such as for railroads or utility lines, have to be established.

Assuming that there is a reason for the state to take property, consider the effects and desirability of a requirement that the state pay *compensation* to property holders. The initial observation to make is that such a requirement cannot readily be justified by the need to provide implicit insurance to owners, for a market in takings insurance would be likely to emerge in the absence of a compensation requirement on the part of the state. If, for example, there is a 0.1% risk per year that a person's property worth $100,000 would be taken, the fair premium for coverage against an uncompensated taking would be $100, and one would expect takings insurance (like today's title insurance) to be sold to cover possible takings. Moreover, note that the fair premium a person would pay of $100 would also equal the savings in taxes he or she would experience if the government does not have to pay compensation for takings. Hence, in an average sense, individuals should be indifferent between government compensation and purchasing takings insurance in a no-compensation regime.

A disadvantage of the compensation requirement is that it may lead property owners to invest socially excessively in property. For example, a person may decide to build a home on land that he owns, despite knowing that there is a chance it will be taken by the state for use for a road; he might build the home because of his knowledge that he will be compensated for the home if the land is taken. However, building the home might not be socially justified, given the probability of use of the land for a road, which would require destruction of the home.

What might justify payment of compensation by government is that this may alter the incentives of public authorities to take property by reducing possible problems of overzealousness and abuse of authority.

However, requiring compensation may also exacerbate potential problems of too little public activity (public authorities do not directly receive the benefits of takings). Therefore, it is not clear whether a compensation requirement would improve the incentives of public authorities. Moreover, it is not argued in general that government needs financial incentives to act in the social interest, so it seems inconsistent to appeal to this reasoning only in the sphere of takings.

I. Property Rights in Information

Legal systems accord property rights in information, including inventions, books, movies, television programs, musical compositions, computer software, chip design, created organisms, and trademarks. The generation and use of such information and therefore the law governing it are growing increasingly important in modern economies. We divide our review of this subject into three parts: First, we discuss certain information, like an invention, that can be used repeatedly to produce something; here we refer briefly to patent, copyright, and trade secret law. Second, we examine diverse other types of information, such as information about where oil is likely to be located, and its legal protection. Third, we consider labels of various types and their protection under trademark law.

1. Inventions, compositions, and similar intellectual works. The classic forms of intellectual works that receive legal property rights protection are inventions and literary, musical, or other artistic compositions.

The well-known description of socially ideal creation and use of such intellectual works is as follows. First, suppose that an intellectual work has already been created. It is socially optimal for the intellectual work to be used by all who place a value on it exceeding the marginal cost of producing or disseminating the good (or service) embodying it. Thus, a mechanical device that has been invented should be used by all who place a value on it exceeding the cost of its manufacture, a book by all who value it more highly than its printing cost, and computer software by all who value it more than the slight cost of downloading it from the Internet. We will call the value that all individuals place on a good embodying an intellectual work, net of the costs of producing or disseminating the good, the optimal social value of an intellectual work given its creation. With this value, the question of whether an intellectual work should be created is simply answered: if the cost of creation of the work is less than its optimal social value (or its optimal expected social value if, as is realistic, the work will not be created for sure), then the intellectual work should be created.

Given this description of social optimality, the advantages and disadvantages of property rights in intellectual works are apparent. In the absence of property rights, a creator of an intellectual work will obtain profits from it only for a limited period — until competitors are able to copy the creator's work. Thus, the profits a creator will be able to garner will tend to be less — perhaps far less — than the optimal social value of an intellectual work. Thus, generation of intellectual works is likely to be suboptimal. But if there exist property rights whereby a creator of an intellectual work obtains a monopoly in goods embodying the work, incentives to produce the works will be enhanced. This spur to creation of intellectual works is the advantage of intellectual property rights.

The major drawback to intellectual property rights, however, is that monopoly pricing leads to socially inadequate production and dissemination of goods embodying intellectual works. Namely, because the monopoly price will exceed the marginal cost of production, there will be individuals who would be willing to pay more for goods than the cost of production but who will not buy them because they will not pay the monopoly price. Surplus will be forgone as a consequence. (Refer to the general discussion of monopoly in Chapter 6, Microeconomics.) This problem can be severe where the monopoly price is much higher than the marginal cost of production. A good example is computer software, which may be sold for hundreds of dollars a copy even though its cost of dissemination is essentially zero.

Another problem (with patent rights in particular) is the race to be the first to develop intellectual works. Given that the rights are awarded to whoever is first, a socially wasteful degree of effort may be devoted to winning the race, for the private award of the entire monopoly profits may easily outweigh the social value of creating a work before a competitor does. Suppose, for example, that one drug firm that is in a race with another spends $1 million to beat by one day the second company to the patent office. This may be quite rational for the drug company to do to obtain the patent prize, as it may be worth more than $1 million in profits, but socially the value of having the patent awarded one day earlier may be negligible.

Patent law and copyright law are the most familiar forms of legal intellectual property rights protection. The extent of protection afforded by each body of law is partial in various dimensions, however, so they might be considered to represent a compromise between providing incentives to generate intellectual works and mitigating the monopoly problem. Patents and copyrights are limited in duration and also in scope. As an example of the latter, the copyright doctrine of fair use often allows a person to copy short portions of a copyrighted work. This probably does not deny the copyright holder significant revenues (a person would be unlikely to purchase a book just to read a few pages), and the transaction costs of the copier having to secure permission would be a waste and might discourage his use.

A distinct form of legal protection is trade secret law, comprising various doctrines of contract and tort law that serve to protect not only processes, formulas, and the like that might be protected by patent or copyright law but also other commercially valuable information, such as customer lists. An example of trade secret law is the enforcement of employment contracts stipulating that employees not use employer trade secrets for their own purposes. A party can obtain trade secret protection without having to incur the expenses and satisfy the legal tests necessary for patent or copyright protection. Also, trade secret protection is not limited in duration (e.g., Coca-Cola's formula has been protected for over a century). However, trade secret protection is, in some respects, weaker than patent protection. Notably, it does not protect against reverse engineering or independent discovery.

An interesting and basic alternative to property rights in intellectual works is for the state to offer *rewards* to creators of intellectual works and for these works then to enter the public domain, to be available to all. Thus, under the reward system, an author of a book would receive a reward from the state for writing the book — possibly based on sales of the book — but any person or firm that wanted to print and sell the book could do so. Like the property rights system, the reward system encourages creation of intellectual works, because the creator gains

---

Box 7-4
The Past and Future (?) of Rewards

Historically, rewards and prizes have at times been used by government to stimulate inventions and to avoid patent monopoly pricing. For instance, Edward Jenner won a large award for his invention of the smallpox vaccine; Napoleon offered a prize for the invention of the canning process; and England offered a reward for a device that would measure longitude.

In today's world, the case for rewards seems appealing. Good examples concern music, movies, and, indeed, virtually all electronically recordable products. They're intrinsically essentially free to distribute — notably, they can be posted on the Internet — but they often sell at distinctly positive prices. Moreover, a lot of money is spent (often fruitlessly) attempting to prevent copying and trading, and a lot of effort is devoted to litigation. This means that the social costs due to the patent and copyright systems are very high. None of these costs is necessary. If a reward system were used in place of intellectual property rights, all electronically recorded material would be available for free.

---

from producing such works. But unlike the property rights system, the reward system results in the optimal dissemination of intellectual works, because the goods embodying the intellectual works will not sell at a monopoly price. For instance, a book will tend to sell at the cost of printing it, software would be free, and so forth, because no one would hold a copyright or a patent. Hence, the reward system may seem to be superior to the intellectual property rights system. A major problem with the reward system, however, is that, in order to determine rewards, the state needs information about the value of intellectual works. To some degree, society does use a system akin to the reward system in that it gives grants and subsidies for basic research and other intellectual works. But society does this largely when these intellectual works do not have direct commercial value.

Optional material

Other types of information. There are many types of information different from the information that we have been discussing. One type of information is that which can be used only a single time — for example, information that oil is located under a particular parcel of land. With regard to this type of information, there is sometimes no need for property rights protection. If the party who has the information can use it himself (e.g., to extract the oil), then once he does so, the issue of others learning it becomes moot; there will be no further value to the information. To the degree, though, that the party is unable to use the information directly (perhaps he cannot conveniently purchase drilling rights), his having property rights in the information might be valuable and beneficially induce the acquisition of information. Moreover, giving property rights in the information will not undesirably reduce the use of information when the optimal use of it is only once. In fact, the legal system usually does furnish property rights protection in such information as where oil is located through trade secret law and allied doctrines of tort and contract law.

Another type of information is that relevant to future market prices. Here, the private and the social value of gaining such information can diverge. For example, a person who first learns that a pest has destroyed much of the cocoa crop and that cocoa prices are therefore going to rise can profit by buying cocoa futures. The social value of his information inheres principally in any beneficial changes in behavior that it brings about. For example, an increase in cocoa futures prices might lead candy producers to reduce wastage of cocoa or to switch from production of chocolate to production of another kind of candy. But the profit that a person with advance information about future cocoa prices makes can easily exceed its social value (e.g., suppose that he obtains his information only an hour before it would otherwise become available, so it has no social value) or fall short of its social value (e.g., suppose that he obtains information early on but that his profits are low because he has limited funds to invest in futures). Hence, it is not evident whether it is socially desirable to encourage acquisition of such information about price movements by giving individuals property rights in the information. The law does not generally discourage such information acquisition (but an exception is regulation of trading based on insider information) and the law often encourages acquisition through trade secret protection.

Last, consider information of a personal nature about individuals. The cost of acquiring this information is the effort to snoop, although the information is sometimes adventitiously acquired, so costless. The social value of the information involves various complexities. The release of information of a personal nature to the outside world generally causes disutility to those persons exposed and utility for others, the net effect of which is ambiguous. Further, a person's behavior may be affected by the prospect of someone else obtaining information about him: he may be deterred from socially undesirable behavior (such as commission of crimes) or from desirable but embarrassing-if-publicly-revealed behavior, and he may make costly efforts to conceal his behavior. Thus, there are reasons why the acquisition and revelation of personal information are socially undesirable, and there are reasons as well why they might be socially beneficial. The law penalizes blackmail and in this way attempts to discourage profit from acquisition of personal information. But otherwise the law does not generally retard the acquisition of personal information. It also extends limited property rights in such information. Notably, an individual who wants to sell to a publisher personal information he has obtained usually can do so.

As this brief discussion has illustrated, the factors bearing on the desirability of protecting property rights in information vary significantly according to the type of information and call for analysis quite different from that concerning information of repetitive value (like the words in a book) that we considered above.

2. Labels. Many goods and services are identified by labels. The use of labels has substantial social value because the quality of goods and services may be hard for consumers to determine directly. Labels enable consumers to make purchase decisions on the basis of product quality without going to the expense of independently determining their quality (if this is even possible). A person who wants to stay at a high-quality hotel in another city can choose such a hotel merely by its label, such as Ritz Hotel; the consumer need not directly investigate the hotel. In addition, sellers will have an incentive to produce goods and services of quality, because consumers will recognize quality through sellers' labels. The existence of property rights in labels — that is, the power of holders of the rights to prevent other sellers from using holders' labels — is necessary for the benefits of labels to be enjoyed.

In view of the social value of property rights in labels, it is not surprising that the legal system allows such rights, according to trademark law. Also, trademarks are of potentially unlimited duration (unlike patents or copyrights), which makes sense because the rationale for their use does not wane over time. The guiding principle of trademark protection is prevention of consumer confusion: a new trademark that is so similar to another (e.g., Liz Clayborne and Liz Claiborne) that it would fool people would be barred, but an identical trademark might be allowed if used in a separate market. Trademarks are usually required to be distinctive words or symbols. Otherwise, normal usage of words and symbols could be encumbered. (If a restaurant obtained a trademark on the two words "good food," other restaurants would be limited in their ability to communicate.)

3. Torts

Here we will examine various versions of a model of accidents involving two types of parties, injurers and victims. We might think, for example, of injurers as drivers of automobiles and of victims as bicyclists, or of injurers as parties conducting blasting operations and of victims as passersby. The two major rules of liability — strict liability and negligence — and certain variations of them will be considered.

We will consider first liability and incentives, then the liability system and insurance, and finally the factor of administrative costs.

A. Unilateral Accidents and Levels of Care

In the first version of the accident model — the one we will emphasize for simplicity — we will suppose that accidents are *unilateral* in nature:

only injurers' exercise of *care* or *precautions* will be assumed to affect accident risks; victims' behavior will not. Where an airplane crashes into a building, for example, the victims presumably could not have done much to prevent harm. In these cases, the accidents may be seen as literally unilateral. Also, other types of accident might be seen as approximately unilateral if the victims' role is believed slight. Consider, for example, automobile-bicycle accidents where bicyclists' actions are believed to be of minor importance in reducing risks. In addition, the social goal will be taken to be minimization of the sum of the costs of care and of expected accident losses. This sum will be called *total social costs*.

1. Social welfare optimum. Before determining how injurers are led to act in different situations, we will find it of interest to identify the level of care that minimizes total costs. This socially optimal level of care will clearly reflect both the costs of exercising care and the reduction in accident risks that it would accomplish. Consider the following example.

Example 7-1

The relationship between injurers' care and the probability of accidents that would cause losses of 100 is as in Table 7-1. To understand why exercising moderate care minimizes total social costs, observe, on one hand, that raising the level of care from none to moderate reduces expected accident losses by 5 but involves costs of only 3. It thus lowers total social costs. On the other hand, observe that raising care above the moderate level to the high level would further reduce expected accident losses by only 2, yet involve additional costs of 3. Hence, it would not be worthwhile.

Table 7-1
Care of Injurers and Accidents

Care level	Cost of care	Probability of accident	Expected accident losses	Total social costs
None	0	15%	15	15
Moderate	3	10%	10	13
High	6	8%	8	14

Note that the example illustrates the obvious point that the optimal level of care may well not result in the lowest possible level of expected accident losses (for that would require the highest level of care). Let's now examine how much care injurers will be led to exercise in various situations.

2. No liability. In the absence of liability, injurers will not exercise any care because exercising care is costly and does not yield them any benefit: they will not bear any expenses if accidents occur, so any reduction in the occurrence of accidents will not matter to them. Total social costs will, therefore, generally exceed their optimal level. In Example 7-1, for instance, they would be 15 rather than 13.

3. Strict liability. Under the *rule of strict liability*, injurers must pay for all accident losses that they cause. Hence, injurers' total costs will equal total social costs, and the last column in Table 7-1 will be injurers' total costs. And because they will seek to minimize their total costs, injurers' goal will be the social goal of minimizing total social costs. Consequently, injurers will be induced to choose the socially optimal level of care. Thus, in Example 7-1, injurers will decide to exercise the moderate level of care.

4. Negligence rule. Under the *negligence rule,* an injurer is held liable for accident losses he causes only if he was negligent — that is, only if his level of care was less than a level specified by courts, called *due care.* If the injurer exercised a level of care that equaled or exceeded due care, he will not be held liable. The negligence rule is said to be *fault-based* because liability is found only if the injurer was at fault in the sense of having been negligent.

If the due-care level is chosen by courts to equal the socially optimal level of care, then injurers will be led to exercise due care, and the outcome will be socially optimal. To see why, first reconsider Example 7-1. Suppose that courts define due care to be the socially optimal, moderate level. Then, if no care is taken, the expected liability of an injurer equals total accident costs, 15 (see Table 7-2). If moderate care is taken, the expected liability of an injurer is zero, and the injurer's total costs equal just the cost of care, 3. If high care is taken, the injurer's expected liability is also zero, and the injurer's total costs equal the costs of high care, 6. Hence, injurers are best off exercising moderate care.

Table 7-2
Negligence Rule

Care level	Cost of care	Liability	Expected liability	Injurer's total costs
None	0	yes	15	15
Moderate	3	no	0	3
High	6	no	0	6

Box 7-5
Is Due Care Really Chosen Optimally?

Do we think that courts and juries would choose the level of care optimally: so as to minimize the sum of costs of care and accident losses? Obviously, they would not be likely to do this in any conscious way. However, there's good reason to believe they decide cases in a manner that's *as if* they're seeking the optimal level of care. For example, they would say a precaution should have been taken if it was pretty easy and would have eliminated a substantial risk, but not if the precaution was very hard to take. When they intuitively compare the cost of a precaution against its benefit in terms of risk reduction, they're implicitly finding the optimal level of precautions.

Optional material

More generally, there are two reasons why injurers will necessarily be led to take due care if it is chosen to equal the optimal level. First, injurers plainly would not take more than due care because they will escape liability by taking merely due care. Taking greater care would therefore be to no advantage, yet would involve additional costs. Second, injurers would not wish to take less than due care, provided that due care is the socially optimal level. If injurers took less than due care, they would be exposed to the risk of liability, so their expected costs would equal total social costs. Thus, injurers would want to choose their level of care so as to minimize total social costs. But this in turn means that they would wish to raise their level of care to the socially optimal point — which, by hypothesis, equals due care and therefore allows them to avoid liability entirely.

5. Liability rules compared. Both forms of liability — strict liability and negligence — result in the same, socially optimal behavior, but they differ in what courts need to know to apply them. Under strict liability, a court need only determine the magnitude of the loss that occurred, whereas under the negligence rule a court must, in addition, determine the level of care actually taken (e.g., a driver's speed) and calculate the socially optimal level of due care (e.g., the appropriately safe speed). To do the latter, in turn, a court needs to know the cost and effectiveness of taking different levels of care in reducing accident risks.

B. Bilateral Accidents and Levels of Care

The analysis of liability when accidents are *bilateral* in nature — that is, when the behavior of both injurers and victims influences accident risk — has been extensively addressed in economically oriented literature. Although we will not discuss this situation here, we mention two conclusions about it. First, victims can be given incentives to behave properly under strict liability if there is a defense of contributory negligence — that is, if victims are able to collect only if they themselves were not negligent in the taking of their own precautions.

Second, under the negligence rule, the defense of contributory negligence is not needed to induce victims to behave appropriately: because injurers are generally led to be nonnegligent, victims bear their own losses and thus are induced to take proper care.

C. Unilateral Accidents, Levels of Care, and Levels of Activity

We will now consider an injurer's *level of activity* — that is, whether or how much he engages in a particular activity. The number of miles an individual drives, for instance, might be interpreted as his level of activity. An injurer's level of activity is to be distinguished from his level of care, which has to do with the precautions he takes *when* engaging in his activity (i.e., the precautions an individual takes when on the road, such as slowing for curves, as opposed to the number of miles he drives).

We will assume for simplicity that an increase in an injurer's activity level will result in a proportionate increase in expected accident losses, given their level of care. Thus, a doubling in the number of miles that individuals drive will result in a doubling in the number of accidents they cause, given the care with which they drive. Or a doubling in the number of times individuals walk their dogs will result in a doubling in the risk that their dogs will bite strangers, given the care taken (e.g., leashing) to prevent attacks. We will also assume that an increase in an injurer's level of activity will result in an increase in his utility (at least up to some point): the more individuals drive or the more they walk their dogs, the greater will be their utility (until their need to drive is met or until walking their dogs turns into a chore).

The social goal will be taken to be maximization of the utility injurers derive from engaging in their activity minus total accident costs — that is, minus their costs of care and expected accident losses.

1. Social welfare optimum. For social welfare to be maximized, an injurer must, as before, choose a level of care that reflects the effect of care in reducing accident losses and the costs of exercising care. But now, in contrast to the earlier case, the injurer should also select his level of activity appropriately, which is to say, the level that appropriately balances the utility he obtains against the additional risks he creates.

Example 7-2

> Assume that Example 7-1 describes the situation each time injurers engage in their activity. In this case, injurers who behave optimally will take moderate care at a cost of 3 and will reduce expected accident losses to 10. Consequently, if an injurer engages in his activity twice, taking optimal care each time, his costs of care will be 6 (i.e., $2 \times 3 = 6$), and the expected accident losses he causes will be 20 (i.e., $2 \times 10 = 20$); if he engages in his activity three times, his costs of care will be 9 and expected accident losses will be 30; and so forth. These figures are shown in the third and fourth columns of Table 7-3. The second column shows the total utility injurers derive from engaging in the activity. Social welfare, the last column, is obtained by subtracting total costs of care and total accident losses from total utility.
>
> The optimal activity level is 2 because social welfare is highest at that level. One way to explain why is as follows: Each

b/c highest social welfare

strict liability

Negligence

b/c marginal utility starts to go down

don't consider social welfare not liable

Table 7-3
Activity Level, Accidents, and Social Welfare

Activity level	Total utility	Total costs of care	Total accident losses	Social welfare
0	0	0	0	0
1	40	3	10	27
2	60	6	20	34
3	69	9	30	30
4	71	12	40	19
5	70	15	50	5

time an injurer engages in the activity, he will increase total accident costs by 13 (i.e., 3 + 10 = 13). Therefore, social welfare will be enhanced by his engaging in the activity another time if and only if the marginal utility he would gain thereby exceeds 13. Because the utility he obtains from engaging the first time is 40, the marginal utility he obtains from the second time is 20, and that from the third time is only 9, it is best that he stop at the second time.

The general point illustrated by this example is that the socially optimal behavior of injurers can be determined in two steps: (1) first by finding the level of care that minimizes total accident costs incurred each time injurers engage in their activity and (2) then by raising the level of activity as long as the marginal utility injurers derive exceeds the increment to total social costs.

2. No liability. In the absence of liability, injurers will fail to take care, as we said before, because exercising care is costly for injurers but does not benefit them because they do not bear liability for accidents that they cause. Moreover, there is an additional problem: injurers will engage in their activity to too great an extent. Indeed, they will continue to engage in it as long as they obtain any additional utility (e.g., individuals will go for drives or walk their dogs on mere whims). By contrast, it would be socially desirable that they engage in their activity only when the additional utility they obtain from doing so exceeds the costs of optimal care plus the expected accident losses they cause. In Example 7-2, if injurers are not liable, they will choose activity level 4, the level at which they cease to gain utility from their activity, rather than the optimal activity level of 2.

3. Strict liability. Under strict liability, injurers will choose both their level of care and their level of activity optimally. Consider first our examples. We already know from our discussion of Example 7-1 that strictly liable injurers will take the moderate level of care each time they engage in their activity. Hence, injurers will bear these costs of 3 and expected liability of 10 each time they engage in their activity. It follows that the last column in Table 7-3 will become injurers' utility, net of their costs of care and expected liability. Thus, injurers will choose the optimal activity level of 2.

More generally, injurers will choose the optimal level of care because doing so will minimize the expected costs they bear each time they engage in their activity. And they will choose the optimal level of activity because they will wish to engage in the activity only when the extra utility they derive exceeds their costs of care plus their added expected liability payments for accident losses caused. (People will walk their dogs only when their utility gain outweighs the disutility of having to leash the dogs and the added liability risk from dog bites.)

Optional material

> Still another way to explain why injurers choose optimal levels of care and of the activity is this: Under strict liability, an injurer's utility, net of his expected costs, will be equal to the measure of social welfare, as he will pay for the accident losses he causes, will naturally enjoy the benefits of engaging in his activity, and will bear the costs of care. Accordingly, injurers will behave so as to maximize social welfare; they will thus choose both the optimal level of care and the optimal level of activity.

4. Negligence rule. As we saw earlier, injurers will be led to take optimal care under the negligence rule, assuming that the level of due care is chosen by courts to equal the optimal level of care. Because they will take due care, however, injurers will escape liability for any accident losses they cause. They will, therefore, not have a reason to consider the effect that engaging in their activity has on accident losses.

Table 7-4
Negligence Rule and Activity Level

Activity level	Total utility	Total costs of care	Total utility minus costs of care
0	0	0	0
1	40	3	37
2	60	6	54
3	69	9	60
4	71	12	59
5	70	15	55

Consequently, injurers will be led to choose excessive activity levels. Specifically, they will engage in their activity whenever the utility they derive net of the cost of care is positive (whenever the pleasure from walking their dogs net of the disutility of leashing them is positive), rather than only when their net utility exceeds the additional expected accident losses they create.

This can be seen in Example 7-2, where, if due care is the optimal, moderate level, injurers will take due care. Because injurers take due care under the negligence rule, they will not be liable for accident losses, and their situation will be that described in Table 7-4.

From the last column in the table, it is evident that injurers will choose the activity level of 3 rather than the optimal activity level of 2: they will increase their activity level from 2 to 3 because this will raise their utility by 9 and their costs of care by only 3; they will not consider that increasing their activity level will also raise expected accident losses by 10 (as can be seen in Table 7-3), for they will not be liable for these.

5. Liability rules compared. Under both strict liability and the negligence rule, injurers are led to take socially optimal levels of care. But under the negligence rule, they engage in their activity to too great an extent because, in contrast to the situation under strict liability, they do not pay for the accident losses that they cause.

The importance of this defect of the negligence rule will clearly depend on the expected magnitude of the losses caused by an activity. If an activity is by its nature very dangerous even when carried out with appropriate precautions, then it may be significant that under the negligence rule, the level of the activity would be excessive. For example, if

> **Box 7-6**
> **The *Restatement* and the Economics**
> **of Strict Liability**
>
> Section 519 of the *Restatement (Second) of Torts* says that "[o]ne who carries on an abnormally dangerous activity is subject to liability for harm . . . although he has exercised the utmost care to prevent the harm." Is this consistent with the economic theory we've discussed? Section 520 of the *Restatement* says that, in deciding whether an activity is abnormally dangerous, one should consider the "extent to which the activity is not a matter of common usage." So, for example, you might be held strictly liable if you do something unusual, like walk on stilts and cause an accident, but not if you do something typical, like travel on roller blades and cause an accident. Does this kind of distinction make economic sense?

the walking of dogs of a vicious breed or if blasting creates high risks of harm despite the use of all reasonable care, it may be of real consequence that under the negligence rule people would walk their dogs excessively (rather than exercising them in a yard or owning dogs of another breed) or firms would blast excessively (rather than employing other methods of excavation). If, however, an activity creates only a low risk of accidents when due care is taken, then the importance of any excess in the level of activity under the negligence rule will be small. This is true of many, and perhaps most, of our everyday activities (e.g., mowing a lawn, playing catch, walking the friendly, domesticated dog).

D. Accidents Involving Firms as Injurers

Let's briefly reconsider liability and deterrence under the assumption that injurers are firms. Our analysis here consists of two parts. The first is concerned with accidents in which the victims are strangers to firms, such as an accident in which a gasoline tanker truck crashes and explodes, harming other vehicles or homes near the roadside. Then we'll consider

Table 7-5
Care of Firms and Accidents

Care level	Cost of care	Probability of accident (%)	Expected accident losses	Total social costs
None	0	9	9	9
Care	2	3	3	5

accidents in which the victims are the customers of firms, for example, an accident in which a water heater that a person purchased ruptures and damages his property. For simplicity, firms will be presumed to maximize profits and to do business in a perfectly competitive environment. This means that the price of a product will equal the total unit costs associated with production, including liability costs.

1. Victims are strangers. In this case, our conclusions about care are essentially the same as we have already discussed — firms will be led to take proper care under both negligence and strict liability rules — but the effect of liability on product price and purchases is a new consideration, as the next example illustrates.

Example 7-3

> Firms' direct costs of production per unit are 10, and the risk of accidents that would cause losses of 100 depends on whether firms take care. The exercise of care reduces expected accident losses by 6 and costs only 2 (see Table 7-5). Thus, it is socially desirable for firms to take care.
>
> Under the negligence rule, firms will have to take care to avoid liability. Firms therefore will take care, and their total costs per unit will be 12 — the direct production costs of 10 plus the costs of care. Accordingly, the product price will also be 12: by assumption, competition will drive the price down to total unit costs.
>
> Firms will take care under strict liability, too, in order to minimize their total unit costs. But these unit costs and thus the price will equal 15, because the unit costs will include expected liability expenses of 3.

As this example shows, product price will be higher under strict liability than under the negligence rule, because under strict liability, firms

Table 7-6
Utility from the Product

Customer	Utility from the product
A	40
B	20
C	17
D	13
E	11

strict liability reduces/shifts supply

bear the costs of accidents that occur. This effect on price has implications for the level of activity — that is, the amount sold by firms. This is illustrated by elaborating the previous example.

Example 7-4

Because the total unit costs of production, including expected accident losses, are 15 in Example 7-3, social welfare (i.e., the total value people obtain from the product minus the production costs, accident losses, and costs of care) will be maximized if production is carried out only when customers obtain utility exceeding 15 per unit. Suppose, for instance, that there are 5 customers who would derive the utilities shown in Table 7-6 from purchasing the product. (Or suppose that a single customer obtains increments to utility, as shown in the table, from purchasing successive units of the product.) Then only customers A, B, and C, who derive utility greater than 15, should purchase the product. The optimal level of production is 3.

Under the negligence rule, the product price will be 12, as we have seen. Hence, customers A–D will purchase the product, so 4 units will be sold, which is socially excessive. Customer D buys the product because he faces a cost of 12, even though the true social cost is 15. So it would be best that D not purchase the product.

Under the strict liability rule, the product price will be 15. So only customers A–C purchase the product, and the level of production is optimal.

The general point of this example is that it is socially optimal for production to proceed only as long as the utility customers derive from consuming additional units exceeds direct production costs plus total accident costs. Therefore, the level of production turns out to be optimal if liability is strict, because then the product price reflects total accident costs. Under the negligence rule, the price is socially too low, and too much is purchased. This is the analogue of the point made earlier that activity levels are too great under the negligence rule.

2. Victims are customers. Firms' behavior in this case will be influenced not only by their potential liability but also by customers' perceptions of product risks, for the latter will affect customers' willingness to make purchases. More precisely, a customer will buy a product only if the utility of the product to him exceeds its perceived full price — the price actually charged in the market plus the perceived expected accident losses that would not be covered by liability payments (which he would have to bear). The expected accident losses that a customer perceives he would have to bear will depend on his information about product risks. Alternative assumptions about customers' information are now considered.

Where customers' knowledge is perfect, firms will be led to take optimal care even in the absence of liability. To see exactly why, observe that, in the absence of liability, customers will bear their losses, and the full price will equal the market price plus expected accident losses. (The full price of a water heater will be seen as its price in the market plus the expected losses due to the possibility that it will rupture.) If a firm were to take less than optimal care, its potential customers would recognize this and factor into the full price the relatively high expected accident losses. Consequently, the firm's customers would go elsewhere. They would prefer to make their purchases from competitor firms exercising optimal care and therefore offering the product at a lower full price, although at a higher market price. This potential loss of customers will lead firms to take optimal care even in the absence of liability. (A similar argument shows why a firm would lose customers if it took more than optimal care.)

Example 7-5

Suppose that the situation is as in Example 7-4 except that the victims are customers, and assume that firms do not face liability for accident losses. A firm that did not take care may be able to set the market price of its product at the direct production cost of 10, but the full price would be at least 19, for the firm's customers would add to the market price the expected accident losses of 9 that they would bear. The firm would thus lose its customers to firms that take care. The price charged by firms that take care would be 12 (because the price would have to include the cost of care of 2), yet the full price would be just 15 (because expected accident losses would amount to only 3). Hence, a firm that did not take care would not survive in competition against firms that did take care.

Where, however, customers do not have enough information to determine product risks at the level of individual firms (e.g., customers cannot ascertain the risk of rupture of a particular firm's water heaters), firms will not take care in the absence of liability. No firm will wish to incur added expenses to make its product safer if customers would not recognize this to be true and reward the firm with their willingness to pay a higher price. Liability will thus be needed to induce firms to take optimal care and to induce customers to purchase the appropriate quantity of products.

What is the likely character of customers' actual information about risks? It will vary with the type of product or service (e.g., more will be known about simple goods and services, such as hammers and haircuts, than about complex ones, such as automobiles and medical care), and also with the nature of the purchaser (e.g., whether a repeat buyer or a one-time purchaser). Remedies to problems of lack of customers' information exist but are not complete. Firms have inappropriate incentives to provide information about the dangerousness of their products and services. In addition, organizations specializing in the collection of information about risks may not be able to earn enough (e.g., through sale of publications like *Consumer Reports*) to finance their activities at a socially desirable scale, in part because individual buyers can pass on the information to others in various ways. Finally, the very capacity of customers to absorb and act on information about the risks they face seems restricted.

E. Risk Aversion, Insurance, and Liability

We will now recognize that the accident problem involves not only the goal of appropriately reducing the risks of accidents but also a second objective: *allocating and spreading the risk of losses from accidents that do occur* so that those who are risk averse do not bear them, in whole or in part.

1. Risk aversion. *Risk aversion* is a term of art, describing an attitude of dislike of financial risk. For example, a risk-averse person prefers to have his present wealth for sure than to face a gamble in which he has a 50% probability of losing $1,000 and a 50% probability of receiving $1,000 — even though the expected value of the gamble is zero (i.e., 50% × $1,000 – 50% × $1,000 = $0).

Why, exactly, would a person be risk averse? A person will be risk averse if the utility value of having more money — say an extra $1,000 — is less than the loss in utility from losing that amount of money.[1] A 50% chance of losing $1,000 will then hurt more in expected terms than a 50% chance of gaining $1,000 will help, so a gamble in which the person loses $1,000 with 50% chance and wins $1,000 with 50% chance will not be desirable.

A risk-neutral person, by contrast, cares only about expected values of risky situations and thus would be indifferent between having his present wealth for sure and the gamble in which he loses $1,000 with a probability of 50% and gains $1,000 with a probability of 50%. Until now, we have assumed for simplicity that individuals are risk neutral. The ex ante measure of well-being of a risk-neutral person is his probability-discounted or expected wealth. The ex ante measure of well-being of a risk-averse person is the expected utility obtained from his wealth.

Risk aversion is most relevant in situations where losses could be large in relation to an actor's assets and thus impinge substantially on the actor's utility. If losses would be modest relative to an actor's assets, the actor would be likely to display a roughly risk-neutral attitude toward them. Thus, large firms might usually be considered as risk-neutral actors in relation to typical types of accidents, for these would cause losses that are small in relation to their assets. (If the harm involved injury to

---

1. *Optional material:* In technical terms, a person for whom the marginal utility of money declines, the more money the person has, is risk averse.

many, due, for example, to injury to thousands of people, the conclusion about large firms might be different.) However, individuals would usually be considered as risk-averse actors in relation to many types of accidents, as these would cause losses that are substantial in relation to their assets.

2. Insurance. Risk-averse parties tend to purchase insurance against risk. For example, a risk averse person who faces a risk of 10% of losing $10,000 will prefer to pay a premium of $1,000 for full coverage against this $10,000 risk than to bear the risk. Note that the premium of $1,000 equals 10% of $10,000 — that is, $1,000 is the expected payment that the insurance company has to make to an insured person. Such a premium that equals the expected payment that the insurer is obligated to make under the terms of an insurance policy is called a *fair premium*. Risk-averse parties will typically want to purchase full insurance coverage if premiums are fair.

An important aspect of insurance is that insureds may be able to affect the risk of loss, as when a person owns fire insurance and can lower the risk of fire by purchasing a fire extinguisher, or when a person owns liability insurance and can lower the risk of incurring liability by taking precautions that reduce the likelihood of causing harm to others. In such situations, there is a problem associated with ownership of insurance, and it is known as the moral hazard. Namely, because the ownership of insurance protects the insured against loss, the insured has less reason to take precautions (i.e., to do what is moral) to prevent loss than otherwise. This is a problem not only for insurance companies — moral hazard increases their costs because it means that they have to make payments more often or in greater amounts. It is a problem also for insureds, because their premiums will reflect the costs of insurers, and thus their premiums will be higher as a consequence of moral hazard.

There are several general features of insurance policies that may mitigate the problem of moral hazard. First, insurance companies may lower premiums if people take precautions. For instance, fire insurance companies may lower premiums for insureds who purchase fire extinguishers. Note that, for a fire insurance company to lower premiums if people purchase fire extinguishers, the insurance company must verify whether or not people really do purchase fire extinguishers.

(Second) insurance companies may reduce or eliminate the amount of coverage if, at the time a claim is made, it is determined that the insured failed to take a precaution that he said he would take, such as have a working sprinkler system. This will induce insureds to take the precautions, for fear of not obtaining coverage if they suffer losses. Note that, for an insurance company to adjust coverage at the time a claim is made on the basis of whether a precaution was taken, the insurance company needs to be able to verify whether the precaution was taken, such as whether a fire victim's sprinkler system was in fact functioning when a fire occurred.

Sometimes, neither of the two insurance features just mentioned is workable because the insurance company cannot obtain information about precautions either when a policy is obtained — and thus cannot link the premium to the exercise of precautions — or when a claim is made — and thus cannot link the insurance coverage payment to the exercise of precautions. Consider, for instance, the behavioral precaution of being careful in handling flammables or the behavioral precaution of driving carefully (e.g., watching for hazards, staying in lane). These behavioral precautions cannot be observed by the insurer when a person buys a policy, so the premium cannot be linked to them. Also, what the behavioral precautions have been might well be difficult to ascertain at the time a claim is made, so it might not be possible to link the amount of coverage to the taking of the precautions.

When insurers cannot link either the premium or the amount of coverage to the taking of precautions, they have another tool available to induce precautions: sale of only incomplete coverage against loss. If coverage is less than complete, such as $80,000 coverage on a $100,000 possible loss, the insured will have a $20,000 financial incentive to prevent loss, for he will bear that amount of the loss. Even though an owner of a home worth $100,000 would know that his lack of behavioral precautions to prevent fire would not affect his premium or the amount of coverage he would obtain if there were a fire, he might still want to take care (e.g., by storing flammables carefully) in order to prevent the $20,000 out-of-pocket expense he would suffer if he sustained the $100,000 loss (as well as to prevent injury to himself, of course). Incomplete coverage is thus often desired by insureds. Although it exposes them to some risk, which they do not like, it has the benefit for them of lowering their premiums — because if they buy incomplete coverage, they will be led to take greater care, lowering the insurer's costs.

3. Liability in the light of risk aversion and insurance. Now let's return to the subject of liability and consider the implications of risk aversion and insurance. Insurance is, of course, a very important feature of our accident and liability system: insurance against losses that parties might sustain as accident victims (so-called first-party insurance) is widely held, as is liability insurance protecting parties against liability judgments. More than *90%* of all payments made to tort victims are paid for by liability insurers.

Three points about liability and insurance are important to make. First, because liability insurers pay for most or all of the losses for which injurers are found liable, the manner in which liability rules alter injurers' behavior is, to a significant degree, indirect, being associated with the terms of their liability insurance policies. But liability still affects incentives to reduce accidents. Notably, liability insurers may reduce premiums for parties who take precautions to reduce risk or may reduce payments to parties who did not take precautions, or liability insurers may sell policies with incomplete coverage, leaving insureds with an incentive to take precautions. Thus, parties have incentives to take precautions due to liability rules. The incentives are either translated ones, having to do with the terms of their liability insurance policies, or direct ones, the result of the incompleteness of insurance coverage.

Second, the availability of liability insurance is usually socially desirable. The particular arguments demonstrating this are roughly as follows. The availability of liability insurance increases the welfare of risk-averse injurers, because it protects them from risk and ameliorates problems that would otherwise arise — namely, they might take excessive care or be discouraged from engaging in desirable activities. Moreover, the availability of liability insurance does not negate injurers' incentives to reduce risk, as we've already noted, although it may reduce them. Nevertheless, there are circumstances in which liability insurance is, in principle, not socially desirable — for example, where injurers' assets are insufficient to pay for harm. (But discussion of this point is beyond our scope.)

Box 7-7
Requiring Liability Insurance

Quite the opposite of preventing the purchase of liability insurance is mandating it — as is done for drivers of cars and for operators of some businesses. Suppose a party is forced to buy substantial coverage against liability, more than the party would voluntarily purchase. Under what circumstances would this requirement backfire and lead to increased risks of accidents? And under what circumstances would it tend to reduce the risks of accidents? Why do you think these requirements to purchase liability coverage exist?

Historically, it is interesting to note that liability insurance was resisted as being against the public interest (as the thinking went, how could society allow wrongdoers to escape punishment by permitting them to be covered by liability insurance?). Indeed, its legality and sale were deferred in some countries until the early twentieth century. Perhaps most notable was the complete ban on liability insurance in the former Soviet Union. Even today, liability insurance is not always permitted. In some jurisdictions, for example, coverage against punitive damages is not permitted.

Third, the availability of accident and liability insurance limits the importance of compensation and the allocation of risk as factors in evaluating the social desirability of liability rules. In particular, society need not rely on the liability system to compensate victims of accidents, for they can be compensated by insurers. Thus, that the typical injurers in some areas of accidents might be large, essentially risk-neutral firms and the victims risk-averse individuals does not constitute an argument in favor of imposing liability to the extent that the individuals are insured against their losses. Moreover, there is no strong reason to favor strict liability or the negligence rule on grounds of the difference in risks they impose on injurers — strict liability imposing more of a risk on injurers than the negligence rule — for injurers can relieve risk by purchasing liability insurance coverage.

F. Liability and Administrative Costs

A third element that needs to be considered in an analysis of the liability system is administrative costs. These are defined to be the legal and other expenses and costs (including time and effort) borne by parties in resolving disputes that arise when harm occurs. It is important to recognize that administrative costs are incurred not only with cases that go to trial but also with cases that settle (more than 90% of cases settle).

What is the magnitude of administrative costs? Existing data suggest that, in the United States, the administrative costs of the liability system are substantial. Many studies find that, averaged over settled and litigated claims, administrative costs approach or exceed the amounts received by victims. That is, for every dollar received by a victim, more than a dollar is spent delivering the dollar to the victim! And even these estimates may be low, for they do not take into full account the time and disutility of the litigants. (It is not clear, however, to what extent these administrative costs should be viewed as intrinsic to the liability system or as resulting from the particular system that has developed in the United States.)

Several implications of administrative costs should be noted. First, the comparison of strict liability and negligence rules may be affected by consideration of administrative costs. On one hand, the number of cases is likely to be higher under strict liability than under the negligence rule, suggesting that administrative costs are higher under strict liability. On the other hand, the cost of resolving each case is likely to be higher under the negligence rule, as negligence will be an issue under that rule but not under strict liability. Therefore, it is not clear on a priori grounds under which rule administrative costs will be higher, but differences in such costs under the rules are relevant to take into account.

Second, the existence of the administrative costs of the liability system suggests that liability will not be socially worthwhile unless the social benefits of the system are sufficiently high. Otherwise, a system without liability, such as a no-fault system, will be best. This point is important because, in fact, the administrative costs of the liability system are so high. Therefore, the benefits of the liability system must be high to warrant its use. The principal benefit of the system may well be deterrence of accidents, not compensation of victims, for the latter would tend to occur through insurance were there no liability system. Accordingly, it seems that the liability system must be justified largely by its ability to reduce accident costs through provision of incentives. Whether, or in what domains, it does reduce accident costs substantially is an empirical question (which unfortunately has been relatively little investigated).

G. Economic Analysis of Tort Law versus Traditional Analysis

Several differences between economic analysis of tort law, as presented above, and the traditional analysis and view of legal scholars, judges, and most lawyers may be noted. First, economic analysis focuses on identifying the effects of liability rules; it is essentially consequentialist in orientation. Traditional analysis, however, is not centered around the question of ascertaining the effects of liability rules; although these effects are often discussed, they are not ordinarily considered in a sustained and organized way.

Second, the goal of liability law, under economic analysis, is the advancement of social well-being through three channels: fostering incentives to reduce risk, properly allocating risks of accidents that do occur, and reducing administrative costs. Moreover, because of the existence of insurance, the chief social advantage of the liability system — its social warrant — is the incentives it provides to reduce accident risk. In contrast, the traditional view is that the primary social function of the liability system is to compensate victims and to achieve corrective justice — in other words, to make wrongdoers pay those they have wronged. From the economic perspective, the view that the liability system is required to compensate victims is problematic because, as just noted, insurance is available to provide compensation. The view that the liability system achieves corrective justice also has problematic aspects, in part because liability insurers typically pay judgments. Thus, wrongdoers are not really punished in the direct way that corrective justice would seem to require.

4. Contracts

This section presents on overview of basic elements of economic analysis of contracts. It is concerned with the definition of contracts and with important aspects of contractual practice and the law of contracts. A focus of the analysis is the determination of aspects of contract law that tend to raise the well-being of the parties to contracts from the ex ante perspective.[2]

A. Definitions and Framework of Analysis

By a *contract* we mean a specification of the actions that named parties are supposed to take at various times, often as a function of the *conditions* that hold. The actions typically pertain to delivery of goods, performance of services, and payments of money, and the conditions include uncertain contingencies, past actions of parties, and messages sent by them. For example, a contract might state that a photographer should, on February 1, take pictures at a wedding and circulate among the guests to obtain a good record of the event, that the buyer should pay the photographer $1,000 within a week of the wedding, that the buyer may cancel if he notifies the photographer by January 1, and that the photographer may cancel if he becomes ill. It is apparent that, because the notions of actions and conditions are broad, the conception of a contract is very general.

A contract is said to be *completely specified* if the list of conditions on which the actions are based is explicitly exhaustive — that is, if the contract provides literally for each possible condition in some relevant universe of conditions. In a contract for a photographer to take wedding photographs, suppose that the universe of conditions is everything that could happen to the photographer (e.g., becoming ill, receiving an offer to take photographs at another wedding the same day, and so forth) and everything that could happen to the wedding couple (e.g., becoming ill, breaking off their marriage, and the like). A completely specified contract would then have to include an explicit provision for each of these possible conditions pertaining to the photographer and the wedding couple. Although, as we will discuss, contracts are far from completely specified in reality, the concept of a completely specified contract will be helpful for clarifying our thinking about contracts.

A contract is said to be *Pareto optimal* if the contract cannot be modified so as to raise the expected well-being of each of the parties to it. Contracts

---

2. The orientation of this material on contracts is different from that of the Contracting chapter, which emphasized how to draft contracts. Here, the primary emphasis is on the effects and social desirability of rules of contract law.

should tend to be Pareto optimal: if a contract can be altered in a way that would raise the expected well-being of each party, we would think that this would be done. For example, suppose that the wedding contract states that the photographer should appear at 10:00 A.M. but that an alternative contract, under which he would arrive at 9:00 A.M. and he would be paid an additional $100, is preferred both by the wedding couple and by the photographer. Then the first contract would not be Pareto optimal, and we would expect the modification to it to be made.

1. Enforcement of contracts. Contracts are assumed to be enforced by *tribunals,* which generally will be interpreted to be state-authorized courts or arbitration organizations. A basic function of tribunals is to decide about *contract formation* — that is, when a valid contract has been made. Given that a contract has been properly made and is deemed valid, tribunals must often engage in contract *interpretation,* notably by filling gaps in contracts and resolving ambiguities. Another function of tribunals concerns *breach* of contract. Tribunals must decide when breach has occurred and impose sanctions, or equivalently award "remedies," for breach. Tribunals may impose two different types of sanctions for breach of a contract by a party to it: they may force a party in breach to pay money *damages* to the other, or they may insist that the contract be performed in a literal sense (e.g., require land to be conveyed, as stipulated in the contract), which is to say, insist on *specific performance* of the contract. Finally, tribunals may also decide to *override* contracts. That is, even though a contract was properly formed and is not invalid on that count, the tribunal may refuse to enforce it and declare it invalid.

2. Social welfare and the welfare of contracting parties. It will generally be assumed that the goal of tribunals is to maximize social welfare. This will usually mean that tribunals act to further the welfare of the parties to the contract, for they will ordinarily be the only parties affected by the contract. If, however, other parties are affected by a contract, then the well-being of these parties outside the contract will also be assumed to be taken into account by the tribunal.

B. Contract Formation

A basic question that a tribunal must answer is, At what stage of interactions between parties does a contract become legally recognized — that is, become enforceable? A general legal rule is that contracts are recognized as valid if and only if both parties have given a clear indication of assent, such as signing their names on a document. This rule has two basic functions suggesting that the rule is in the interests of parties who want to make contracts.

First, the rule plainly allows two parties to make an enforceable contract when they both so desire and for each to know that this is so. An important virtue of this point is that the parties will often immediately have an incentive to act in the many ways that will raise the value of their contractual relationship. For instance, a party that promises to build something, knowing that he has a valid contract, may immediately begin plans for construction, buy materials, hire workers, and so forth.

Second, the rule protects each party against becoming legally obligated against that party's wishes, because the rule requires mutual assent for a contract to be recognized. Thus, the rule prevents the formation of what would be undesirable contracts (e.g., suppose that a person were

---

Box 7-8
Leaky Basements, Mineral Deposits,
and the Duty to Disclose

One issue about contract formation is when you should have the obligation to disclose information in contracting. Economics suggests that there should often be such a duty, such as about the leaky basement of a house you're selling. This way the buyer will know what he's getting and avoid storing valuables in the basement. But economics also says that sometimes there shouldn't be a disclosure obligation. For instance, suppose (as happened in a case) that a mineral company did an aerial survey and figured out that there were valuable mineral deposits under a farmer's land. To make the company disclose this to the farmer might make the company pay so much for mineral rights as to negate its incentive to conduct aerial surveys. Thus, allowing nondisclosure might be good. (And why doesn't this logic apply to leaky basements?)

to become obligated to have something built that did not really suit his purposes). Also, were individuals subject to the risk of becoming contractually bound, without their assent, because they engaged in negotiations with others, then the search and negotiation process would be chilled. This would tend to negatively affect contract formation and would not be desired by potential parties to contracts.

C. Incompleteness of Contracts

Let's now assume that a contract has been formed and ask about its likely character. A feature of contracts that will be seen to be of considerable importance is that they are significantly incomplete. Contracts typically omit all manner of variables and contingencies that are of potential relevance to contracting parties. A contract to take pictures at a wedding would be likely to fail to include many outcomes that might make it difficult or impossible for the photographer to perform, as well as many circumstances that would alter the couples' desire for photographs or for the type of record they want to be made.

There are several reasons for the incompleteness of contracts. One is simply the cost of writing more complete contracts. Parties may not include terms in a contract, at least not in a detailed, desirable way, because of the cost of evaluating, agreeing upon, and writing terms. In particular, parties will tend not to specify terms for events of low probability, because the expected loss from this type of exclusion will be minimal whereas the cost of including such terms would be borne with certainty. For example, it might take 15 minutes to discuss and include a term about what to do if the photographer is involved in a car accident on the way to the wedding, but if the likelihood of such an event is quite low, it will not be worth the parties' while to include a provision for such an outcome in the contract.

A second reason for incompleteness is that some variables (e.g., effort levels, technical production difficulties, and the like) cannot be verified by tribunals. If the value of the variable cannot be verified, then were the parties to include it, one of the parties would generally find it in his interest to make a claim about the value of the variable, causing problems. For example, if the contract specifies that payment need not be made for a service if it is performed poorly and if the quality of performance cannot be verified by the tribunal, the buyer would always find it in his interest to claim that performance was subpar in order to escape having to pay. Of course, many such variables can be made verifiable (e.g., effort could be made verifiable through videotaping), but that would involve expense.

A third reason for the incompleteness of contracts is that the expected consequences of incompleteness may not be very harmful to contracting parties. Another reason why incompleteness may not matter is that a tribunal might interpret the contract in a desirable manner. In addition, as we shall see, the prospect of having to pay damages for breach of contract may serve as an implicit substitute for more detailed terms. Furthermore, the opportunity to renegotiate a contract often furnishes a way for parties to alter terms in the light of circumstances for which contractual provisions had not been made.

D. Interpretation of Contracts

Given that parties leave contracts incomplete, questions naturally arise about interpretation toward completeness of contracts by tribunals. As a general matter, parties will want incomplete contracts to be interpreted in the way that they would have written them had they spent the time and effort to write more detailed terms. For example, suppose that a builder and a buyer do not include a term in their contract stating whether the builder is to perform if material prices rise steeply, and suppose that, had they included the term, it would have relieved the builder of having to perform in this circumstance. The parties would want the tribunals to interpret the incomplete contract in this way should prices rise steeply.

E. Damage Measures for Breach of Contract

When parties breach a contract, they often have to pay damages in consequence. The *damage measure,* the formula governing what they should pay, can be determined by the tribunal, or it can be stipulated in advance by the parties to the contract (so-called liquidated damages). One would expect parties to specify their own damage measure when it would better serve their purposes than the measure the tribunal would employ and otherwise to allow the tribunal to select the damage measure. In either case, we now examine the functioning and utility of damage measures to contracting parties.

1. Incentives to perform. It is clear that damage measures provide parties incentives to perform by threatening them with having to pay damages if they do not. To illustrate, suppose that a buyer wants a custom desk built and that the measure of damages for breach is $800. The seller would be induced to build the desk if his construction cost is less than $800 but would commit breach if his construction cost would be higher than $800. Thus, a particular damage measure provides a particular degree of incentive to perform. And, in general, the higher the damage measure is, the greater the incentive to perform.

2. Completely specified contracts. A question that naturally arises is, What measure of damages provides the best incentive to perform for the parties? That is, what damage measure would most raise their expected well-being from contracting? It might seem that a very high damage measure would be best, for that would give a very strong motivation to obey a contract. This idea is correct if a contract is truly completely specified. In this case, a very high damage measure — so high that no party would ever breach a contract — would be in the parties' mutual interests, because they would then be assured that exactly the contract they want would be obeyed.

Let's illustrate with a contract for the building of the desk, and let's assume that the buyer places a value of $1,000 on having the desk. If such a contract were Pareto optimal and completely specified, it can be shown to have the following simple character: the seller is to make the desk if the production cost would be less than $1,000, and the seller is excused from performance if the production cost would exceed $1,000. In essence, the explanation is that the buyer would not be willing to pay enough to the seller to induce him to include terms calling for performance when the production cost would be high.

Note two points about the outcome if the damage measure for breach is high enough to guarantee performance of the terms in this contract. First, the seller will be led to construct the desk when the production cost would be less than $1,000; otherwise, he would have to pay very high damages. Second, the seller will *not* be led to construct the desk when the production cost would exceed $1,000, for the contract does not call for this, and thus *no damages* will be paid by the seller when he fails to construct the desk in such circumstances.

The general point of importance illustrated by the preceding example is this: under a damage measure that is sufficiently high to necessarily induce performance of a Pareto optimal completely specified contract, it is true not only that performance is always guaranteed when called for but also that there is no risk of a party's having to perform when performing would be onerous and no risk of having to bear high damages for breach. The latter is so because, whenever performance would be onerous, the contract, being completely specified and Pareto optimal, will not call for performance.

3. Incomplete contracts. When contracts are not completely specified, then damage measures that are so high that they always lead to performance or lead to performance too often are usually not desirable for the parties. Instead, moderate damages tend to be mutually desirable, because they will allow a party to commit breach when performance of the incomplete contract would be difficult.

To explain, let's reconsider the example from above. Suppose that the contract states simply that the seller shall make a desk for the buyer. The contract does not have specific terms because of, say, the cost of taking the time to include them. Given this incomplete contract calling for performance under all circumstances, a high measure of damages would be needed to guarantee performance. For instance, suppose that production costs could be as high as $2,000. Then the damage measure for breach would have to exceed $2,000 (e.g., $3,000) in order to guarantee performance.

A damage measure like $3,000 that is so high as to result in performance of the incomplete contract all the time would result in outcomes very different from that under the Pareto optimal complete contract. Under the latter contract, we know that the desk would be constructed only when its production cost is less than the buyer's valuation of $1,000, whereas under the incomplete contract with a $3,000-damage measure, the desk would be built even when the production cost exceeds $1,000. This suggests what will now be illustrated, that the parties will be worse off because of the excessive performance under a very high damage

measure like $3,000 and that a moderate damage measure of $1,000 —
namely, the *expectation measure*, the measure necessary to make the victim
of the breach whole — will be superior in the eyes of both parties to the
contract.

Let's elaborate the example in order to flesh out the above points. Suppose that there are two possible production costs: a normal production
cost of $300, the likelihood of which is 90%, and a high production cost of
$2,000, the likelihood of which is 10%. The parties initially contemplate a
contract with $3,000 as damages for breach and with a contract price, to
be paid at the outset, of $700. Because the damages are so high, the seller
will definitely produce the desk. In particular, if production cost is $2,000
he will produce at that cost rather than pay $3,000 in damages. Hence,
the value of the contract to the buyer is simply $300 (i.e., $1,000 – $700 =
$300), as he knows that there will be no breach. The seller's expected
profit is $230 (i.e., $700 – 90% × $300 – 10% × $2,000 = $230).

Now we claim that *both* parties would want to switch from the high
damage measure of $3,000 to the expectation measure of $1,000, even
though this will result in the seller breaching when production cost is
$2,000. Note first that the buyer will not be worse off if damages are
lowered to his expectation, for if he does not receive the desk, he will
obtain $1,000 in damages, which is, by assumption, equivalent to receiv-
ing the desk. Hence, the value to the buyer of a contract with the same
price of $700 and the $1,000 damage measure must be the same, $300.
However, the seller will be better off, as he will be able to pay $1,000 in
damages rather than bear the production cost of $2,000 when it is high.
In particular, the expected value of the contract to the seller will be $330
(i.e., $700 – 90% × $300 – 10% × $1,000 = $330), so he is better off by $100.
This increase suggests that the seller can lower the price he charges
somewhat and still remain better off while making the buyer definitely
better off than under the original contract. Indeed, if the price is $650 and
the $1,000 damage measure is employed, both parties will be better off.
The buyer's value will be $350 (i.e., $1,000 – $650 = $350), which is better
than $300, and the seller's expected value will be $280 (i.e., $650 – 90% ×
$300 – 10% × $1,000 = $280), which is better than $230.

The methods of argument just used can be employed to demonstrate
that, in very general circumstances, both parties will always elect to alter

a contract in which the damage measure is not the expectation measure to one in which it is the expectation measure, usually with a price adjustment. In the example, the intuition was that the seller would reduce the price in order to have the damage measure lowered from a high level to the expectation measure. It is also true that the buyer would be willing to pay a higher price to raise the damage measure to the expectation measure if the damage measure were lower, such that the seller might commit breach when the production cost is below his valuation.

4. Moderate damage measures as substitutes for better specified contracts. An interpretation of significance of the foregoing is that moderate damage measures function as substitutes for detailed contracts. It has been seen that, if a contract leaves out terms stating when contracts should be performed and when not, use of a properly chosen moderate damage measure will lead to performance in approximately the circumstances that the parties would have named in a completely specified contract. That is because, on one hand, performance will be induced when it is not too burdensome to perform, which is when a completely specified contract would have stipulated performance. And, on the other hand, performance will not be induced when it would be difficult to perform, which is when a completely specified contract would have excused a party from having to perform. Therefore, the opportunity of the parties to employ moderate damage measures enables them to write contracts that lack great detail but that, nevertheless, lead to performance and to nonperformance when they want.

5. Is breach and payment of damages immoral? The discussion above sheds light on the often-discussed question of whether breach of contract and payment of damages is immoral, similar to breaking a promise. To understand and evaluate this assertion, let's assume that the type of promise that ought to be kept is the completely specified contract that the parties could be imagined to make. This assumption is a natural one, for it is only the completely specified contract that is explicit about and thus is able to reflect the desires of the parties as to each of the circumstances of possible relevance to them. It would be unnatural to interpret an incomplete contract as embodying the desires of the parties in a particular circumstance if the parties would have stipulated something different from what the incomplete contract implies should hold for that circumstance. When an incomplete contract is employed by parties, it is for reasons of convenience or practicality, and it would thus be strange to view it as reflecting the true desires of the parties in all circumstances.

Given, then, the assumption that the completely specified contract represents the promise of the parties that ought to be kept and that incomplete contracts are not necessarily the promises that ought to be kept, we can see that the view that it is immoral to breach contracts and pay damages is confused and may well represent the opposite of the truth. Consider the incomplete contract for the making of the desk that names no contingencies. Under the expectation measure, breach of this contract will occur whenever production cost exceeds $1,000. In such instances, breach is encouraged when the damage measure is moderate and the nonperformance is exactly what would have been allowed in the completely specified contract that represents the real wishes of the parties and the promise that they would want met. Thus, the breach induced by the damage measure is seen to *satisfy* the true promise of the parties, not to abrogate it. Hence, the appropriate view of breach under moderate damage measures seems very different from the view that breach under such damage measures is immoral, which fails to take into account and appreciate the significance of the incompleteness of contracts.

6. Incentives to rely. Let's now return to our consideration of damage measures and consider their effect on so-called *reliance* of contracting parties, by which we mean the various actions that parties can take that will raise the value of performance of the contract. For example, the buyer of the custom desk may order bookshelves to match the desk, which will increase the value to him of having the desk; a person who contracts for a band to appear at his club may advertise the event and thus enhance the profits he will make if the band appears; and so forth. Reliance activities are manifold and substantially augment the value of contracts in general. Because damage measures tend to lead to performance, they also provide parties with incentives to engage in reliance activities. This is a significant beneficial effect of damage measures that is distinct from their direct effect on when there will be performance.

7. Risk bearing. Another important function of damage measures concerns the allocation of risk. Notably, because the payment of damages compensates to one or another degree the victim of a breach, the measure might be mutually desirable as an implicit form of insurance if the victim is risk averse.

However, the prospect of having to pay damages also constitutes a risk for a party who might be led to commit breach and that party might be risk averse as well. For example, consider a contract between a buyer for whom performance is worth $100,000 and a risk-averse seller for whom the usual production cost is $10,000 but could be much higher and exceed $100,000 with a probability of 20%. Under the expectation measure, the seller faces the risk of having to pay damages of $100,000 with a probability of 20% and may find this risk hard to bear. If so, the seller might demand a very high price if the expectation measure is to be employed and propose instead that a more detailed contract be written in which, if production costs become very high, he is excused from performance rather than having to pay large damages. Such a contract would require that the buyer be able to verify that production costs have in fact risen. The parties may be willing to incur these verification costs in order to avoid the bearing of risk that the use of the expectation measure would involve for the seller.

A full consideration of damage measures, then, must reflect how these measures distribute risk and the willingness of both parties to the contract to bear risk.

F. Specific Performance

As observed at the outset, an alternative to a damage measure for breach of contract is specific performance: requiring a party to satisfy his contractual obligation. The interpretation of specific performance depends on the nature of the contractual obligation. Usually, specific performance refers to an obligation to deliver a good or to perform a service, in which case it means that exactly this must be done. If the contractual obligation is for a party to pay a given amount (e.g., for an insurance company to pay coverage to an insured), then the meaning of specific performance is to require the party to pay money. Specific performance can be enforced with a sufficiently high threat or by exercise of the state's police powers (e.g., a sheriff removes a person from the land that he promised to convey). Note, too, that if a monetary penalty can be employed to induce

---

Box 7-9
The Puzzle of Specific Performance

From the economic perspective, it's not at all clear why specific performance would be a good remedy rather than money damages, and no good explanation has been offered (but see the discussion in the optional material). Adding to the puzzle is that other legal systems, such as the French and the German systems, resort to specific performance in approximately the same circumstances as Anglo-American law does but through very different doctrines and legal principles.

---

performance, specific performance is equivalent to a damage measure with a high level of damages.

1. Incentives to perform. What we said above about damage measures bears on the desirability of specific performance. Namely, if contracts are incomplete, then, for the reasons we gave favoring moderate damage measures such as the expectation measure, specific performance ordinarily would not be desired by the parties. Specific performance will often result in performance of contracts when doing so would be onerous and when performance would not have been stipulated in a completely specified contract. Were a contract completely specified, specific performance would be desired by the parties. But note that specific performance would never constitute an undue burden for the performing party, because any difficult contingency would constitute an excuse for him. However, contracts are in fact incomplete, so this point about the desirability of specific performance is a hypothetical one.

2. Ability to enforce. The ability of tribunals to enforce specific performance depends on the type of contractual obligation. If the obligation is to perform a service or to make something, enforcement means forcing a person to undertake particular actions and thus may entail special difficulties, especially if the person is recalcitrant. If the obligation is to convey something that exists, such as land, specific performance does not involve that difficulty but does require the thing to be removed from the holder and given to the buyer. Specific performance does not require, as damage measures do, that the assets of the party in breach be found and that the party be forced to pay. Thus, where the obligation is to convey something that exists, it is possible that specific performance is easier for a tribunal to enforce than payment of damages.

Optional material

Possible desirability of specific performance. Why might specific performance be desirable for contracting parties? We can only loosely sketch an answer here, applying it to the particular context of contracts for conveyance of land (or for conveyance of something else that already exists and does not have to be produced). Under specific performance, a buyer of land will definitely receive it, and there might be no drawback analogous to excessive performance of a contract to produce something, where the seller would bear production costs exceeding the value of the good to the buyer. Excessive performance in relation to a contract to convey land would be conveyance of land to a buyer who would retain it even though a third party would pay more for it than the buyer's valuation. This, though, might not occur under specific performance, for the buyer might be expected to sell to a third party who values the land more than he does. Thus, specific performance would result only in the buyer receiving the land and retaining it when he values it more highly than a third party does.

However, it might be asked why the expectation measure would not also result in that outcome, for if the seller has to pay the buyer his valuation in the event of breach, the seller will sell to a third party only if this party offers more than the buyer's valuation. The expectation measure might not result in this outcome, though, because the tribunal might underestimate the buyer's valuation. Yet if this is the case, why wouldn't the buyer name as liquidated damages an amount equal to his valuation? The buyer might not want to do this because he might not want to reveal his true valuation to the seller, for this would lead the seller to raise his price. Hence, specific performance, which does not reveal his valuation, might be preferred by the buyer. Also, as noted above, it is possible that damage measures are more difficult to enforce than conveyance of the land.

G. Renegotiation

Heretofore, the possibility that contracts might be renegotiated when difficulties arise has not been explicitly considered. For example, if construction cost is high relative to the value of performance and the damage measure would induce performance, might not the seller renegotiate with the buyer and pay him to be excused from having to perform? There are appealing reasons to consider such renegotiation. The main one is this: because the parties, having made an initial contract, know of each other's existence and know many particulars of the contractual situation, they would be expected to tend to renegotiate if problems arise. That is, they would find it relatively cheap to renegotiate, and they would have the time to do so because they could locate each other fairly easily.

However, before discussing the implications of renegotiation, let's briefly note why renegotiation may not occur. One reason is simply that, at the time that difficulties are experienced, one party might benefit from acting quickly, but the parties may not be in contact with each other, or arranging immediate renegotiation might be costly. A producer might benefit from acting quickly because, for instance, a problem may occur during the course of production and the producer may have to decide on the spot whether to abort the process or to proceed at greater cost. Or a new bid may be heard and have to be immediately answered. A second problem with renegotiation is that, even if the parties are in contact with each other, a breakdown in bargaining may occur.

Nevertheless, let's assume in the remainder of this section that, when difficulties arise and a mutually beneficial renegotiated contract exists in principle, it will be made.

1. Performance. If contracts will be renegotiated when difficulties arise, then performance of contracts will occur whenever this would be mutually beneficial, despite the incompleteness of contracts.

Let's illustrate with the example of the production contract for the desk worth $1,000. Recall our statement that, in a Pareto optimal completely specified contract, the parties would have stipulated performance when production cost is less than $1,000 but not when it is more. Suppose, however, that an incomplete contract does not mention any contingencies and, initially, that the remedy for breach is specific performance. In the absence of renegotiation, the seller would be led to make the desk when the production cost exceeds $1,000 as well as when the cost is less than $1,000. However, the contract would be renegotiated whenever the cost exceeds $1,000. For instance, if the cost would be $1,500, the seller could pay the buyer $1,250 for an agreement to allow him not to perform. This would be mutually beneficial because $1,250 exceeds the $1,000 value of performance to the buyer and because $1,250 is less than the production cost of performance for the seller.

In general, whatever the degree of incompleteness of the contract and whatever the remedy for breach, renegotiation will lead to performance exactly when this would have been stipulated in a Pareto optimal completely specified contract. Therefore, renegotiation reduces the need for complete contracts and serves as an implicit substitute for them. (In this sense, renegotiation serves a purpose similar to that of damage measures.)

2. Risk bearing. Although renegotiation of contracts may tend to result in performance in appropriate circumstances and thus reduces the need for damage measures to accomplish this, renegotiation may not cure problems of undesirable risk bearing. For example, if specific performance or a very high damage measure is the remedy for breach of a production contract, the seller may have to pay a very large amount to the buyer to be excused from performance when the cost of performance would be great. This would constitute a large risk for the seller, which he might not want to bear. Therefore, the seller might much prefer the expectation measure as the remedy for breach, because it would limit his risk. Such risk-bearing factors associated with renegotiation of contracts need to taken into account in assessing renegotiation as a device that might aid contracting parties when problematic contingencies arise.

3. Cost. Another point about renegotiation is its cost. Here we note that it might be thought that the expectation measure (as well as other moderate damage measures) involves less cost than renegotiation does. Under the expectation measure, one possibility is that there will be performance rather than, perhaps, renegotiation for performance with attendant cost. The other possibility is that there will be breach and payment of damages rather than, perhaps, renegotiation to be excused from performance. In this case, damage measures will involve lower cost than renegotiation, assuming that the amount of damages is clear and thus that settlement will be a smooth process.

H. Legal Overriding of Contracts

A basic rationale for legislative or judicial overriding of contracts is the existence of harmful externalities. Contracts that are likely to harm third parties — for example, agreements to commit crimes, price-fixing compacts, and certain simple sales contracts (such as ones for machine guns) — are often not enforced. Of course, the harm to third parties must tend to exceed the benefits of a contract to the parties themselves for it to be socially desirable not to enforce contracts. Thus, a contract between a person who wants to have a party and a band might cause some disturbance to neighbors who would prefer to enjoy a quiet evening, but if the disturbance is not great, the contract would, on net, be beneficial and be enforced.

Another general rationale for nonenforcement of contracts is to prevent a loss in welfare to one or both of the parties to contracts (as opposed to third parties). This concern may motivate nonenforcement when a party lacks relevant information (as when a person buys food that is mislabeled or a security that is not correctly described) and, as a result, is made worse off by the transaction. Similarly, an incompetent person or a child might make a contract that makes him worse off, and transactions by such individuals are generally nonenforceable.

Two other rationales that are offered for not enforcing contracts may be noted. One is that contracts sometimes are not enforced because they involve the sale of things that are said to be inalienable, such as human organs, babies, and voting rights. However, it seems that wherever the justification of inalienability is adduced, the previous two rationales — externality and losses in welfare to the parties themselves — apply (perhaps in subtle form), so one might doubt whether inalienability stands for a distinct rationale for failing to enforce a contract. For example, the sale of human organs might be thought undesirable because some individuals will sell their own organs (e.g., kidneys) without realizing the detrimental consequences to themselves (i.e., the contracting parties will be made worse off because of lack of information), because some individuals will be allowed to die earlier than necessary in order for their organs to be harvested (i.e., the contracting parties will be made worse off because of the contract-induced behavior of others), and because the very existence of the market will be understood by individuals as eroding norms of respect for human life (a harmful externality), where these norms themselves are welfare enhancing because they reduce violence and encourage the giving of aid in emergencies and the like.

Similarly, contracts are sometimes not enforced because of paternalism (e.g., a person is not allowed to purchase certain drugs or a child is not allowed to purchase pornographic material). This rationale, like that of inalienability, often seems reducible to the two previous rationales concerning externalities and harm to the contracting parties themselves. If a person is not allowed to purchase drugs, the justification may lie in the possibility that he or she does not understand the true properties of the drugs or that using them (as in the case of addictive drugs) may result in problems for third parties.

I. Extralegal Means of Enforcement

There are means of contract enforcement apart from the state-authorized courts that should be mentioned.

1. Private adjudication. We said at the outset that the tribunals under discussion include those of private arbitration. Private adjudication can be better for the parties than the courts are, in that parties can specify their adjudicators to be those who have special knowledge, can avoid juries, and can stipulate any kind of procedure they desire. For these reasons, it is socially desirable for courts generally to enforce the judgments of private adjudication. This is, in fact, usually the case.

2. Reputation. We have not mentioned reputation as a factor in the contractual context, but it is, of course, important. The prospect of suffering harm to one's reputation can serve to induce parties to adhere to contracts. However, this reputational factor is unlikely to lead to enforcement that is as good as that achieved through tribunals. Tribunals obtain fairly detailed information about contractual situations (e.g., about the true magnitude of harm to the victim of a breach) and more information that would tend to be embodied in a party's reputation. If a party committed a breach and paid too little, it is not clear that his reputation would reflect that difference, so he might not be led to pay the right amount even though he would be led to by a tribunal. Similarly, if a party wants his contract interpreted by the tribunals (e.g., to excuse him because of problems he is facing), tribunals might do this knowing his true situation, but would his excuse be recognized and he not be penalized reputationally?

Additionally, it is not evident that reputational incentives of parties are necessarily strong enough to induce adherence to contracts. Consider a party who is not going to be transacting in the future but who is presently making a large contract that it would benefit him greatly to breach. He may well rationally do so, despite the loss to his reputation.

5. Civil Litigation

We here take up the basic theory of litigation and consider three stages of litigation: (1) the potential plaintiff decides whether to bring a suit against the defendant, (2) if suit is brought, the plaintiff and the defendant decide whether or not they will settle the case, and (3) if the parties do not settle the case, they go to trial. In each stage, we discuss how the parties behave and then how this compares to what is socially desirable. A theme of emphasis will be that the private incentives of parties in litigation may diverge significantly from the socially appropriate incentives, given that litigation is a costly activity.

A. Bringing of Suit

By a *suit*, we will mean the taking of a costly initial step that is a prerequisite to a further legal proceeding. One may interpret suit as a formal legal step, such as the filing of a complaint, or as an informal step, such as, notably, engaging a lawyer. Bringing a suit involves costs, including the plaintiff's time and energy, legal services, and possibly filing fees. For simplicity, it will be assumed, unless otherwise noted, that the costs associated with suit are fixed.

1. Private incentive to sue. The plaintiff will sue when the cost of suit is less than the expected benefits from suit. (We assume that parties are risk neutral unless otherwise noted.) The expected benefits from suit involve possible settlement payments or winnings from trial. Thus, the lower the cost of suit, the greater the likelihood of winning at trial, and the greater the plaintiff's loss, the more likely suit is.

2. Private and socially desirable suit. We now take up the question of how the amount of suit that parties are motivated to bring compares to the socially optimal amount of suit. The main point that we wish to make is that the private incentive to bring suit is fundamentally misaligned with the socially optimal incentive to do so and the deviation between them could be in the direction of either too much or too little suit. The reasons for this conclusion may be understood as follows.

On one hand, there is a divergence between social and private costs that can lead to socially excessive suit. Specifically, when a plaintiff contemplates bringing suit, he bears only his own costs. He does not take into account the defendant's costs or the state's costs that his suit will engender. Hence, the plaintiff might be led to bring suit when the total costs would make this undesirable.

On the other hand, there is a difference between the social and the private benefits of suit that may lead to a socially inadequate level of suit or may reinforce the cost-related tendency toward excessive suit. The plaintiff would not usually be expected to treat as a benefit to himself the social benefits flowing from suit — notably, its deterrent effect on the behavior of injurers (and, more generally, other factors as well). What the plaintiff does consider as the benefit from suit is the gain he would obtain from prevailing. This private gain is not a social benefit but, instead, a transfer from the defendant. It could be either larger or smaller than the social benefit.

To clarify these points, let's consider for concreteness the setting studied in the discussion of torts, in which injurers can exercise care to lower the risk of accidents. Let's suppose that the social welfare goal is to minimize total social costs, comprised of the costs of precautions, the losses due to accidents that occur, and also the costs of suit and litigation. Thus, the socially optimal amount of suit is that which minimizes total social costs. We want to show that the amount of suit that private parties find it in their interest to bring could be above or below the socially optimal amount. An example of each possibility follows.

To illustrate that socially excessive suit may arise, let's suppose that the loss a victim would suffer in an accident is $10,000, that a victim's cost of bringing suit is $3,000 and an injurer's cost of defending is $2,000, that the probability of accidents is 10%, and that there is no precaution that injurers can take to lower accident risk.

A victim will bring suit whenever an accident occurs, for suing will cost a victim only $3,000 and yield him $10,000. From the social perspective, this outcome is undesirable. Suit creates no beneficial deterrent, as injurers cannot do anything to lower risk. Yet suit does generate legal costs: the expected legal cost is $500 — that is, 10% × ($3,000 + $2,000) = $500. The bringing of suit is not socially desirable in this example because there are no incentives toward safety created by the prospect of suit. This fact is of no moment to a victim, nor is the injurer's litigation cost. A victim brings suit for his private gain of $10,000.

In this example, there was no deterrent benefit whatever from the bringing of suit, but it should be obvious that the point of the example would hold if the deterrent benefit were positive but not very large.

Let's now consider the opposite possibility, that suit will not be brought even though it would be best that it be brought.

Suppose here that the loss a victim suffers in an accident is $1,000 and that an expenditure of $10 by an injurer will reduce the probability of an accident from 10% to 1%. The costs of suit and defending against suit are as in the previous example.

In this case, victims will not bring suit, as doing so will cost them $3,000 but yield them only $1,000. Hence, injurers will have no reason to take care to reduce risk, and the total social cost will be $100 (i.e., 10% × $1,000 = $100).

It would be desirable for a victim to bring suit, however. If he did, the injurer would be led to spend $10 to lower risk to 1%, and the total social cost would be only $70 — that is, $10 + 1% × ($1,000 + $5,000) = $70. The bringing of suit is socially worthwhile because of the significant reduction in accident losses that would result. Observe that this is true even though the total legal cost of $5,000 exceeds the victim's loss of $1,000. This is because the high cost of suit would only rarely be incurred as a result of the deterrent effect of the prospect of suit. But the victim does not take the deterrence-related benefits of suit into account. The victim looks only to his own gain from suit, which is small.

Here, as emphasized, a victim does not bring suit because his private gain from suit — the harm he has sustained — is not sufficient to outweigh his cost, even though the general deterrent that would be engendered by the bringing of suit would so reduce accident loss that the bringing of suit would be socially worthwhile.

Optional material

Negligence rule and the private versus the socially optimal amount of suit. In a perfectly working negligence system, a harmful outcome that is not the result of negligence would never result in suit — because the victim would know he would lose against a nonnegligent injurer. This implies that it would be desirable for the state to subsidize suits, for then victims would always be willing to bring suit and thus injurers would be led by this threat to take due care. Because no suits would actually result, no litigation costs would, in fact, be incurred by society. Of course, the negligence system does not operate perfectly in practice. Victims sometimes bring suit against nonnegligent injurers, and injurers sometimes act negligently. Thus, problems of excessive suit may well exist under the negligence rule, but it is plausible that they are not as serious as they are under strict liability.

We now mention a number of issues that bear on the foregoing discussion and its interpretation.

a. Practical importance of the divergence. The difference between private and social costs of suit is often large, at least in percentage terms. As emphasized, the private cost divergence is that victims do not take into account injurers' and the state's litigation costs. Thus, it is not unreasonable to expect that victims may fail to take into account half or more of total litigation costs.

The difference between the private and the social benefits of suit can also be substantial. First, many harms are large and give the victim significant incentives to sue, yet deterrence effects may be relatively small for a variety of reasons. To illustrate, let's consider automobile accident litigation. We know that harms from automobile accidents are sufficient to generate a tremendous volume of suit: it is estimated that they comprise about 50% of all tort litigation. However, intuition suggests that

Box 7-10
The Lesson from New Zealand

In the mid-1970s New Zealand undertook a bold experiment: it eliminated the right to sue for all personal injuries, including those resulting from automobile accidents. In this way, New Zealand eliminated a lot of legal expenses. Yet the accident rate did not measurably increase. (Compensation is still accomplished through private and social insurance.) We can interpret this New Zealand policy as solving the problem that the private incentive to use the legal system exceeded the social reason to use it.

liability-related deterrence of these accidents may be modest. Individuals have good reasons, apart from wanting to avoid liability, not to cause automobile accidents: they may be injured themselves, and they face fines for traffic violations and serious criminal penalties for grossly irresponsible behavior, such as drunkenness. Given that these incentives toward avoidance of automobile accidents exist and given that the deterrent due to liability is dulled by ownership of liability insurance, one wonders how much the threat of tort liability adds to deterrence.

The opposite possibility — that the volume of suit is socially inadequate — is also of practical significance. Recall the earlier example in which an individual's losses are relatively low, so suit would not be brought, but in which the frequency of harmful events can be fairly cheaply reduced. This example seems to be of relevance. One can readily imagine situations in which firms know that the harms that they cause will not be of sufficient importance to be worth a typical victim's while to pursue, even though the incidence of the harms can be decreased substantially by modest expenditures. (Consider, for example, low-level pollution damage, such as more frequent peeling of paint in a neighborhood near a factory, which the factory could eliminate by installing inexpensive smoke scrubbers.) One can also envision situations in which, even though the magnitude of harm might be high, the expected value of suit is still low because of difficulty in proving causation. (Suppose, for instance, that the pollution from the factory can produce cancer but that this connection is hard to demonstrate.) If, once causation were established, many other suits could easily be brought, then it might be socially valuable for suit to be filed in the case at hand even though this would not be advantageous to the plaintiff.

Optional material

> **Cost of suit leads to inadequate precautions.** An issue that we have not yet discussed is that, even if injurers are always sued, their level of precautions will tend to be inadequate, given the costs of suit. The damages that injurers will have to pay equal the direct harm they cause their victims, but the full social costs of an accident include also the litigation costs associated with suit: The full costs that society incurs when harm leads to suit is not only the direct harm but also the resources absorbed in the litigation process. Thus, for injurers' incentives to take precautions to be correct, injurers should bear, in addition to the direct harm caused to victims, the litigation costs borne by victims and by the state (injurers bear their own litigation costs already). If, for example, the harm is $10,000 and the litigation costs of the victim and the state are $3,000 and $1,000, respectively, the injurer should pay $14,000, not $10,000. This point is not insignificant, because the litigation costs of victims and courts are substantial as a percentage of actual losses.

3. Corrective policy. It should be straightforward in principle for the state to remedy an imbalance between the privately determined and the socially best level of litigation. If there is excessive litigation, the state can discourage it by imposing a properly chosen fee for bringing suit or by some other device to make suit more expensive. The state could also refuse to allow unwanted categories of suit to be brought. If there is inadequate litigation, the state can subsidize or otherwise encourage suit.

However, the state requires a great deal of information to be able to assess the socially correct volume of suit. To determine whether suit is socially desirable, the state must ascertain not only the costs of litigation for both sides but also the deterrent effect of the prospect of suit. This

means that the state needs to deduce the nature and the cost of the opportunities for preventing harm.

Optional material

It should be noted that, by contrast, for the state to ameliorate
the problem of inadequate precautions, a corrective policy that
will be helpful is easily identified and should not be difficult to
implement. Namely, when suit is brought, the defendant should
have to pay more than the harm done. As explained above, he
should also have to pay the victim's and the state's litigation
costs, for only then will he be bearing the full social cost associated with harm.

B. Settlement versus Trial

Assuming that suit has been brought, we now take up the question of
whether parties will reach a settlement or go to trial. A settlement is a
legally enforceable agreement, usually involving a payment from the
defendant to the plaintiff, in which the plaintiff agrees not to pursue his
claim further. If the parties do not reach a settlement, we assume that
they go to trial — that is, that the court determines the outcome of their
case. We discuss here two different scenarios describing whether settlement occurs and then consider the socially optimal versus the private
decision whether to settle.

1. Simple scenario. Let's assume for simplicity that the plaintiff and
the defendant each has somehow formed beliefs — which may differ —
about the trial outcome. Then we can discuss settlement possibilities in
terms of two quantities. Consider first the minimum amount that the
plaintiff would accept in settlement, his so-called reservation amount.
Assuming that the plaintiff is risk neutral, this reservation amount equals
his expected gain from trial minus the cost of going to trial. For instance,
if the plaintiff believes that he will prevail with a probability of 70% and
would then obtain $100,000 and if the trial would cost him $20,000, the
minimum he would accept in settlement is $50,000 (i.e., 70% × $100,000 −
$20,000 = $50,000). If he were offered anything less than this amount, he
would be better off going to trial.

The other quantity is the defendant's reservation amount, the maximum amount that the defendant would be willing to pay in settlement.

Box 7-11
The Priest-Klein Insight

Two law and economics professors, George Priest and Ben Klein, wrote an article emphasizing the point that the cases that go to trial are *not* representative of the population of disputes, most of which settle. The cases that wind up going to trial tend to be ones in which there is real uncertainty, either about who is going to win or about the amount of damages. (Why?) If it's pretty clear what's going to happen, a case is very likely to settle. Thus, for instance, we might see that the cases in some area of dispute that go to trial are won about 50% of the time by each side — since it's the unclear cases that wind up in trial — even though most disputes would be won by plaintiffs, but they generally settle.

This is his expected loss from trial plus his cost of going to trial. If the defendant believes that the odds of the plaintiff's winning are, say, only 50% and if the defendant's trial costs would be $25,000, then he would pay at most $75,000 in settlement (i.e., 50% × $100,000 + $25,000 = $75,000).

It is evident that if the plaintiff's reservation amount is less than the defendant's reservation amount, a mutually beneficial settlement is possible: a settlement equal to any amount in between these two figures would be preferable to a trial for each party. Thus, if the plaintiff's minimum acceptable amount is $50,000 and the defendant's reservation amount is $75,000, any amount in between, such as $60,000, would be preferred by each to going to trial.

However, if the plaintiff's reservation amount exceeds the most that the defendant will pay, settlement cannot occur. Suppose, for instance, that the defendant thought the plaintiff's chances of winning were only 20%. Then the defendant's maximum amount would be $45,000 (i.e., $20,000 + $25,000 = $45,000). Thus, the most he would pay is less than the minimum $50,000 that the plaintiff would be willing to accept, and settlement could not occur.

Can more be said about when a mutually beneficial settlement will and will not exist? That is, under what conditions will the plaintiff's minimum acceptable demand be less than the defendant's maximum acceptable payment? It is clear that, if the plaintiff and the defendant have the same beliefs about the trial outcome, there should always exist a mutually beneficial settlement, because they can escape trial costs by settling. Suppose that they both believe that $50,000 is the expected judgment the defendant will have to pay at trial. Then any trial costs that the plaintiff would bear would lead to his willingness to accept a figure lower than $50,000. If, for instance, his trial costs would be $10,000, he would accept $40,000 rather than at least $50,000. Conversely, any trial costs the defendant would have to bear would increase above $50,000 the amount he would be willing to pay. If his trial costs would be $10,000, he would be willing to pay at least $60,000 rather than at least $50,000. Thus, the settlement range would be from $40,000 to $60,000. For the possibility of settlement to be eliminated, the plaintiff's reservation amount must rise from $40,000 and/or the defendant's reservation amount must fall from $60,000, such that the plaintiff's reservation amount turns out to exceed the defendant's reservation amount. This can occur only if they have different beliefs about the trial outcome. This line of thought suggests the following conclusion: a mutually beneficial settlement amount exists as long as the plaintiff's and defendant's estimates of the expected judgment do not diverge too much. Indeed, it can be shown that *a mutually beneficial settlement exists as long as the plaintiff's estimate of the expected judgment does not exceed the defendant's estimate by more than the sum of their costs of trial.*[3] Let's illustrate.

Example 7-6

Consider the situation from above in which the plaintiff's expected gain from suit is $70,000 (i.e., 70% × $100,000 = $70,000), his costs of trial are $20,000, the defendant's expected

---

3. *Optional material:* It may be helpful to express this algebraically. Let A be the judgment amount, P_p the plaintiff's estimate of the probability of winning, P_d the defendant's estimate of the probability of winning, C_p the plaintiff's litigation costs, and C_d the defendant's litigation costs. The plaintiff's reservation amount is $P_p A - C_p$, and the defendant's reservation amount is $P_d A + C_d$. There will be a settlement as long as $P_p A - C_p \le P_d A + C_d$, which is equivalent to $P_p A - P_d A \le C_p + C_d$.

loss is $50,000 (i.e., 50% × $100,000 = $50,000), and his trial costs are $25,000. Here, we observed that mutually beneficial settlements exist, for the plaintiff would accept as little as $50,000 and the defendant would pay as much as $75,000. Notice that it is also true that the difference between the plaintiff's view of the expected judgment and defendant's estimate of the expected judgment is $20,000 (i.e., $70,000 – $50,000 = $20,000) and that this is less than the sum of their costs of trial, $45,000 (i.e., $20,000 + $25,000 = $45,000). This is consistent with the italicized statement in the preceding paragraph. Moreover, we observed that, if the defendant's estimate of the expected judgment is $20,000, he would pay only $45,000 and thus that no settlement exists. In this case, notice that the difference between the plaintiff's and defendant's estimates of the expected judgment is $50,000 (i.e., $70,000 – $20,000 = $50,000), which exceeds the $45,000 sum in litigation costs, so the nonexistence of a settlement amount is again consistent with the italicized statement.

A number of comments may be made to help us interpret and understand the discussion and conclusions reached in the simple scenario.

a. Does existence of a mutually beneficial settlement amount imply that settlement will occur? Although we know that there cannot be a settlement when a mutually beneficial settlement amount *does not* exist, what can be said about the outcome when a mutually beneficial settlement amount *does* exist? The answer is that there may or may not be a settlement, depending on the nature of bargaining between the parties and the information they have about each other. This will be discussed below.

b. Parties' beliefs. From the above discussion, it is evident that what leads to trial is not that a plaintiff is confident of winning but that he is *more* confident of winning than the defendant thinks he has a right to be. A plaintiff's belief that he is very likely to win does not itself suggest that trial will occur, as might naively be thought. If the plaintiff is likely to win, it is true that he will ask for more in settlement from the defendant than he would otherwise. But it is also true that, if the defendant agrees that the plaintiff is likely to win, the defendant will be willing to pay more in settlement. What makes for trial is a refusal of the defendant to pay what the plaintiff demands, and this will be the case when the defendant does not believe the plaintiff's demand is warranted.

What would we expect the parties' beliefs about the likelihood of trial outcomes to be? The parties may, and often will, be in possession of different information about a case when it begins. However, the parties may elect to share information, or they may be forced to do so through the discovery process. And parties often can independently acquire information that the other side possesses. To the degree that the parties do come to similar beliefs, settlement increases in likelihood.

c. Risk aversion. The possibility that parties are risk averse leads to a greater tendency toward settlement. The reason is that a trial is a risky venture because its outcome is unknown. This means that settlement is more attractive to a risk-averse party than to a risk-neutral party. Further, as the degree of risk aversion of either party increases or as the risk increases (e.g., as the size of the judgment or the size of legal fees increases), settlement should become more likely, other things being equal.

2. Scenario with explicit bargaining. The foregoing scenario that we have discussed was simple in two important respects, among others. First, the bargaining process was not explicit. Although the range of possible settlements was determined, whether a bargain in the range would be reached, and where so, was not predicted. Second, the origin of differences in beliefs was not explained. It was assumed that the parties somehow come to their beliefs. More sophisticated accounts of settlement versus trial attempt to remedy these gaps and thus to provide additional insight into the settlement process (but achieve less than might at first appear).

Optional material

An important version of such accounts is that in which bargaining consists of a single offer and that offer is made by a party, given lack of knowledge about the opposing side. For concreteness, assume that the plaintiff makes a single offer to the defendant but does not know the probability of defendant liability, whereas the defendant does know this (because, say, he has private information about his level of care). In this situation, we can determine the rational offer for the plaintiff to make and then whether or not it will be accepted. This is illustrated as follows.

Example 7-7

If the plaintiff prevails, he will obtain a judgment of $100,000; his legal costs will be $10,000. There are three, equally numerous types of defendants: those who would lose with a probability of 60%, those who would lose with a probability of 50%, and those who would lose with a probability of only 20%. The plaintiff cannot tell these types of defendants apart. The expected gain from trial for a plaintiff depends on which type of defendant the plaintiff in fact faces: if the likelihood of success is 60%, the plaintiff's net expected gain from trial would be $50,000; if the likelihood of success is 50%, the plaintiff's net expected gain would be $40,000; and if the likelihood of success is 20%, the plaintiff's net expected gain would be $10,000. If the legal costs for a defendant would be $10,000, the plaintiff could demand and obtain as much as $70,000 from the first kind of defendant, $60,000 from the second type, and $30,000 from the third. It follows that the plaintiff's rational settlement demand is $60,000: if he demands $60,000, his demand will be accepted two-thirds of the time (by the first and second types of defendants) and he will go to trial one-third of the time, so his expected gain would be $43,333 (i.e., 2/3 × $60,000 + 1/3 × $10,000). In contrast, if the plaintiff asks for only $30,000, although his offer would always be accepted, his gain would be only $30,000; and if he asks for $70,000, he would obtain this only one-third of the time, so his expected gain would be only $40,000. A consequence of $60,000 being the rational offer for the plaintiff to make is that, in the cases where the defendant would lose with only a 20% chance, the defendant will spurn the offer and there will be a trial.

Note that, in this example and in general, the rational offer for the plaintiff to make may be such that there will be a chance of trial. In essence, the rational offer for the plaintiff to make may not be so low as to produce a yes answer from any and all possible types of defendants. To ask for so little is usually not in the interest of the plaintiff. This feature of the outcome — that trial may result — may be considered to be due to asymmetry of information: if the plaintiff knew the type of defendant he faced, he would ask for a different amount from each type — namely, the maximum that the defendant would be willing to pay rather than go to trial. It is, therefore, the asymmetry of information that leads the rational plaintiff to ask for more than some defendants are willing to pay, and thus to the possibility of trial.

3. Actual frequency of settlement. In fact, the vast majority of cases settle. Recent data on state courts show that, in fiscal year 1992, more than 96% of civil cases did not go to trial (Ostrom and Kauder, 1996). Similarly, recent data on federal courts demonstrate that, for fiscal year 1995, almost 97% of federal civil cases were resolved without trial (Administrative Office, 1995). These figures may, however, overstate or understate the true rate: because cases that are not tried may have been dismissed by a court, 96% is the settlement rate plus the dismissal rate, not the settlement rate. Yet, because many disputes are settled before any complaint is filed, 96% may understate the settlement rate. In any event, the vast majority of cases do settle.

That cases tend to settle does not mean that they settle without legal expenses having been borne. Settlement may occur only after a considerable amount has been spent gathering information and preparing for trial.

4. Private versus socially desirable settlement. The private and the social incentives to settle may diverge for a number of reasons related to those explaining the difference between the private and the social incentives to sue.

Notably, the parties may have a socially insufficient motive to settle, because they do not take all of society's trial costs into account. Because the parties involved in litigation do not bear all the costs of a trial — such as the salaries of judges and ancillary personnel, the forgone value of juror time, the implicit rent on court buildings — the parties save less by settling than society does.

Optional material

A second reason that the private incentive to settle may be socially inadequate concerns asymmetric information. As discussed, asymmetric information leads parties to fail to settle because they may misgauge each other's situation. That the parties may misgauge each other's situation, however, does not constitute any obvious justification for social resources to be expended on a trial proceeding.

A third factor suggesting that private incentives to settle may diverge from social incentives is that settlement may affect deterrence (can you say why?). The parties themselves would usually not be thought to consider deterrence as an important factor in settlement versus trial. For them, the event has occurred, and it would be irrational to give deterrence of others any weight.

5. Legal policy. Legal policy bearing on settlement versus trial appears generally to foster settlement. This is accomplished by allowing parties to engage in discovery, sometimes requiring them to participate in nonbinding arbitration prior to trial, to hold settlement conferences, and so forth. The justification that one usually sees offered for the promotion of settlement is that it clears court dockets and saves public and private expense. This justification comports with economic analysis in the obvious sense that the parties do not consider the court's time and other public costs associated with trial as a saving from settlement. The possibility that trial ought to be held despite the parties' wishes to settle receives relatively little attention. One wonders, for example, about the wisdom of promoting settlement — let alone allowing it — in situations where deterrence is likely to be compromised because the identity and/or important aspects of the defendants' conduct do not become public knowledge.

C. Trial

For a variety of reasons, expenditures will tend to increase a litigant's chances of prevailing at trial or will influence beneficially the magnitude or character of the judgment. A party will generally make a litigation expenditure as long as it costs less than the expected benefit it yields. To assess the expected benefit from a particular step, a party will often have to consider not only the court's reaction to it but also the other litigant's reaction to it.

1. Private versus socially desirable litigation expenditures. There are several sources of divergence between social and private incentives to spend during litigation. First, litigants may spend in ways that largely offset each other and thus have little social value. A classic instance is where both parties devote effort to legal arguments of roughly equivalent weight but supportive of opposite claims, and another is where both hire experts who produce equally convincing reports favoring opposite assertions.

Second, expenditures that are not offsetting may mislead the court rather than enhance the accuracy of outcomes. For example, a guilty defendant may be able to escape liability for harm for which he was responsible. This possibility dilutes deterrence. Legal expenditures resulting in such outcomes have negative social value even though they have positive private value.

Third, expenditures that are not offsetting and that do not mislead courts may not be socially optimal in magnitude. By analogy to what was stressed about the bringing of suits, the parties decide on their expenditures based on how they influence the litigation outcome, without regard to the influence (if any) on incentives to reduce harm. This could lead to expenditures that are too great or too small relative to what is socially correct.

2. Legal policy. Several means of controlling litigation expenditures exist, given the basic form of legal rules and legal procedure. Expenditures can be discouraged through monetary disincentives. They can also be regulated through constraints on the time parties are given to prepare for trial, restrictions on discovery, limits on the length of permitted submissions and the number of testifying experts, and so forth. In fact, controls on expenditures seem to be made largely through such forms of regulation of the pretrial and trial processes rather than through financial inducements.

In addition, litigation expenditures could be controlled through major changes in substantive legal rules. A notable example of a change in a legal rule would be one that stated that damages should be based on a table rather than on presentations of evidence (which are often elaborate).

Finally, litigation expenditures can be controlled through substantial changes in legal procedure. A possibility that would be desirable in some circumstances would be for certain types of evidence to be produced, not by the parties, but by court-appointed experts. Especially where private knowledge of the parties is not needed to develop the evidence, court direction of the acquisition of information might be more beneficial than acquisition of information by the parties, which might both mislead courts and result in duplication of effort.

6. Public Law Enforcement and Criminal Law

We consider here public enforcement of law: the use of inspectors, tax auditors, police, prosecutors, and other enforcement agents to detect and to sanction violators of legal rules. Of course, private parties also play an important role in law enforcement, by providing information to public authorities and also by initiating their own legal actions (notably, tort suits). But to maintain focus, we restrict attention here to public enforcement activity. We also briefly discuss aspects of criminal law in the light of the theory of public law enforcement.

A. Basic Framework

Let's assume the following: an individual (or a firm) chooses whether to commit a harmful act; if he commits the act, he obtains some gain and also faces the risk of being caught, found liable, and sanctioned. The rule of liability could be either strict — under which the individual is definitely sanctioned for the harmful act — or fault based — under which he is sanctioned only if his behavior was judged undesirable. (As we know, not all harmful acts are undesirable, because they may result in greater benefits.) The sanction that he suffers could be a monetary fine or an imprisonment term.   *whether to harm*

Whether an individual decides to commit a harmful act is assumed to be determined by a calculation. He will commit the act if doing so would raise his expected position, taking into account the gain he would derive and the probability, form, and level of sanction that he would then face.   *cost to public*

We will suppose for simplicity that fines are socially costless to employ because they are mere transfers of money, whereas imprisonment involves positive social costs because of the expense associated with the operation of prisons and the disutility due to imprisonment.   *reg. choice*

The enforcement authority's problem is to maximize social welfare by choosing the probability of detection, the level of sanctions, the form of sanctions, and the rule of liability.

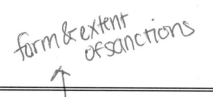
B. Enforcement Given the Probability of Detection

We consider here optimal law enforcement, assuming that the probability of detection is fixed. Thus, we ask about the optimal form and level of sanctions under strict and fault-based liability and about how the two liability rules compare.

1. Strict liability. Assume initially that fines are the form of sanction and that individuals are risk neutral. The fine must be inflated when there is only a probability of having to pay it; otherwise, deterrence will be too low. Appropriate deterrence requires that the fine be inflated enough so that the expected fine equals the harm (for then a person will commit an act only when the gain exceeds the harm, will fail to take a precaution only when its cost exceeds the harm, and so forth). To illustrate, suppose that a person pays a fine for causing harm only half the time he does so and that the harm is $1,000. For the expected fine to equal the harm of $1,000, the fine that is paid when the person is caught must be $2,000, for the expected fine is then $1,000 (i.e., 0.5 × $2,000 = $1,000). Likewise, if the person is caught and has to pay a fine only one-third of the time, the fine that he must pay when caught must be $3,000 in order

---

Box 7-12
The Probability Multiplier

The idea that you need to multiply the penalty to accomplish proper deterrence when there's a chance of escaping detection is of ancient vintage. The Bible, and indeed prebiblical codes, sometimes prescribed higher penalties when the probability of escaping detection was high — for instance, for stealing at night. This multiplier policy sometimes conflicts with intuition, though. What does it imply about the optimal penalty for a flagrant, intentional act, such as purposely harming property in full view of witnesses, as opposed to an act like accidentally harming property when no one happens to be around? Nevertheless, the idea of the probability multiplier is being increasingly applied in the enforcement arena.

for the expected fine to equal the harm. More generally, the formula for the appropriate fine is the harm (H) multiplied by the reciprocal of the probability of sanctions (P):

$$\text{appropriate fine} = H \times (1/P).$$

[handwritten annotation: ↗ harm ; ↗ probability of sanctions]

It should be observed that this recipe for the optimal fine means that if the probability is very low, the fine will be very high. For instance, if the probability of a fine for the harm of $1,000 is only 0.01 (i.e., 1%), the optimal fine is $100,000. If a person does not have the wealth to pay such a fine, then it is unworkable, and deterrence will be too low.

Optional material

> If individuals are risk averse with regard to fines, the optimal fine will tend to be lower than in the risk-neutral case for two reasons. First, this reduces the bearing of risk by individuals who commit the harmful act. Second, because risk-averse individuals are more easily deterred than risk-neutral individuals, the fine does not need to be as high as before to achieve any desired degree of deterrence.

Next assume that imprisonment is the form of sanction. Then the optimal sanction will also be an inflated one, reflecting the probability of sanctions. Of particular note as well is that strict liability is a very costly liability rule, for whenever a party causes harm and suffers imprisonment, social costs are incurred.

2. Fault-based liability. Assume again that fines are the form of sanction but that liability is fault based. Then the same formula as for the optimal fine under strict liability — namely, H × (1/P), the harm multiplied by the reciprocal of the probability of detection — will tend to lead to compliance with the fault standard. That is, it can be shown that, if a person bears an expected fine of the harm H for undesirable behavior, he will not engage in such behavior.

If imprisonment is the form of sanction and the magnitude of the sanction is inflated properly, undesirable acts will be deterred. If deterrence occurs, then sanctions are not actually imposed. Notably, if a person takes necessary and desirable steps to avoid doing harm and harm still occurs, the person will be exonerated and not suffer sanctions. Thus, even though the sanction of imprisonment is costly to impose, social costs will not actually be incurred where sanctions are high enough to deter undesirable behavior.

3. Comparison of liability rules. When sanctions are monetary and costless to impose, both strict liability and fault-based liability may deter, and without social cost. However, fault-based liability requires a determination of fault. When the sanction is imprisonment and thus is socially costly, fault-based liability has a fundamental advantage over strict liability. This is because, when a person is deterred from an undesirable act under fault-based liability, the costs of imposing imprisonment are not incurred when harm occurs. But the costs of imposing imprisonment are incurred when harm occurs under strict liability.

C. Enforcement When the Probability of Detection Is Variable

We now consider the optimal system of enforcement when the state decides on the probability of detection by choosing a level of enforcement effort. (Because the points of importance here do not depend much on the liability rule, we will, for simplicity, assume that the rule is strict.)

An important point is that there is a basic social advantage in employing a low-probability-, high-magnitude-of-sanction enforcement policy. The state can lower its enforcement costs if the probability of sanctions is low. To avoid dilution of deterrence from low sanctions, however, the magnitude of sanctions has to be raised. For example, if the state wants to control pollution violations in a river, it can conserve enforcement costs by inspecting for pollution on a random basis using only a small force of enforcement agents rather than monitoring very often, which would require a large corps of agents. But if inspection occurs with only a low probability, then the magnitude of the fine for polluters who are caught has to be raised significantly above harm — to $H \times (1/P)$, if that is possible — in order to maintain appropriate deterrence.

Optional material

> A curious theoretical point is that, if individuals are risk neutral, it is best for the state to lower the probability and raise the fine to the point that the fine equals a person's entire wealth. The basic explanation for this conclusion is that, if the fine were not

maximal, society could save enforcement costs by simultaneously raising the fine and lowering the probability without affecting the level of deterrence. Suppose, for example, that the fine initially is $5,000, that a person's wealth is $10,000, and that the probability of sanctions is 0.20. Then double the fine to $10,000, and halve enforcement effort; the probability of sanctions is now 0.10. Although the expected fine is unchanged (i.e., 0.20 × $5,000 = 0.10 × $10,000 = $1,000), enforcement expenditures are reduced. Thus, society is better off. For reasons that we cannot explain here, this extreme result that sanctions should be maximal does not hold if individuals are risk averse or under many other variations of assumption. But the extreme result dramatically illustrates the force of the point that there is a social advantage in employing a low-probability-, high-magnitude-of-sanction enforcement policy.

Another point worth noting is that, under fairly general circumstances, it is not advantageous for society to spend enough on enforcement effort to achieve perfect deterrence or even a very high level of deterrence. It will usually be best for society to countenance some degree — and perhaps a great deal — of underdeterrence in order to save enforcement expenses.

It follows from what we just said that *a person's willingness to commit an act that is sanctioned does not mean that the person's act is socially desirable.* It

---

Box 7-13
Nonmonetary Sanctions Other Than Imprisonment

We have not discussed nonmonetary sanctions apart from imprisonment, but they are of potential use. For example, electronic monitoring may be much less expensive to administer than imprisonment, and exposure to public humiliation (e.g., through publication of the names of individuals who have not paid their taxes) is an inexpensive sanction. As a general rule, forms of sanctions should be selected in the order of their effectiveness per dollar of social cost.

may well be that the act is undesirable and is undertaken only because the probability of sanctions and their level are not sufficient to deter. If a firm decides to pollute, it may well be that the pollution is socially undesirable (because its cost exceeds the expense of prevention) and the pollution occurs only because the probability of sanctions and their magnitude are insufficient to deter the firm. If a person commits a crime, it may be true — indeed, it almost always is true — that the act is socially undesirable and is committed only because the probability and magnitude of sanctions are insufficient to deter. Thus, the situation stands in contrast to one where a person pays a price for a good in a market. In this context, a person's purchase is interpreted as socially desirable, for it indicates that the person values the good more than its cost of production, because the person must pay the price with certainty and the price is at least equal to the cost of production. When a person violates the law and bears sanctions only with a probability, the expected sanction may well be lower than the social harm in which his act results, so his willingness to commit the act that violates the law does not imply that the benefit obtained exceeds the social harm.

D. Monetary Sanctions versus Imprisonment

Now consider the question of the form of sanctions that should be imposed. When is it best to employ monetary sanctions and when imprisonment? The gist of the answer is this: if adequate deterrence can be achieved against some harmful act by use of monetary sanctions alone, then only those sanctions should be utilized. It would be socially wasteful to substitute imprisonment for monetary sanctions, for imprisonment is a socially more expensive form of sanction. Hence, imprisonment should be employed only if the maximum monetary sanction has already been imposed and the achievement of greater deterrence is worth the cost of use of imprisonment.

E. Incapacitation

Our discussion of public enforcement has assumed that the threat of sanctions reduces harm by discouraging individuals from causing harm — that is, by deterring them. However, an entirely different way for society to reduce harm is by imposing sanctions that remove parties from positions in which they are able to cause harm — that is, by incapacitating them. Imprisonment is the primary incapacitative sanction, and we will continue to restrict attention to it. (Other examples of incapacitative sanctions exist. For instance, individuals can lose their drivers licenses, preventing them from doing harm while driving; businesses can lose their right to operate in certain domains; and so forth.)

To better understand the role of public enforcement when sanctions are incapacitative, suppose that the sole function of prison is to incapacitate — in other words, that imprisonment does not deter. Then it will be socially best to put a person in jail and to keep him there if — but only if — the expected harm he would cause if he was not in jail exceeds the cost of jail.

A point of interest is that, in principle, the incapacitative rationale might lead society to imprison a person just because it is concluded that he is dangerous — which is to say, even if he has not committed a bad act. This would be true if there were some means to predict accurately a person's dangerousness independently of his actual behavior. In practice, however, that a person has committed a harmful act may be the best basis for predicting his future behavior.

F. Criminal Law

The subject of criminal law may be viewed in the light of the theory of public law enforcement. In particular, that the acts in the core area of crime — robbery, murder, rape, and so forth — are punished by the sanction of imprisonment makes basic sense. Were society to rely on monetary penalties alone in relation to these acts, deterrence would be grossly inadequate. Notably, the probability of sanctions for many of these acts is small, making the monetary sanction necessary for even tolerably good deterrence very large. But the assets of many individuals who might commit criminal acts is quite low. Hence, the threat of imprisonment is needed for deterrence. Moreover, the incapacitative aspect of imprisonment is valuable because of difficulties in deterring many of the individuals who are prone to commit criminal acts.

When we turn to examine important doctrines of criminal law, it appears that they often seem justifiable from the standpoint of rational enforcement policy. A bedrock feature of criminal law is that punishment is not based on a strict liability for doing harm but, rather, is premised on a finding that a person's act was undesirable. For example, punishment is imposed, not for just any act that results in a death, but for only a certain class of such acts, notably for murder. This faultlike aspect of criminal law comports with rational enforcement policy. As we have stressed, when the socially costly sanction of imprisonment is employed, the fault system is desirable because it results in less frequent imposition of punishment than is true under strict liability.

The focus on intent in criminal law, another of its important elements, is also consonant in at least a rough way with rational enforcement policy. Those who intend harm may be harder to deter than those who do not intend harm, because those who intend harm generally obtain higher benefits from their acts (e.g., a person who murders generally does so for a strong reason and is thus harder to deter than a person who kills by accident). Those who intend harm also often are more likely to hide their acts (because the acts are frequently planned) than those who do not intend harm. Thus, deterrence of those who intend harm requires higher sanctions than deterrence of those who do not intend harm. Moreover, those who intend harm usually do more harm than those who act without intent, so intended acts are more important to deter and thus more worth the while of society bearing the costs of sanctions to deter. It also may be the case that those who intend harm mark themselves as having a character and disposition to commit similar acts in the future. If so, they may be worthwhile imprisoning on the incapacitative rationale.

Another hallmark of criminal law is the punishment of acts that do not do harm but have the potential of doing harm — namely, the punishment of attempts. That attempts are punished is an implicit way of raising the likelihood of sanctions for undesirable acts. Given the inability of society to deter adequately acts falling into the category of crime because of the expense of law enforcement, it makes sense for society to avail itself of the opportunity to impose sanctions when it learns that bad acts have been committed, even if, by luck, the acts turn out not to cause harm in the instance.

We have just emphasized the congruence between aspects of criminal law and enforcement in reality, and the theory of optimal law enforcement. However, there is also much about criminal law that is in tension with the theory of optimal law enforcement, or at least a relatively simple version of it. For example, the magnitude of sanctions for certain acts seems too low given the need to deter and the possibilities for accomplishing deterrence (could we not deter tax cheating by imposing sanctions higher than those we tend to use?), and the magnitude of sanctions for other acts seems too high given our relative inability to accomplish deterrence or useful incapacitation thereby.

We also note that we did not mention in our discussion of optimal law enforcement notions of appropriate punishment from the standpoint of moral desert. These notions influence criminal law in fact, and they would play a role in a more expansive, economically oriented analysis of criminal law. If individuals have a desire to punish to a particular extent, this should weigh in the determination of the best level of punishment, along with considerations of deterrence, incapacitation, and the costs of imposing punishment. We also did not mention the symbolic effects of punishment, that it may be said to reinforce valuable social norms. This influence, too, would enter into a broader economic treatment of criminal law.

7. Welfare Economics

A. Framework of Welfare Economics

We described the basic framework of welfare economics in Chapter 6, Microeconomics, and will not repeat it here. Recall, however, that we emphasized several points. First, the notion of the utility or well-being of a person is completely general and includes anything that a person cares about. Second, the concept of a measure of social welfare is built up from the utilities of individuals and is presumed not to depend on factors other than their utilities. Third, there is no single preferred or objective measure of social welfare. An analyst can examine any measure of social welfare and determine what social policy would follow from promoting the measure under consideration. Fourth, many measures of social welfare that are studied reflect a preference for distributional equity, that is, for equality of well-being among individuals, other things being equal. Fifth, distributional equity under any measure of social welfare is better pursued through our income tax (and welfare) system than through any other social policy. Let's amplify slightly on some of these points now.

B. Distributional Objectives Should Not Affect Legal Policy, Given Income Taxation

As just mentioned, distributional objectives are best pursued through the income tax system. The main reason is that the income tax can be employed in principle to meet distributional objectives, whereas using legal rules to satisfy distributional objectives may interfere with the other purposes of the rules. Suppose, for example, that the negligence rule is a cheaper form of liability in some domain than strict liability is — because, say, the negligence rule leads to a lower volume of litigation — but that the negligence rule leaves a poor group of individuals worse off than strict liability does, because they often will not collect under the negligence rule for harms suffered, but would under strict liability. If such effects on the income of the poor lowers social welfare on distributional grounds, this problem can be remedied by suitable changes in the income

---

Box 7-14
What If the Wrong People Control the Income Tax System?

Since the core economic argument against using the law to redistribute is that the income tax system can do that better, the question naturally arises, What if the wrong people — whoever you think they are — control the income tax system? Isn't there, then, an argument for redistributing through the law? The answer is, Not really. Suppose, for instance, that you want the poor to have more wealth, so you make it easier for them to bring suit and collect large judgments. But if the people in control of taxes don't want the poor to get more, presumably they can just raise taxes on the poor (or reduce credits that the poor enjoy) so as to counter the change you sought to effect.

tax (e.g., by lowering taxes imposed on the less well off or by giving them money). If the poor are helped instead by use of strict liability, then the volume of litigation is increased unnecessarily. It is better to help the poor directly, through use of the income tax system, than to do it by means of choice of strict liability when that choice is otherwise undesirable because of its effects on the volume of litigation.

The above argument is the central one for use of the income tax rather than legal rules to accomplish distributional objectives, but there are important supporting arguments that should also be mentioned. One is that legal rules often influence only a small subset of the population, so the rules cannot help very many individuals as compared with the income tax, which can help any large group of individuals. Another is that the groups that legal rules influence (such as the victims of accidents of some type) are typically heterogeneous in their wealth or need for money, so the choice of legal rules is a blunt instrument for accomplishing distributional objectives relative to the income tax. An additional argument is that the legal system is a very expensive way to accomplish distributional goals. Transferring funds to individuals via the legal system may cost about 100% of the funds transferred, as noted earlier, whereas the administrative costs of the tax system are less than 5%. Still another argument is that the choice of legal rules may be negated by price changes. If, for instance, the quality of a product is regulated in order to help those who buy it (say, the quality of housing for the poor is mandated to be higher than it would otherwise be), the price of housing will tend to rise as a consequence, so, in the end, the intended beneficiaries will be no better off.

All this implies that even though distributional objectives may be, and generally are felt to be, important in the measure of social welfare under consideration, they should not influence the choice of legal rules under broad assumptions.

C. Normative Analysis Based on Notions of Fairness (Apart from the Purely Distributional)

Normative analysis of legal rules that one encounters that is not economic in orientation may be — and generally tends to be — based in part on conceptions of fairness. For example, the justification for imposing tort liability may be based on the idea of corrective justice: when A wrongly harms B, A should make B whole. Or the justification for imposing a criminal sanction may be based on the retributive conception of correct punishment: the punishment of a wrongdoer should be in proportion to the gravity of his act. Such notions of fairness are many; some are fairly general (such as the ones just mentioned), and some are quite specific. They typically share the property, however, that they are not defined in terms of the well-being of individuals and are, in fact, not dependent on the consequences of their use. For instance, the idea that punishment should reflect the gravity of the act is not premised on how proportionality of punishment affects the well-being of any person or on whether it promotes deterrence or incapacitation.

Because the goal of satisfying notions of fairness is different from advancing the utilities of individuals, pursuit of the goal can lead to the reduction of individuals' well-being. For instance, individuals might be made better off if the sanction for some harmful act is very high because the act is hard to detect. Thus, it might be best if the penalty for tax evasion is relatively high in order to discourage evasion, given the low probability of its detection. However, if a notion of fair punishment for tax evasion constrains the penalty to be low, we may suffer as a result of inadequate tax collection. Thus, promoting a goal of fair punishment can lower the well-being of individuals.

Indeed, it can be shown that, in principle, the pursuit of any notion of the social good that is not based positively and exclusively on the well-being of individuals will, in some circumstances, make *everyone* worse off: all individuals will want policy A to be chosen over B, yet the notion of the social good will require B to be chosen. This result implies that a person who wants to respect the unanimous choices of individuals must, on grounds of consistency, reject any notion of the social good that does not depend positively and exclusively on the utilities of individuals.

D. Remarks

Several remarks about the foregoing conclusion will help to reconcile it with intuition and explain readers' probable resistance to it.

1. Notions of fairness as tastes. Individuals may have a preference for adhering to a notion of fairness. Individuals may want, for example, punishment to fit the crime and feel unhappy if that is not the case. To the extent that this is a taste of individuals, it would enter into their utilities and thus into the determination of social welfare under the framework of welfare economics. Notice, however, that this channel of influence of a conception of fairness on the choice of policy is very different from what is envisioned by philosophers and most proponents of the use of such notions. They suggest that the notions have normative weight *independently* of whether, or the extent to which, individuals in the population happen to have a taste for the satisfaction of the notions.

2. Functional role of notions of fairness. It is apparent that notions of fairness tend to have a functional role in the sense that they promote social welfare, conventionally conceived, in some average sense. For instance, punishing in proportion to the gravity of an act usually tends to lead to good outcomes, for worse acts are more important than others to discourage; corrective justice tends to promote deterrence and also accomplishes compensation of victims; and the keeping of promises promotes cooperative behavior.

These notions of fairness, which constitute our ideas of morality, thus involve great social advantages. Were people not to have moral notions instilled in them, it is apparent that society as we know it could not function. Thus, from the point of view of welfare economics, it is desirable that individuals believe in these notions of fairness and that social resources be employed to instill them. However, this does *not* imply that an analyst, in thinking about legal policy, should give a notion of fairness independent weight of its own.

8. Criticism of Economic Analysis of Law

The subject of economic analysis of law has been criticized for reasons already discussed concerning the distribution of income and fairness. There are additional reasons for criticism, and we comment on three of them here.

A. Inability to Predict Human Behavior and Irrationality

One species of complaint is that human behavior is very hard to predict, so economic models may not tell us what the effects of legal rules are. This point is doubtlessly true, but it cannot be taken as a criticism of economic analysis except to the degree that such analysis fails to use the best model of human behavior. If the assumptions about human behavior that are employed produce the best approximations of actual behavior but do not predict well in some circumstances, this is unfortunate, but what is the alternative? If we want to predict outcomes, we must, by definition, use the best predictor.

B. Indeterminacy of Recommendations

Economic analysis of law is often said to be indeterminate in its recommendations. Three sources of indeterminacy may be identified, and each, for different reasons, seems invalid as a criticism of economic analysis of law. First, we may be unable to predict the effects of a legal policy choice. The response to this point is that, although often true to this or that extent, it does not constitute a demerit of economic analysis per se. It would constitute a criticism only if there were better methods of prediction than those used by the economic analyst. Second, it is sometimes said that economic analysis is indeterminate because of its malleability — that the list of variables that an analyst can consider is long and up to the analyst to decide upon. It is true that many different variables could be considered by an analyst. But the choice of what to consider in an analysis should properly be regarded as governed by practicality and convenience, not as imparting any arbitrariness to analysis in principle. Third, it is often said that economic analysis is indeterminate because there is no objective method for weighing competing interests of individuals. It is correct that there is no objective method for balancing the interests of individuals. But there is still much that can be said about choice of policy given a measure of social welfare, and the criticism simply fails to recognize that.

C. Political Bias

Last, let's mention the criticism that economic analysis has a particular political orientation, that it is a conservative view, a view that endorses the status quo. An answer to this criticism is that one must separate the political views and the tilts asserted to be evident in the work of particular individuals who are influential in a field from a claim that the field itself has an intrinsic political orientation. It seems plain that economic analysis of law, being based on welfare economics, does not have any such orientation and, notably, is not associated with any view about the virtue of distributional equity in the social welfare measure.

9. Suggestions for Further Reading

Several general books that we recommend are Cooter and Ulen (2007) and Polinsky (2003), undergraduate textbooks covering the subject matter of this chapter, Posner (2007), a wide-ranging book on economic analysis of law, and Shavell (2004), a book on the subject matter of this chapter. Two books that focus on economic analysis of tort law are Landes and Posner (1987) and Shavell (1987). The following list includes works cited in the text as well as several others of possible interest to the reader.

Cesare Beccaria, *An Essay on Crimes and Punishments* (Albany, N.Y.: W. C. Little, 1872; originally published 1770).

Gary Becker, Crime and Punishment: An Economic Approach, 76 *Journal of Political Economy* 169–217 (1968).

Jeremy Bentham, An Introduction to the Principles of Morals and Legislation, in *The Utilitarians* (Garden City, N.Y.: Anchor Books, 1973; originally published 1789).

Guido Calabresi, *The Costs of Accidents* (New Haven: Yale University Press, 1970).

Ronald Coase, The Problem of Social Cost, 3 *Journal of Law and Economics* 1–44 (1960).

Robert Cooter and Thomas Ulen, *Law and Economics*, 5th ed. (Reading, Mass.: Addison-Wesley, 2007).

Louis Kaplow and Steven Shavell, Why the Legal System Is Less Efficient Than the Income Tax in Redistributing Income, 23 *Journal of Legal Studies* 667–681 (1994).

Louis Kaplow and Steven Shavell, Fairness versus Welfare, 114 *Harvard Law Review* 961–1388 (2001).

William Landes and Richard Posner, *The Economic Structure of Tort Law* (Cambridge, Mass.: Harvard University Press, 1987).

New Palgrave Dictionary of Economics and the Law, ed. Peter Newman (New York: Stockton Press, 1998).

A. Mitchell Polinsky, *An Introduction to Law and Economics*, 3rd ed. (New York: Aspen Publishers, 2003).

A. Mitchell Polinsky and Steven Shavell (eds.), *Handbook of Law and Economics* Vols. 1 and 2 (Amsterdam, The Netherlands: North Holland 2007).

Richard Posner, *Economic Analysis of Law* (Boston: Little, Brown, 1972).

Richard Posner, *Economic Analysis of Law,* 7th ed. (New York: Aspen Publishers, 2007).

Steven Shavell, *Economic Analysis of Accident Law* (Cambridge, Mass.: Harvard University Press, 1987).

Steven Shavell, Foundations of Economic Analysis of Law (Cambridge, Mass.: Harvard University Press, 2004).

8
Statistical Analysis

Statistics is the scientific study of methods for gathering, analyzing and utilizing numerical facts, i.e., data.[1] Students who major in natural or social scientific disciplines, engineering, or business, typically encounter statistics in a required course or courses presenting a version of statistics specifically designed for their particular discipline. These courses differ quite significantly from one field to another, both in content and in level of presentation, reflecting differing varieties of statistical practice within the different fields. While we cannot here aspire to reproduce in detail the content of all (or even any single one) of these courses, there is a core set of concepts, arguments and techniques that one would expect to find in all of them and that can be at least introduced in a chapter-length presentation such as the present one.

Unlike the typical statistics course, our focus here will not be on preparing you to perform research, but on teaching you enough about the various forms of statistical argumentation for you to become effective consumers and critics of research work done by others. As we shall see, statistical claims, though typically presented in courts as resulting from

---

1. The word *statistics* actually has three separate but related meanings. When used as the name of a discipline, as in *if you study statistics, you'll be a more effective lawyer*, it has the meaning given in the text. A second, often encountered, meaning is a reference to numbers that can be analyzed using the science of statistics, as in *each year, the Justice Department publishes statistics on the incidence of all types of felonies*. A third, technical, meaning of statistics will be introduced later in the chapter.

445

the strict application of statistical methodology, often depend on the exercise of a good deal of subjective judgment on the part of the researcher or statistician making them. Knowledge of where such subjectivity enters is crucial to the effective critique of such claims. A major goal of this chapter is to make plain for you where methodology leaves off and subjectivity begins.

1. One-Variable Descriptive Statistics

How have mutual funds performed over the past year? This question can be answered in a number of ways. For example, a list of all mutual funds and their yields for the year could be compiled. In fact, major

---

Box 8-1
Statistics in Litigation

A recent development in the law of evidence has made statistics more important than ever before to litigators. In *Daubert v. Merrell Dow*, 509 U.S. 579 (1993), the Court held that judges were to act as gatekeepers for scientific evidence: judges would review the scientific methods underlying proffered evidence, and only if they deemed the methods acceptable could the evidence be introduced at trial. Often, at least one of the critical methodological issues to be reviewed is a matter of statistics. Later cases — *General Electric Co. v. Joiner*, 522 U.S. 136 (1996), and *Kumho Tire Co. v. Carmichael*, 526 U.S. 137 (1999) — have expanded the scope of the *Daubert* review to cover all expert testimony.

Daubert and its progeny represent the Supreme Court's attempt to come to grips with the problem of so-called "junk science" in the courtroom — wherein impressionable juries decide cases on the basis of nonstandard "science" presented by hired experts with impressive credentials. The problem is still common, however, in large part because most judges are untutored in the scientific methods that they've been delegated to police.

newspapers (e.g., the *New York Times* and the *Wall Street Journal*) do just that, and the list takes up five or more pages, even though it's printed in very small type. Despite the huge amount of information that the list contains, for many purposes it isn't very helpful. Suppose that you're thinking about investing in a particular fund and want to compare its performance last year with that of mutual funds overall before making your decision. The complete list wouldn't be of much help unless you spent a lot of time organizing and summarizing the information in it. The newspapers spare their readers this onerous task by providing a variety of summaries, in words, numbers, and pictures. (Remarkably, one of these summaries encapsulates the entire body of information in a single number: the average rate of return for all mutual funds for the year.) Most readers use the list itself only to look up the performance of a few funds that they're particularly interested in. Then they turn their attention to the summaries, which they're likely to find much more useful.

Many other questions that arise every day invite similar treatment: What was the starting salary for last year's law school graduates? How much do female engineers earn? What is the prognosis for Hodgkin's disease patients treated with chemotherapy? Although a list of all of the available information would be of some value in each case, one or more summaries would probably better serve the questioner. Best of all, would be a well-crafted picture of the data. Even where data sets are small, the old saying "a picture is worth a thousand words" (or in this case, a thousand *numbers*) will often be true. Data presented in a well chosen graphic or pictorial form will typically be much more easy to assimilate (and rhetorically persuasive, if that is your purpose) than the same data presented in simple tabular form. Hence the ubiquity in newspapers, journals, books, and classrooms of a wide variety of statistical graphics. The subfield of statistics concerned with producing and analyzing informative/persuasive pictures and verbal summaries of data is called *descriptive statistics*.

A. Making Sense of Data

No concept is more basic to descriptive statistics (indeed, to all of statistics) than that of *data*. For the purposes of statistics, data are just bits of information presented in terms of *individuals* and *variables*. Individuals are the things that the information is *about*. Any object of study can be an individual: a person, a school, a state (e.g., Alabama), an act (e.g., arson), and so forth. A variable can be any *property* of individuals under study, as long as the individuals differ in some way with respect to the property and their differences can in some practical way be measured or ascertained. Height can be a variable because rulers, yardsticks, etc. offer practical ways of measuring it. Greediness, though a property of individuals, cannot function as a variable unless an investigator devises a practical way of measuring it. An investigator who develops such a measurement technique is said to have *operationalized* the concept of greediness. (If a law professor wants to use statistical methods to test the hypothesis that the sociability of law students is correlated with their job choices, she would first have to operationalize sociability. Can you think of a way she might do this?)

Variables come in two types. A variable that's measured numerically, such as height, weight, blood pressure, GPA, or price, is a *quantitative variable*. In Table 8-1, for example, five-year rate of return is a quantitative variable. A variable that requires that each individual be assigned to one of several specified or implied categories, such as gender, race, or marital status, on the other hand, is a *categorical variable*. In Table 8-2, chosen weapon is a categorical variable.

A collection of values of a given variable for more than one individual is a *one-variable data set*. Table 8-1 presents a one-variable data set, Table 8-2 presents a summary of another one-variable data set. (What does the one-variable data set summarized in Table 8-2 look like?) Combining two or more one-variable data sets for the same individuals produces a *multivariate data set* (see Table 8-3). The number of variables in a multivariate data set can be very large. The U.S. Census, for example, consists of hundreds of data points for each individual surveyed. Picturing, analyzing, and applying data become increasingly difficult as the number of variables in a data set increases, though spreadsheets and statistics programs are now available to perform the necessary calculations.

B. Histograms and Frequency Distributions

A one-variable quantitative data set can be represented pictorially in several ways. The type of picture most commonly used by statisticians is

Table 8-1
Quantitative Variable: Five-Year Rates of Return for a Group of Mutual Funds (hypothetical data)

Load mutual fund	5-Year rate of return (%)	No-load mutual fund	5-Year rate of return (%)
AIM Advisor	16.20	Accessor	21.90
American Express	26.70	American Century	9.50
BB&T Growth	21.10	Excelsior	24.30
Chase Vista	21.70	Fidelity Puritan	15.10
DU Winthrop	10.00	Heartland Value	12.50
Dreyfus Premier	-8.00	Janus Enterprise	23.80
Fidelity Select	18.30	J.P. Morgan US	13.00
Galaxy Equity	18.40	Meridian Fund	12.70
Guardian	23.60	Mutual Beacon	17.40
Kemper	9.00	PIMCO Stocks Plus	16.40
Lexington Strategic	-11.00	Ryders OTC	40.90
MainStay	22.40	Standish Equity	19.30
MFS Research	21.20	T. Rowe Price Equity	20.70
One Group	21.90	Vanguard Utilities	-16.60
Parkstone	9.70	Westcore	15.80
Principal Balanced	12.80		
Smith Barney	21.30		
United Continental	12.30		
Van Eck Gold	-14.20		
Zwieg Strategy	10.50		

Table 8-2
Categorical Variable:
Homicides by Chosen Weapon, 1998

Type of weapon	No. of homicides
Handgun	7,361
Knife	1,877
Fist	949
Blunt object	741
Shotgun	619
Rifle	538

Source: *Uniform Crime Reports* (1999).

a kind of bar graph called a *histogram*. Histograms are such useful tools for describing and analyzing data that, as an early step in analyzing a data set, statisticians routinely construct and scrutinize a histogram for each quantitative variable contained in it.

Table 8-3
A Multivariate Data Set: Education, Income, and Poverty

| | Public school enrollment | | | Educational attainment, 1990 | | |
| | Fall | | | | Percent | |
County	1998-1999	1994-1995	1990	Persons 25 years and over	High school graduate or higher	Bachelor's degree or higher
Maine	210.080	212.225	212.465	795.613	78.8	18.8
Androscoggin	16,472	17,438	17,664	66,785	71.8	12.6
Aroostook	13,349	14,653	16,509	55,738	70.9	12.5
Cumberland	39,693	37,475	37,559	159,876	85.0	27.6
Franklin	5,348	5,471	5,575	17,980	79.7	17.7
Hancock	8,198	8,354	7,565	31,475	83.3	21.4
Kennebec	18,361	18,735	20,441	74,858	78.9	18.1
Knox	4,744	4,842	5,837	24,778	80.8	19.8
Lincoln	6,236	6,353	5,037	20,674	81.4	22.2
Oxford	10,673	10,585	9,814	34,779	76.9	12.7
Penobscot	24,571	25,473	24,756	91,410	79.1	17.7
Piscataquis	3,173	3,473	4,057	12,248	75.4	12.3
Sagadahoc	6,952	6,991	5,885	21,573	81.1	21.6
Somerset	9,316	9,821	10,066	31,726	71.9	10.5
Waldo	5,240	5,226	6,404	21,295	77.4	16.8
Washington	5,428	6,359	6,777	23,087	73.2	12.7
York	32,326	31,276	28,519	107,331	79.5	19.0
Maryland	841,671	790,938	703,379	3,122,665	78.4	26.5
Allegany	10,978	11,303	10,872	49,857	71.0	11.8
Anne Arundel	74,079	70,588	63,918	276,130	81.1	24.6
Baltimore	105,914	99,231	85,386	473,574	78.4	25.0
Calvert	15,241	12,819	9,659	32,408	79.3	17.6
Caroline	5,685	5,290	4,616	17,510	66.8	10.8
Carroll	27,224	24,515	21,115	79,153	78.5	19.6
Cecil	15,550	14,258	12,628	44,944	72.2	12.1
Charles	22,263	20,419	18,228	60,821	81.0	16.2
Dorchester	5,143	5,165	4,821	20,861	64.7	10.9
Frederick	35,383	31,655	26,088	94,994	80.4	22.0
Garrett	5,082	5,104	5,306	17,908	68.4	9.5
Harford	38,909	35,956	30,153	115,199	81.6	21.5
Howard	41,858	36,125	29,545	122,454	91.1	46.9
Kent	2,891	2,794	2,595	11,822	81.4	16.9
Montgomery	127,933	117,082	101,083	512,839	90.6	49.9
Prince George's	130,259	118,478	106,064	458,296	83.2	25.5
Queen Anne's	6,888	6,020	5,498	22,993	76.8	19.9
St. Mary's	14,743	13,428	12,800	45,592	77.1	16.8
Somerset	3,113	3,339	3,698	15,901	61.2	9.6
Talbot	4,590	4,340	3,829	21,903	76.5	23.0
Washington	20,159	19,510	18,459	81,140	69.3	11.4
Wicomico	14,330	13,652	11,738	47,231	72.1	18.5
Worcester	6,916	6,439	5,241	24,828	70.8	14.8
Independent city						
Baltimore city	106,540	113,428	110,039	474,307	60.7	15.5
Massachusetts	937,647	893,727	830,138	3,965,223	80.0	27.2
Barnstable	28,788	30,964	26,042	133,951	88.4	28.1
Berkshire	15,802	21,204	20,346	92,609	77.9	20.9
Bristol	84,296	82,475	80,028	327,994	65.0	15.9
Dukes	2,543	2,182	1,796	8,245	90.4	32.1
Essex	116,844	105,625	94,592	445,994	80.2	25.9
Franklin	11,907	11,813	10,925	46,559	82.4	24.2
Hampden	77,037	71,919	69,898	292,806	73.6	17.6
Hampshire	20,100	20,772	18,531	85,463	83.0	31.9
Middlesex	206,094	189,963	177,247	941,201	84.3	35.4
Nantucket	1,238	1,042	764	4,316	89.4	32.9
Norfolk	95758	88154	77929	421102	88.0	34.4
Plymouth	78989	77360	73465	276957	83.8	22.2
Suffolk	79,258	73,551	72,355	427,138	85.4	27.7
Worcester	118,993	116,703	106,220	457,888	77.4	22.2

Table 8-3
A Multivariate Data Set: Education, Income, and Poverty (continued)

	Median household income			Persons below poverty level, 1997				
				Number			Percent	
			Percent	Persons of all ages		Persons	Person	Persons
	1997	1989	change,		Net change,	under	of all	under
	(dollars)	(dollars)	1989-1997	Total	1989 1997	18 years	ages	18 years
	33,140	27,854	19.0	132,809	4,343	44,122	0.7	14.9
	34,242	26,979	26.9	10,732	−840	3,575	10.7	14.5
	29,124	22,230	31.0	11,152	−724	3,562	15.0	19.6
	41,393	32,286	28.2	20,432	1,660	6,366	8.1	11.3
	30,712	24,432	25.7	3,643	163	1,247	12.7	17.6
	33,397	25,247	32.3	4,974	428	1,626	10.1	14.5
	35,559	28,616	24.3	12,040	576	4,046	10.6	14.7
	33,478	25,405	31.8	4,050	−149	1,347	10.8	15.5
	35,696	28,373	25.8	3,067	184	1,117	9.6	15.3
	30,688	24,535	25.1	6,663	219	2,313	12.3	17.4
	33,574	26,631	26.1	17,229	−866	5,486	12.1	16.4
	28,599	22,132	29.2	2,488	−312	850	13.6	19.1
	39,991	31,948	25.2	2,795	410	980	7.8	11.0
	28,300	22,829	24.0	7,840	768	2,806	14.9	20.6
	29,812	23,148	28.8	5,279	80	1,820	14.3	19.5
	25,673	19,993	28.4	6,252	−348	2,106	17.7	24.5
	39,288	32,432	21.1	14,173	3,094	4,875	8.0	11.3
	45,289	39,386	15.0	484,987	99,691	194,703	9.5	14.9
	28,794	21,546	33.6	11,209	−656	4,011	15.9	24.2
	56,147	45,147	24.4	24,894	6,503	11,893	5.3	9.7
	44,715	38,837	15.1	54,891	17,737	20,936	7.6	12.8
	57,017	47,608	19.8	4,815	2,161	2,212	6.6	10.4
	32,902	27,758	18.5	3,772	652	1,649	12.8	20.4
	55,906	42,378	31.9	7,320	2,792	2,996	4.9	7.2
	44,650	36,019	24.0	7,375	2,169	3,359	9.0	14.2
	54,110	46,415	16.6	8,757	3,750	4,407	7.4	12.2
	29,361	24,922	17.8	4,629	414	1,825	15.5	25.3
	53,415	41,382	29.1	10,695	3,640	4,448	5.8	8.6
	30,197	22,733	32.8	4,605	563	1,957	15.8	24.2
	52,231	41,680	25.3	13,841	4,719	5,813	6.4	9.6
	68,024	54,348	25.2	10,503	4,719	4,187	4.4	6.6
	36,391	30,104	20.9	1,949	6	703	10.7	17.1
	62,130	54,089	14.9	47,141	15,490	18,201	5.6	8.8
	47,882	43,127	11.0	71,557	30,275	30,164	9.3	15.1
	48,226	39,190	23.1	3,016	781	1,151	7.5	11.3
	49,495	37,158	33.2	7,628	2,235	3,528	8.8	13.2
	26,867	23,379	14.9	4,344	1,179	1,453	21.8	29.1
	39,663	31,885	24.4	3,224	660	1,208	9.7	16.7
	37,327	29,632	26.0	12,284	1,710	4,762	10.1	15.7
	34,827	28,512	22.1	10,793	2,214	4,431	13.5	21.6
	32,815	27,586	19.0	5,106	1,323	2,119	11.9	21.8
	27,713	24,045	15.3	150,937	−5,347	57,290	23.7	34.4
	43,015	36,952	16.4	649,293	129,954	250,244	10.7	17.0
	40,791	31,766	28.4	18,547	4,751	6,912	8.9	15.5
	37,284	30,470	22.4	14,783	3,223	5,577	11.3	18.2
	38,866	31,520	23.3	61,556	16,389	25,043	11.9	18.8
	50,852	31,994	27.7	931	162	319	6.7	10.1
	44,187	37,913	16.5	74,648	13,877	29,994	10.6	17.0
	38,330	30,350	26.3	7,461	838	2,922	10.5	16.5
	36,746	31,100	18.2	72,537	15,200	31,647	16.6	26.9
	42,287	34,154	23.8	12,798	−886	3,500	9.4	11.3
	53,268	43,847	21.5	103,324	20,385	33,979	7.3	10.9
	48,151	40,331	19.4	340	—	106	4.2	6.0
	54,528	46,215	18.0	32,148	5,013	9,828	5.0	7.0
	49,165	40,905	20.2	40,461	12,308	16,935	8.6	13.2
	36,260	29,399	23.3	129,133	14,385	51,621	20.7	35.4
	40,489	35,774	13.2	80,628	24,011	31,862	11.1	16.8

Table 8-4
Five-Year Rates of Return for a Group of
Mutual Funds: Frequency Distribution

Five-year rate of return		No. of
At least	But less than	funds
−20%	−10%	3
−10%	0%	1
0%	10%	3
10%	20%	15
20%	30%	12
30%	40%	0
40%	50%	1

Let's see how histograms are constructed:

How to . . .

> *. . . construct a histogram (using the data in Table 8-1)*
> 1. We define and list the names of sufficient equal-sized categories to allow every score in the data set to be placed into one and only one category.[2] Let's use seven categories, those listed in Table 8-4.
> 2. Next, we tally the number of scores that fall into each category and note the tallies next to their respective category names to create a table called a *frequency distribution*.[3] (As used here, frequency means the number of values in a given category.)
> 3. We label the horizontal axis (x-axis) of a graph with the name of the variable and its unit of measurement (which in our example are five-year rate of return and percent, respectively) and mark off a scale that appropriately reflects the category

---

2. There is no "right" number of categories to use in creating a histogram, but a good starting point is the square root of the number of individuals in the data set.

3. A variation in histogram construction you should be aware of is the use of a *probability distribution* table giving the percentage of individuals in the data set who fall into each category, instead of the actual number of the individuals in each category as in the frequency distribution table. The resulting histograms look the same whether a probability distribution table or a frequency distribution table is used in their construction.

Figure 8-1
Histogram Created from Frequency
Distribution in Table 8-4

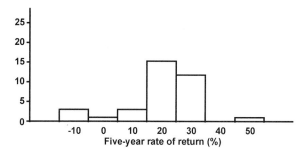

boundaries. We label the vertical axis (y-axis) frequency, note the unit of measurement (i.e., number of mutual funds), and mark off a scale appropriate for the frequencies (number of scores) in the various categories of our distribution.

4. Our last step is to construct, for each category, a column that spans its interval along the x-axis and extends upward from the x-axis to the level on the y-axis that reflects the frequency for the category. The bars will be proportional in height and area to the frequencies for the categories they represent. (See Figure 8-1.)

What does a statistician look for when inspecting a histogram? The answer is, first and foremost, its shape — more specifically, an approximate match between the histogram's overall shape and the shape of one of the entries in the statistician's mental catalog of ideal shapes that histograms often resemble.

One simple ideal shape is the rectangle. The histogram in Figure 8-2 is an example of a rectangular histogram, the graphic equivalent of a *rectangular distribution*. (What can you say about a data set whose histogram resembles a rectangle?)

A more interesting shape in the statisticians' mental catalog is the one in Figure 8-3: the *normal curve*, which is the graphic equivalent of a *normal distribution*. We can't expect a histogram of an actual data set to look exactly like a normal curve. After all, a normal curve is smooth because it's an ideal shape, whereas a histogram, any histogram, is bumpy, because, by definition, it's made up of columns. So, the most we can expect is for

Figure 8-2
A Rectangular Histogram

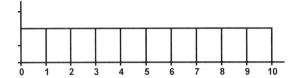

Figure 8-3
A Normal Curve

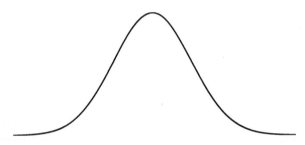

the histogram's overall shape to more or less resemble a normal curve (see Figure 8-4). The degree to which a histogram resembles a normal curve is of great interest: if the distribution of the data portrayed in the histogram matches a normal distribution well enough to be accepted and treated as such, a number of important practical consequences follow. We'll go into these later in the chapter.

Even when the shape of a histogram doesn't come anywhere near matching an ideal shape, it's amenable to description in statistical language. For example, in contrast to a normal curve (which can be divided into two mirror-image halves by an appropriately placed line and thus is symmetric), some histograms are highly asymmetric. Such histograms may be either right-skewed or left-skewed (see Figure 8-5). A histogram constructed from data on income, for example, is likely to be right-skewed. (Why?) One constructed from scores on an easy multiple-choice test, on the other hand, is almost certain to be left-skewed. (Why?)

Another feature of overall histogram shape that statisticians pay attention to is "hilliness." Some histograms are relatively flat, while mounds, or peaks, are obvious in some others. These mounded histograms can be further characterized on the basis of the number of mounds that are apparent: a one-mound histogram is *unimodal,* a two-mound histogram

Figure 8-4
A Histogram Resembling a Normal Curve

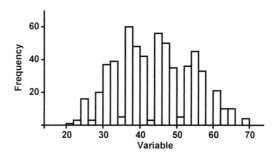

Figure 8-5
Skewed Histograms

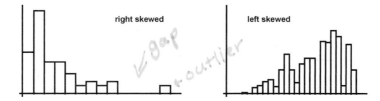

is *bimodal* (see Figure 8-6), and so on.[4] A histogram reflecting the heights of students in a law school classroom is likely to be bimodal. (Why?) What about a histogram that represents years of post-operative survival for 50-year-old male patients who have undergone risky, but potentially lifesaving heart surgery? Multimodality is often a clue that the data have been gathered from subpopulations that differ from one another in some important way.

In addition to looking at the overall shape of a histogram, a statistician checks for *gaps* and *outliers*. A gap naturally raises the question of why few scores (or none at all) have values in that particular range. Outliers are values that are much lower or higher than the other values in a data set. Sometimes they're the result of measurement error (due to the use of a broken measuring instrument, for example, or to the misreading of a question by a survey participant), in which case statisticians may decide to exclude the outliers from the analysis. But sometimes outliers are legitimate, "real" scores. They're simply a reflection of the fact that,

---

4. *"Modal"* is used in this context because the most frequently occurring score in a distribution is called the *mode* of the distribution.

Box 8-2
The Impact of Alternative Forms of Presentation

The way in which data are presented can have a profound effect on the impact they will have. Any given data set can be presented in myriad ways, and the presentations can vary drastically from one another in appearance. Because all are representations of the same data, it might be tempting to think that differences in appearance are merely cosmetic. But appearance can — and often does — make a crucial difference. Consider the table and the two bar graphs below — three different presentations of the same data. Bar Graph B is a standard unbiased pictorial representation of the data in table A. Bar Graph C presents the same data using a common graphic trick (the y-axis scale does not go to zero). It's a fair bet that graph C would convey a more positive impression of revenue growth than either the table or graph B to most audiences. The enormous persuasive effect that cleverly crafted images of data can have on unsuspecting individuals, such as jurors, voters and consumers, has been recognized for the past hundred years or so. In response, a whole field of pictorial representation and misrepresentation has developed. It behooves lawyers presenting quantitative information to be as sensitive to the rhetorical nuances of visual representations of data as they are to those of verbal descriptions of the same basic set of facts. (If you'd like to explore this topic further, the books by Hamilton and Tufte cited at the end of the chapter would be good starting points.)

A.	Year	Revenues
	1998	$50,000,000
	1999	$50,500,000
	2000	$51,500,000
	2001	$52,500,000
	2002	$53,500,000

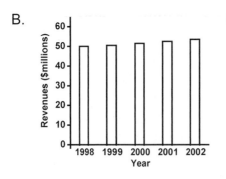

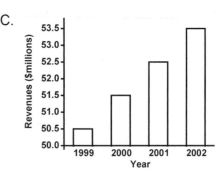

Figure 8-6
A Bimodal Histogram

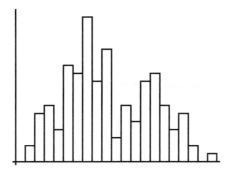

for the variable in question, extreme values, though rare, do occur. Outliers are a concern because of the very large effects that they can have on the results of formal statistical calculations. Whether to retain or to discard outliers from a particular analysis is a decision that has to be made case by case.

C. Numerical Descriptors/Summaries of Distributions

Two sorts of numerical descriptors of distributions are in common use: measures of central tendency and measures of variability.

1. Measures of central tendency. Very often, a description of a distribution includes a measure of its central tendency (i.e., its center, or average), most commonly its *mean or median*. The mean is just the arithmetic average of the values in the distribution. More formally, the mean of a distribution consisting of n values $x_1, x_2, \ldots, x_n$ is:

$$(x_1 + x_2 + \ldots + x_n)/n$$

The *median* on the other hand is just the middle value in a distribution, or, if the distribution contains an even number of values, the average of the middle two values.

The mean and median are both in common use. Does it matter which one is reported as a measure of central tendency? For a perfectly symmetric distribution, the answer is no, for the simple reason that the mean and the median are the same: both are equal to the value at the exact center of the distribution. Such is not the case for a skewed distribution, however. As can be seen in Figure 8-7, in a skewed distribution the mean

Figure 8-7
Mean and Median in a Skewed Distribution

shifts away from the location of most of the values to a value in the direction of the skew, whereas the median remains near the range of values where the majority of data points are concentrated. This disparity reflects a fundamental difference between the mean and the median — means are much more responsive than are medians to the presence of unusually high or low scores in a distribution. So, if a measure that represents the majority of the data and that isn't influenced by a few unusual scores is suitable to the purpose at hand, the median is a better choice than the mean. Indeed, it's the median that's typically reported for well-known skewed distributions, such as housing prices and salaries. Otherwise, the mean is usually more appropriate, because it's sensitive to all scores in the distribution and also, as we'll soon see, because it plays so central a role in inferential statistics. (What's your best guess at the shape of the distribution of wrongful death tort damages? Would the mean of this distribution be a useful summary statistic?)

An example will help to illustrate the importance of the difference between the mean and the median.

Example 8-1

Mary Starchway, the president of Starchway Cookies, is defending against a claim of gender discrimination in pay at her company. The company has 20 employees (including Ms. Starchway), 10 men and 10 women. Ms. Starchway reports that the average (mean) salary is the same for the men and the women at her company: $60,000. In reviewing the salaries, listed in Table 8-5, you note that the median is $40,000 for the women but $50,000 for the men. Do either the means or the medians

Table 8-5
Current Salaries of Starchway Employees

Gender	Salary ($000s)									
Men	25	25	50	50	50	50	75	75	100	100
Women	20	20	20	40	40	40	50	50	70	250

reasonably represent these salary data? When Ms. Starchway gives herself, but no one else, a raise next year, what will happen to these averages? Does it look as if there might be gender discrimination in wages at Starchway Cookies?

An important moral to derive from Example 8-1 is that when you're presented with an argument that relies on quantitative data, it can be a very bad idea for you to be satisfied with a summary statistic such as the mean or the median (or even both), for it will often fail to reveal critical features of the data. Rather, and especially in adversarial situations, you should insist on inspecting the actual data from which the summary statistics have been derived.

2. Measures of variability or spread. The values in some distributions are bunched very tightly around a central value, while those in others are widely dispersed (see Figure 8-8). When values are tightly bunched within a narrow range, either the mean or the median may provide a reasonable description of the data. As variability increases (i.e., as the scores spread out over an increasingly large range), the mean and the median become less useful as summaries, because, on average, they fall further and further away from the individual scores. For this reason,

Figure 8-8
Data Dispersion

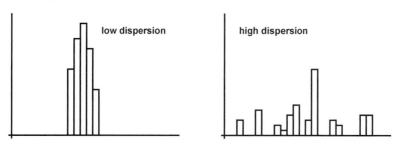

low dispersion

high dispersion

statisticians and researchers commonly supplement a measure of central tendency with a measure of the dispersion of the data.

One measure of dispersion, the simplest one, is the *range,* which is just the difference between the lowest and the highest values in the data set. (What's the range for the Starchway salaries?) However, as a descriptor, the range is severely limited, because it provides little or no information about the majority of the data points. Data sets can have the same range even though their distributions bear very little resemblance to one another.

The most frequently used measure of variability, the *standard deviation,* reflects all of the values in a data set. Let's work through an example to get a better feel for how the standard deviation is calculated and to see one way in which it can be used.

Example 8-2

> Hector wants to know how much variability there was in the returns on large-cap common stocks on the Ames Stock Exchange last year. The standard deviation is what he needs, and we will calculate it for him from the data in Table 8-6. (You'll probably want to follow along in Table 8-7 as we do the calculations.)
>
> 1. To begin, we calculate last year's mean return for all Ames large-cap common stocks, and we find that it's 10%.
>
> 2. For each stock, we subtract the mean return, 10%, from its actual return to get its deviation (see Figure 8-9).
>
> 3. We square each stock's deviation.
>
> 4. We add all the squared deviations and find that the total is 720.

Table 8-6
Last Year's Returns on All Large-Cap Common
Stocks on the Ames Stock Exchange

Stock	Investment return (%)	Stock	Investment return (%)
1	+16	6	+28
2	−1	7	−5
3	+12	8	+12
4	+11	9	+9
5	+8	10	+10

Table 8-7

Calculating the Standard Deviation for Last Year's Returns on All Large-Cap Common Stocks on the Ames Stock Exchange

Stock	Score value	Score value − Mean = Deviation	Squared deviation
1	+16	+16 − 10 = 6	6^2 = 36
2	−1	−1 − 10 = −11	-11^2 = 121
3	+12	+12 − 10 = 2	2^2 = 4
4	+11	+11 − 10 = 1	1^2 = 1
5	+8	+8 − 10 = −2	-2^2 = 4
6	+28	+28 − 10 = 18	18^2 = 324
7	−5	−5 − 10 = −15	-15^2 = 225
8	+12	+12 − 10 = 2	2^2 = 4
9	+9	+9 − 10 = −1	-1^2 = 1
10	+10	+10 − 10 = 0	0^2 = 0

100 (sum of score values)

100/10 = 10 (mean)

720 (sum of squared deviations)

720/10 = 72 (mean squared deviation)

$\sqrt{72}$ = ~8.5 (standard deviation)

$$\frac{\sqrt{(x-m)^2 + (y-m)^2}}{\#}$$

Figure 8-9
Deviation from the Mean

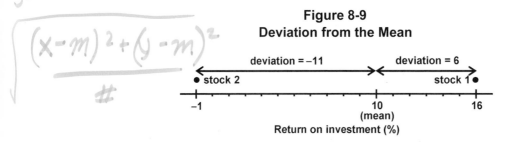

deviation = −11   deviation = 6

● stock 2   stock 1 ●

−1   10   16
                   (mean)
        Return on investment (%)

5. We divide the sum of the squared deviations, 720, by the number of stocks, 10. The result is 72, which is the average (mean) of the squared deviations or *variance*. (What would the result have been if we had averaged the deviations themselves rather than the squared deviations?)[5]

6. Our last step is to find the square root of the variance, 72. This yields the standard deviation, which turns out to be about 8.5.

These days, fortunately, such calculations are generally done by computers. Doing them manually a couple of times is useful, though, because we're able to see just which characteristic features of a distribution are actually reflected in its standard deviation. Notice in the example that we just worked through, for instance, that almost all of the variability reflected in the standard deviation derives from three data points, those for stocks 2, 6, and 7. That these three data points are outliers is very obvious when we look at Figure 8-10, a dot plot of Hector's data.

Figure 8-10
Dot Plot of Data from Table 8-6

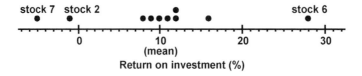

stock 7   stock 2   ●   stock 6
   ●   ●   ●●●●●   ●   ●

          0   10   20   30
                      (mean)
            Return on investment (%)

---

5. When computing a population standard deviation from data on every member of the population, n is the appropriate divisor — here, 10. When computing a sample standard deviation in order to estimate a population standard deviation, n-1 would be the appropriate divisor.

It should be clear from this example that the standard deviation, like the mean, is very responsive to the presence of unusually high or low values in a distribution. Example 8-3 is a problem for you to tackle on your own.

Example 8-3

Last year's returns on small-cap stocks from the Ames Stock Exchange are listed in Table 8-8. What's the standard deviation? (Do the calculation by hand.) Make a dot plot of the data. Are there outliers? If the small-cap stocks and the large-cap stocks on the Ames Stock Exchange continue to perform as they did last year, according to the data used in our two examples, what are the relative merits of investing in Ames small-cap and large-cap stocks?

Summing up . . .

To compute a standard deviation

1. For a data set of n scores with values $x_1, x_2, \ldots x_n$, subtract the mean of the scores from the value of each score to find the score's deviation from the mean. (For simplicity, *deviation from the mean* will from now on be shortened to *deviation*.)
2. Square each deviation.
3. Add all the squared deviations.
4. Divide the sum of the squared deviations by n if you have data on every member of the population, or by n-1 if your data is confined to a sample of the population, to get the average squared deviation, or variance, of the data set.

Table 8-8
Last Year's Returns on All Small-Cap Common Stocks on the Ames Stock Exchange

Stock	Investment return (%)	Stock	Investment return (%)
1	+14	6	+14
2	+28	7	−24
3	+16	8	+17
4	+11	9	+30
5	−13	10	+17

5. Find the square root of the variance. The result is the standard deviation.

Generalizations about the standard deviation
1. The standard deviation measures spread about the mean and thus should be used only in conjunction with a reported mean.
2. Like the mean, the standard deviation isn't a "resistant" measure; it's heavily influenced by outliers.
3. The standard deviation equals zero only when all the scores in the data set have the same value.
4. Chebychev's Rule: for any data set, at least 75% of the data points lie within 2 standard deviations of the mean (i.e., within the range bounded by the mean minus 2 standard deviations and the mean plus 2 standard deviations) and at least 89% lie within 3 standard deviations of the mean.[6] (Does this rule hold for the Ames Stock Exchange data?)

D. The Normal Distribution

Researchers are often interested in determining where a given data point falls relative to the others in a data set. They could get at least a rough idea from Chebychev's Rule, but predictions based on the shape of a distribution are likely to be more accurate. When a distribution's shape resembles the ideal normal curve closely enough for the distribution to be treated as normal — and in practice, distributions are very commonly assumed to be approximately normal — predictions about where particular values fall relative to others can be quite accurate.

The normal distribution, rather than being a single distribution, is actually a family of distributions, which look quite similar when represented graphically as curves. The reason for the resemblance is that the curves are derived from very similar mathematical formulas that differ only in the values of 2 variables, the mean and the standard deviation. For each possible combination of mean and standard deviation, there's a unique normal distribution, which, when graphed, produces a version of the familiar bell-shaped curve. A common practice is to use

---

6. This rule is named after Pafnuty Chebychev, a nineteenth-century Russian mathematician.

Figure 8-11
Two Members of the Family of Normal Curves

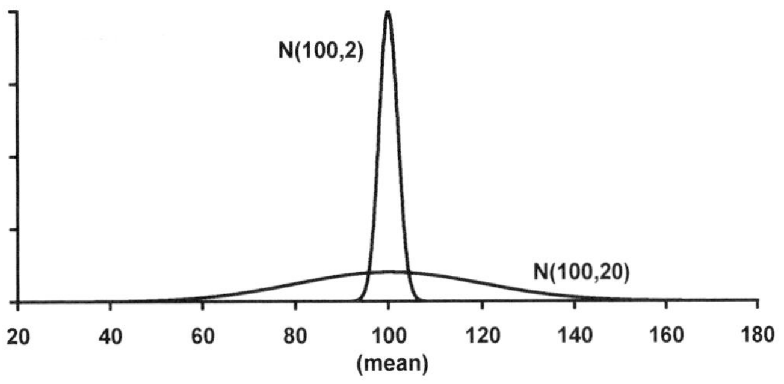

the notation N(μ,σ), where μ ('mu') is the mean and σ ('sigma') is the standard deviation, to designate individual normal distributions. For example, N(7,5) would be a reference to the normal distribution with mean 7 and standard deviation 5. The larger the standard deviation of any given normal distribution relative to its mean, the more spread out the distribution looks when it's represented graphically as a curve (see Figure 8-11).

While true normal distributions are theoretical constructs representing mathematical ideals, they and their graphic counterparts, normal curves, are central in statistics, because, as it turns out, many naturally occurring distributions resemble (i.e., approximate) true normal distributions and are treated as if they are normal, and because, as we shall see, they play an important role in the theory of hypothesis testing and estimation. The assumption that a distribution is "normal enough" is a powerful one. All inferences based on it are only as valid as the assumption itself.[7]

---

7. A natural question is: How close to being perfectly normally distributed must the data be for them to be considered normally distributed? This issue is often a crucial one for statisticians, and complex tests have been devised to assess the precise degree of the match, or *fit*, between the distribution of any given data and the normal distribution. Nevertheless, even though such a determination can be made, deciding whether to accept any particular degree of fit as "close enough" is a matter of judgment, not method, with due consideration given to the purpose of the analysis at hand.

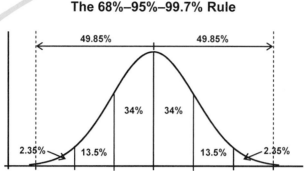

Figure 8-12
The 68%–95%–99.7% Rule

Properties of . . .

. . . normal distributions and normal curves

1. All normal curves are similar in appearance: bell shaped and symmetric.

2. The mean, the median, and the mode of every normal distribution have the same value: mean = median = mode. (The mode is the most frequently occurring value in the distribution and corresponds to the highest point of the curve.)

3. The 68%–95%–99.7% Rule: in every normal distribution, about 68% of the values are within 1 standard deviation of the mean (i.e., within the range bounded by the mean minus 1 standard deviation and the mean plus 1 standard deviation), about 95% are within 2 standard deviations, and about 99.7% are within 3 standard deviations (see Figure 8-12).[8]

The 68%–95%–99.7% Rule enables us to solve an interesting class of problems, those of the sort illustrated by the following example.

Example 8-4

Suppose that the distribution of heights of 20-year-old American men is known to be approximately normal and to have a mean of 5 feet 9 inches (i.e., 69 inches) and a standard deviation of 3 inches — in other words, N(69,3). What percentage of 20-year-old men are taller than 6 feet (i.e., 72 inches)?

---

8. You might want to compare these percentages to those in Chebychev's Rule, which, as you'll remember, applies to all distributions, not just to normal distributions.

We know from the 68%–95%–99.7% Rule that the heights of about 68% of the men will be within 3 inches (i.e., 1 standard deviation) of the mean, 69 inches. So 68% of the men will be from 66 inches to 72 inches tall. The remaining 32% will be either shorter than 66 inches or taller than 72 inches. Because a normal distribution is symmetric, half of the 32% (16%) must be shorter than 66 inches and the other half (the other 16%) taller than 72 inches. Thus, the answer to the question is 16%.

E. Z-Scores and the Z-Table

The preceding example was relatively easy to work through because the difference between the mean (69 inches) and the value of interest (72 inches) was exactly 1 standard deviation (3 inches). In the vast majority of real-life situations, however, the difference between the two values doesn't translate into a whole number of standard deviations. In such cases, while an approximate answer can be derived using the 68%-95%-99.7% Rule, a much more exact answer can be obtained using z-scores and a z-table.[9]

How to . . .

. . . calculate a z-score
1. Subtract the mean of the distribution from any given value to get a deviation score.
2. Divide the deviation score by the standard deviation of the distribution. The result is the z-score for the given value.

A z-score tells how far, as measured in standard deviations, any given value is from the mean of a distribution. It also tells whether the value is larger than or smaller than the mean: the value is larger than the mean if the z-score is positive and smaller if the z-score is negative.

Let's work through an example.

Example 8-5

What is the z-score for a height of 72 inches in the distribution described in the previous example?

---

9. Z-scores are also known as *standard scores*. Transforming raw scores on a variable into standard scores is called standardizing the data. This is sometimes done in order to allow direct comparison of values taken from different normal distributions.

1. We subtract 69 inches (the mean) from 72 inches (the height that we're interested in) and find that the difference (the deviation score) is 3 inches.

2. The next step is to divide 3 inches (the deviation) by 3 inches (the standard deviation score). The result is 1.0. So z = 1.0 for a height of 72 inches. In other words, a height of 72 inches is exactly 1 standard deviation larger than the mean height of 69 inches.

What if we wanted to know the percentage of 20-year-old American men who are taller than 74 inches? Figuring out the z-score is simple enough: $(74 - 69)/3 = 1.67$. But how do we use this number? To solve this problem, we need to use the z-table (see Z-Table on page 487). The z-table provides, for any given z-score, the proportion of individuals in a normal distribution who would be expected to have a z-score *less* than the given z-score.

Example 8-6

Given the distribution of heights from Example 4, to find the percentage of 20-year-old American men who are taller than 74 inches, using the z-table (see Z-Table on page 487)

1. We calculate the z-score (we've already done this) and find that it's 1.67.

2. We find 1.6 (the z-score through its first decimal place) in the far-left column of the z-table (see Z-Table on page 487).

3. We move across the row that 1.6 is on until we reach the column labeled .07 (the second decimal place of the z-score) at the top.

4. The number in the cell where the row and the column for our z-score of 1.67 intersect, .9525, gives us the proportion of 20-year-old American men who would be expected to have a height the z-score of which is less than 1.67, i.e. the proportion of men who are shorter than 74 inches.

5. We convert the proportion, .9525, to a percentage by moving the decimal two places to the right, and we get 95.25%. Thus, 95.25% of 20-year-old American men are 74 inches or shorter.

6. If 95.25% are 74 inches or shorter, then the remainder, 4.75% (i.e., 100.00% − 95.25% = 4.75%), of 20-year-old Ameri-

can men are taller than 74 inches. And this is the answer to our question.

This is one way in which z-scores can be used. We'll revisit them, as well as the normality assumption, a little later in the chapter.

2. One-Variable Inferential Statistics

One-variable inferential statistics is the science of using data derived from a relatively small number of individuals to make educated guesses about some characteristic of a larger group from which the individuals were selected. The smaller group is called a *sample*, the larger group is called a *population*, and the manner in which the smaller group was selected is referred to as the sampling method. Sampling is done in the service of the two fundamental procedures of inferential statistics: hypothesis testing and estimation. We'll cover both of these topics, but before we do, we should focus a little more closely on samples and sampling and touch on the issue of validity in relation to sample data.

A. Samples and Sampling

A data set may contain scores on one or more variables for *all* of the individuals — that is, the entire population — the researcher is interested in studying. Such a data set is called a *census*. For example, a company's employment records contain a census of its employees' salaries, and a university registrar's office contains a census of student grades. Though the U.S. census aspires to be a true census, it doesn't achieve this goal. (See Box 8-3.)

Often, however, gathering complete information isn't a viable option. The task may be prohibitively expensive (e.g., a pollster would like to know what *all* Americans think of lawyers but can afford to ask only 500 or 1,000 people), practically impossible (e.g., a pharmaceutical company would like to know what would happen if everyone with a stomach ulcer were treated with a new drug that it is developing), or truly impossible (e.g., a stock market analyst would like to know at what level the S&P 500 stock index will be for each of the next twenty weeks). In such situations, the best the researcher can do is measure the variable of interest for some subset of the population under investigation and, by applying

---

Box 8-3
Is the U.S. Census a True Census?

"The ideal of 'count every resident once, and only once' is the correct target. I also must admit that the U.S. Census never has, and likely never will, achieve that goal." (The Director of the Census). Some people are just too difficult to contact, and even when contacted, many refuse to participate. The Census relies primarily on a mail survey which in 2010 produced a 74% response rate, with follow up visits to households that did not return their forms. In addition, for counting groups that the mail survey is known to undercount, sampling is performed to adjust the estimates (except for purposes of Congressional apportionment —see *Department of Commerce v. U.S. House of Representatives*, 525 U.S. 316 (1999)). Despite spending $14 billion (about $50 per person counted), millions of residents are not counted and millions of other residents end up being counted more than once. These inaccuracies have political significance, as the uncounted residents in the decennial census aren't randomly distributed throughout society. Rather, certain minorities, immigrants, and the poor — individuals from groups that traditionally are overwhelmingly Democratic — are disproportionately missed.

---

techniques of statistical inference to the resulting measurements, try to make educated guesses about what the measurements on all the other individuals in the population would be if they were actually collected.

The distinction between sample and population is crucial to inferential statistics. To help maintain the distinction, statisticians call numerical descriptors of populations *parameters* and numerical descriptors of samples *statistics*. For instance, population mean (μ), population variance (σ^2), and population standard deviation (σ) are parameters, whereas sample mean ($\bar{x}$), sample variance (s^2), and sample standard deviation (s) are statistics. The goal of sampling is to select a sample sufficiently representative of the population that statistics derived from it provide accurate estimations of the population parameters.

Because a sample is intended to represent a population, for it to work well in statistical inference, it must be typical of the population with respect to the variable being studied. For any variable, the degree to which the sample distribution resembles the population distribution is the *representativeness of the sample*. Analysts and researchers can't search through the population to find perfectly typical subsets of individuals, so they rely on randomization to produce an approximately representative sample. A *simple random sample* is one that's selected in such a way that it was no more and no less likely to be selected than was any other possible sample of the same size — in other words, all possible samples of the given size had the same likelihood of being selected. Note that this is not the same thing as a sample in which each *individual* has the same chance of being selected. (Do you see the difference?) Randomization can be achieved in a variety of ways, ranging from drawing slips of paper from a box containing one slip for each member of the population (a method suitable for sampling from small populations) to using random number generating computer programs. All sound methods do, however, have something in common: their starting point, which is always a carefully constructed definition of the relevant population.

Randomization doesn't guarantee representativeness. It does, however, allow analysts to control for bias and apply statistical techniques to the data collected. If a sample isn't random, or at least approximately so, it isn't appropriate for use in making statistical inferences about the underlying population from which the sample was derived.

To avoid the expense involved in random sampling, many social science studies gather data from *convenience samples*. These are samples that comprise individuals who have been chosen because they were relatively accessible. For example, college students enrolled in psychology courses account for the majority of individuals in samples used for psychology experiments. The researchers who rely on such samples would like to claim that they learn facts, not simply about the nature of college students, but about general human nature. Whether an inference of this kind is justified depends on the answer to the question: With respect to the variable being investigated, how representative of the population of all humans is a sample of college students enrolled in psychology courses likely to be? And this is a question to be answered by informal argument, not by application of statistical techniques.

Consider the following examples. Are the sampling methods described likely to yield truly representative samples of the populations of interest?

- To determine whether her constituents favor a proposed gun-control bill, a Congresswoman tallies the views expressed in letters from her constituents.
- To determine the percentage of motorists who drive while under the influence of alcohol, the state police administer a Breathalyzer test to the driver of every twentieth car passing a highway checkpoint.
- To determine what a town's residents would be willing to pay to preserve the local environment, a company interested in building a chemical factory near the town surveys the shoppers at a nearby Wal-Mart.
- The Student Life Committee at Legal Eagle Law School would like to know how important the opportunity to travel is to students' choice of future employment. The committee polls the law students taking a class in international trade at the school.
- To select a jury pool, county officials call the home phone numbers of randomly selected registered voters between 12:00 noon and 5:00 P.M. on weekdays (Mondays through Fridays) and summon any eligible adult who answers.
- To determine how many apples in a crate are rotten, a grocer inspects the ones at the top of the crate.

B. Survey Data and Validity

If the results of statistical inference are to be sound, not only must the sampling technique be proper, but the measurements of the variable in question must be valid as well. *Validity* is the extent to which a measuring instrument measures what it's intended to measure. (Is a polygraph a valid device for detecting lying? Is the LSAT a valid test of aptitude for law school?) If the data on which we base our statistical inferences are invalid, then we'll be unable to accurately generalize about population characteristics. Validity is a particularly acute problem in *survey design and analysis,* because there often are good reasons to suspect that survey responses don't reflect the true views of respondents.

Although much of the data that appear in law and public policy settings are derived from surveys, the study of valid survey design has remained relatively undeveloped. Most surveys are designed to be *face valid.* That is, they consist of questions that request directly and obviously the information desired (e.g., How old are you? What was your income last year? How happy are you at law school? Who do you intend to vote for in the upcoming presidential election?). The responses are compiled, and the results from the samples are offered as truths about the age, income, level of satisfaction, and voting proclivities of the respective populations. The designers of face-valid surveys often ignore well-established truths about the complexity of the relationship between what people report their beliefs, attitudes, and behaviors to be when they participate in surveys and what their beliefs, attitudes, and behaviors actually are. Yet accepting the accuracy of sampling (routinely reported as a margin of error — e.g., a margin of error of ±3 percentage points — when the survey results are presented) as a measure of the validity of survey results is commonplace.

The validity problem is obvious with some survey questions (e.g., How often have you used the following substances in the past month: cocaine, heroin, PCP?). But even relatively innocuous questions (e.g., How old are you? What was your income last year?) are unlikely, for a variety of reasons, to yield completely reliable data. Sometimes, for example, all it takes is a small alteration in wording to bring about a major change in the distribution of responses to a question. Compare (1) with (2): (1) Do you think the United States should forbid public speeches against democracy? (2) Do you think the United States should allow public speeches against democracy? You might think that a *yes* answer to the first is equivalent to a *no* answer to the second, but in the survey from which these questions were taken, only 20% of respondents answered *yes* to the first question whereas 45% of respondents answered *no* to the second question. Indeed, polls regularly find much less public support for "a constitutional amendment prohibiting abortion" than they do for "a constitutional amendment protecting the life of an unborn child."

Sophisticated survey designers are well aware of such problems, however, it's often in the interest of the party sponsoring a survey for a question to be posed in a form that produces less valid responses. Compare, for example, two questions designed to obtain information about the pervasiveness of harassment at law firms: (1) Have you ever observed or do you know of anyone else who has ever observed an incident of harassment at your law firm? (2) Have you been harassed at your law firm? Which is likely to be the question of choice for an interest group committed to combatting harassment?

A key point to remember in interpreting survey data is that people who take part in surveys aren't simply tools of the surveyor, single-mindedly committed to following instructions and providing useful data. Rather, they come with concerns of their own, which are often in tension with the goals of the survey designer. The *resulting motivational bias* is a serious threat to the validity of survey work. Some survey participants may, for example, be set on presenting a positive image (or at least not a negative image) of themselves. Think about how valid their responses would be to these questions: How many times per month do you watch X-rated movies? How often do you attend religious services? Other survey participants may want to further their own personal or political goals. Imagine tax lawyers polled about their views of the social desirability of simplifying the tax code, or doctors polled about the social desirability of caps on malpractice liability.[10] The result is likely to be seriously biased responses.

The way in which survey questions are put to participants can also introduce bias or exacerbate biases arising from other causes. Imagine, for example, a survey conducted face to face in which an attractive interviewer poses questions that require the participant to provide potentially embarrassing information.

---

10. In some instances, survey participants' opposing goals are very specific. This may be the case, for example, when potential jurors for a high-profile case, many of whom will have a strong, unexpressed desire to sit on the jury, fill out juror questionnaires. Similar tensions arise when people complete employment or mental health questionnaires.

Box 8-4
Sampling Validity

National Survey Finds Adultery Less
Common among Married Americans
Than Previously Thought

A national survey of American sexual practices has revealed that only 7% of married Americans have committed adultery within the past five years (margin of error ±2%). Previous estimates had ranged from 20% to 40%.

The above is based on press coverage of a widely reported academic study conducted in the 1990s. Some (though very few) newspapers did go on to reveal that this finding was derived from the frequency of yes and no responses to the question — Have you committed adultery within the past five years? — that an interviewer posed to all married respondents in their homes and in the presence of their spouses. Is this a valid measure of the frequency of adultery? (The cited margin of error, ±2 percentage points, is *not* an indication that the actual rate of adultery was between 5% and 9%. Rather, it's a measure of *sampling error* — an indication that, based on the sample results, had the entire population of married people been asked the same question under the same circumstances, it's very likely that between 5% and 9% would have answered yes.)

Although the way in which the question about adultery was put to survey participants may seem like an extreme example of surveyor insensitivity, consider the following: A prominent AIDS researcher reported that gay men who are infected with HIV are unlikely to know it. He based this claim on a survey of gay men done at popular gay nightclubs. Each was asked his HIV status, and gave a sample of blood. After pairing the survey responses and the results of the blood tests, the researcher calculated the percentage of HIV-infected respondents who had correctly identified themselves as HIV positive. Can you offer an alternative explanation for the results of this investigation?

Even data collected from respondents who have the intention of cooperating fully with the surveyor can be biased for any of a number of reasons. For example, respondents may discern from the way a question is worded (e.g., Do you believe that the Salvation Army should receive additional funding to continue its good works?) what sort of answer the survey designer is hoping to get, and often they are all too happy to oblige. Bias that arises in this way has been dubbed *acquiescence bias.*

Motivational and acquiescence biases can be very difficult to detect and control for. For this important reason (among others), people who do serious survey research conduct pilot studies — preliminary studies in which the planned survey instrument is administered to a small sample of respondents who are then individually interviewed at length about what the experience was like. Using this information, the designers can then revise their survey questions. Another important reason for conducting pilot studies is to uncover questions that could cause cognitive difficulties for the respondents. Perhaps some questions could be perceived as being vague, or ambiguous. Maybe some contain unfamiliar words. Yet others might be difficult or impossible for respondents to answer because of the type or nature of the information requested (e.g., On average, how many hours per week do your children watch television? Over the past six months, what have you seen on television or read in the newspaper about tobacco litigation?).

Although survey data regularly suffer from serious sampling and validity problems, they're often the only sort of data available on a host of important public and private questions. Indeed, our democratic system itself requires surveys in the form of elections whereby a non-random sample of the population selects those who will govern the nation. Every major election in the United States is flawed by substantial sampling errors, validity problems, or both. But what alternatives do we have for eliciting information about the public will? Despite their serious shortcomings, surveys will persist into the foreseeable future as a major source of social data.

C. Hypothesis Testing

Now that we've explored, a little, where data come from, let's see how they're used in statistical inference. Consider the following scenario:

John and Mary, two law students, are discussing the cost of living in Lawville. Mary claims that the average rent paid by local law students is $1,100 a month. (Though John's probably correct in assuming that Mary's use of 'average' refers to the mean rent, he perhaps should have her verify that she isn't referring to the median rent.) Since he is currently taking a statistics course, John decides to test Mary's claim by surveying 100 of their fellow students, sampled randomly, about the rent they pay. The resulting sample of 100 rents has a mean of $1,145 and a standard deviation of $150. Data in hand, he approaches Mary.

JOHN: Sorry, Mary, but my survey shows you are wrong about the average rent.

MARY: (After looking at the results) No it doesn't; $1,145 is pretty close to $1,100, so you don't have any good evidence that I'm wrong. After all, if I flip a coin 20 times, I would expect to get, on average, 10 heads and 10 tails. But I wouldn't be surprised if I got 8 heads and 12 tails or, for that matter, 13 heads and 7 tails. And I certainly wouldn't decide on the basis of such outcomes that heads and tails weren't equally likely. So your experiment doesn't shake my belief that the real mean rent is $1,100.

JOHN: But what would you say if you got 19 heads and 1 tail? Or 1 head and 19 tails? You'd be pretty likely to conclude that the coin wasn't evenly balanced, wouldn't you? If you were right about the mean rent and it actually is $1,100, the chance is only about 1 in 385 that I would have come up with a random sample of 100 rents that has a mean rent $45 or more away from $1,100 ($1,055 or less, or $1,145 or more). So I reject your hypothesis.

This example illustrates the basic logic underlying statistical hypothesis testing. We begin with a claim — a hypothesis — about a population mean (i.e., that it has some particular value).[11] We select a random

---

11. There are methods for testing claims about any parameter, but the population mean is, by far, the one that is tested most often. There are also hypothesis tests which utilize two samples, but these are outside the scope of this chapter.

sample from the relevant population and calculate its mean. If the sample mean is so different from the hypothesized population mean that it's highly unlikely that we would have obtained such a sample mean if the hypothesis had, indeed, been true, then we conclude that we have good evidence against the hypothesis. On the other hand, if the sample mean doesn't seem particularly unlikely, even though it differs from the hypothesized population mean, all we can conclude is that we don't have good evidence that the hypothesis is false.

So how did John conclude that the chance was about 1 in 385 that his sample would have had a mean $45 or more away from $1,100 if Mary's claim (that the mean rent of the population of all student rents is $1,100) were correct? He calculated a z-score from his data and used the z-table to determine how likely such a z-score would be. The formula he used to calculate the z-score is (almost) as follows:

$$z = \frac{\bar{x} - \mu}{\sigma / \sqrt{n}}$$

Don't let this formula put you off. The numerator is just the difference between the sample mean ($\bar{x}$ = $1,145) and the hypothetical population mean (μ = $1,100). The denominator is the population standard deviation divided by the square root of the sample size. BUT WAIT — John doesn't know the population standard deviation, and it is not given in Mary's hypothesis. This is the typical state of affairs in hypothesis testing situations. After all, if one needs to hypothesize the mean of a population, it's hardly likely that one would happen to know its standard deviation! The way forward is to use the standard deviation of the sample one has taken as an estimate of the population standard deviation.[12] So, John calculated z as 1,145 – 1,100 divided by 150/10 (check to see if you can identify all these numbers!) which equals 3.

The next step is for John to determine, using the z-table, how unlikely it would be for him to get a result with a z-score as far away from the hypothesized mean as 3 standard deviations. John looked up 3 in the z-table. He found that the table entry corresponding to a z-score of 3 is

---

12. This is okay, as long as the sample size is > 30.

0.9987, which is equivalent to 99.87%. This means that about 99.87% of the time, he could expect the sample mean to be less than 3 standard deviations above the population mean. So, the chance of getting a result 3 or more standard deviations above the mean is only about .13%. Now what about the chance of getting a score as far away from the population mean as 3 standard deviations in the other direction, i.e., a z-score of –3 or lower? The z-table gives the answer as .0013 or .13%. So adding together the chances of a z-score greater than or equal to 3 and a z-score less than or equal to –3 gives a total probability of .0026 (.26%) or about 1 out of 385 as the probability of getting a sample mean as far as $45 away from the hypothesized mean, if the hypothesis were true.

The hypothesis being tested is often referred to as the *null hypothesis*. The reason for this choice of language is the frequent use of hypothesis testing in the following kind of scientific situation: *A drug company researcher, Dr. Johnson, creates a new ointment which she has reason to believe will lessen the time it takes for minor cuts to heal. The company has data on the average time of healing of a standard cut — 52 hours with a standard deviation of 7 hours. To test the ointment, Dr. Johnson applies it to cuts newly inflicted on a group of volunteers. Their cuts heal on average in 50 hours. Is this good evidence that the ointment is effective? The null hypothesis is that the ointment is ineffective, i.e., that the population mean for cuts treated with the new ointment is not different from the population mean for cuts allowed to heal on their own.*[13]

Often, in science the goal of an experiment is to see if some new treatment or drug or intervention makes a positive difference. If it does, that's a scientific discovery, and results in fame and fortune, or

---

13. In this situation, Dr. Johnson would be tempted to use a variant of the standard hypothesis test that, for purposes of rejecting the null hypothesis, only counts sample means that are unusually low, given the truth of the null hypothesis. Such a hypothesis test, a type of *one-tailed hypothesis test,* is sometimes employed when a researcher has strong reason to think that the actual population mean could not be higher than the mean given in the null hypothesis, and so a sample mean higher than that in the null hypothesis will just result in that sample being rejected as chance error. (As you may have guessed, there is also a one-tailed test that counts just sample means *higher* than the hypothesized mean.) As it is easier to achieve a given level of statistical significance using a one-tailed test than a two-tailed test (the standard test), the justification for using a one-tailed test should be carefully evaluated.

at least, a publication for the scientist. If the treatment doesn't make a difference — cuts don't heal faster, patients don't live longer, etc. — then in the typical case, that's not news and no fame, fortune, or even publication, results. The natural way for statisticians to approach the question of whether some intervention makes a difference is to use data to test the hypothesis that there is *no* difference (the null hypothesis) and to decide there probably *is* a difference if the null hypothesis is shown to be very unlikely. So, the scientist is usually eager to find a large enough difference between the background level and the sample result with the proposed treatment to be able to claim that there is very good evidence against the null hypothesis of no difference. A difference large enough to allow the scientist to make this latter claim is called a *statistically significant difference.*

A *statistically significant difference* between a hypothesized population mean and the mean of a random sample is a difference large enough to justify the claim that the sample was taken from a population with a mean different from the hypothesized mean. But just how large does a difference have to be in order to be statistically significant? It depends. The most common standard used by a majority of scientific journals (and courts) requires that the difference be large enough that it would have occurred by chance only 5% of the time or less if the null hypothesis (that there is no difference) were in fact true. When this standard of significance is met, the result is said to be significant at the 0.05 level or, equivalently, that the null hypothesis is *rejected at the 5% level of significance.* If you check the z-table, you'll see that the 0.05 level of significance corresponds to a z less than −1.96 or greater than 1.96. (Remember that setting the standard of statistical significance at .05 means that we have chosen to reject the null hypothesis if we observe a sample mean which is so far from the mean stated in the null hypothesis that we get such a sample mean less than 5% of the time when the null hypothesis is true.)

It's important to realize that nothing in the definition of statistical significance singles out 0.05 as *the* level that must be met for the null hypothesis to be rejected. Indeed, such a one-size-fits-all approach has come under increasing fire lately. As some scientists and statisticians have pointed out, a decision to reject the null hypothesis is a practical one: the null hypothesis should be rejected only if the data meet a standard

Figure 8-13
Hypothesis Testing: Possible Outcomes

Null hypothesis

	True	False
Do not reject null hypothesis	**A** Null is true. Test says do not reject.	**C** Null is false. Test says do not reject.
Reject null hypothesis	**B** Null is true. Test says reject.	**D** Null is false. Test says reject.

Result of hypothesis testing

Type II error (handwritten annotation pointing to box C)

Type I error (handwritten annotation pointing to box B)

that makes sense in terms of the nature and circumstances of the issue at hand, and the appropriate cutoff between significant and nonsignificant should be the significance level corresponding to this standard.[14]

Type I and Type II errors. When you test a hypothesis, there are four possible outcomes that can result from your test (see Figure 8-13). Boxes A and D show accurate test results. In A, we do not reject the null hypothesis when it is in fact true, and in D we reject the null hypothesis when it is in fact false. In B and C, however, our hypothesis test leads us to make an error. In C we fail to reject a false null hypothesis and in B we *do* reject a true null hypothesis. The sort of error made in B is called a Type I error. In Dr. Johnson's experiments this would be concluding that the salve is effective when it isn't. The sort of error made in C is called a Type II error. For Dr. Johnson, this would be concluding that she has insufficient evidence that the salve is effective when in fact it *is* effective. (Now would be a good time for you to identify the Type I and Type II errors in the rent example.)

---

14. In some contexts, researchers prefer to report a specific probability (p) of getting a particular result rather than a significance level at which the null hypothesis can be rejected: for example, $p = 0.016$ rather than *significant at the 0.05 level*.

Box 8-5
Hypothesis Testing with Proportions

In many legal contexts — notably in cases concerning allegations of discrimination — the question arises as to whether a group of employees or voters or jurors reflects the demographic characteristics of the population as a whole. Consider, for example, the case of *Castaneda v. Partida*, 430 U.S. 482 (1976). The criminal defendant alleged that Mexican-Americans were underrepresented on grand juries in Hidalgo County, Texas, where he was convicted of burglary with intent to rape. The county's population was 79% Mexican-American, but of the 870 residents summoned for jury duty, only 339 (i.e., 39%) were Mexican-American. How likely would such a large disparity be if the jury pool had been drawn randomly from the population (i.e., had been a true random sample of the population) of Hidalgo County?

We can use the z-test to answer this question, but because the data is given in percentages, we calculate z using a formula that looks somewhat different from the one we used earlier:

$$z = \frac{\hat{p} - p}{\sqrt{p(1-p)} / \sqrt{n}}$$

where $\hat{p}$ is the sample percentage converted to its decimal equivalent (e.g., the percentage of Mexican-Americans in the sample of jurors, 39%, converted to 0.39), p is the population percentage converted to a decimal (e.g., the percentage of Mexican-Americans in the population of Hidalgo County, 79%, converted to 0.79), and n is the sample size (e.g., the number of jurors in the sample, 870). Using this formula, what is your answer to the question posed above?

For Dr. Johnson's drug company, a Type I error would result in beginning product development on an ineffective salve while a Type II error would result in missing the chance to develop an effective product. Which sort of error is of greater consequence to the drug company? Suppose that it is very costly for them to begin development of a new product and that ultimately if a product is ineffective that product cannot be marketed. In such a case the company would want to set standards for its product testing that will make Type I errors rare. Unfortunately, setting the standard of statistical significance in such a way as to make Type I errors less likely necessarily increases the risk of committing Type II errors and vice versa. (Do you see why this must be true?)

In a criminal trial, the null hypothesis is "defendant is innocent." Rejecting a true null hypothesis (e.g. finding guilty when innocent) is a Type I error. Failing to reject a null hypothesis that is in fact false (e.g. finding innocent when guilty) is a Type II error. A crucial question for criminal procedure is where we should set the balance between these two types of errors.

FDA regulation of drugs also requires a balancing of Type I and Type II errors. If the FDA begins with the null hypothesis that a given drug is not safe, is a Type I or Type II error likely to be of more concern to the agency?

D. Estimation

Estimation enables us to use sample data to make educated guesses about population parameters. Suppose that John wanted to estimate from his sample data the mean rent paid by law students in Lawville.[15] What would be his best guess? An obvious choice is $1,145, the mean of his sample. Indeed, this would be an acceptable estimate for most purposes, though it's very unlikely to be exactly right. (Why?) The sample mean provides a *point estimate* (so called because it's a single value — i.e., a point — in the entire spectrum of possible values) of the parameter. A point estimate by itself generally isn't as useful as an *interval estimate*, which specifies both a range of values and the probability that the true

---

15. Other parameters can be estimated, but the mean is estimated much more often than any of the others.

value of the parameter is somewhere within this range. John could, for example, use his data to calculate an interval in such a way that, on average, 95% of intervals calculated in this way will contain the actual population mean. Let's do this for him. First, we divide the sample standard deviation by the square root of the sample size — $150/10 = 15$. Then we multiply this result by 1.96 to get 29.4. The desired 95% confidence interval is the interval from John's sample mean minus 29.4 to his sample mean plus 29.4, which is the interval 1115.6 to 1174.4. For a 99% confidence interval, replace 1.96 by 2.57 in the above calculation. As you can see, producing a confidence interval is not difficult! What *is* difficult is coming to understand why an interval produced in this way has the valuable property it has, namely, that 95% of intervals constructed like this (take a random sample of 30 or more individuals from the population of interest and use the mean and standard deviation of that sample in the above set of calculations) will, on average contain the actual mean of the population. This is a task beyond the scope of our text (but an explanation is to be found in chapters 18 and 19 of the De Veaux suggested reading).

E. Statistical Significance and the Real World

Before wrapping up, we should return for a final, brief visit to Legal Eagle Law School.

Mary and John are chatting as they head for the cafeteria.

MARY: So maybe I was wrong. But I wasn't far wrong. Who cares if I was off by $45 or so?

There is truth in Mary's comment, which illustrates an important point: a statistically significant difference doesn't necessarily have any *practical* significance. It may have little or no real-world importance even if it's statistically significant at a very high level. This is very commonly the case when the sample from which the data have been obtained is large.

In some fields, though, very small differences, even 0.1%, can be of enormous significance, and it's extremely important to be certain that the differences are real. This is the case, for example, when two treatments for a widespread illness are compared. Let's say that a certain kind of pos-

Box 8-6
Potential Pitfalls in Hypothesis Testing

Suppose that Mello, a soft-drink company, wants "scientific evidence" that consumers prefer its new lemon-lime soft drink to the lemon-lime drink of a rival company. And suppose that the new drink has been formulated so as to taste exactly like its competitor. Mello hires twenty independent researchers who are unknown to each other. Each researcher conducts taste tests in which randomly chosen consumers taste the two drinks from unlabeled glasses and are rewarded with a six-pack of the soft drink they like better. When Mello receives the results of the twenty experiments, it shreds nineteen of the reports and keeps one, which it claims offers "scientific evidence" at the 0.05 level of significance, that consumers prefer its new soft drink to that of the rival company. Given that the retained study does, in fact, conclude at the 0.05 level of significance that consumers prefer Mello's lemon-lime drink, is the company's claim consistent with what you know of the logic of hypothesis testing?

A more troubling version of this problem routinely occurs in well-established areas of scientific research. Because scientific journals, almost without exception, will publish only research that finds "significant" differences, studies that don't reject the null hypothesis are often filed away, never to see the light of day. Suppose that 100 researchers in different parts of the world, unknown to each other, are studying whether an over-the-counter drug can cause birth defects in infants born to women who took the drug during pregnancy. Eventually, five papers on the effects of the drug are published in scientific journals. Given what you know of the practices of scientific journals, will these five papers together present an accurate view of the harmful effects of the drug? This problem, which is of serious concern to those who base arguments on published scientific research, including tort lawyers, has been dubbed the *file drawer problem.*

A related problem is the *cancer cluster problem.* States annually publish the incidence of each major type of cancer for each of their counties. Suppose that a state has 25 counties and that incidence data are listed for 10 types of cancer. A tort lawyer scans the list and observes that the incidence of liver cancer in one county is significantly above the state-wide incidence (0.05 significance level). Is this good evidence that some unusual agent that causes liver cancer is at work in that county? What if the list had been a national list that provided incidence data for the same 10 types of cancer in 1,000 counties?

sibly fatal heart disease can be treated with treatment A or treatment B. And suppose further that a series of clinical trials produces statistically significant results suggesting that the survival rates associated with the two treatments are 67.2% and 67.3%. Although it might appear that the difference of 0.1% is unimportant, if 1 million people suffer from the type of heart disease in question, using the better treatment will save, on average, 1,000 lives a year.

3. Suggestions for Further Reading

Jelke Bethlehem, *Applied Survey Methods: A Statistical Perspective* (Hoboken, NJ: John Wiley & Sons, 2009). A thorough introduction to survey design and analysis.

Richard D. De Veaux, Paul F. Velleman, and David E. Bock, *Intro Stats*, 3rd ed. (Reading, MA: Addison Wesley, 2008). If you are having difficulty with any of the topics covered in this chapter, this college text is a good place to look for simple explanations with many worked problems.

Lawrence C. Hamilton, *Statistics with STATA: Version 10*, 7th ed. (Pacific Grove, CA: Duxbury Press, 2008). If you want to perform data analysis on your own, you will need a statistics software package. Stata is an easy to use program for beginners, and Hamilton provides an excellent introduction to its use.

David Salsburg, *The Lady Tasting Tea: How Statistics Revolutionized Science in the Twentieth Century* (New York, NY: W.H. Freeman, 2001). A thoroughly engaging portrayal of the people and events responsible for the development of modern statistical analysis.

Nassim Nicholas Taleb, *The Black Swan: the Impact of the Highly Improbable*, 2nd ed. (New York, NY: Random House Trade Paperbacks, 2010). An influential and thought-provoking critique of some standard uses of statistics in finance.

Edward R. Tufte, *The Visual Display of Quantitative Information*, 2nd ed. (Cheshire, CT: Graphics Press, 2001). A modern classic updated.

Z-Table

z	.00	.01	.02	.03	.04	.05	.06	.07	.08	.09
-3.4	.0003	.0003	.0003	.0003	.0003	.0003	.0003	.0003	.0003	.0002
-3.3	.0005	.0005	.0005	.0004	.0004	.0004	.0004	.0004	.0004	.0003
-3.2	.0007	.0007	.0006	.0006	.0006	.0006	.0006	.0005	.0005	.0005
-3.1	.0010	.0009	.0009	.0009	.0008	.0008	.0008	.0008	.0007	.0007
-3.0	.0013	.0013	.0013	.0012	.0012	.0011	.0011	.0011	.0010	.0010
-2.9	.0019	.0018	.0018	.0017	.0016	.0016	.0015	.0015	.0014	.0014
-2.8	.0026	.0025	.0024	.0023	.0023	.0022	.0021	.0021	.0020	.0019
-2.7	.0035	.0034	.0033	.0032	.0031	.0030	.0029	.0028	.0027	.0026
-2.6	.0047	.0045	.0044	.0043	.0041	.0040	.0039	.0038	.0037	.0036
-2.5	.0062	.0060	.0059	.0057	.0055	.0054	.0052	.0051	.0049	.0048
-2.4	.0082	.0080	.0078	.0075	.0073	.0071	.0069	.0068	.0066	.0064
-2.3	.0107	.0104	.0102	.0099	.0096	.0094	.0091	.0089	.0087	.0084
-2.2	.0139	.0136	.0132	.0129	.0125	.0122	.0119	.0116	.0113	.0110
-2.1	.0179	.0174	.0170	.0166	.0162	.0158	.0154	.0150	.0146	.0143
-2.0	.0228	.0222	.0217	.0212	.0207	.0202	.0197	.0192	.0188	.0183
-1.9	.0287	.0281	.0274	.0268	.0262	.0256	.0250	.0244	.0239	.0233
-1.8	.0359	.0351	.0344	.0336	.0329	.0322	.0314	.0307	.0301	.0294
-1.7	.0446	.0436	.0427	.0418	.0409	.0401	.0392	.0384	.0375	.0367
-1.6	.0548	.0537	.0526	.0516	.0505	.0495	.0485	.0475	.0465	.0455
-1.5	.0668	.0655	.0643	.0630	.0618	.0606	.0594	.0582	.0571	.0559
-1.4	.0808	.0793	.0778	.0764	.0749	.0735	.0721	.0708	.0694	.0681
-1.3	.0968	.0951	.0934	.0918	.0901	.0885	.0869	.0853	.0838	.0823
-1.2	.1151	.1131	.1112	.1093	.1075	.1056	.1038	.1020	.1003	.0985
-1.1	.1357	.1335	.1314	.1292	.1271	.1251	.1230	.1210	.1190	.1170
-1.0	.1587	.1562	.1539	.1515	.1492	.1469	.1446	.1423	.1401	.1379
-0.9	.1841	.1814	.1788	.1762	.1736	.1711	.1685	.1660	.1635	.1611
-0.8	.2119	.2090	.2061	.2033	.2005	.1977	.1949	.1922	.1894	.1867
-0.7	.2420	.2389	.2358	.2327	.2296	.2266	.2236	.2206	.2177	.2148
-0.6	.2743	.2709	.2676	.2643	.2611	.2578	.2546	.2514	.2483	.2451
-0.5	.3085	.3050	.3015	.2981	.2946	.2912	.2877	.2843	.2810	.2776
-0.4	.3446	.3409	.3372	.3336	.3300	.3264	.3228	.3192	.3156	.3121
-0.3	.3821	.3783	.3745	.3707	.3669	.3632	.3594	.3557	.3520	.3483
-0.2	.4207	.4168	.4129	.4090	.4052	.4013	.3974	.3936	.3897	.3859
-0.1	.4602	.4562	.4522	.4483	.4443	.4404	.4364	.4325	.4286	.4247
-0.0	.5000	.4960	.4920	.4880	.4840	.4801	.4761	.4721	.4681	.4641
0.0	.5000	.5040	.5080	.5120	.5160	.5199	.5239	.5279	.5319	.5359
0.1	.5398	.5438	.5478	.5517	.5557	.5596	.5636	.5675	.5714	.5753
0.2	.5793	.5832	.5871	.5910	.5948	.5987	.6026	.6064	.6103	.6141
0.3	.6179	.6217	.6255	.6293	.6331	.6368	.6406	.6443	.6480	.6517
0.4	.6554	.6591	.6628	.6664	.6700	.6736	.6772	.6808	.6844	.6879
0.5	.6915	.6950	.6985	.7019	.7054	.7088	.7123	.7157	.7190	.7224
0.6	.7257	.7291	.7324	.7357	.7389	.7422	.7454	.7486	.7517	.7549
0.7	.7580	.7611	.7642	.7673	.7704	.7734	.7764	.7794	.7823	.7852
0.8	.7881	.7910	.7939	.7967	.7995	.8023	.8051	.8078	.8106	.8133
0.9	.8159	.8186	.8212	.8238	.8264	.8289	.8315	.8340	.8365	.8389
1.0	.8413	.8438	.8461	.8485	.8508	.8531	.8554	.8577	.8599	.8621
1.1	.8643	.8665	.8686	.8708	.8729	.8749	.8770	.8790	.8810	.8830
1.2	.8849	.8869	.8888	.8907	.8925	.8944	.8962	.8980	.8997	.9015
1.3	.9032	.9049	.9066	.9082	.9099	.9115	.9131	.9147	.9162	.9177
1.4	.9192	.9207	.9222	.9236	.9251	.9265	.9279	.9292	.9306	.9319
1.5	.9332	.9345	.9357	.9370	.9382	.9394	.9406	.9418	.9429	.9441
1.6	.9452	.9463	.9474	.9484	.9495	.9505	.9515	.9525	.9535	.9545
1.7	.9554	.9564	.9573	.9582	.9591	.9599	.9608	.9616	.9625	.9633
1.8	.9641	.9649	.9656	.9664	.9671	.9678	.9686	.9693	.9699	.9706
1.9	.9713	.9719	.9726	.9732	.9738	.9744	.9750	.9756	.9761	.9767
2.0	.9772	.9778	.9783	.9788	.9793	.9798	.9803	.9808	.9812	.9817
2.1	.9821	.9826	.9830	.9834	.9838	.9842	.9846	.9850	.9854	.9857
2.2	.9861	.9864	.9868	.9871	.9875	.9878	.9881	.9884	.9887	.9890
2.3	.9893	.9896	.9898	.9901	.9904	.9906	.9909	.9911	.9913	.9916
2.4	.9918	.9920	.9922	.9925	.9927	.9929	.9931	.9932	.9934	.9936
2.5	.9938	.9940	.9941	.9943	.9945	.9946	.9948	.9949	.9951	.9952
2.6	.9953	.9955	.9956	.9957	.9959	.9960	.9961	.9962	.9963	.9964
2.7	.9965	.9966	.9967	.9968	.9969	.9970	.9971	.9972	.9973	.9974
2.8	.9974	.9975	.9976	.9977	.9977	.9978	.9979	.9979	.9980	.9981
2.9	.9981	.9982	.9982	.9983	.9984	.9984	.9985	.9985	.9986	.9986
3.0	.9987	.9987	.9987	.9988	.9988	.9989	.9989	.9989	.9990	.9990
3.1	.9990	.9991	.9991	.9991	.9992	.9992	.9992	.9992	.9993	.9993
3.2	.9993	.9993	.9994	.9994	.9994	.9994	.9994	.9995	.9995	.9995
3.3	.9995	.9995	.9995	.9996	.9996	.9996	.9996	.9996	.9996	.9997
3.4	.9997	.9997	.9997	.9997	.9997	.9997	.9997	.9997	.9997	.9998

9
Multivariate Statistics

Some methods for performing three fundamental tasks of statistical analysis — data description, hypothesis testing, and estimation — on one-variable (i.e., univariate) data sets were introduced in the last chapter. Now the focus shifts from univariate analysis and univariate data sets to multivariate analysis and multivariate data sets — those composed of values, or scores, on two or more variables for each of a set of individuals.

1. Bivariate Statistics

The simplest form of multivariate statistics — bivariate statistics — probes the relationship between just two variables. The data set of interest consists of paired values, one score on each of the two variables for every individual in the set. Important questions in many fields seem to be natural candidates for bivariate analysis: Do high LSAT scores indicate that students will do well in law school? Is smoking bad for your health? Do grade-school students learn better in smaller classes? Does wearing a seat belt decrease the chance of sustaining serious injuries in car wrecks? Are the prices of stocks with high P/E ratios likely to decline? Such questions arise when a party wants to be able to predict or manipulate a variable using information about its relation to some other variable with which it is associated.[1]

---

1. Although any combination of categorical or quantitative variables can be analyzed with bivariate methods, we'll consider here only situations where both variables are quantitative.

A. Scatterplots

The most common form of pictorial presentation of bivariate data sets is the scatterplot, a type of graph on which each individual's scores on both variables are plotted as a single point. The pattern created by the points in a scatterplot can reveal the nature of the relationship between the two variables.

The Starchway scenario presented in the preceding chapter provides a good example of a situation where a scatterplot may be a helpful way to analyze data. To refresh your memory, Mary Starchway is defending against a claim of gender discrimination in pay at her company, Starchway Cookies.

Example 9-1

Ms. Starchway claims that the gender differential for wages at her company is a by-product of paying higher salaries to employees with more experience. (Indeed, a common defense in such cases is that the difference in pay is due, not to discrimination, but to innocent practices, such as tying salary to education level, giving a raise every year to all employees, and so forth.) To support her contention, she puts together a table, listing each employee's gender, salary, and number of years of relevant experience (see Table 9-1).[2] As a first step in evaluating Ms. Starchway's claim, we can construct a scatterplot from the data for the two quantitative variables — salary and relevant experience.

How to . . .

. . . construct a scatterplot

To construct a scatterplot for two quantitative variables measured on the same set of individuals:

---

2. Even though there are three variables, this can be considered a bivariate case. The reason is that our immediate concern is with only two variables (salary and experience). Thus, for the moment we can ignore the other variable (gender). However, if we wanted to know whether gender has an impact on the relationship between salary and experience, we could plot salary against experience for males and females separately.

Table 9-1
Gender, Salary, and Experience
of Starchway Employees

Employee	Gender	Salary ($000s)	Experience (no. of years)
1	m	25	2
2	m	50	4
3	f	40	4
4	m	75	5
5	f	40	7
6	f	50	13
7	f	20	1
8	m	50	4
9	m	50	4
10	f	70	15
11	m	25	1
12	f	20	2
13	f	250	6
14	m	100	9
15	m	75	6
16	m	50	5
17	f	20	1
18	f	50	3
19	m	100	7
20	f	40	5

1. Label the x-axis of a graph with the name of one variable and its unit of measurement.

2. Select an appropriate scale for the x-axis (a scale that allows the axis to accommodate all scores on the variable), and mark and label the axis accordingly.

3. Do the same along the y-axis for the other variable.

4. For each individual in the data set, place a mark at the point where a vertical line drawn through the value of the x-axis variable would intersect a horizontal line drawn through the value of the y-axis variable.

Applying these steps to the data in Table 9-1 gives us Figure 9-1.

Does salary appear to go up as experience increases, as would be consistent with Ms. Starchway's claim? Well, it looks as if there may be such a tendency. However, several exceptions

Figure 9-1
Starchway Employees: Salary and Experience

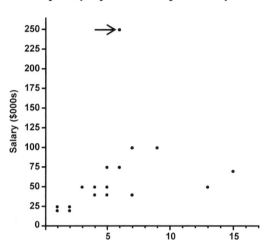

are clearly apparent. The two employees with the most relevant experience do not by any means have the highest salaries. And the employee with the highest salary by far, has what looks to be only about average experience.

When analyzing scatterplots, statisticians bring to the task a mental set of ideal shapes, just as they do when approaching graphic presentations of single-variable data. The difference is that the entries in this second mental catalog represent ideal relationships between two variables rather than ideal distributions of one variable. The most important shape for describing scatterplots is, without a doubt, the straight line. When all the points in a scatterplot can be connected by a single straight line, we say the two variables plotted in the scatterplot have a perfect linear relationship. In practice, however, bivariate data virtually always fall short of perfect linearity, and statisticians have to decide, case by case, whether the relationship between the two variables is "linear enough" to treat it as linear.

B. Linear Relationships

As you may remember from math classes you've taken, every equation for a straight line has the simple form $y = a + bx$, where a and b are constants and x and y are variables, one plotted on the x-axis and the other

Figure 9-2
Temperature Scales: A Linear Relationship

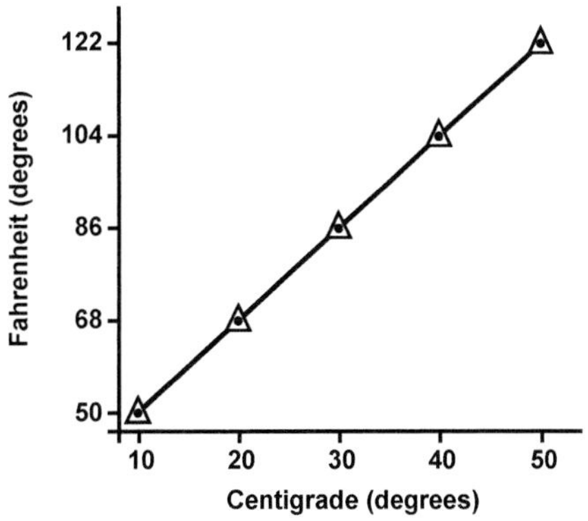

on the y-axis. When two variables are linearly related, such an equation can be used to calculate y (the value, or score, on the variable represented along the y-axis) from any given x (value, or score, on the variable represented along the x-axis) and vice versa. In the case of the two variables in Figure 9-2 (the two scales of temperature measurement, Fahrenheit and Centigrade), the linear equation is °F = 32 + (9/5 × °C). Hence, for any given temperature in degrees Fahrenheit, we can calculate the equivalent temperature in degrees Centigrade, and for any given temperature in degrees Centigrade, we can calculate the equivalent temperature in degrees Fahrenheit. In other words, the relationship between Fahrenheit and Centigrade is one of complete predictability.

Unfortunately, such perfect relationships are virtually always the result of a definitional connection, as is the case for the Fahrenheit and Centigrade scales. When we construct scatterplots from actual data, what we see are generally much less tidy arrangements of points, such as those in Figure 9-3.

All six scatterplots in Figure 9-3 more or less resemble perfect linearity — that is, the shape of each one is more or less a straight line. To describe them with qualitative language, scatterplot A exhibits no apparent linear relationship, scatterplot B reflects a weak linear relationship, scatterplots C and D represent moderately linear relationships, and scatterplots E and F suggest strong linear relationships. A strong linear relationship means that there's a linear equation that will enable us to do a very good job of predicting the value of either variable from

Figure 9-3
Bivariate Data: Scatterplots

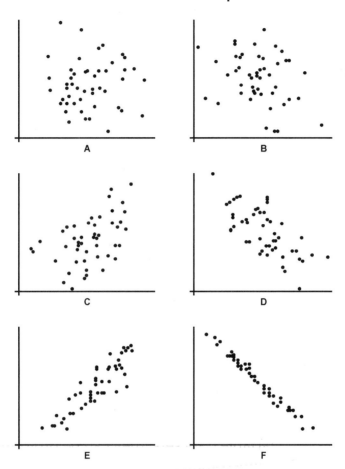

the corresponding value of the other variable. In contrast, if a linear relationship is weak or nonexistent, there is no linear equation that will be of much use.

C. The Pearson Correlation Coefficient

Although the strength of the linearity of a relationship between two quantitative variables can be roughly estimated simply by inspecting a scatterplot, a precise measure, the Pearson correlation coefficient, is generally calculated. This coefficient, r, is a number between -1.0 and $+1.0$ that describes not only the strength of the linear relationship between two variables, but also its direction, positive or negative.

Variables may be correlated positively, negatively, or not at all. Two variables are *positively correlated* if above-average values of one tend to accompany above-average values of the other, and below-average values of one tend to accompany below-average values of the other. Education and income, for example, are positively correlated, as are height and weight. A positive correlation coefficient (i.e., one that's greater than 0 but less than or equal to +1.0) indicates that variables are positively correlated. Two variables are *negatively correlated* if below-average values of one tend to accompany above-average values of the other and vice versa. A country's mortality rate and its GNP, for example, are negatively correlated. A negative correlation coefficient (i.e., one that's less than 0 but greater than or equal to –1.0) signifies that variables are negatively correlated. The closer to +1.0, in the case of positive correlations, or –1.0 in the case of negative correlations, the stronger the linear relationship. A correlation coefficient of 0 or close to 0 indicates the absence of a linear relationship between the two variables.[3]

To get a feel for correlation coefficients, let's look again at the scatterplots in Figure 9-3. Note how our qualitative descriptions pair up with the quantitative descriptions (i.e., their correlation coefficients) of the depicted linear relationships (see Table 9-2).

Correlation coefficients must be interpreted with some degree of care, for they are subject to a number of distorting influences. For example, just like means of single-variable data sets, they can be profoundly affected by outliers. For a clear illustration of this phenomenon, let's look again at Figure 9-1: the correlation coefficient between experience and salary calculated from the data plotted there turns out to be 0.3289, which is far from the 0.6030 that's obtained if the data for the single (but extreme) outlying point are excluded from the calculation.

How are correlation coefficients calculated?

---

3. Because correlation coefficients are derived from sample values, the concerns pointed out in the previous chapter regarding the relationship between sample values and population values apply here as well. In particular, confidence intervals can be calculated for a correlation coefficient derived from sample data and the hypothesis that two variables are correlated (i.e., that their correlation coefficient is different from 0) can be tested by using sample data. The methods for doing so are, however, beyond the scope of this chapter.

Table 9-2
Qualitative and Quantitative Descriptions of the
Scatterplots Pictured in Figure 9-3

Scatterplot	Qualitative description	Quantitative description
A	none	$r = 0.00$
B	weak negative	$r = -0.30$
C	moderate positive	$r = 0.50$
D	moderate negative	$r = -0.70$
E	strong positive	$r = 0.90$
F	very strong negative	$r = -0.99$

How to . . .

. . . calculate the Pearson correlation coefficient

1. For a data set consisting of n individuals and two variables, X and Y, calculate the mean and standard deviation for each of the 2 variables.

2. For each individual in the data set, calculate the z-score for the value of variable X:

$$z_{X_1} = (X_1 - \bar{x}) / s_X$$

$$z_{X_2} = (X_2 - \bar{x}) / s_X$$

$$\ldots$$

$$z_{X_n} = (X_n - \bar{x}) / s_X$$

3. For each individual, calculate the z-score for the value of variable Y:

$$z_{Y_1} = (Y_1 - \bar{y}) / s_Y$$

$$z_{Y_2} = (Y_2 - \bar{y}) / s_Y$$

$$\ldots$$

$$z_{Y_n} = (Y_n - \bar{y}) / s_Y$$

4. Multiply each individual's two z-scores to get the product:

$$z_{X_1} \times z_{Y_1}$$

$$z_{X_2} \times z_{Y_2}$$

$$\ldots$$

$$z_{X_n} \times z_{Y_n}$$

5. Add the products of the z-scores:

$$\left(z_{X_1} \times z_{Y_1}\right) + \left(z_{X_2} \times z_{Y_2}\right) + \ldots + \left(z_{X_n} \times z_{Y_n}\right)$$

6. Divide the sum by n – 1 to arrive at the Pearson correlation coefficient:

$$r = \frac{\left(z_{X_1} \times z_{Y_1}\right) + \left(z_{X_2} \times z_{Y_2}\right) + \ldots + \left(z_{X_n} \times z_{Y_n}\right)}{n - 1}$$

Obviously, calculating the correlation coefficient can be a messy affair for all but the smallest of data sets. Fortunately, computer programs now assume the burden. The task is manageable for small data sets, however, and working through the calculations by hand at least once can be very informative. See if you can figure out what the impact on the correlation coefficient would be of adding an individual to the data set whose score on both variables was very high relative to other scores on those variables. How about adding an individual whose score was very high on one of the variables and very low on the other?

1. Correlation and causation. It can be very tempting to think of correlation as an indicator of causation. After all, why would the value of one variable increase — or, for that matter, decrease — in direct proportion to an increase (or decrease) in the value of another variable unless some causal mechanism were at work? When a bicyclist pedals faster, for example, her heart rate increases, and when the demand for gasoline rises, consumers are charged more for it. On the other hand, when the supply of air conditioners decreases, their price goes up, and when the number of people using seatbelts increases, the number of highway fatalities goes down. In all these instances, it's plausible to think that a change in the value of one variable is responsible for — causes — the change in the other.

A few moments of reflection, however, are enough to realize that a correlation between two variables, even a very strong correlation, doesn't necessarily mean that a change in one of the variables would cause a corresponding change in the other variable. Consider, for example, LSAT scores and first-year law school grades. Although there's a modest to moderate correlation between them, it's certainly not true that scoring high on the LSAT *causes* a law student to get high grades in the first year of law school. More plausibly, a third variable — probably some sort of ability that enables people to do well (or poorly) on the LSAT as well as on first-year exams — accounts for the correlation. In the same vein, hand size and foot size are highly correlated, though surely not because bigger hands cause bigger feet or vice versa but because some of the genes that influence the size of one also influence the size of the other. Situations like these illustrate what is known as the *common response problem.*

Sometimes, even though a causal relationship exists between two correlated variables, its strength may be difficult to estimate because one or more other, unaccounted for, variables are also contributing to the correlation. The length of one's rap sheet, for example, is negatively correlated with one's yearly salary. But are these variables correlated because employers are prejudiced against hiring repeat offenders? Or because the time repeat offenders spend committing crimes or serving sentences cuts into the time they can devote to devote to education or employment? Or because the character of career criminals isn't compatible with success in high-paying jobs? Clearly, it's a mistake to infer that the strength of the causal relationship between rap-sheet length and yearly salary is similar to the strength of their correlation.

When a correlation coefficient misleads as to the strength of a causal connection between two correlated variables — because it reflects not only the relationship between those variables but also the influence of one or more other variables whose individual effects can't easily be isolated and assessed — there is said to be *confounding*. More generally, confounding is said to occur whenever a causal inference based on a data set is determined to be ill-founded because of the operation of a variable or variables not accounted for in the making of the inference. And the unaccounted for variables are variously referred to as *confounders* or *lurking variables.*

Box 9-1
Correlation: Some Illustrations

College grades and first-year law school grades	<0.30
LSAT scores and first-year law school grades	~0.40
Heights of fraternal twins	~0.50
Heights of identical twins	~0.95

Here's another example of confounding: for high schools in the United States, average teacher's salary and average student SAT scores are moderately to highly correlated. Will paying teachers more result in improved student SAT scores? What are some potential confounders that might explain the apparent strength of this relationship?

Confounders are widely prevalent, and they have the potential to lead the unwary astray. But you'll avoid falling into the trap if you let this maxim be your guide: correlation doesn't imply causation; even a very strong correlation between two variables isn't in and of itself conclusive

---

Box 9-2
Simpson's Paradox — Categorical Data
and Confounding

You are presented with the following categorical data: over the past 5 years, 3,000 out of 10,000 women applicants for graduate study at Ames University were accepted, while 3,500 out of 10,000 male applicants were accepted. Using the z-test for proportions, you determine that the difference in acceptance rates is highly statistically significant. You conclude that there is a prima facie case for gender discrimination in graduate admissions at Ames University.

Further inquiry elicits the following information: There are three graduate schools at Ames: the law school, the medical school and the business school. When broken down by school, the admissions data looks like this: for the medical school, 300 of 3,000 male applicants were accepted (10%), versus 900 of 6,000 female applicants (15%); for the law school, 1,200 out of 3,000 males (40%) were accepted, versus 1,500 out of 3,000 females (50%), for the business school 2,000 males were accepted out of 4,000 male applicants (50%) versus 600 females out of 1,000 (60%).

So, when the data is broken down by school, each of the 3 schools is found to admit a higher percentage of its female applicants than of its male applicants. Do you wish to reconsider your initial assessment of the probability of gender discrimination?

evidence that a change in one causes a change in the other. The implication is that you shouldn't rely solely on correlational analysis if you want
to investigate causal relationships between variables.

The field of experimental methodology is largely concerned with the
making of sound causal inferences from controlled observations. Most
of the time, however, the data encountered in law and social policy making haven't been derived from experiments. When causation is a critical
issue, and you don't have experimental evidence, you must do the best
that you can with correlational data sets. Commonly, this will involve
gathering data on many variables and looking for patterns in the correlations among them. Further analysis will require the use of multiple
regression (which will be addressed a little later) or some other statistical
method appropriate for multivariate data analysis.

Just as correlation doesn't imply causation, causation doesn't imply
correlation. Correlation reflects a linear relationship. If the association
between two variables is nonlinear, the correlation coefficient may be
small, or even zero, even though the causal relationship is quite strong.
The data from psychological research on motivation and performance
provide what has become a famous example of this phenomenon (see
Figure 9-4). When motivation is weak, performance is poor, and as motivation becomes stronger, performance improves — but only up to a
point. Performance level eventually drops off, because of factors such as
anxiety resulting from excessive motivation. (For example, if your life
were at stake, your performance would likely be seriously impaired,
even though you'd be extremely highly motivated to perform well.) The
causal relationship between motivation and performance is unmistak-
able. Nevertheless, the correlation between the two is zero.

2. Correlation and prediction. Although correlation doesn't imply causation, it does imply that a value of either variable for a given individual
can be used to predict the value of the other variable for that individual.
And the higher the absolute value of the correlation coefficient for the
two variables, the better the prediction. Consider for a moment LSAT
scores and first-year law school grades, which we concluded aren't caus-
ally related despite being moderately correlated. Is it, then, a mistake
to make a rough prediction about a student's first-year grades from the
student's LSAT score? No, it isn't. What a positive correlation says about

Figure 9-4
Motivation and Performance: The Inverted U

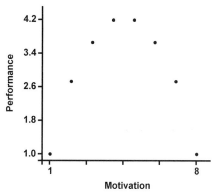

the relationship between variables is that higher values of one variable tend to be paired with higher values of the other variable and lower values with lower values. Thus, for example, predicting that first-year GPA will be higher than average for a student whose LSAT score was higher than average and lower than average for a student whose LSAT score was lower than average would be perfectly justifiable (and even more specific predictions are possible, though we will need the material in the next section to make them).

A lack of information about causation simply implies that we can't predictably change the value of one of two correlated variables by intervening and manipulating the value of the other one. Imagine, for example, that we could persuade the LSAT scorers to raise a student's score. Could we conclude that the student's first-year GPA would be higher than it would have been had the LSAT score not been bumped upward? Though we might not be tempted to answer this question in the affirmative, we could probably be more easily led to believe, solely on the basis of correlational studies, that drinking wine is good for the heart or that increasing teachers' salaries will improve student performance.

D. Simple Linear Regression

Correlational analysis is useful for roughly identifying the strength and direction of a linear relationship between two variables. So, when a loose, qualitative prediction (e.g., that Mary will be taller than average) is good enough, as is sometimes the case, correlational analysis is up to the task.

Box 9-3
Correlational Analysis:
A Controversial Application

A recent book by a well known public health researcher offers the following advice to parents — "It is
well known that the earlier a child takes his first drink, the
more likely he will be an alcoholic in later life, so do all
you can to delay your child's first experience of alcohol."
Is this advice justified by the cited results?

Often, however, a more specific, quantitative prediction is desirable or
necessary. In such cases we would like to identify the specific linear
equation that is likely to produce, on average, the best estimates of the
value of the variable to be predicted, given our data.

Simple linear regression is a technique for deriving and using this
optimal linear equation. The variable whose value is to be predicted is
called the *response variable*, and the variable from which the prediction is
made is the *explanatory variable*. Because linear regression depends only
on correlational information and correlation is bidirectional (i.e., if A is
correlated with B, then B is correlated with A), either of the correlated
variables may be designated the response variable.

Here's an example of the use of a simple linear regression equation.

Example 9-2

Hazel, a 40-year-old mother, is 66 inches tall, and she'd like
to know how tall her 6-year-old daughter, Emily, will be at age
20. She knows that daughter's height and mother's height are
correlated and thus that it's possible to predict daughter's height
from mother's height,[4] but she doesn't know how to do it. So
she turns to us.

We just happen to have a simple regression equation for
predicting the height (in inches) of a 20-year-old daughter (let's

---

4. Mother's height could just as easily be predicted from daughter's height, in
which case mother's height would be the response variable and daughter's height
the explanatory variable.

call this height E) from the height (in inches) of her mother at age 40 years (H):[5]

$$E = 28 \text{ inches} + (0.6 \times H)$$

We also know that Hazel, at age 40 years, is 66 inches tall, so we plug 66 into the equation:

$$E = 28 + (0.6 \times 66)$$
$$= 28 + 39.6$$
$$= 67.6$$

We can tell Hazel that Emily is predicted to be 67.6 inches tall when she's 20 years old.

As you may have noticed, the equation that we just used has the general form of a linear equation, y = a + bx, where x and y represent variables and a and b are constants. And because a linear equation is the formula for a straight line, when pairs of values for the two variables of any given simple regression equation are plotted in a scatterplot, they lie on a perfectly straight line,[6] called the *regression line* for that particular regression equation. The value of one of the constants, a, determines where the regression line intersects the y-axis. Hence, a is known as the *y-intercept*. The value of the other constant, b, which is called the *regression coefficient*, determines the direction of the regression line. B is also referred to as the *slope* of the regression line. When b is a positive value, we can be certain both that the line goes *upward* from left to right and that y (the value predicted for the response variable) *increases* as x increases. When b is negative, on the other hand, the line goes *downward* from left to right and y *decreases* as x increases.

---

5. This equation was derived from the heights of 500 pairs of mothers and daughters. The actual derivation was a complicated, messy task — one that's best left to computers.

6. If this concept isn't familiar, take a moment to check it out. Label the y-axis of a graph daughter's height and the x-axis mother's height. Choose three or four values for mother's height, calculate daughter's height for each, and plot the pairs of heights. You can also plot the pair of values from the example (x = 66.0, y = 67.6). A single straight line can be drawn through all of the plotted points.

Every linear equation has a corresponding regression line (and every regression line has a corresponding linear equation). Hence, for any two correlated variables, finding the best linear equation for prediction (i.e., the one that yields the best predictions possible) is equivalent to finding the straight line that comes closest to the points of the scatterplot.[7] The closeness of the regression line to the points on the scatterplot is known as the *fit* of the regression line to the data. The fit is perfect when all the points fall squarely on the line. For fit to be perfect, the correlation must be perfect — that is, the correlation coefficient between the explanatory variable and the response variable must be exactly +1.0 or –1.0. Otherwise, the degree of fit depends on the definition of closeness adopted. We'll illustrate this definitional problem in the following example.

Example 9-3

We've just been informed that the personnel file on one Starchway employee, employee 21, was inadvertently left out of the batch of files provided to us when we did our initial analysis of salaries at the company. Even though the file still isn't available and we don't know anything particular about the employee, we'd like to estimate the employee's salary.

Our best guess at employee 21's salary is $60,000, the mean of the salary distribution.[8] (In the absence of additional useful information, the best guess at an unknown value from a distribution is, for most purposes, the mean of the distribution.)

Employee 21's personnel file has been delivered to us. We can't, however, find any record of the employee's current salary, though we can determine that the employee has 9 years of relevant experience. What's our best estimate now?

Knowing that experience and salary are correlated and knowing how much relevant experience employee 21 has, we can apply linear regression analysis to make an estimate of the employee's salary that's likely to be better than our original estimate. We'll treat salary, which we'll designate S, as the re-

---

7. As we'll see in a moment, *best* and *closest* require further elucidation to function as regression criteria.

8. An argument could be made, of course, that a more appropriate estimate would be the mean calculated with Ms. Starchway's salary excluded.

sponse variable, and relevant experience, E, as the explanatory variable, so,

$$S = a + (b \times E)$$

where we will determine from our data what values for the two constants, a and b, yield the best linear equation for prediction.

The best linear equation for prediction will be the one that describes the line that lies closest to the points in the scatterplot of salary and experience (Figure 9-1). Figure 9-5 offers some candidate regression lines. As you can see, it's not obvious which line fits the description "closest to the points," because each line is closer to some points than any of the other lines, but further from others. What we need is a measure of overall closeness, one that in some way takes into account all the distances between the data points and the line. The sum of the distances between each point and the line might seem the obvious candidate, but for technical reasons, the sum of the *squared* distances is preferred.[9] Thus, from a statistical perspective, the line that's closest to all the data points and thus the best choice for the regression line is the one for which the sum of the squared distances between the data points and the line is the smallest possible. This line is called the *least squares regression line*, and the equation for the line is the *least squares regression equation*.

Example 9-3 *(continued)*

The least squares regression equation for our data on Starchway salary and experience turns out to be

$$S = 35,278.89 + 4,754.06(E)$$

where S is salary (in dollars) and E is relevant experience (in years). The constant b (4,754.06) in this equation can be interpreted as a measure of how much 1 year of relevant experience is worth, on average, in terms of salary. In other words, every year of relevant experience that a Starchway employee has is worth an average of $4,754.06 in salary. The constant a (35,278.89) can be interpreted as the starting salary of a worker with no experience. The line itself can be seen on the scatterplot

---

9. Specifically, we use the vertical distance between each point and the line.

Figure 9-5
Candidate Regression Lines

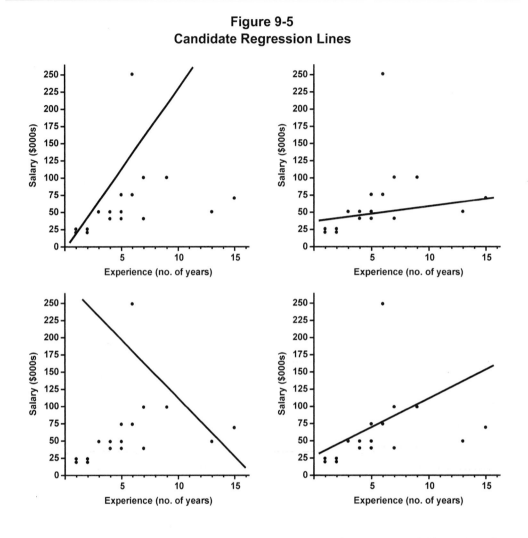

in Figure 9-6. So our best estimate of employee 21's salary from linear regression analysis is

$$S = 35,278.89 + (4,754.06 \times E)$$
$$= 35,278.89 + (4,754.06 \times 9)$$
$$= 78,065.43$$

How good is our new prediction likely to be? It depends on how strongly the explanatory variable (experience) is correlated with the response variable (salary). The correlation coefficient of 0.3289 for experience and salary indicates that the correlation between the two variables

Figure 9-6
Starchway Salaries: The Best-Fitting Line

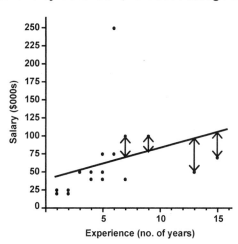

is weakly positive. We can't, then, expect our prediction to be very accurate. To get a sense of the overall accuracy of our regression equation, we can compare the estimated salaries calculated from the equation for employees 1–20 with the actual salaries, which we know.

Let's look at Table 9-3, where the actual salary of each employee is listed along with the corresponding estimate calculated from the regression equation and the residual for each of the two estimates of salary — the regression-generated estimate and the mean of all employee salaries. (A residual is simply the difference between a true value and an estimated value.) It's immediately apparent from the residuals that the regression estimates certainly aren't perfect, though they do seem, on average, to be better estimates than the mean is.

A statistic, R^2, is frequently used to express the accuracy of the estimates provided by a regression equation. All the information necessary to calculate R^2 for our regression equation is in Table 9-3.

How to . . .

> **. . . calculate R-squared**
>
> 1. Using the mean of each response variable as an estimate of its residual, add the squared residuals for all variables to find the total sum of squares (TSS):

Table 9-3
Starchway Salaries: The Residuals

Employee	Actual salary ($)	Regression derived estimate ($)	Regression residual ($)	Residual using mean ($60,000) as estimate ($)
1	25,000	44,787.01	−19,787.01	−35,000
2	50,000	54,295.13	−4,295.13	−10,000
3	40,000	54,295.13	−14,295.13	−20,000
4	75,000	59,049.19	15,950.81	15,000
5	40,000	68,557.31	−28,557.31	20,000
6	50,000	97,081.67	−47,081.67	10,000
7	20,000	40,032.95	−20,032.95	40,000
8	50,000	73,311.37	−23,311.37	10,000
9	50,000	73,311.37	−23.311.37	10,000
10	70,000	106,589.79	36,589.79	10,000
11	25,000	40,032.95	−15,032.95	35,000
12	20,000	44,787.01	−24,787.01	40,000
13	250,000	63,803.25	186,196.75	190,000
14	100,000	78,065.43	21,934.57	40,000
15	75,000	63,803.25	11,196.75	15,000
16	50,000	59,049.19	−9,049.19	10,000
17	20,000	40,032.95	−20,032.95	40,000
18	50,000	49,541.07	458.93	10,000
19	100,000	68,557.31	31,442.69	40,000
20	40,000	59,049.19	−19,049.19	20,000

$$TSS = \text{residual}_{(mean)_1}^{2} + \text{residual}_{(mean)_2}^{2} + \ldots$$
$$+ \text{residual}_{(mean)_n}^{2}$$

2. Then, using the estimated residual derived for each variable from the regression equation, add the squared residuals for all variables to get the sum of squared residuals (SSR):

$$SSR = \text{residual}_{(regression)_1}^{2} + \text{residual}_{(regression)_2}^{2} + \ldots$$
$$+ \text{residual}_{(regression)_n}^{2}$$

3. Subtract the sum of the squared residuals from the total sum of squares to find the reduction in the total that's achieved by estimating with the regression equation rather than with the mean, and divide the difference by the total sum of squares to get the proportionate reduction, which is R-squared:

$$R^2 = \frac{TSS - SSR}{TSS}$$

4. Optionally, convert the calculated R-squared to a percent. When expressed as a percent, R-squared is often referred to as the *percentage of variance explained.* (Why is this term appropriate? Think about how the total sum of squares is related to variance.)

$$R^2 (\%) = \frac{TSS - SSR}{TSS} \times 100$$

An R-squared of 0 indicates that the error in the estimate calculated from the regression equation is no less than that associated with the mean as estimate. In other words, the explanatory variable is of no use at all in predicting the response variable. An R-squared of 1.0, on the other hand, indicates that there is no error in the regression-generated estimates and thus that the explanatory variable predicts the response variable perfectly.

So what is R-squared for our Starchway regression?

Example 9-4

1. Calculate the TSS:

Square the residuals resulting from using the mean as estimator and add them together TSS = 48,900,000,000.

2. Then calculate the SSR:

Square the residuals resulting from using the regression equation as estimator and add them together SSR = 43,609,000,000.

3. Subtract the SSR from the TSS:

48,900,000,000 – 43,609,000,000 = 5,291,000,000 the reduction in the squared errors resulting from using the regression equation.

4. Calculate R^2

$$\frac{5,291,000,000}{48,900,000,000} = .1082$$

5. Convert R^2 to a percent reduction in squared error .1082 × 100 = 10.82%.

We now know that the equation will reduce the average squared error about 11%. Put another way, the equation explains about 11% of the variation in employees' salaries.[10] Remember, though, that this R-squared was calculated from a given data set and therefore, claiming that it applies to predictions made about individuals outside the given data set is a matter of inference, which involves problems of randomness, sample size, and so forth.

You may have noticed that the R-squared for our Starchway regression is exactly equal to the square of the correlation coefficient, r, for salary and experience: $R^2 = 0.1082$ and $r^2 = 0.3289^2 = 0.1082$. That the two are identical is no accident. Rather, it's the result of a general phenomenon that relates correlation and simple regression. (Are you surprised that the statistic is dubbed R-squared?)

E. Residuals

Residuals are of interest for much more than their role in calculating R-squared. Let's return to the Starchway residuals for the regression estimates. A simple way to visually organize them is to plot them as in Figure 9-7. A plot of this sort is particularly useful for identifying individuals in the data set for whom the explanatory variable is especially poor at predicting the actual response variable. Such individuals are routinely accorded special attention, because unusual residuals suggest that these individuals may be subject to some factor that doesn't generally

---

10. *Explains* is commonly used in this context even though use of the word generally isn't justified. It should be clear from what you know about how R-squared is calculated that the claim of explanation goes beyond the available evidence. Think back to the temperature example that we considered earlier in the chapter. The R-squared for a regression equation that predicts Fahrenheit temperatures from Celsius temperatures would be 1.0 — that is, the equation would be perfect in its predictions. But would you say that Celsius temperature perfectly *explains* Fahrenheit temperature?

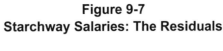

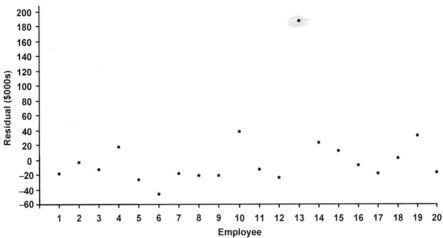

affect the others in the data set. A residual that's far out of line with the majority poses a problem analogous to the one posed by outliers in one-variable distributions. As with outliers, such residuals may arise from legitimate, valid values of the variable in question. But because of their disproportionate effect on the results of a variety of statistical analyses of the data, the data values that produced them are scrutinized care-fully and may be excluded from certain statistical calculations. Because the least squares regression equation is designed to minimize squared errors, the problem of unusual values can be particularly acute in the regression context. A list of individuals that generate unusual residuals, or *influential observations,* as they're often referred to, usually appears on the regression printout.

From the plot of the Starchway residuals, the residual associated with the salary for employee 13, Mary Starchway, appears to be just as influ-ential as the salary itself was as an outlier. Do all outliers in one-variable data sets appear as influential observations in regression analyses? (Do all influential observations in regression analyses appears as outliers in one-variable data sets?)

Plots such as Figure 9-7 for the Starchway data can also reveal patterns in residuals that suggest that some important variable other than the two in the regression equation is at play. Plotting the residuals against

Figure 9-8
Hypothetical Stock Index: Regression Residuals

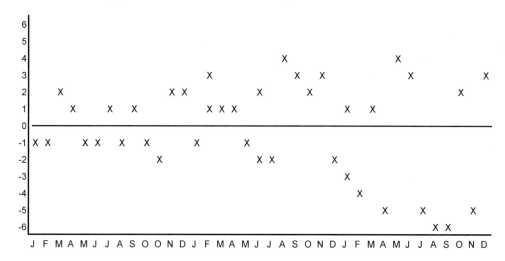

the times at which the matching observations were made, for example, might yield a pattern like the one in Figure 9-8. The regression equation we're using predicted past values very well but appears to be doing much worse recently. Is some new factor affecting the relationship between the response variable and the predictor variable?

F. Limitations of Linear Regression

Linear regression analysis has important limitations. For example, although the relationship between two variables may take any of a number of forms, a linear equation is an effective predictor only if the relationship is approximately linear (i.e., only if the scatterplot has a roughly linear appearance). The larger the absolute value of the correlation coefficient of the two variables, the better the linear regression equation is in its predictions.

A second limitation is that a linear regression equation predicts the same value for the response variable for all individuals with a given value on the explanatory variable. For example, using the regression equation on page 504, a height of 67.6 inches is predicted at age 20 for every daughter whose mother at age 40 was 66.0 inches tall. It takes just a moment, though, to realize that this pattern of outcomes is extremely unlikely. Rather, the daughters of mothers who were 66.0 inches when they were 40 years old constitute a subpopulation of all daughters. And because this subpopulation has a height distribution of its own, no single predicted value can possibly be correct for all its members. In fact, for any given value of an explanatory variable, variability in the value of the response variable is the norm rather than the exception. For this reason, error is virtually unavoidable in regression analysis.

2. Multiple Regression

Multiple regression may be viewed as an extension of simple regression to data sets with more than two variables. To accommodate the additional data, the regression equation is expanded to include more than one explanatory variable $(x_1, x_2, \ldots, x_n)$, each paired with its own regression coefficient $(b_1, b_2, \ldots, b_n)$. Thus, the general form of a multiple regression equation is $y = a + x_1 b_1 + x_2 b_2 + \ldots + x_n b_n$. For example, a multiple regression equation for predicting life expectancy (the response variable) for 25-year-old males on the basis of four explanatory variables — systolic blood pressure, cigarette smoking, weight, and formal education — might be

$$L = 51 - (0.03 \times P) - (0.2 \times C) - (0.1 \times W) + (0.3 \times S)$$

where L represents life expectancy in number of years, P represents systolic blood pressure in millimeters of mercury (mm Hg), C represents cigarette smoking in number of packs per week, W represents weight in percent above ideal, and S represents formal schooling in number of years. Just as with simple regression, a predicted score for an individual is calculated by multiplying the individual's score on each explanatory variable by its regression coefficient and then adding all the products plus the value of the y intercept (the value of the constant a) together. (What's the predicted life expectancy of a 25-year-old male who has a systolic blood pressure of 90 mm Hg, weighs 10% more than the ideal, smokes 4 packs of cigarettes a week, and has completed 19 years of school? Can you explain the negative coefficient for the cigarette-smoking variable?)

As with simple regression, the best equation for a multiple regression analysis is the one whose calculated intercept and coefficients (a and $b_1, b_2, \ldots, b_n$, respectively) minimize the sum of the squared errors of prediction. This equation, the *OLS multiple regression equation*, can be evaluated in much the same way as the simple linear regression equation was: by comparing, for each individual in the data set, its prediction of the response variable, y, with the alternative prediction of the response variable, its mean. If we knew nothing about a particular 25-year-old male, we would predict an average life expectancy for him. But if we knew something about his blood pressure, our prediction would be better. And if we also knew whether or how much he smokes, it would be better still. In fact, the more *relevant* information we have, the better our prediction would be, because multiple regression uses the additional information to improve predictive accuracy.

Multiple regression is eminently suited to the task of analyzing complex phenomena that result from the interplay of many variables. Crime rates, law school grades, employee salaries, business profits, inflation, and election outcomes are just a few examples. For such phenomena to be fully understood, not only must the contributory factors be identified, but the relative contribution of each must be quantified. For example, we might want to know what impact a change in the unemployment rate would have on the violent crime rate. Using a *simple* regression approach, we would check to see that unemployment and crime rate are correlated, and then produce a simple linear regression equation relating the two. Such an approach, while better than nothing, is subject to the common response problem (perhaps unemployment doesn't cause crime, but some third variable, e.g. lack of education, causes both to move together) and the problem of confounding variables (for example, both unemployment and crime have seasonal components).

Remember, as we emphasized above, correlation doesn't imply causation. To fully understand the relationship between unemployment and crime we have to account for the impacts on both of other related variables like education and season, and this is not possible within the restricted domain of simple regression. Multiple regression, on the other hand, allows us to take account of all additional relevant factors for which we have data. We develop a multiple regression equation that includes all relevant explanatory variables (or at least as many as practicable) and then focus on the coefficient of the variable of interest — here, the unemployment rate. This coefficient, unlike the simple regression coefficient, reflects the magnitude of the relationship between the unemployment rate and crime, when the influence of the other predictor variables is accounted for.

Consider the following regression equation (which, admittedly, falls far short of the ideal of including all relevant variables), where C represents the crime rate (in number of crimes per 100,000 population), T represents the average monthly temperature (in degrees Fahrenheit), D represents the high school dropout rate (in percent), and U represents the unemployment rate (in percent):

$$C = 200 + 1.2T + 2D + 40U$$

The analyst would conclude that, when temperature and dropout rate are controlled for (i.e., accounted for), each 1.0 percentage point increase in the unemployment rate is associated with, on average, an additional 40 violent crimes per 100,000 population.

Multiple regression is also used for prediction of a response variable, just as was simple linear regression. The difference is that, with multiple regression, enormous amounts of additional information can be brought to bear. Equations created to predict the future course of the U.S. economy contain literally thousands of explanatory variables.

A. Multiple Regression and Discrimination Litigation

Multiple regression analysis is often used in discrimination litigation to isolate the impact of a single explanatory variable on a response variable, such as the decision to hire. In litigation of a claim of gender discrimination in wages, for example, a plaintiff could make a prima facie case by pointing out that the average wage for women at the defendant company is less than the average wage for men. The defense might argue that the discrepancy has arisen not because of discrimination, but simply because the women on the company's payroll happen to have, on average, less education and experience than the men do and the defendant, perfectly legitimately, rewards its employees who have more education and experience by paying them higher wages. In other words, the average wage is higher for the men because they are, as a group, more educated and more experienced employees. The plaintiff would love to be able to rebut this argument with data on women employees whose experience and education are comparable to men's but whose wages are lower. Unfortunately, in a particular workforce, there may be few women for whom such a direct comparison is possible. Multiple regression analysis, via a mathematically complex averaging process, is able to generate precisely the sort of comparison that the plaintiff has in mind.

Using data on the relevant variables from the defendant's employment records, the plaintiff would construct a multiple regression equation with wage as the response variable. Letting W stand for wage in dollars, S for number of years of schooling (or education), E for number of years of experience, and G for gender,[11] suppose that the multiple regression equation that the plaintiff ended up with turned out to be:

$$W = 23{,}000 + (2{,}000 \times S) + (3{,}100 \times E) - (7{,}000 \times G)$$

This regression equation predicts, for example, that the average salary for female employees with 16 years of education and 6 years of experience would be $66,600:

$$23{,}000 + (2{,}000 \times 16) + (3{,}100 \times 6) - (7{,}000 \times 1) = \$66{,}600$$

The prediction for male employees with the same amount of education and experience, on the other hand, would be $73,600:

$$23{,}000 + (2{,}000 \times 16) + (3{,}100 \times 6) + (7{,}000 \times 0) = \$73{,}600$$

It's easy to see that, for any combination of education and experience, the average female employee would be paid $7,000 less than the average male with exactly the same combination of education and experience. Or, to put it into statistical language, after controlling for education

---

11. Gender is a categorical variable, and for this reason, it receives special treatment (as does any categorical variable included as an explanatory variable in a regression equation). Because there are two possible "values" of gender, female and male, one (female) was assigned a numerical value of 1 and the other (male) a numerical value of 0. A categorical variable whose possible values are assigned numerical values of 0 and 1 for the purpose of inclusion in multiple regression equations is known as a *dummy variable*. It doesn't matter which non-numerical "value" the 0 or the 1 is applied to which gender; the assignment is arbitrary. In the equation here, 1 could just as well have been assigned to male and 0 to female. Had this been the case, the gender coefficient would have turned out to be +7,000 instead of -7,000. In other words, male employees will have been found to make $7,000 more than their female counterparts rather than female employees making $7,000 less than their male counterparts.

and experience, women employees are paid $7,000 less than men. And this is exactly the type of demonstration that the plaintiff was hoping to present.

Let's look at an example of this sort of application of multiple regression analysis from an actual case.

Example 9-5

Bazemore et al. v. Friday et al., 478 U.S. 385 (1986)

This case centered around an allegation of racial discrimination in salary at the North Carolina Agricultural Extension Service. The average annual salary of black employees was substantially below that of whites. However, blacks tended to have less education and job experience. Data on salary, race, and legitimate factors that affect wages (education and job experience among others) were analyzed by multiple regression to determine whether the racial disparity in salary remained when the other factors were controlled for. Table 9-4 summarizes the explanatory variables that were included in the equation to predict annual salary, the scoring system for these variables, and the regression results. When all other factors were controlled for, being white added, on average, about $395 to salary.

The standard error of an estimated regression coefficient is a version of the standard deviation, as applied to estimated regression coefficients. It provides a measure of how closely sample-based estimates of a particular regression coefficient will cluster around the actual population regression coefficient. The larger the sample, the smaller the standard error of the regression coefficient will be and the smaller the difference between the coefficient for the sample and the coefficient for the population is likely to be.

There's always a possibility that what regression analysis identifies as an association between a response variable and an explanatory variable is only an apparent association not a genuine association — the result of unknowingly working with a sample that's unusual in some way and thus not truly representative of the population. For this reason, standard practice is to test each regression coefficient to determine whether there's good reason to think that the corresponding coefficient for the population

Table 9-4
Bazemore et al. v. Friday et al.: Explanatory Variables and Scoring System Used in Multiple Regression Analysis

Explanatory variables and scoring system

Variable	Score
Education	
master's degree (MS)	1 if person has master's degree; 0 otherwise
Employment	
tenure (TENURE)	number of years with the Service as of 1975
Position	
chairman (CHM)	1 if chairman; 0 otherwise
agent (AGENT)	1 if agent; 0 otherwise
associate (ASSOC)	1 if associate agent; 0 otherwise
Race (WHITE)	1 if white; 0 otherwise

Results

Response variable: annual salary

Explanatory variable	Coefficient	Standard error
MS	898.55	140.36
TENURE	59.06	8.47
CHM	5,221.19	232.28
AGENT	2,404.44	170.58
ASSOC	918.82	174.42
WHITE	394.80	137.67
CONSTANT	9,291.51	(none given)

Adjusted R-squared: 0.76

isn't 0. A null hypothesis is formulated for each regression coefficient — i.e., that the regression coefficient is 0 (i.e., $b_x = 0$) — and the hypothesis is tested. In this setting, the t test is the appropriate test.

How to . . .

> *. . . perform a t test*
> 1. Divide the regression coefficient for the sample, b_x, by its standard error to calculate its t score (the distance, measured in standard errors, that the coefficient is from 0).[12]

$$t = \frac{b_x}{\text{standard error for } b_x}$$

← coefficient

← std error

---

12. Calculating a t score no doubt reminds you of calculating a z-score. The processes are quite similar, but the t table is a bit more complicated to use than the z-table is.

2. Subtract the number of regression coefficients (which we'll abbreviate as c for the sake of simplicity), including the constant, in the equation being tested, from n, the number of individuals in the sample from which the regression equation was derived, to find the number of degrees of freedom (df):[13]

$$\text{df} = n - c \quad \text{← sample size} \quad \text{← # of coefficients}$$

(handwritten annotations: "degrees of freedom →" pointing to df; "← sample size", "# of coefficients")

3. Look in the t table (see end of chapter) to find the t score that corresponds to the number of degrees of freedom at the 0.05 significance level (or whatever significance level has been set as the standard to be met). To do this, look in the column labeled df for the appropriate number. Look across that row until you reach the column labeled 0.05. The number in this cell is the t score for the number of degrees of freedom at the 0.05 significance level.

4. If the calculated t score for the regression coefficient is greater than the t score in the table, you can reject the null hypothesis (i.e., $b_x = 0$) and conclude that the regression coefficient for x is statistically significant at the 0.05 level.

Let's test the null hypothesis for one of the regression coefficients — tenure — from the *Bazemore* case.

Example 9-6

1. We divide the regression coefficient for tenure by the corresponding standard error to get the coefficient's t score:

$$t = \frac{59.06}{8.47}$$
$$= 6.97$$

2. Then, to determine the number of degrees of freedom, we subtract the number of regression coefficients (which is 7, including the constant) from the sample size (which, though not specified earlier, is 568):

---

13. Degrees of freedom is a technical concept, the explanation of which is beyond the scope of this chapter. You don't, however, have to understand it to be able to use the t table, but you do need to know that it's derived from the size of the sample, n, from which the regression equation was derived.

$$df = 568 - 7$$
$$= 561$$

3. Our next step is to find the t score that corresponds to 561 degrees of freedom at the 0.05 significance level. But when we look down the column labeled df in the t table, we see that no numbers between 120 and infinity are listed. Let's be conservative and thus opt to use the t score for 120 degrees of freedom. Locating the cell where the row for 120 degrees of freedom intersects with the column for the 0.05 significance level, we find that the t score is 1.980.

4. Because the t score that we calculated (6.97) is greater than the t score corresponding to 120 degrees of freedom at the 0.05 significance level (1.980), we can reject the null hypothesis (i.e., $b_{tenure} = 0$) and conclude that the regression coefficient for tenure is statistically significant at the 0.05 level.[14]

What if a regression coefficient fails to pass the t test at the desired level of significance? In such an event, we can't conclude that the explanatory variable associated with it has a statistically significant effect on the response variable when all the other explanatory variables in the equation are controlled for. Failure to reach the specified level of significance is most troubling when the variable is the one of particular interest. For example, finding that the coefficient for race in the Bazemore case didn't meet the criterion for statistical significance would be a serious blow to the plaintiff's case.[15] If the coefficient that fails the t test is for an explanatory variable other than the one that's the focus of the inquiry, calculating a new regression equation from which the questioned variable is omitted and noting the impact that the omission has on R-squared would be appropriate. If the change in R-squared is small, the revised equation may well be preferable. The decision is ultimately a judgment

---

14. In fact, all of the regression coefficients in the Bazemore equation are significant at the 0.05 level. You might want to verify this claim by testing the null hypothesis for each of the other regression coefficients.

15. There would, however, be room for argument over the appropriateness of a 0.05 significance level in a civil case, where the overall evidentiary standard is preponderance of the evidence.

call by the analyst, taking into consideration nonstatistical matters, such as the nature of the underlying scientific theory.

B. Things That Can Go Wrong

In our experience, badly conducted regression analysis is the norm rather than the exception in social science and law. Because of the substantial leeway accorded the analyst in choosing explanatory variables and finding or generating data, it is possible for sophisticated analysts to represent a much more favorable view of their preferred theories than would be justified by a more balanced treatment of the evidence. Less sophisticated researchers too often miss the mark, in their case, because of a failure to appreciate the considerable subtleties and complexities of regression analysis. In the following sections we will present the deviations from sound practice that you will most frequently encounter, along with some idea of the distortions that may result and what to do about them

1. Omission of important explanatory variables. Whether important explanatory variables have been omitted from a regression equation is an issue that is at the heart of many discrimination cases. For example, in *EEOC v. Sears*, 839 F.2d 302 (1988). Sears, the defendant in a sex discrimination suit, claimed that women were less likely to be in high-paying jobs in commission sales at Sears because, as a group, they lacked interest in work of this type, not because Sears discriminated against women in hiring. According to the defense's theory, a woman who expressed an interest in commission sales would have about the same chance as a man of getting such a position, but this would only be revealed in the regression analysis if interest were included as an explanatory variable. If interest is correlated with being female and if interest is an important determinant of employment in commission sales, then excluding interest from the regression equation would lead to an incorrect estimate of the effect that being female has on the chance of getting a job in commission sales.

It's important to note here that the problem arises not simply because a variable with the potential to affect hiring is left out of the equation. Many factors affect hiring decisions, ones that are measurable as well as ones that aren't. For the most part, they can be ignored as long as they aren't correlated with the variables that are included. The regression may have less explanatory power overall (i.e., a smaller R-squared), but the interpretation of the significance and magnitude of the coefficients of the included variables won't be tainted. However, when the omitted variable is significantly correlated with one or more included variables, then the regression coefficients of the correlated variables will be biased.

As an example of the consequences of omitting an important variable that's correlated with an included variable, consider this equation for hourly wage, which includes as explanatory variables education (E), age (A), race (R; 1 if the individual is white, 0 otherwise), and marital status (M; 1 if the individual is married, 0 if not):

$$W = -12 + (1.2 \times E) + (0.2 \times A) + (1.5 \times R) + (1.7 \times M)$$

According to these estimates, married men earn, on average, $1.70 an hour more than unmarried men with the same characteristics. However, if we omit age from the equation but otherwise use the same data, the equation becomes:

$$W = -6 + (1.2 \times E) + (1.3 \times R) + (3.2 \times M)$$

Now the implication is that married men are paid, not $1.70 an hour more, but $3.20 an hour more than their unmarried counterparts. When age is omitted from the equation, its effect is picked up by the coefficients of the other variables in the model.

Notice that the coefficient for education didn't change and the one for race changed only slightly. The reason for this is that the correlation between education and age is weak (once people complete their education), as is the correlation between race and age. However, the correlation between marital status and age is fairly strong: older men are more likely than younger men to be married. The effect of age on earnings is rolled into the marriage coefficient, and the result is an artificially inflated estimate of the influence of marriage on wage.

2. Inclusion of irrelevant variables. Obviously, when the goal is to explain the response variable, the ideal is for all of the variables at play in producing the observed variation in the response variable (and only these variables) to be included in the regression model. Typically, this standard is quite difficult to achieve. Variables are included and excluded as the analysis proceeds, and different models are tested against the data. Candidates for inclusion as explanatory variables come from two sources:

preexisting theories about the phenomenon being investigated and data sets that allow for the statistical testing of possible associations. Such possibly relevant variables are included in trial regressions. Depending on the sizes of the resulting regression coefficients, the magnitude of the R-squared, and the levels of significance revealed by the t-tests, they may be included in or excluded from the final regression model.

A problem is inherent in this approach. If too many variables are tested for possible relevance, a small percentage of them will, simply because of sampling error, appear to be significant when in fact they aren't. If these variables are erroneously included in the final regression model, not only will spurious relationships be presented as real, but the coefficients calculated for the variables that *are* relevant will, on average, be worse estimates of the corresponding population coefficients.

3. Multicollinearity. Most economic variables are correlated with one another to some extent. For instance, number of years of work experience and age are highly correlated for college-educated men. If both age and experience are included in a wage equation, isolating the effect of age on wage from the effect of work experience on wage may be difficult, and statistically, neither variable may appear to be a significant determinant of wage. This type of problem is the result of multicollinearity. Although the temptation may be to drop one of the variables creating the problem, doing so may introduce bias if both variables are important determinants of wage.

Multicollinearity can be used to make effects that would otherwise be statistically significant disappear. For example, we can define makeup use as a variable. Since makeup use and being female are highly correlated, including both variables in a wage regression is likely to yield an insignificant effect of being female on wage. Although this example may seem silly and extreme, an econometrician can, quite easily and subtly, add in variables that will make the variable of concern appear insignificant. In contrast, including fewer variables will increase the apparent importance of the variables that are retained. Usually, the solution to multicollinearity is to obtain better, more refined data — not to throw out important variables.

4. Two-way causation. Do police have a damping effect on the violent crime rate? Most people would say that the answer is obviously yes. It might seem obvious then that, in a multiple regression equation with police (number per 1,000 residents) as an explanatory variable and violent crime rate (e.g., number of violent crimes per 1,000 residents) as the response variable, the regression coefficient for police should be negative, an indication that the violent crime rate decreases as police presence increases. Surprisingly, however, the coefficient is likely to be near 0 or even positive — while it is true that sending more police to a particular area will tend to reduce the crime rate in that area, it is also true that more police will be sent to areas that have higher crime rates. Changing the concentration of police changes the crime rate (more police, fewer crimes) but changing the crime rate changes the concentration of police (as the crime rate drops in a particular area, police are shifted away from that area). This is an example of the two-way causation problem, which arises when an explanatory variable causes changes in a response variable, while at the same time changes in the response variable cause changes in the explanatory variable. In such a situation, the regression coefficient for the explanatory variable in question is biased. Solving a two-way causation problem is, generally, not easy, and the methods are outside the scope of this text.[16]

Another instance of the simultaneity problem occurs in the following situation: a researcher hypothesizes that the more money spent per pupil on primary and high school education in a school district, the better the resulting education. Yet, when the researcher produces a regression equation with achievement test scores as the response variable and per pupil spending as an explanatory variable, the regression coefficient on per pupil spending is negative, indicating that the less money spent per pupil, the better on average the achievement test scores. Can you use the two way causation idea to explain this result?

3. Suggestions for Further Reading

Many complexities of multivariate statistics were glossed over or, indeed, entirely omitted from this chapter. If you'd like to delve deeper into the

---

16. Chapters 10 & 11 of the Stock and Watson text cited on the following page present the two most common approaches to the problem of two-way causation.

subject — whether out of pure intellectual curiosity or out of a practical need to know more — the following works will be helpful.

Laurence G. Grimm and Paul R. Yarnold, eds., *Reading and Understanding Multivariate Statistics* (Washington, D.C.: American Psychological Association, 1995). Presents chapter-length treatments of a variety of approaches to multivariate data that may be used as substitutes for, or supplements to, standard OLS regression written for the beginning social science graduate student with very little background in math.

Laurence G. Grimm and Paul R. Yarnold, eds., *Reading and Understanding More Multivariate Statistics* (Washington, D.C.: American Psychological Association, 2000).

James H. Stock and Mark W. Watson, *Introduction to Econometrics* 2nd ed. (Boston, MA: Addison-Wesley, 2006). Slightly less sophisticated than Wooldridge, but with a concluding section of 70 pages presenting the theoretical foundation of econometrics at a graduate level. Also contains a number of thoughtful problems together with solutions to aid self-study.

Jeffrey M. Wooldridge, *Introductory Econometrics: A Modern Approach* 4th ed. (Mason, OH: South-Western Thomson Learning, 2008). A self-contained presentation at the undergraduate level that assumes only a basic knowledge of algebra.

T - Table (abbreviated)

df	.10	.05	.01
1	6.314	12.706	63.657
2	2.920	4.303	9.925
3	2.353	3.182	5.841
4	2.132	2.776	4.604
5	2.015	2.571	4.032
6	1.943	2.447	3.707
7	1.895	2.365	3.499
8	1.860	2.306	3.355
9	1.833	2.262	3.250
10	1.812	2.228	3.169
11	1.796	2.201	3.106
12	1.782	2.179	3.055
13	1.771	2.160	3.012
14	1.761	2.145	2.977
15	1.753	2.131	2.947
16	1.746	2.120	2.921
17	1.740	2.110	2.898
18	1.734	2.101	2.878
19	1.729	2.093	2.861
20	1.725	2.086	2.845
21	1.721	2.080	2.831
22	1.717	2.074	2.819
23	1.714	2.069	2.807
24	1.711	2.064	2.797
25	1.708	2.060	2.787
26	1.706	2.056	2.779
27	1.703	2.052	2.771
28	1.701	2.048	2.763
29	1.699	2.045	2.756
30	1.697	2.042	2.750
40	1.684	2.021	2.704
60	1.671	2.000	2.660
120	1.658	1.980	2.617
∞	1.645	1.960	2.576

Glossary of Statistical Terms

The 68%-95%-99.7% Rule: In every normal distribution, about 68% of the values are within 1 standard deviation of the mean, about 95% of the values are within 2 standard deviations, and about 99.7 percent are within 3 standard deviations.

Acquiescence Bias: Bias induced by survey respondents' desire to give the answers the survey designer seems to want.

Chebychev's Rule: For any data set, at least 75% of the data points lie within 2 standard deviations of the mean and at least 89% lie within 3 standard deviations of the mean.

Central Limit Theorem: The theorem postulates that the distribution of the means of random samples of size n from a given population approximates a normal distribution, that it has the same mean as the population from which the samples were drawn and that it has a standard deviation which equals the population standard deviation divided by the square root of n.

Common Response Problem: A problem which arises when correlational data are used in an effort to determine causal relationships. If A and B have a strong correlation, is it the result of a direct causal connection between them, or because both are responding to changes in a third, unaccounted for, variable?

Confidence Interval: A range of values constructed from sample data in such a way as to have a specific probability of including a true population parameter of interest, as in a 95% confidence interval for the mean, which is constructed in such a way that 95% of intervals so constructed will, on average, contain the true population mean.

Confounders: Also called lurking variables, confounders are the unaccounted for variables that produce confounding.

Confounding: There is said to be confounding when a causal inference is determined to be ill-founded because of the operation of a variable or variables not accounted for in the making of the inference.

Correlation: Two variables are positively correlated if above average values of one tend to accompany above average values of the other, and below average values of one tend to accompany below average values of the other. Two variables are negatively correlated if above average values of one tend to accompany below average values of the other, and vice versa. The stronger the correlation between two variables, the better will be predictions of the value of one of the variables from the value of the other.

> **Pearson Correlation Coefficient:** A number between –1.0 and +1.0 that describes the strength and direction of the linear relationship between two variables. An r of –1.0 indicates a perfect negative relationship, +1.0, a perfect positive relationship.

Curve: The graphic representation of a distribution.

> **Normal Curve:** The graphic representation of a normal distribution; it is unimodal and can be divided into two mirror-image halves by an appropriately placed line and thus is symmetric.

> **Unimodal Curve:** A curve characterized by a single mound.

> **Bimodal Curve:** A curve characterized by two mounds.

Data: Bits of information presented in terms of individuals (the units the data are about) and variables (the properties under examination).

> **Survey Data:** Data derived by direct questioning of individuals from the population being studied.

Data Set: A collection of values of one or more variables for more than one individual.

> **Bivariate Data Set:** A data set consisting of paired values, one score on each of two variables for every individual in the data set.
>
> **Census:** A data set containing scores on one or more variables for all of the individuals — the entire population — of interest.
>
> **Multivariate Data Set:** A collection of values that combine two or more one-variable data sets for the same individuals.
>
> **One-Variable (Univariate) Data Set:** A collection of values of a given variable for more than one individual.

Distribution: The way the values of a variable in a sample or population are related to one another, as is revealed by a histogram or a dot plot.

> **Normal Distribution:** A distribution that has the shape of a normal curve.
>
> **Rectangular Distribution:** A distribution that has the shape of a rectangle.
>
> **Skewed Distribution:** A non-symmetric distribution with values spread out more in one direction than the other.

Estimator: Any determinate method for producing an estimate from sample data.

Estimation: The use of sample data to make an educated guess about a parameter value of the population from which a sample was drawn.

> **Interval Estimate:** An estimate that specifies both a range of values and the probability that the true value of the parameter is somewhere within this range.
>
> **Point Estimate:** A single value guess at the value of a parameter.

Gaps: Regions in a distribution where there are no or few scores.

Histogram: A kind of bar graph used to pictorially represent a one-variable quantitative data set.

Hypothesis: In statistical hypothesis testing, a claim about the value of a population parameter.

> **Null Hypothesis:** The hypothesis that there is no difference between a given, or hypothesized, population parameter and the value of that parameter in the population from which the investigator has drawn a sample.

Individuals: Individuals are the units that data are about. Any object of study can be an individual — a person (e.g. a 24 year old man), a state (e.g. Georgia), an act (e.g. buying a car), a law (e.g. an anti-discrimination statute), etc.

Influential Observations: Unusual data points which have a large influence on estimates of regression coefficients.

(Simple) Linear Regression: A technique for deriving and using the linear equation that will produce, on average, the best estimates of a variable that can be obtained using another variable with which it is correlated.

Linear Relationship: When two variables are linearly related, the value of one can be used to estimate the value of the other via an equation of the form $x = a + by$, where x and y are the variables and a and b are constants. The stronger the linear relationship between the variables, the better the estimates will be.

Measures of Central Tendency

> **Median:** The middle value in a distribution (or, if the distribution contains an even number of values, the average of the middle two values).

> **Mean:** The arithmetic average of the values in a distribution.

> **Mode:** The most frequently occurring value in a distribution.

Measures of Variability or Dispersion

> **Range:** The difference between the lowest and the highest values in the data set.

Standard Deviation: The square root of the variance.

Variance: The mean of the squared deviations from the mean of the values in the data set.

Multicollinearity: A problem which arises in multiple regression analysis when an explanatory variable is very closely correlated with other explanatory variables in the same equation. The estimates of the regression coefficients of the correlated variables will be unreliable.

Motivational Bias: A type of bias in survey data resulting from respondents answering survey questions untruthfully in an effort to promote various respondent goals inconsistent with those of the surveyor.

Operationalization: Development of practical measurement techniques or standards that allow for the translation into variables of the properties being studied.

Outliers: Values that are much lower or higher than the other values in a data set.

Parameters: The numerical descriptors of a population.

Population: The entire set of individuals to be studied.

R^2: A statistic used to express the accuracy of the estimates provided by a regression equation.

Representativeness (of a sample): The representativeness of a sample is the degree to which the sample distribution resembles the distribution of the population from which the sample was taken.

Residual: The difference between a true value and an estimated value.

Sample: A group of individuals selected from the population under study.

Convenience Sample: A sample that comprises individuals who have been chosen because they were relatively accessible.

Simple Random Sample: A sample selected in such a way that it was no more and no less likely to be selected than was any other possible sample of the same size from the population being studied.

Scatterplot: A type of graph on which bivariate data sets are pictorially presented by plotting each individual's scores on both variables as a single point in a two dimensional Cartesian space.

Standard Error: The standard deviation of the sampling distribution of a statistic. The term is also often used to refer to an estimate of the standard deviation of a sampling distribution derived entirely from sample values.

Statistics: The scientific study of methods for gathering, analyzing and utilizing numerical facts.

Descriptive Statistics: The subfield of statistics concerned with producing and analyzing informative/persuasive pictures and verbal summaries of data.

Inferential Statistics: The science of using sample data to make accurate claims about the populations from which the samples are drawn.

(As opposed to Parameters): Numerical descriptors of samples as e.g. the sample mean and the sample standard deviation.

Statistically Significant Difference: A large enough difference between a given population parameter and a statistic computed from a random sample to justify the claim that the sample was taken from a population with a different parameter value, or, a large enough difference between statistics computed from two different samples to justify the claim that the samples were taken from different populations.

Type I Error: The rejection of the null hypothesis when it is, in fact, true.

Type II Error: Failure to reject the null hypothesis when it is, in fact, false.

Validity: The extent to which a measuring instrument measures what it's intended to measure.

> **Face Validity:** A survey is said to be face valid when it consists of questions that request directly and obviously the information desired by the surveyor.

Variable: A variable can be any property of individuals under study (e.g. height, wealth, aversion to risk, etc), as long as the individuals differ in some way with respect to the property and the differences can be measured or ascertained in some practical way.

> **Categorical Variable:** A variable that requires that each individual be assigned to one of several specified or implied categories, such as gender, race, or marital status.

> **Explanatory Variable:** A variable used as a predictor in a regression equation. Sometimes referred to as an independent variable.

> **Quantitative Variable:** A variable that is measured numerically, such as height, blood pressure, or income.

> **Response Variable:** The variable whose value is to be predicted. Sometimes referred to as the dependent variable.

z-Score: The distance, measured in standard deviations, of a given value from the mean of a distribution. Sometimes referred to as a standard score.

Index